GREEK PAINTED POTTERY

GREEK PAINTED POTTERY

Third edition

R. M. Cook

London and New York

First published 1960
by Methuen & Co Ltd
Reprinted with corrections 1966
Second Edition 1972
Reprinted 1977

First published by
Routledge in 1992

Third Edition first published 1997
by Routledge
11 New Fetter Lane, London EC4P 4EE

Simultaneously published in the USA and Canada
by Routledge
29 West 35th Street, New York, NY 10001

© 1960, 1972, 1997 R. M. Cook

Typeset in Garamond by
Florencetype Ltd, Stoodleigh, Devon

Printed and bound in Great Britain by
Redwood Books Ltd, Trowbridge, Wiltshire

British Library Cataloguing in Publication Data
A catalogue record for this book is available from the British Library

Library of Congress Cataloguing in Publication Data
A catalogue record for this book has been requested

ISBN 0–415–13859–0 (hbk)
ISBN 0–415–13860–4 (pbk)

To Kathleen Cook

CONTENTS

———— ·◆· ————

	List of illustrations	xi
	Acknowledgements	xxiii
	Note on orthography	xxv
I	Introduction	1
II	The Protogeometric style	5
	Introduction	5
	Athens	7
	Protogeometric outside Attica	10
III	The Geometric style	15
	Introduction	15
	Athens	18
	The Argolid	23
	Corinth	24
	Laconia	26
	Western Greece	27
	Boeotia	28
	Euboea	29
	The Cyclades	30
	Thessaly	33
	The East Greek region	33
	Crete	36
	Italy	38
IV	The Orientalizing and black-figure styles	41
	Introduction	41
	Corinth	46
	Athens	63
	The Argolid	88
	Laconia	88
	Boeotia	96
	Euboea	98
	The Cyclades	100
	The East Greek region	109
	Thasos	134
	Crete	135

— Contents —

	Italy	138
	The Eastern fringes	153
V	The Red-figure style	155
	Introduction	155
	Attica	158
	Corinth	178
	Boeotia	179
	Etruria	180
	South Italy	182
VI	Hellenistic pottery with painted decoration	193
	Introduction	193
	West Slope ware	195
	The Lagynos group	196
	Hadra ware	197
	Canosa ware	199
	Centuripae ware	200
VII	Black-painted and Relief wares	201
	General comments	201
	Reserved and painted decoration	202
	Impressed decoration	203
	Relief decoration	204
VIII	Shapes	207
	General comments	207
	Amphorae	209
	Hydria	213
	Oinochoai	214
	Kraters	217
	Lekythoi etc.	220
	Pyxides	223
	Cups	223
	Plates and dishes	227
	Lids	229
IX	Technique	231
	The standard processes	231
	Other processes	237
	Local clays	238
	Mending	240
X	Inscriptions	241
	General comments	241
	Inscriptions before firing	242
	Inscriptions after firing	246

— Contents —

XI   Chronology   249
Introduction   249
Relative chronology   249
Absolute chronology   251
The reconciliation of relative and absolute chronologies   258

XII   The pottery industry   259

XIII Uses for other studies   263
Dating   263
Trade   264
Political relations   265
Prosperity   265
Iconography   265

XIV Practical comments   267
Handling   267
Examination   267
Taking notes   270
Drawing and photographing   270
Cleaning   272
Mending   272
Collecting   273

XV   The history of the study of vase-painting   275

List of abbreviations   313
Note on museums   317
Note on sites   323
Glossary   325
Bibliography   331
Index   357
Plates   *opposite page* 376

ILLUSTRATIONS

———— •◆• ————

Numbers in square brackets after the descriptions of the plates indicate the pages on which the plate in question is discussed.

PLATES AT END OF BOOK

1   A   Attic Protogeometric cup: ht 14.7 cm. 10th cent. BC. Athens, Agora Mus. P.3953.   [8, 9, 18, 224]
Photo: Agora Excavations, American School of Classical Studies at Athens.

     B   Attic Protogeometric 'tea-cup': ht 9.2 cm. 10th cent. BC. Athens, Agora Mus. P.7076.   [8–9, 18, 225]
Photo: Agora Excavations, American School of Classical Studies at Athens.

     C   Attic Protogeometric lekythos: ht 15.5 cm. Early 10th cent. BC. Athens, Agora Mus. P.5863.   [9, 221]

     D   Attic Protogeometric oinochoe: ht 30 cm. Late 10th cent. BC. Athens, Agora Mus. P.6676.   [7, 8, 15, 215]
Photo: Agora Excavations, American School of Classical Studies at Athens.

2   A   Myceanaean 'amphora': ht 52.5 cm. 14th cent. BC (LH IIIA). British Museum 70.10–8.124 (A.828).   [8, 9, 210]
Photo: British Museum.

     B   Attic Protogeometric amphora: ht 46 cm. 10th cent. BC. Athens, Ceramicus Mus. 586.   [8, 9, 15, 18, 210]
Photo: German Archaeological Institute, Athens.

3   A   Attic Geometric amphora: ht 72.2 cm. *c.*875–850 BC. Athens, Ceramicus Mus. 254.   [15, 18, 19, 210]
Photo: German Archaeological Institute, Athens.

     B   Attic Geometric amphora: ht 77.5 cm. Middle or later 9th cent. BC. Athens, Ceramicus Mus. 2140.   [15, 18, 19, 210]
Photo: German Archaeological Institute, Athens.

4   A   Attic Geometric amphora: ht 155 cm. By the Dipylon painter: *c.* 760 BC. Athens, N.M. 804   [15, 20, 21–22, 210]
Photo: National Museum, Athens.

     B   Attic Geometric oinochoe: ht (with lid) 80 cm. Workshop of Dipylon painter: *c.* 750 BC. Athens, N.M. 266. [16, 19, 20, 21, 216]
Photo: National Museum, Athens.

xi

5   Detail of Plate 4A.   [21, 64]
    Photo: J. M. Cook.

6   A Attic Geometric pyxis: ht (with lid) 19.5 cm, *c.* 740 BC. Athens,
      Agora Mus. P.4784.   [15, 20, 223]
      Photo: Agora Excavations, American School of Classical Studies at
      Athens.
   B Theran Geometric amphora: ht 28 cm, *c.* 700 BC. Edinburgh
      1900.65.   [31]
      Photo: Royal Scottish Museum, Edinburgh.

7   A Rhodian Geometric oinochoe: ht 21.9 cm. Bird kotyle workshop:
      late 8th or early 7th cent. BC. British Museum 60.4–4.10.
                      [9, 35, 216]
      Photo: British Museum.
   B Cretan Protogeometric B hydria: ht 27.7 cm. Later 9th cent. BC.
      Heraklion (Fortetsa 493).   [36]
      Photo: G. M. Young.

8   A Corinthian Geometric cup: ht 6.7 cm. Later 9th cent. BC. Corinth
      CP.865.   [18, 24, 224]
   B Corinthian Geometric kotyle: ht 10.5 cm, *c.* 740–730 BC. Athens,
      N.M. 14476.   [25, 62, 226]
   C Protocorinthian oinochoe: ht 33.4 cm, *c.* 720–690 BC. (EPC). Naples
      128199.   [25, 47, 215]
      Photo: National Museum, Naples.

9   A Protocorinthian aryballos: ht 7.5 cm, *c.* 720–690 BC. (EPC). Naples
      128321.   [47, 222]
      Photo: National Museum, Naples.
   B Protocorinthian aryballos (detail): ht of field 3 cm. By the Ajax
      painter: *c.* 675 BC. (MPC). Boston 95.12.   [49–50, 270]
      From H. G. G. Payne, *Protokorinthische Vasenmalerei*, pl. 11.1
      (Verlag Heinrich Keller).
   C Protocorinthian aryballos (detail): ht of field 2 cm. By the Chigi
      (or Macmillan) painter: *c.* 650 BC. (MPC). British Museum
      89.4–18.1.   [50–51, 167]
      From *JHS* 1890, pl. 2.
   D Protocorinthian aryballos: ht 5.2 cm, *c.* 675 BC (MPC). Boston
      95.13.   [47, 49, 222]
      Photo: Museum of Fine Arts, Boston.

10 A Protocorinthian kotyle: ht 19 cm. By the Hound painter: *c.* 660 BC
      (MPC). British Museum 60.4–4.18.   [49, 51]
      Photo: British Museum.
   B Ripe Corinthian aryballos: ht 7.8 cm. By the Heraldic Riders
      painter: *c.* 600 BC (EC). British Museum 1958. 1–14.1.
                     [47, 54, 57, 222]
      Photo: British Museum.

C Ripe Corinthian alabastron: ht 9.7 cm, *c.* 625–600 BC (EC). Cambridge G.28. [54, 55, 222]
Photo: R. Johnson.

11 A Transitional Corinthian olpe: ht 27.5 cm, *c.* 640–625 BC (Tr.) Oxford 1879.100. [54, 217]
Photo: Ashmolean Museum, Oxford.

B Ripe Corinthian oinochoe (some repainting): ht 38 cm, *c.* 625–600 BC (EC). Paris, Bibliothèque Nationale 4756. [54, 55, 215]
Photo: Bibliothèque Nationale.

12 A Ripe Corinthian kotyle (detail): ht of field 6 cm. By the Samos painter: *c.* 580 BC (MC). Boston 95.14. [58]
Photo: Museum of Fine Arts, Boston.

B Ripe Corinthian kotyle (detail): ht of field *c.* 6.5 cm. By the Samos painter: *c.* 580 BC. Louvre CA.3044. [57, 58]
Photo: Louvre Museum.

C Ripe Corinthian column-krater: ht 46 cm, *c.* 600 BC (EC). Louvre E.635 (Camp. 33). [56, 58, 115, 218]
Photo: Louvre Museum.

13 Ripe Corinthian red-ground column-krater (detail): combined ht of fields *c.* 20 cm. By the Cavalcade painter: *c.* 570 BC (LCI). Vatican 126. [60]
Photo: Alinari.

14 A Protoattic hydria: ht 52.5 cm. By the Analatos painter: *c.* 700 BC. Athens, N.M. 2696. [63–65, 67, 213]
Photo: J. M. Cook.

B Protoattic krater: ht 39 cm. By the Analatos painter: *c.* 690 BC. Munich 6077. [65]
Photo: Antikensammlungen, Munich.

15 A Protoattic amphora: scale *c.* 1:4. By the Ram Jug painter: *c.* 660–650 BC. Berlin A.9. [67]
After *CVA Berlin* I, pl. 5 (C. H. Beck'sche Verlagsbuchhandlung).

B Attic Bf dinos? (fragment): scale *c.* 1:1. By Sophilos: *c.* 590–580 BC. Istanbul 4514. [72]
From C. Blinkenberg, *Lindos* I, pl. 127.2629 (Verlag Walter de Gruyter & Co.).

16 Protoattic amphora: ht 108.5 cm, *c.* 660 BC. New York 11.210.1. [67]
Photo: Metropolitan Museum, New York.

17 Protoattic amphora: ht 122 cm. By the Nessos painter: *c.* 615 BC. Athens, N.M. 1002. [69–70]
Photo: National Museum, Athens.

18 Attic Bf dinos and stand: total ht 93 cm. By the Gorgon painter: *c.* 590 BC. Louvre E.874 (Camp. 30). [71, 208, 220]
Photo: Giraudon.

19   A Attic Bf volute-krater: ht 66 cm. The François vase. By Clitias:
         c. 570 BC. Florence 4209.   [73–74, 219]
         Photo: Soprintendenza Antichità, Florence.
      B Detail of lip from the other side: ht of upper field 5.6 cm.
         Photo: Soprintendenza Antichità, Florence.
20   A Attic Bf hydria:ht *c.* 25 cm. By the Polos painter: *c.* 600–570 BC.
                                                                          [76]
         Photo: National Museum, Athens.
      B Attic Bf amphora: ht 38.8 cm. Tyrrhenian group, by the Timiades
         painter: *c.* 570–560 BC. British Museum 97.7–27.2.   [75–76, 210]
         Photo: British Museum.
21   A Attic Bf one-piece amphora: ht 54 cm. *c.* 600 BC. Munich 1360.
                                                                 [71, 76–77, 212]
         Photo: Antikensammlungen, Munich.
      B Attic Bf Panathenaic amphora: ht 61.2 cm. The Burgon amphora,
         c. 560 BC. British Museum, uninventoried (B.130).
                                                      [80, 86–87, 211, 254, 281]
         Photo: British Museum.
22   Attic Bf one-piece amphora: ht 61 cm. By Exekias: *c.* 530 BC. Vatican
      344.   [77, 82, 210, 212]
      Photo: Alinari.
23   Attic Bf amphora: ht 33 cm. By the Amasis painter: *c.* 530 BC. Paris,
      Bibliothèque Nationale 678 (Cat. 222).   [81, 84, 210, 211]
      Photo: Giraudon.
24   A Attic Bf cup: ht 9.5 cm. Comast group, manner of the KX painter:
         c. 580–570 BC. New York 22.139.22.   [74–75, 224]
         Photo: Metropolitan Museum, New York.
      B Attic Bf Siana cup: ht 13 cm. By the C painter: *c.* 570–560 BC.
         British Museum 67.5–8.940 (B.382).   [75, 224]
         Photo: British Museum.
25   A Attic Bf lip cup: ht 12.4 cm, *c.* 550–530 BC. Manchester Mus.
         iii. H.45.   [78–79, 80, 224, 242]
         Photo: H. Spencer.
      B Attic Bf band cup: ht 13.3 cm, *c.* 550–530 BC. Manchester Mus.
         iii. H.39.   [79, 80, 224]
         Photo: H. Spencer.
26   A–B Laconian cup: diam. (without handles) 22 cm. By the Taranto
         Fishes painter: early 6th cent. BC. Taranto I.G. 4806.   [91]
         Photos: National Museum, Taranto. ·
27   A–B Laconian cup: diam. (without handles) 17.8 cm. By the Rider
         painter: *c.* 550–540 BC. British Museum 42.4–7.7 (B.1).   [92]
         Photos: British Museum.
28   A Boeotian Bird cup: ht 21 cm. Mid–6th cent. BC. Munich 2238.
                                                                    [96–97]

Photo: Antikensammlungen, Munich.

B Eretrian amphora: ht 75 cm, *c.* 625–600 BC. Athens, N.M. 12077.
[99]

Photo: J. Boardman.

29 A–C Linear Island amphora: ht 43.5 cm. Early 7th cent. BC. Thera.
[100–101, 211]

Photos: German Archaeological Institute, Athens.

D East Greek Bird bowl: ht 5 cm, *c.* 675–650 BC. Oxford 1928.313.
[110, 224]

Photo: Ashmolean Museum, Oxford.

30 A Wild Goat style oinochoe: ht 30 cm, *c.* 630 BC. Berlin F.295.
[112, 216]

Photo: Staatliche Museen, Berlin.

B Wild Goat style oinochoe: ht 36 cm, *c.* 625–600 BC. British Museum
67.5–8.928.   [112–13, 208, 215]

Photo: British Museum.

31 A Wild Goat style oinochoe (detail): ht of field *c.* 6.5 cm, *c.* 625 BC.
Zurich, Technische Hochschule.   [114]

Photo: F. Brommer.

B Wild Goat style krater (detail): ht of field *c.* 3.7 cm, *c.* 600–575 BC.
Tübingen 1473.   [114]

Photo: Archaeological Institute, Tübingen University.

C Chiot Wild Goat style bowl (fragment): ht of field 7.8 cm,
c. 615–600 BC. British Museum 1924.12–1.84.   [119]

D Clazomenian sarcophagus (detail): ht of field *c.* 17 cm, *c.* 515–500
BC. Vienna IV. 1865.   [130]

From *Antike Denkmaler* I, pl. 45.

32 A Fikellura amphora: ht 30.5 cm. By the Running Man painter:
c. 540–520 BC. Birmingham University V. 58.   [125]

Photo: Department of Ancient History and Archaeology, Birmingham University.

B Clazomenian Bf amphora: ht (as preserved) 31 cm. By the Petrie
painter: *c.* 540–530 BC. British Museum 88.2–8.69.   [128–9]

Photo: British Museum.

33 A East Greek situla: ht (as restored) 47.6 cm, *c.* 575–550 BC.
Philadelphia 29.71.189.   [131–2]

Photo: University Museum, Philadelphia.

B East Greek Bf cup: diam. (without handles) 23.5 cm, *c.* 550 BC.
Louvre F.68 (Camp. 623).   [123]

Photo: Louvre Museum.

34 Etruscan Bf amphora: ht 35.1 cm. Pontic class, by the Paris painter:
c. 540–530 BC. New York 55.7.   [147]

Photo: Metropolitan Museum, New York.

35 Caeretan hydria: ht 44 cm, *c.* 520–510 BC. Dunedin E.53.61. [151, 214]

36 'Chalcidian' column-krater: ht 45.7 cm. By the Inscription painter: *c.* 550–530 BC. Würzburg K.160. [149, 218]
Photo: Martin von Wagner Museum, Würzburg.

37 A Attic Rf Nolan amphora (detail): scale *c.* 4:1. By the Berlin painter: 500–490 BC. Manchester Mus. iii. I. 40 (formerly Tarporley). [155, 233]
Photo: A. Cambitoglou.
B Attic Rf bell-krater (fragment): scale *c.* 2:3. By the Peleus painter: *c.* 440 BC. Cambridge, Mus. of Classical Archaeology UP.131 [172, 234, 234]
Photo: R. Johnson.

38 Attic Rf one-piece amphora: ht of field 18.1 cm. By the Andocides painter: *c.* 520 BC. Munich 2301. [158–9, 162, 226]
Photo: Antikensammlungen, Munich.

39 Attic Rf one-piece amphora: ht of field 24.2 cm. By Euthymides: 510–500 BC. Munich 2307. [159, 162, 243]
Photo: Antikensammlungen, Munich.

40 Attic Rf cup (fragment – inside): greatest length *c.* 18.7 cm. By Onesimos (the Panaitios painter): 500–490 BC. Bowdoin College 30.1. [163, 164]
Photos: Museum of Fine Arts, Bowdoin College and D. von Bothmer.

41 Attic Rf amphora of Panathenaic shape (detail): ht of figure *c.* 27 cm. By the Berlin painter: *c.* 490 BC. Munich 2311 [163, 164]
From J. D. Beazley, *der Berliner Maler*, pl. 6 (Verlag Heinrich Keller).

42 Attic Rf pointed amphora: ht of field 24.7 cm. By the Cleophrades painter: 500–490 BC. Munich 2344. [163–4, 165]
Photo: Antikensammlungen, Munich.

43 Attic Rf cup: diam. (without handles) 32.2 cm. By the Brygos painter: 490–480 BC. Würzburg K.479. [163–4]
Photo: Martin von Wagner Museum, Würzburg.

44 Attic Rf bell-krater: ht 37.1 cm. By the Pan painter: *c.* 470 BC. Boston 10.185. [166, 171, 219]
Photo: Museum of Fine Arts, Boston.

45 Attic Rf pelike: ht 41 cm. By the Chicago painter: 460–450 BC. Lecce 570. [166, 169, 212]
Photo: G. Guido.

46 A Attic Rf amphora: ht 58.1 cm. By the Peleus painter: *c.* 440 BC. British Museum 47.9–9.7 (E.271). [172, 173, 211]
Photo: British Museum.
B Attic Rf squat lekythos: ht 19.4 cm. By the Midias painter: 410–400 BC. British Museum 56.5–12.15 (E.697). [174, 175, 221]
Photo: British Museum.

47 Attic Rf squat lekythos (detail): ht of field 9.2 cm. By the Eretria painter: 430–420 BC. Berlin F.2471. [172]
From Furtwängler, *la Collection Sabouroff*, pl. 55.

48 A Attic Rf bell-krater: ht 31.5 cm. By the Dinos painter: 420–410 BC.
Philadelphia MS.5682. [172, 174, 219]
Photo: University Museum, Philadelphia.

B Attic Rf bell-krater (detail): ht of second figure 15.4 cm. By the
Lycaon painter: *c.* 440 BC. Warsaw (once Goluchow, Czartoryski
43). [172]
From J. D. Beazley, *Greek Vases in Poland*, pl. 25 (Clarendon Press).

49 A Attic Wg lekythos: ht 38.7 cm. By the Achilles painter: 450–440
BC. British Museum 91.8–6.85 (D.51). [168, 172, 173, 221]
Photo: British Museum.

B Attic Wg lekythos: ht 31.5 cm. By the Reed painter: 420–410 BC.
British Museum 73.8–20.303 (D.73). [174, 221]
Photo: British Museum.

50 Attic Rf pelike: ht (as made up) 28.7 cm. By the Jena painter: *c.* 380
BC. Exeter University. [176]
Photo: B. B. Shefton.

51 Attic Rf pelike: ht 42.5 cm. By the Marsyas painter: *c.* 350 BC. British
Museum 62.5–30.1 (E.424). [177, 212]
Photo: British Museum.

52 A Apulian Rf volute-krater (detail): combined ht of fields *c.* 29 cm.
By the Sisyphus painter: 430–420 BC. Munich 3268. [183, 186]
Photo: Antikensammlungen, Munich.

B Lucanian Rf bell-krater (detail): ht of field *c.* 17 cm. By the Amykos
painter: 440–430 BC. Denver, Colorado. [183, 188]
Photo: Hesperia Art, Baltimore.

53 Apulian Rf calyx-krater (detail): ht of field 28.5 cm. By the Lycurgus
painter: 360–350 BC. British Museum 49.6–23.48 (F.271). [183, 187]
Photo: British Museum.

54 Lucanian Rf amphora of Panathenaic shape: ht 81 cm. By the Primato
painter: *c.* 340 BC. Ipswich 1921/120. [183, 188, 210]
Photo: Ipswich Museum.

55 A Campanian Rf kotyle: ht 29.5 cm. By the CA painter: *c.* 330 BC.
Athens, N.M. 1423. [183, 189]
Photo: National Museum, Athens.

B Paestan Rf bell-krater (detail): ht of field 16.3 cm. By Asteas:
c. 350 BC. British Museum (F.188). [183, 185]
Photo: British Museum.

56 A West Slope amphora: ht 17.4 cm. First half of 2nd cent. BC. Athens,
Agora P.600. [193, 195]
Photo: Agora Excavations, American School of Classical Studies at
Athens.

B Gnathian (Apulian) bell-krater: ht 22.2 cm. Group of the Louvre
Bottle: *c.* 330 BC. Oxford 1939.72. [191, 193, 219]
Photo: Ashmolean Museum, Oxford.

FIGURES

1 Late Mycenaean cup: ht 9 cm, *c.* 1150 BC. (LH IIIc).
Athens, N.M.   8
From A. Furtwängler and G. Loeschcke, *Mykenische Vasen,*
pl. 28. no. 241.

2 Cup with pendent semicircles: ht 8 cm. Cycladic or Euboean:
9th or early 8th cent. BC. Mykonos A.1465 (from Rheneia).   11

3 Cycladic Geometric amphora: ht 42 cm. Wheel group,
c. 725–700 BC. Thera (J.16).   32

4 A Protocorinthian kotyle: ht 7.5 cm. Subgeometric style:
first half of 7th cent. BC. Syracuse.
From *NSc* 1893, 474.

   B Protocorinthian cup: ht *c.* 5 cm. Subgeometric style:
mid-7th cent. BC. Syracuse.   48
From *NSc* 1893, 476

5 A Protocorinthian aryballos: ht 6.2 cm. Linear style: third
quarter of 7th cent. BC. (LPC–Tr). Athens, N.M.
After K. F. Johansen, *les Vases sicyoniens,* pl. 15.8 (Librairie
Ancienne Edouard Champion and Librairie V. Pio–Poul
Branner).

   B Protocorinthian aryballos: ht *c.* 8 cm. Linear style: third
quarter of 7th cent. BC. (LPC–Tr).   49
From H. G. G. Payne, *Necrocorinthia,* fig. 8b
(Clarendon Press).

6 Protocorinthian and Ripe Corinthian lions.   53
   A Beginning of 7th cent. BC (MPC).
   B *c.* 675 BC (MPC)
   C *c.* 660–650 BC (MPC).
   D *c.* 650–640 BC (LPC).
   E *c.* 650–640 BC (LPC).
   F *c.* 640–625 BC (Tx).
   G *c.* 625–600 BC (EC).
   H *c.* 615–600 BC (EC).
   I *c.* 600–580 BC (MC).
      A–B from Johansen, op. cit., pl. 20.3*c* and pl. 22.2*b*; C–I
from Payne, op. cit., fig. 7, pl. 9.1, pl. 10.8, pl. 11 *bis* 2,
pl. 25.2, fig. 11, pl. 30.4. (To help comparison A, C, F, H
and I are reproduced in reverse.)

7 Ripe Corinthian red-ground column-krater (fragment):
scale 1:1, *c.* 565 BC. Delphi.   59

8 Details to supplement Plate 14A. A. Neck. B. Belly.   64
From *JdI* 1887, pl. 3.

9 Protoattic oinochoe: ht 17.3 cm, *c.* 700–675 BC. British

	Museum 65.7–20.1.	66
	From *JdI* 1887, 48, fig. 8.	
10	Attic Bf bowl (details of panels): scale *c.* 1:2. By the Nessos painter, *c.* 605 BC. Berlin F. 1682.	70
	From *AZ* 1882, pl. 9.	
11	Laconian lakaina: ht *c.* 17.5 cm. Third quarter of 7th cent. BC. Sparta	89
	After a photo by E. A. Lane.	
12	Laconian animals: scale *c.*1 1:1. Third quarter of 7th cent. BC. Sparta.	90
	After a photo by E. A. Lane	
13	Boeotian kantharos (detail): scale *c.* 2:5. Cabiran style, by the Mystae painter: early 4th cent. BC. Once Berlin Inv. 3286.	98
	From P. Wolters, *das Kabirenheiligtum bei Theben* I, pl. 28.3 (Verlag Walter de Gruyter & Co.).	
14	Cycladic oinochoe (detail of shoulder): ht of field 7 cm. Ad group: first quarter of 7th cent. BC. Kimolos, C. Mustakas.	102
	From *AM* 1954/5, Beil. 61 (Verlag Gebr. Mann).	
15	Cycladic amphora (detail of neck): scale *c.* 3:7. Heraldic group: first or perhaps second quarter of 7th cent. BC. Athens, N.M. 11708.	104
	From *Thera* II, fig. 420*a*.	
16	Cycladic amphora (details of shoulder, front and back): scale 2:3. Protome group: mid-7th cent. BC. Mykonos C.1.	105
17	'Melian' amphora: ht (without lid) 45.5 cm. Early 6th cent. BC. Athens, N.M. 914.	107
	From *JdI* 1887, pl. 12.	
18	Wild Goat style oinochoe (details of shoulder): scale 2:3. Late Bf style: first quarter of 6th cent. BC. Delos B.6002.	115
19	East Greek lotus flowers and buds.	116
	A Middle Wild Goat style: *c.* 630–600 BC.	
	B Middle Wild Goat style: *c.* 615–600 BC.	
	C–D Late Wild Goat style: early 6th cent. BC.	
	E Fikellura: middle and later 6th cent. BC.	
20	Chiot chalice: ht 14 cm. Chalice style: late in first quarter of 6th cent. BC. Louvre A.330(1).	121
	After A. de Longpérier, *Musée Napoléon III*, pl. 52.	
21	Fikellura amphora: ht 29 cm, *c.* 540 BC. British Museum 61.4–25.47.	124
	From J. Boehlau, *aus ionischen und italischen Nekropolen*, fig. 25 (Teubner).	
22	Fikellura amphoriskos (details of body): scale *c.* 2:3 *c.* 520 BC. Rhodes 12396.	126

23   Vroulian cup: ht 7 cm. Early or middle 6th cent. BC. British
Museum 61.4–25.41.   133

24   Cretan and 'Melian' lotus flowers and buds.   136
A–D Cretan: early 7th cent. BC.
E 'Melian': late 7th–early 6th cent. BC.
A–D, after J. K. Brock, *Fortetsa*, Analysis of Patterns,
15*a*, *s*, *m*, *o* (Cambridge University Press).

25   'Phoenician' palmette: scale 1:2 Etruscocorinthian: late
7th cent. BC. Cambridge GR.12.52.   140

26   Etruscocorinthian olpe: ht 26.8 cm. By the Bearded Sphinx
painter: late 7th cent. BC. Boston 13.71.   143
From Payne, op. cit., fig. 93.

27   Etruscan bucchero kantharos: ht 11.6 cm. Later 7th or early
6th cent. BC. Cambridge, R. M. Cook.   146

28   Attic Rf cup (inside): diam. of field 10.7 cm. By Oltos:
520–510 BC. Oxford 516.   159
From *CVA Oxford* I, pl. 93.2 (Clarendon Press).

29   Attic Rf cup (inside): diam. of field 9.8 cm. By Epictetus:
c. 500 BC. Boston 10.212.   160
From J. D. Beazley, *Attic Red-figured Vases in American
Museums*, fig. 9 (Harvard University Press).
A Attic Bf cup–type A: ht 13 cm, *c*. 530 BC. Munich 2044.
After A. Furtwängler and K. Reichhold, *Griechische
Vasenmalerei* I, p. 227 (Verlagsanstalt F. Bruckmann AG).
B Attic Rf cup–type B: ht 11.7 cm, 490–480 BC. Boston
01.8034.   162
From L. D. Caskey and J. D. Beazley, *Attic Vase Paintings
in the Museum of Fine Arts, Boston*, fig. 24 (Museum of Fine
Arts, Boston).

31   Attic Rf cup (detail of outside): ht of field 9.5 cm. By the
Penthesilea painter: 470–460 BC. Hamburg 1900.164.   166
From Furtwängler and Reichhold, op. cit., pl. 56.6.

32   Attic Rf calyx-krater (detail): scale *c*. 2:5. By the Niobid
painter: *c*. 460 BC. Louvre G.341 (MNC 511).   167
From Furtwängler and Reichhold, op. cit., pl. 165.

33   Attic Rf volute-krater (detail): ht of field 21.5 cm. By the
painter of the Woolly Satyrs: *c*. 460 BC. New York 07.286.84.   170
From Furtwängler and Reichhold, op. cit., pl. 116.

34   Attic Rf bell-krater (detail of back): scale 1:2. By the Filotrano
painter: mid-4th cent. BC. Cambridge Mus. of Classical
Archaeology 206 (formerly Hope 314).   178
After Furtwängler and Reichhold, op. cit., II, Fig. 52.

35   Apulian Rf voluke-krater (detail of neck): scale *c*. 1:2. By the
Darius painter: *c*. 330 BC. Naples 3254.   184

36 Paestan Rf handle ornament of bell-krater. Later
    4th cent. BC.   190
37 Light-ground lagynos: ht 19 cm. Later 2nd or early 1st
    cent. BC. Vienna IV, 3880.   197
    From K. Masner, *die Sammlung antiker Vasen und*
    Terracotten im k.k. oest. Museum, fig. 34.
38 Attic Bf Nikosthenic amphora: ht 31 cm, *c.* 530 BC.
    Louvre F.103 (Camp. 564).   212
    After *Diagonal* I, 197 fig. 4*a* (Jay Hambridge).
39 Attic Rf hydria ('kalpis'): ht 27.75 cm, 450–440 BC.
    Boston 91.224.   214
    After Caskey, *Geometry of Greek Vases*, 113, no. 67.
    (Museum of Fine Arts, Boston.)
40 Attic Rf stamnos: ht 33.1 cm, *c.* 450 BC. Boston 01.8082. 220
    After L. D. Caskey, op. cit., 97, no. 54.
41 Conjectural restoration of a Greek kiln.   235
42 Main structure of system of dating.   256
43 Cross-dating of some archaic schools.   257
44 Inside of sherd showing wheel-marks.   281

ACKNOWLEDGEMENTS

———— •◆• ————

It is impossible to assess and acknowledge all debts to the work and assistance of others. Here I mention by name only those who have been so kind as to read and criticize my text. Professors J. M. Cook and Mrs K. Cook have been through most of it, and I thank them first. Next and no less sincerely I thank those who have looked at one part or another – Sir John Beazley, Mr J. C. Belshé, Miss M. Bimson, Mr J. Boardman, Mr J. K. Brock, Mr. P. E. Corbett, Professor J. A. Davison, Mr V. R. d'A. Desborough, Dr M. I. Finley, Dr J. M. Hemelrijk, Dr L. H. Jeffery, Professor A. W. Lawrence, Dr S. R. Nockolds, Mr A. Purves, Dr F. H. Stubbings, Professor A. D. Trendall, Mrs A. D. Ure, Professor A. J. B. Wace, Professor T. B. L. Webster and Mr A. G. Woodhead. If more often than not I have rejected their advice, I hope that they will set it down to obstinacy and not to ingratitude.

The help I have had with the illustrations is more easily summarized. For advice and the loan or procuring of photographs I am obliged to Professor A. D. Trendall, Mr P. E. Corbett, and Mr E. A. Lane; to Sir John Beazley, Professor J. M. Cook, Mr R. A. Higgins, Mrs S. Karouzou, Dr L. Talcott; to Professor P. Amandry, Dr M. Bernardini, Mr J. Boardman, Dr D. von Bothmer, Mr J. K. Brock, Dr G. Buchner, Professor F. Brommer, Mr T. Burton Brown, Dr A. Cambitoglou, Dr G. Caputo, Mr V. R. d'A. Desborough, Mr P. Devambez, Dr N. Himmelmann, Dr R. Lullies, Professor H. Möbius, Mr R. Oddy, Dr C. N. Schmalz, Mr B. B. Shefton, Dr F. J. Tritsch, Mrs A. D. Ure, Dr C. C. Vermeule, Mr J. B. Ward Perkins, Dr R. S. Young; and not least to Mr R. Johnson and Mr S. C. Collard. Permission to reproduce photographs and drawings has been given courteously by the authorities of museums and by other institutions and persons: the names may be found at the beginning and end of many entries in the list of illustrations. Some plates and figures are taken from other works by the generosity of publishers and authors. It is a pleasure to record my debt for these and other kindnesses.

Lastly I thank Mr Peter Wait for his patience.

FURTHER ACKNOWLEDGEMENTS

In revising this book for its corrected first edition and still more for the second I have been aided by many colleagues. Of those who have read and criticized various passages I am indebted most to Mr J. N. Coldstream, next to Professor A. D. Trendall, Professor F. Villard, Dr J. V. Noble and Dr J. W. Hayes, and further to Mr B. F. Cook and Dr B. A. Sparkes. For help over photographs I add the name of Dr D. Willers, and for much practical assistance those of Mr B. D. Thompson, Mr E. E. Jones and Mrs G. J. Blake. To them and many others I offer my honest thanks.

STILL FURTHER ACKNOWLEDGEMENTS

When revising in 1989 for a Greek translation (Ελληνική Αγγεωγραφία) I consulted Professor J. N. Coldstream yet again, Mr P. J. Callaghan, Dr P. Dupont, Dr C. A. Morgan, Dr T. B. Rasmussen and Dr N. J. Spivey. I am properly grateful to them. There has of course been some more revising for the present edition and in this I am indebted to an anonymous referee for some helpful suggestions.

NOTE ON ORTHOGRAPHY

——— ·◆· ———

The rendering of Greek names and words into English is difficult. For a long time Classical scholars have tended to reject more and more of the Latin forms that are naturalized and familiar. 'Pheidias', for instance, is now almost regular in learned works, and 'Thoukydides' has made his appearance. Such innovations are pedantic and often objectionable. First, the Greek alphabet is not the same as the English, so that any system of transliteration must be arbitrary. Secondly, English spelling has its own patterns, which decency should respect. The Greek name Ἡρακλῆς may serve as an example. Most students of the Classics now render it 'Herakles', though English usage prefers a 'c' rather than a 'k' in such a position and there is the compelling analogy of 'Heraclea', 'Heraclitus' and 'Pericles'. So I have kept to 'Heracles'. But in the names of shapes I have (as I see) been timid, writing 'krater' where Payne wrote 'crater', and repeating learned plurals like 'amphorae' instead of risking 'amphoras'. The French do these things better.

CHAPTER I

INTRODUCTION

——— ·•· ———

Greek pottery differs in character from the pottery of other civilizations, and those who have formed their tastes on porcelain may at first sight find it surprising. Though they liked a shiny surface, the Greeks did not use a high glaze. Their shapes, designed to be useful, are constructed with a clean and vigorous precision of contour. The decoration, which is arranged in a band round the pot to confine or emphasize its structure, in appearance as well as in fact keeps to the plane of the surface. Of the decorative motives the human figure becomes the most important; it is drawn with a neat economy of line, and though in time the roundness of the body is suggested, movement and grouping usually avoid the implication of depth. The whole effect shows a considered and logical planning, which imposed a strict discipline on artists and left little room for virtuosity.

Besides a sound artistic tradition Greek potters had other advantages. During much of the period covered in this survey there was a large class of customers of moderate wealth for whom painted pots were near the limit of luxury. So fine pottery was a profitable industry and offered not only employment but opportunity to artists even of the first rank. In the Protogeometric and Geometric periods it was one of the few forms of art generally practised. In the seventh century sculpture and free painting appeared; but statues had the special difficulty of being in three dimensions, and reliefs and pictures differed from vase-paintings in little more than a larger scale and a wider choice of colours. It was not till the fifth century that free painting began to draw away, and vase-painting at last declined to a minor art.

In the Late Bronze Age the Mycenaean style of pottery became universal throughout the Greek world and was welcomed beyond. It was based on a Cretan model, which, with its flowing shapes and freely spreading decoration of plants and sea creatures, appeals immediately to modern taste. But the Mycenaean potters did not have a genuine understanding of the subtleties of curve and spacing, and the history of their pottery is one of steady decline into rigid composition and stiffer and clumsier forms. By the mid-eleventh century, when the Bronze Age in Greece was passing into the Iron Age, all that remained was a lifeless and limited repertory of simple ornaments generally arranged in bands. At this point a revival began. The new Protogeometric style (Plates 1 and 2B) remodelled the shapes and decoration it inherited and gave them precision and dignity; the weary

I

spiral for instance was converted into neat sets of compass-drawn concentric circles, and the sagging shapes were tautened and defined. What caused this artistic revolution is unknown, for Attica where it flourished most strongly was according to tradition the only major province of Greece to escape the invasions of the Dorians and other tribes; its originators may even have believed that they were doing no more than restore the decadent Mycenaean style to its ancient vigour. The effects however are clear. By its strong sense of logical order, which is the antithesis of the spontaneity of the models that inspired Mycenaean, the new spirit determined the course of Greek art till its decay.

The Protogeometric style succeeded Mycenaean throughout Greek lands and in time evolved into what is defined as Geometric. But parochialism was growing and some local schools lagged behind others or strayed off on their own. At Athens, which led the development, a climax was reached in the ninth century in such harmonious exercises as the pot illustrated on Plate 3B, where the abstract decoration (notably the hatched meander) with its nice balance of dark and light is economically but lucidly disposed to emphasize the strongly articulated shape. Further development led some Attic workshops to a vulgar profusion of ornament that obscured the shape (Plate 4B), and Corinth to a neat and delicate mannerism (Plate 8B). As the eighth century advanced, Greek vase-painting was ready for a change and Oriental art, with which the Greeks were already acquainted, showed that other styles than the Geometric were possible.

The Oriental examples – metalwork, ivories and textiles – came chiefly from Syria, where there flourished a competent and tasteless hotch-potch of the artistic achievements of Nearer Asia and Egypt. Fortunately the Greeks were not overwhelmed by its sophisticated senility – good sense or the strength of tradition saved them – and instead they selected suitable motives and adapted them. Without the Oriental influence Greek vase-painting of the seventh century would have had a smaller fauna and a floral ornament that was rarer or at least more abstract. But even if the black-figure technique, unknown to the pottery of the Orient, was derived from Oriental metalwork or inlays, the evolution of the human figure from the austerely stylized silhouette of Geometric would have been similar, though perhaps slower. The new style widened the divisions between local schools. Corinth, which now took the lead, developed the black-figure technique, in which the figure is drawn in silhouette but enlivened by incised – that is engraved – detail and touches of added colour, and with it created an elegant miniature style (Plate 9B). At Athens there were two generations of ambitious exuberance which preferred to draw in outline (Plate 16). The cities of Asiatic Greece were content with unadventurous mediocrity (Plate 31). Other schools in their own time and way followed or defied their betters, and gradually the smaller and less successful faded away.

In the later seventh century Corinth forced the pace by switching to a cheap and showy style which greatly increased her production (Plate 11B), and this example was uncritically and sometimes disastrously imitated by her competitors (Plate 20A and Figure 18). So the black-figure technique became almost ubiquitous. But the Corinthian staple was an animal style, and during the early sixth century Athens created a new artistic standard based partly on improved technique and partly on the more regular use of human figures (Plates 19, 22 and 23). About the middle of the century Corinth was in turn eliminated and such other local schools as were left did not survive much longer. Once again there was a single style of vase-painting among the Greeks, with the difference that it was no longer universal but the monopoly of a dominant local school.

The black-figure style was well fitted for the representation of action, but Attic vase-painters were now ambitious to express mood and to experiment in anatomy. This was made possible by the red-figure technique, which replaced the convention of silhouette and engraving by the freer method of outline drawing with painted linear detail (Plates 38–39). The red-figure style, the first manifestation of the Classical spirit, was established in the late sixth century and by the middle of the fifth had driven out its older rival: its achievement during this time was extraordinary (Plates 37–45). Meanwhile free painting was adventuring towards perspective, modelling and subtler expressions of human feeling, and soon the painters of pottery were faced with a dangerous choice, to stand still and stagnate or to advance out of their depth. Though a respectable compromise was contrived, vase-painting in the later fifth century was no longer a creative art, and during the fourth century at Athens and soon after in South Italy (where new red-figure schools had sprouted) the long tradition withered away. Hellenistic vase-painters, if they can be called that, mostly made do with a few tatty ornaments from the conventional stock.

Greek art is the source of most Western art, and no branch of it has survived in such quantity as the painted pottery. But there is no need for historical reasons to justify the study of this pottery. It is one of the few subjects of archaeology that can give aesthetic enjoyment.

CHAPTER II

THE PROTOGEOMETRIC STYLE

— .•. —

INTRODUCTION

The first monumental achievement of Hellenic art was the Geometric style. It is best represented by the painted pottery, of which much has survived. A glance at Plate 3B shows its character. The decoration, in dark paint on a lighter surface, is carefully planned in bands of simple ornament which emphasize the shape of the pot. The individual elements of the ornament are unimportant, it is their cumulative effect that concerns the artist. To an unusual degree the style depends on composition without regard to the detail.

There is an essential contrast between the Geometric style and the Mycenaean style of the Late Bronze Age which preceded it. A typical sample of each is illustrated in Plate 2A and Plate 3B. The Mycenaean artist conceived his pot as a single whole; the contour has a flowing continuous curve, the painted decoration may embrace the full field in freehand balance. His Geometric successor observes a more orderly system: his pot is composed of clearly articulated parts, and the pattern is plotted exactly in bands of linear regularity. The intermediate stage, which was late in receiving its recognition, bears the cumbrous name of Protogeometric. This Protogeometric style (see Plates 1 and 2B) is not simply the transition from Mycenaean to Geometric proper, but a separate entity with its own standards. It has a sober easy discipline, firm but not finicky, with a conscious preference for definition of shape and ornament and for mechanical rather than individual forms. The shapes are solid and neat, and the articulation of the parts is clear without being punctilious. The decoration depends on broad contrasts of dark and light with a modicum of simple balanced ornament. The effect, as is evident in the amphora of Plate 2B, is direct, bold and harmonious, thoroughly satisfactory if not inspiring. In its own limited way it cannot be bettered, and by its standard the·Geometric style – and much of later Greek pottery – is fussy and pedantic.

The creation of the Protogeometric style marks a new era in the art of the Greek lands. Its trend towards geometrical precision has evoked comparisons with Middle Helladic wares some five hundred years earlier: a natural taste for Geometric forms in art, it has been suggested, was inherent in the early population of Greece, had been suppressed by the creators of the Mycenaean culture, and now on its collapse re-emerged.

A safer statement is that the ultimately Cretan characteristics of Mycenaean art had now been bred out, and for the evolution of a fresh style the Geometric method was as obvious and handy as any other. In fact it had been preparing since the fourteenth century, when the Cretan culture broke down and Mycenaean artists were left to their own limited resources. The freshly sketched forms of plants and marine animals which distinguished Cretan vase-painting become in Mycenaean more and more conventional, their disposition more and more stereotyped. Technically Mycenaean pottery maintained its high standard, but its artistic ability contracted: shapes became clumsier, decorative motifs fewer and more abstract, and particularly in the 'Close style' a growing tendency towards banded decoration was reinforced by the use of such compact linear motifs as sets of concentric arcs and fine scale pattern. The last phase, the Submycenaean, was current (anyhow at Athens) in the earlier eleventh century; even technical quality is declining. Here bottom is reached: recovery, when it comes, is in a new direction. Submycenaean and Protogeometric have much in common, but in one vestiges of the old naturalistic forms are visible, the other is purely abstract. In other words the one looks backwards, the other has hope for the future.

Another theory sees in the geometrical impulse the effect of a new people. Ancient Greek tradition makes much of the Dorian invasion of southern Greece, which it dated about the same time that archaeologists now date the end of the Mycenaean period. The proposition that the Dorians brought the Geometric or the Protogeometric style with them from Macedonia or the Danube has therefore been attractive. But first, the centre of both these styles was in Attica, the one important district of Old Greece that according to tradition was not touched by the Dorians – a difficulty which one or two scholars have resolved by assuming some unremembered invasion of Attica. The second and graver objection is that there is a satisfactorily continuous evolution from Mycenaean to Geometric art.

The Mycenaean style, centred in the Argolid, though produced more widely, had been remarkably uniform, but before its end local variations became apparent and divergence continued sluggishly in the succeeding Submycenaean. The local workshops, it seems, kept to a common tradition, now decaying, but were increasingly isolated from each other, though at the beginning of the Protogeometric some communication is implied by the general adoption of the compass to draw circles; the replacement of the stirrup vase by the lekythos may be rather earlier. (Crete, of course eccentric, did not accept circles until the tenth century and it retained the stirrup vase.) In the new Protogeometric style Attica shows the most vigour and originality, and its influence is strong in the Argolid, Corinth and part of Boeotia at least, in the Cyclades, and in the new Greek settlements on the east of the Aegean. Another grouping comprises Euboea, Skyros,

Thessaly and perhaps eastern Boeotia. What is called Western Greek is at home in Laconia, Messenia, Elis, Achaea, Aetolia, Acarnania and Ithaca, but the coherence of this group may be exaggerated. Crete stays apart, with regional variations of its own: here Mycenaean had affected, but not ousted, the old Minoan tradition, and this was still active in Protogeometric. Generally, too, lack of contact or local conservatism meant that development was not uniform, even in the same group.

It is usually assumed that in Attica Protogeometric began in the middle of the eleventh century and in fifty years or so was spreading to other members of the Attic group. (These dates are speculative and may be up to fifty years too early.) Elsewhere, except in Euboea, Thessaly and Crete, evidence is still insufficient, but for convenience the transition from Submycenaean – that is, the point at which potters now take a more positive attitude to tradition – is most often put in the tenth century. In Athens Geometric supersedes Protogeometric around 900 BC and in the rest of the Attic group not much later. These dates are conventional. In Central (but apparently not in Eastern) Crete Protogeometric ends around 850 BC. In the Euboean and the Western groups it persists till near the middle of the eighth century. Only in the Attic group is there an evolution from Protogeometric to Geometric; in the other groups Geometric generally appears as a foreign intrusion, so that their Protogeometric might have been described more accurately as Pregeometric, and indeed the term 'Dark Age' has been proposed for the Western Greek series.

ATHENS

At Athens – thanks to the excavations of the Germans in the Ceramicus and the Americans in the Agora – there is evidence enough to trace in detail the history of the Protogeometric style. This is fortunate, since the Attic school is of primary importance, both for artistic quality and as the parent of Geometric, so that anyhow it deserves much fuller treatment.

The Attic pioneers of Protogeometric pottery were evidently determined that the decoration should harmonize with and be generally subsidiary to clear well-designed shapes. Two principles were in use, both inherited from Mycenaean, light-ground and dark-ground. The amphora of Plate 2B is a fair specimen of the light-ground manner, which sometimes invades the neck also: it is used mainly on large vases, and becomes less popular towards the end of the style. The sparse ornaments and bands of dark paint only emphasize the prevailing light tone. Plate 1 illustrates the complementary dark-ground manner, which on the oinochoe (D) is carried to an extreme that might be called the black style. It is no accident that such ornaments as concentric circles and chequers and even cross-hatching are composed equivalently of dark and light, and so can be interpreted according to their

Figure 1 Late Mycenaean cup.
Ht 9 cm, *c.* 1150 BC (LH IIIc).

context either as light ornaments on a dark ground or as dark ornaments on a light ground. The normal decoration emphasizes the shoulder of closed vases, the field between the handles of open vases; large closed pots may have a second decorative field round the middle of the belly – so some amphorae have concentric circles where that of Plate 2B has its wavy lines. Towards the end of the black style shifts the main field to mid-belly, and in anticipation of Geometric makes experiments with ornament on the neck (so on Plate 1D).

The ornaments, few and simple, are derived from Mycenaean. Typical are sets of concentric circles and semicircles, drawn with a compass and multiple brush in contrast to the freehand spirals and arcs of Mycenaean which they replace (cf. Plate 2A and Figure 1 with Plates 2B and 1A): at the centre of these circles is a dot or a solid core – this usually early – or an hour-glass ornament as on Plate 2B, and the sets are sometimes divided by pendent groups of tongues. Cross-hatched triangles, lozenges and panels are common, and small chequers (see Plate 1A–B). Besides these are lesser ornaments – solid triangles set in a row like teeth or alternate and separated by oblique strokes (or 'opposed diagonals'), zigzags, and the wavy lines popular on the bellies of amphorae. It is a simple repertory, and simply and sensibly used: thus of the major motives semicircles and cross-hatched triangles belong to the strongly curving shoulders of closed pots, full circles to more rectangular fields. The composition is symmetrically balanced. Either there is a continuous row of – say – semicircles (so on

Plate 2B, and divided by dots on Plate 1C); or a central panel is flanked by free ornaments (Plate 1A) or by other panels (Plate 1B). Occasionally the field is divided into an upper and a lower register. The more elaborate products, with several panels or the alternation of semicircles and cross-hatched triangles, are generally later. Protogeometric is a severely abstract style, direct and calculated, and the extremely rare organic forms are introduced in unusual places or without conviction: so on an amphora from the Ceramicus a little silhouette horse stands shyly under the wavy lines to one side of the handle frieze, amusing but irrelevant.

The commonest shapes are neck-amphorae with vertical or horizontal handles (now the standard container of the ashes in Attic graves), krater, trefoil-mouthed oinochoe, lekythos (which already in Submycenaean was superseding the stirrup vase), cup, 'tea-cup', spherical pyxis and kalathos (sometimes provided with a handle). Most of these shapes are inherited from Mycenaean, though modified and remodelled as can be seen by the comparison of Plate 2B with Plate 2A or Plate 1A with Figure 1. In general contours are tauter and more clearly, if not yet sharply, defined; and there is a tendency from globular to ovoid forms with a higher belly. Necks are now larger and stronger, and feet more firmly marked and even – on cups, kraters and many 'tea-cups' – boldly conical: high incurving feet, found in some Protogeometric schools, are alien to Attica. The pots illustrated on Plates 1 and 2B show the clean vigour of the new profiles; there is nothing niggling about them.

The technique is similar to Mycenaean, though not as good as the best work in that style. The clay, sometimes gritty, varies from a pale to a mid-brown: the larger light-ground pots, which are generally pale, seem often to have a thin coating of a finer yellowish slip. The paint ranges from dark-brown to near black, sometimes accidentally fired to red. In ornaments a variation in its density often shows the brush running dry; but there was some deliberate dilution, notably in the zigzag that frequently runs above a row of concentric circles or round a lip (as on Plate 1B). Both paint and unpainted surface have a sheen, now often worn off. Generally the later vases, particularly of the black style, are the most careful, and their darker clay, blackish paint and strong sheen are indistinguishable from much Early Geometric work.

The Attic Protogeometric style began about 1050 BC, perhaps with some initial prompting from Cyprus, and after a short spell of experiment established its canon. In the tenth century the elongation of shapes led to a shift of decorative emphasis from shoulder to neck, and there appears some effort for elegance in the now popular black style and the elaborate panel decoration; but since each shape had its own system or systems of decoration, this evolution was not uniform. The end of the style, which came about 900 BC, was as rapid as its beginning. A few exports have been noticed.

PROTOGEOMETRIC OUTSIDE ATTICA

Knowledge of Protogeometric schools outside Attica has been growing in recent years and, though most are still shadowy, it is becoming clear that they were more independent than had been supposed. The summary that follows can only be provisional.

The *Argolid*, which had been the dominant artistic region of the Late Bronze Age, produced the only Protogeometric school comparable with Attic, to which it remained close; generally this must have been due to imitation by Argive. From *Corinth* there are so far only a few modest dark-ground pieces, related to Attic or Argive, and the apparent survival of Protogeometric for a generation or so longer suggests that its school was a minor one. This connection of the north-east Peloponnese with Attica may seem curious to believers in ethnic solutions. Less surprising is the influence of Argive in *Arcadia*, where such Protogeometric as there is looks a cross between Argive and Laconian. In *Boeotia* a few Attic imports have been recognized and so some local imitation might be expected, though in the eastern districts Euboean influence would not be unlikely. What little is known from the *Southern Cyclades* suggests Attic models, and the absence of earlier Protogeometric may be accidental.

Much Protogeometric has been found in *Rhodes* and *Cos*. Once again the style is modelled on Attic (and possibly Argive), and there are some admirable pieces. Gradually local variations appeared, for instance an excess of latticing and (as in some of the Cyclades) the linking of grouped circles by bands of zigzag or straight lines. This Dodecanesian school seems to have received some new influences when Geometric was beginning at Athens, though a proper Geometric style did not succeed for another fifty years. At *Smyrna*, *Samos* and *Miletus*, and also in *Caria*, the earliest Protogeometric was very like Attic. Finds elsewhere in *Ionia* and *Aeolis* are too few for useful conclusions, whether because the early levels have not been explored or because Greek settlement in those parts had hardly begun. Imports and local imitations are reported – perhaps too hopefully – at Sardis in Lydia.

For *Euboea* the excavation of Lefkandi has been informative. A Protogeometric style is thought to have started independently at the same time as at Athens. This Early phase is unambitious, with decoration little more than a wavy line. In the Middle Protogeometric, around the end of the eleventh century, so new finds are showing, Attic example and local talent produced an enterprising school, which with its rich variety of shapes and ornaments (including a precocious tree) had effects outside Euboea. The Late Protogeometric which followed became more conventional, though it retained or perhaps introduced some uncanonical forms – notably the jug with cut-away neck, which came from Thessaly, and the PSC cup, so-called for its pendent semicircles, disposed in two sets which often

Figure 2 Cup with pendent semicircles (PSC cup).
Ht 8 cm. Cycladic or Euboean, 9th or early 8th century BC.

intersect (Figure 2). By the end of the tenth century stagnation had set in and a simplified Protogeometric style, inelegantly and unnecessarily dubbed Subprotogeometric, persisted until the mid-eighth century, occasionally borrowing something from Athens, where the style was now Geometric. Artistically Euboean Protogeometric has a rough vigour, though the Late Protogeometric PSC cups (Figure 2) have some elegance and more historical importance, since they were exported to Cyprus and the Levant and to Etruria and are reasonably interpreted as evidence of Euboean commercial enterprise. *Skyros* seems dependent on Euboea and Thessaly. For the *Northern Cyclades* scanty finds show some connection, not necessarily subordinate, with Euboean; but when the Geometric style had been established, they soon joined the other Cyclades in a style based on Attic, though still retaining the PSC cup.

Thessaly was for long on the border of the Greek world. In the Late Bronze Age Mycenaean pottery had been made there and a Protogeometric style is apparent by the end of the eleventh century. Fairly soon, if not from the start, contact with Euboea is evident and, perhaps through Euboean, with Attic. At the same time local traditions survived, especially in inland districts. Notable peculiarities are cut-away necks and trigger handles. It has been suggested that the use of the compass to draw circles originated in Thessaly: if so, Athens appropriated it quickly.

Macedonia, not yet reckoned Greek, had imported Mycenaean but retained its native tradition. That tradition continued in the Iron Age, but at some time a Protogeometric style took root beside it. The quality varies, perhaps according to remoteness. Some examples are respectable enough, but others are barbaric with their impoverished decoration and clumsy shapes. Typical are cups with deep bowl and high lip, decorated with sets of pendent semicircles or three-quarter circles; sometimes consisting of only two arcs. Such influences as can be detected suggest that Mecedonian derived from Thessalian or Euboean. On some sites at least it lasted till about 600 BC when Corinthian imports became numerous.

For *Laconia* we have a fair number of sherds, nearly all from sanctuaries, but hardly any complete pots. The decoration is clumsy and later often crowded, with frequent cross-hatching on the lip of cups (the commonest shape among the finds), sets of squarish panels between the handles, and dark paint below. The motifs are mostly rectilinear, the favourite being the cross-hatched triangle. Horizontal grooving of the body is a peculiarity of this school, the clay is darker than usual elsewhere, and the deep-brown to blackish paint often has a metallic sheen. There may be Attic influence, perhaps through Argive, in the occasional use of circles, but generally this looks a conservative style of separate origin, wherever that origin may be. The closest connections in system of decoration and motifs are with *Messenia*, where the sequence goes back to the Late Bronze Age. There, too, cross-hatched panels and triangles are frequent and, as further north, sets of semicircles sometimes both hang from the top and rest on the bottom of a panel. The clay, which varies in colour, is usually soft and flaky. Finds are too few to determine how much uniformity there was in different localities. Too little is known of *Elis, Achaea, Aetolia* and *Acarnania* for any useful characterization, though it seems that in their pottery coastal settlements of Achaea differed from inland ones and had some connections with Aetolian settlements across the gulf. Lastly, *Ithaca* (which has been more prolific) had a related, but distinctive Protogeometric style. Its favourite ornaments are cross-hatched lozenges and triangles, sometimes fringed, vertical zigzags and, less frequently, concentric circles and semicircles and loops. In all this Western Greek region the Protogeometric (or, if one prefers, the Dark Age) style lasted without much change until near the middle of the eighth century; perhaps not so long in Ithaca.

In *Crete* the material is relatively plentiful, but here the antecedents were different. In other parts of the Greek world the style of the Late Bronze Age had been uniformly Mycenaean, but in Crete the older Minoan tradition was tenacious and had partially resisted the mainland style. Now in turn there was resistance to Protogeometric. In Eastern Crete Subminoan continued into the ninth century, but in Central Crete, though, Protogeometric was accepted in the early tenth, if with reservations. There we still find the stirrup vase, kalathos, pyxis with high steep sides, duck vases, and the deep cup which turns into a kind of bell-krater. Other common shapes are squat trefoil-mouthed oinochoe, amphora with very short neck or collar, and a footless amphora which tends to acquire a long inward curve towards it flat base. The decoration, in light or dark style, is lax. The commonest ornaments are concentric circles, often floating loosely in the field and filled with an oblique hour-glass, and thick bands of paint to separate zones are used more freely than elsewhere. Another characteristic motif is the double horizontal zigzag. Clearly the Protogeometric style did not originate in Crete, but evident signs of foreign influence are few though there are some imported Attic pots. It lasted at Cnossus till the middle of the ninth century and in remoter places probably longer.

CHAPTER III

THE GEOMETRIC
STYLE

—— ·◆· ——

INTRODUCTION

A conscious insistence that shape should be clearly defined and decoration
have an abstract regularity distinguishes the Protogeometric from the
Mycenaean style. Geometric takes these tendencies a stage further: contrast
the two amphorae of Plates 2B and 3B. Geometric ornament has recurred
again and again throughout the history of art, but the almost mathematical logic of the Greeks makes theirs the pre-eminent if not the only
Geometric style. The shape of the pot, analysed into its component parts,
is carefully balanced. The decoration is placed and designed to emphasize
the shape. Here is a style so self-disciplined that it can be monumental.

The Protogeometric amphora of Plate 2B is a sober but easy-going work,
plump in shape and ingenuous in decoration. Its Geometric counterpart
(Plate 3B) has drawn itself in and the band of meander, compact and
rigid, advertises the restriction. To suit the new shape and the new feeling
for shape the decorative emphasis is shifted from shoulder to belly and
neck – Protogeometric groping towards this is shown on the late oinochoe
of Plate 1D, and a transitional stage on Plate 3A. The ornaments change in
sympathy. The groundling semicircles vanish; the loosely spaced rows of
full circles survive only in backward schools; and the firm, continuous
meander becomes the characteristic Geometric motive. The difference
between Protogeometric and Geometric is sharp, but the transition –
though rapid – was evolutionary and there is no sign of artistic prompting
from outside. Older theories that the Dorians brought in the new style
and particularly the meander were still ignorant of the nature or even the
existence of Protogeometric and of the foreshadowing in it of Geometric.

The strict Geometric formula was simple and its ideal easily and quickly
reached. Further development in the eighth century tried to complicate the
decoration. The ornamental fields were multiplied till sometimes they
covered almost the whole surface of the pot, panels and vertical strips interrupted the horizontal rhythm, and some new ornaments, though still regular
and abstract, were invented. In the hands of a master this development
allowed a subtler and mellow grandeur, as on the amphora of Plate 4A.
Here the principal field, set in its proper structural place, still dominates the decoration of the pot, though the shape has lost much of its
primary importance. But more mediocre pieces, such as those of Plate 6A

15

and even of Plate 4B, are restless displays of decoration. The strength of the Geometric conventions is becoming a weakness, since painters rigidly limited in their repertory of ornament let themselves indulge in new and ostentatious arrangements which often ignore or contradict the shape. But progress was made with the figures, human and animal, which first appear regularly in the eighth century. These figures, drawn in silhouette, were quickly geometricized into abstract types, but the problems of pictorial composition set a satisfying task to the more ambitious artists who gradually lost interest in enriching the subsidiary decoration. In Attica their austerer models educated the pioneers of the new art of the seventh century.

No style of pottery has been more successful than mature Greek Geometric in adjusting decoration to the shape of the pot. It achieves its aim by precise planning, assisted by quite simple, almost mechanical ornament. The recipe is easy and calls for no special artistic ability, and for that reason there is till near the end little bad Geometric pottery. This impersonal self-sufficient style flourished for about two centuries, and its end when it came was due less to the impact of outside forces than to its own internal exhaustion. On the artists of the next stage of Greek vase-painting – except in the Subgeometric schools which in most areas continued a watered Geometric tradition for another generation or more – its chief influence lies in the discipline and sense of order which it had implanted in Greek art.

In most other Geometric schools the initiative came from Athens, directly or indirectly, and they continued to borrow from Athens, if only intermittently, till in the later eighth century they found Corinthian novelties more congenial or experimented on their own. The first proselyte was the Argolid, which welcomed Geometric at its start, and Corinth and Boeotia were not much later; these schools followed Attic development through its Middle phases too, though with their own modifications and characteristics – Argive robust, Corinthian unassuming and Boeotian provincial. Attic Middle Geometric had also a wider influence. From the start it was imitated closely in the Cyclades and with some reservation in the East Greek region, and in Euboea Atticizing pottery is found along with its Subprotogeometric; rather later, Crete accepted the new style; and towards the end intimations of it have been discerned in Thessaly and, apparently by way of Argos, in Arcadia and Laconia, though in these schools a costive Protogeometric was still prevalent. At the same time the other Western Greek schools, also still Suptrotogeometric, were beginning to look to Corinth as a guide, though in varying degree. So by the Late stage Geometric had become universal. At first the models had been generally Attic, except at Corinth, which was now exploiting a delicate mannerism, and among its western adherents; but soon an often wilful independence became usual, though there was some copying – even at

Athens – of neat Corinthian formulas. There is also local Late Geometric of Greek type in Italy and Sicily, of which some looks like the work of immigrants and some native imitation: the style of the earlier specimens is or resembles Euboean, of the later increasingly Corinthian. Geometric is regarded as ending when an Orientalizing style begins to establish itself; this is, of course, a simplification, since the old style (now called Subgeometric) may continue for a while alongside the new, though gradually becoming feebler. Anyhow, in the acceptance of Orientalizing Corinth was the pioneer, followed soon by Athens, the Cyclades and Crete: Euboea, the East Greek region and Laconia lagged further behind; and the rest of Western Greece and Thessaly more or less dropped out. Incidentally, the stylistic divisions devised for Attic are commonly applied to the other schools, some of which therefore have no Early or even Middle Geometric.

Such, in outline, is the current orthodoxy about the development and demarcation of the Geometric schools. For Athens it is fairly sound and for Argos, Corinth and Euboea not much less so, but elsewhere new finds may well be upsetting. As for chronology, 900 BC for the beginning of Geometric at Athens is a vague conjecture, but as good as present evidence allows; later dates are progressively less arbitrary, till one is not far from calendar accuracy in putting the establishment of an Orientalizing style at Corinth at 720 and in Athens at 700 BC, though for some of the other schools dating is still hazy.

Technical competence is generally no higher than in Protogeometric. The clay, aiming at a clear medium-brown, is fairly fine. A paler slip was used occasionally in Early Geometric, at least in Attic, and more regularly in some Late Geometric schools. The dark paint has some sheen. It is often deliberately diluted for hatching. Towards the end white is sometimes applied over dark paint, but normally (except in Crete) only for small or subordinate ornament. Very rarely a linear pattern, such as a zigzag, is incised on a dark band. The throwing and the trimming of pots are accurate and assured. The control of firing is still erratic.

In painted pottery Greek Geometric art expressed itself most fully. There was no sculpture or architecture worth the name, and free painting – if it existed – can hardly have been more distinguished. The bronze and still more the terracotta figurines, which were numerous, have not the same concentration of purpose. Metalwork with decoration in relief or engraved, though in the eighth century attracting some competent artists, did not offer enough scope in its small fields. Textiles have naturally perished, but it is hard to believe that their decoration had the tectonic quality that characterizes much of the pottery. Geometric art was in its way a perfection of the potter's craft.

ATHENS

Of the various Geometric styles that of Athens is both the best-known and the best. Its evolution, which covers the two centuries from roughly 900 to 700 BC, may be divided into three stages. The divisions, though conventional, are convenient and can be further subdivided. The number of specimens is large. Graves and stratified deposits have been recorded, notably in the Ceramicus cemetery and the Agora at Athens and also at Eleusis.

Early Geometric (*c.* 900–*c.* 850 BC)

About the end of the tenth century the Protogeometric style passed into the Geometric style proper. As usually happens, progress was not uniform; and pots in the older style were made at the same time as pieces of more distinctly Geometric quality. But the trend is to shapes with less swelling curves, and on the flatter fields that result the decoration, now regularly in the dark-ground scheme, becomes a little bolder. Circular motives give way to rectilinear, particularly the meander, which is used both as a short strip in a panel and repeated to form a continuous band. It appears first in the battlement form and built of parallel strands (Plate 3A) – conceivably an angular version of the wavy lines of Protogeometric (Plate 2B) – or else stuffed with dots; but soon it is regularly involuted and hatched (as on Plate 3B), and this form becomes the characteristic ornament of Attic Geometric. Attempts have been made to derive the meander from contemporary cultures outside Greece, but the parallels suggested are both unsatisfactory and unnecessary. An ornament of such simple form could have been though out independently by Greek artists, and the general aspect of the earlier Geometric period suggests a style developing in thoughtful isolation.

As for shapes, amphorae grow slimmer and stiffer and – partly by lengthening the neck – rather taller. The oinochoe in contrast becomes squatter and more solid in the body, and its neck is more emphatic. The pedestalled krater continues. The cup, which at first falls behind the kantharos in popularity, gives up the Protogeometric high foot for an abrupt broad base as if the pot had been sawn off a little way up the body (compare for the effect Plates 1A and 8A). Among new shapes the most curious is an ovoid pyxis with pointed base, in defiance of the general trend towards stability. The lekythos is replaced by a squat narrow-necked oinochoe. The decoration is re-arranged in rough correspondence to the shape. Thus on the three forms of the amphora the position of the handles determines that of the main decorative field. Where – on the survivors of the Protogeometric favourite – the handles cling to the belly, the emphasis is now regularly on a panel stretching between them. The more modern amphorae with handles either set on the shoulder or reaching up to the neck have panels respectively on shoulder or neck, at first smallish and starkly framed. An example of the latter type, which soon became canonical, is shown on Plate 3A. Here the panel on the neck is wider than usual and the ornament round the belly has become of equal importance: the Early Geometric painter was tiring of austerity. For the same reason the reserved bands which complete the decoration become finer and more numerous. The repertory of ornaments is still small – the meander of both types and the set of horizontal zigzags, which soon take the principal places, the row of solid triangles, and for a time the triangles between oblique strokes; concentric circles remain fashionable only on kraters and belly-handled amphorae. The arrangement, loosely spaced in Protogeometric, becomes neater and more compact. The total effect, simple as it is, shows a clear and firm artistic conception.

Middle Geometric (*c.* 850–*c.* 760 BC)

The trends just described are logically fulfilled about the middle of the ninth century. The amphora on Plate 3B has already been mentioned as typical of the Geometric style in general. Here the forms inherited from earlier phases have been refined, the composition is more precise. The neck, because of the position of the handles, carries the principal decoration: note how the top of the panel is exactly level with the upper junction of the handles. To balance the decorative effect a second field is reserved on the belly, and filled with the same ornaments. Below come neat groups of reserved bands. The dark ground still covers most of the surface of the pot, but is no longer oppressive. There is a similar refinement of the shape. The transition from body to neck, which before was slurred, is now sharply articulated; the proportions are carefully harmonized; and the whole has a more architectural quality. There is little room in this style for original invention and less for virtuosity. For his effects the artist depends on logical planning and the careful repetition of simple ornament. In consequence the general level of attainment was remarkably uniform.

This solution, admirable in its way, had narrow limits. Further development took two courses. One continued to lighten the dark tone of the pot by inserting more bands of ornament and reserved stripes. The other revived the system of dividing a large field into panels (a later and more thoroughgoing version is presented by Plate 4B, on the shoulder): such panelling had been current in Protogeometric (Plate 1A–B), but in earlier Geometric was more or less restricted to narrow strips of chevrons acting as side frames. Both changes weakened the connection of shape and decoration; the pot tends to be regarded as a surface to be covered rather than a shape to be accentuated. This effect is more evident in Late Geometric, as on Plate 6A; here the vertical stress of the panels has no structural relevance, though excusable because of the formlessness of this pyxis. But change was gradual, and particularly on less ambitious pieces the severer style was never wholly superseded.

The repertory of ornament grows richer during this stage. Among early novelties are opposed triangles between vertical strokes (illustrated in a coarse version on Plate 7A) and in the eighth century there are added small circles linked tangentially (as on Plate 6B) and the string of lozenges with a central dot (Plate 5, in the next field to the bottom). More important was the introduction of animate figures. These had appeared even before Middle Geometric, though very rarely and unobtrusively. But with the eighth century the horses, birds and human figures are displayed more boldly, first in subsidiary and then in major panels. Such organic forms do not naturally belong to the severe and abstract Geometric environment, and some time was needed to adapt them. So the earlier representations have a greater freedom than is permitted later (as for instance on Plate 5).

The shapes generally become more clearly articulated and the greatest diameter of the body tends to be higher. There are also changes in types. The flat pyxis, later often embellished with horses on the lid (Plate 6A), is popular from the beginning of Middle Geometric, and subsequent innovations include the mug and the kantharos with high handles.

Production was increasing in the eighth century, to judge by the number of surviving pots, and there is some decline in the quality of technique and draughtsmanship; but judged by purely abstract standards Attic Geometric comes to its perfection in the Middle phase.

Late Geometric (*c.* 760–*c.* 700 BC)

In Late Geometric the enrichment of decoration goes still further so that almost the whole surface of the pot may be covered (Plate 4B), and the division of fields becomes more popular, now often in a series of squarish panels (Plate 6A) which usually are filled with a hatched swastika or quatrefoil. Meanders may be more complex, justifiably where they give extra height to a principal field (as on the neck of the oinochoe of Plate 4B); the tapestry design is invented for the same purpose (Plate 4B, on the belly); the row of hatched leaves is frequent (Plate 4A, near the bottom); and other common innovations are chequers, too strident for the half-tone principles of Geometric decoration, cross-hatched batons, derived from the plastic ribbing of the walls of pots, and snakes, which are drawn in regular undulation and more often without head or tail. Some of the earlier works of this phase still have a disciplined assurance and even grandeur (Plate 4A and to some degree 4B), in others the style is overblown and soon both invention and diligence decay. Painters, especially on smaller pots, lost interest in the old Geometric tradition and the style breaks up.

Ambitious artists turned increasingly to human figures and actions. The standards were set with uncompromising assurance by the painter of the so-called Dipylon amphora in Athens (Plate 4A), made about the middle of the eighth century. Its full height is over a metre and a half. The dark areas are limited to the underside of the moulded lip, the junction of neck and body, and the base, though here broken by reserved bands. The rest of the surface is covered with broad and narrow bands of ornament, which except between the handles run continuously round the pot. This field between the handles (Plate 5) gets further emphasis from its subject, a scene of human figures, which have now been reduced to the canonical Geometric form, inorganic and abstract and still in silhouette. Silhouettes to be intelligible must have intelligible outlines and this, rather than incompetence of draughtsmanship or some primitive vision, determined the conventions which govern figure scenes. Here we have a scene of lamentation round the bier, on which the dead man or, more probably, woman lies covered by a pall, but for clarity the pall is lifted and cut away in steps – rectangular of course – to reveal the corpse. Around are the mourners, careful not to overlap. Their structure consists, again for clarity, of profile head and legs and frontal thorax, and each shows both arms and normally both legs. Even the corpse conforms to this scheme, with the addition of limp fingers set like the teeth of a comb. Here there are no signs of sex, except for the swords of the two men on the far left, though elsewhere women were sometimes distinguished by their breasts – little projections below the armpits – and later still by cross-hatched skirts. The technique of full silhouette (soon enlivened by a circular eye) is in uneasy contrast to the half-tones of the hatched meanders, though the filling ornaments between and around the figures give some relief. For figures Geometric perspective is satisfactory, but such objects as chariots raise difficulties of logic: sometimes one wheel is shown, sometimes both but side by side, and the front rail though viewed in profile is drawn as a wide loop. At first these figure scenes occur most commonly on large amphorae and stemmed kraters, which were set upright over the grave as markers and possibly also as chutes for food and drink, but later they appear on smaller shapes too, some perhaps intended for the use of the living. Besides the mourning at the bier the favourite subjects are processions of chariots and fighting by land and sea. In a few instances students have tried to demonstrate that some legendary or mythological scene is depicted, but all in all Geometric subjects appear to be of a general character and indeed paucity of detail would have made it difficult to indicate a particular incident. Even so, the attendance of chariots at battles, not a military practice of the time, shows that the painters sometimes added a heroic flavour.

Animals appear as well as men but except for the horse not normally in human company. The favourites are deer, goats, and birds. Towards the end of the century Orientalizing creatures occasionally stray in. On the neck of the Dipylon amphora (Plate 4A) are deer grazing and recumbent goats with heads turned back and legs tucked under. These are the two usual postures, of which the second may be an early import from the East. But the animals are repeated as a pattern and do not detract from the main scene, which lies between the handles and is heavily framed by vertical strips of meander – an untectonic use of this ornament which becomes commoner as Geometric principles fail.

The Dipylon painter, who is the first recognizable personality in Greek art, left little or nothing to improve on within the conventions he set, and his rivals and successors, much less sensitive, might give their women skirts and strands of hair but tended to clumsiness and such mannerisms as swaying buttocks. In compensation they gradually reduced the importance of the subsidiary decoration. The ordinary amphora, for instance, which becomes the principal vehicle of the figure style, often has a relatively deeper main field on the body and for the rest plain stripes enlivened with a few narrow rows of zigzags and chevrons. This trend, which shows the influence of Corinthian ornament, leads to the new style of the seventh century and the abandonment of geometry for an organic approach to human anatomy.

The big grave amphorae (Plate 4A) and kraters are the spectacular Late Geometric shapes. The commonest, though, are the ordinary amphora (which tends to grow narrower), the oinochoe with trefoil mouth, the bell-mouthed oinochoe (or pitcher) often with a fancy knob to its saucer-like lid (Plate 4B), the mug, cups of various types, the kantharos with high handles, the kotyle, the cup or bowl with high lip and sometimes a tall stand, and the plate. Bell-mouthed oinochoe, bowl, plate and kotyle (which imitates Corinthian in decoration as well as shape) are novelties. On the whole the shapes in Late Geometric are treated with less respect than before, and it is not surprising that plastic snakes are soon permitted to crawl up the handles or round the shoulder or the lip. The snake is one of the many creatures that have been associated with cults of the dead, but it is rash to make much of this ceramic fashion, prevalent perhaps through two generations, for serpents plastic and painted. Often they have become no more than abstract decoration, though of course protrusions on the lip must have made some pots impracticable for household use.

Technique declines after the Early stage, but even then firing or painting was often uneven, as is shown by the reddening of the dark paint. On the whole Attic Geometric clay is a little browner than Protogeometric, at least till its Late stage. The use of a yellowish slip persisted, though infrequently, into Early Geometric. Towards the end of Late Geometric there is an occasional use of added white for detail.

Of all the Geometric schools that of Athens was the most powerful and till near its end the most admired. Attic exports are fairly frequent in Aegina and Boeotia, and they occur also in the Cyclades, Thessaly and Crete, and during the eighth century even in Cyprus, Syria, Macedonia, South Italy and Sicily. Attic influence is strong in Boeotian and Cycladic, and affects Argive, Corinthian, East Greek, Cretan and Thessalian. It is not till the third quarter of the eighth century that the tide set the other way, and Corinthian imports and imitations became frequent. But already the Orientalizing style was imminent. In Attica, which was no longer the pioneer, this new style emerges about 700 BC; and though conservative painters clung to the old tradition, their Subgeometric – that is, belated, or mannered Geometric – did not survive more than ten or twenty years.

THE ARGOLID

Argive Geometric

The plain of Argos was the centre of the Mycenaean culture and it remained important during the early Iron Age. Much pottery has been found at Argos, Mycenae and Tiryns, and some at Asine and the Argive Heraeum (between two and three miles south-east of Mycenae). Argos, the principal city of the area, was evidently the metropolis of the school, though in the Late stage there are some signs of independence, especially at Asine.

This Argive Geometric, which follows a respectable Protogeometric style, begins about the same time as Attic. Judged by pretensions, it is the second most important Geometric school. Its Early and Middle stages follow Attic, though showing less enterprise. The Late stage, roughly from 750 to 690 BC, develops on its own. Here the division of fields into panels is often excessive, anyhow at first. In the many figure scenes horses are common, sometimes paired and with a man or manger between them and large fishes floating in the field. Women often have two or three long strings dangling in front of their skirts. Meanders are plentiful, a favourite variety being the step meander, which by its diagonal slant tends to unbalance the composition, and hatching comes to be at right angles instead of oblique. Of the subsidiary ornaments the increasingly popular rows of massed zigzags, horizontal or vertical, deserve notice. The effect tends to be heavy, if not lumpish. The final phase admits a few Orientalizing motifs and sometimes gives its figures more solidly constructed heads and even outlined faces. A less ambitious style without figures but adding a few simple Orientalizing motifs to the traditional stock continues into the second quarter of the seventh century; but it is best called Subgeometric.

Of the shapes the most important are amphora, krater (rarely with a high stem), cup, pyxis and oinochoe: in the Late stage and in Subgeometric the krater predominates. The technique is competent. The clay, which often has white inclusions and a greenish tinge, is rather coarser than Attic. The Argive school was evidently influenced by Attic and later by Corinthian.

In turn it had some influence on Arcadia, and a little on Sparta and perhaps too at an early stage on Corinth. There was a little export to neighbouring districts and a few fragments have been recognized at Tarentum and at Megara Hyblaea in Sicily.

'Argive Monochrome'

A pale unpainted ware has also been assigned to the Argolid and called 'Argive Monochrome'. The commonest shapes are the conical oinochoe (generally with arching body) and a small jug. The decoration is rarely more than incised or pricked zigzags and wavy lines. The clay is about the colour of putty. Most of these pots are shaped by hand, not on the wheel. This simple ware appears to have been made not only in the Argolid but also in Corinth and Attica and probably elsewhere too. Its main period is the eighth and seventh centuries, but a similar monochrome was being made much earlier and it is not rare in the sixth century.

CORINTH

We still know very little of Mycenaean and early Iron Age Corinth. A few Protogeometric pots have been found, akin to Attic and Argive but apparently local. The Geometric style is clearer, especially towards its end. It is a simple and neat school, which may be divided into three phases – Early (*c.* 875–*c.* 825 BC), Middle *c.* 825–*c.* 750 BC), and Late (*c.* 750–*c.* 720 BC).

Of the *Early Geometric* not much has survived. The commonest shapes seem to be trefoil-mouthed oinochoai and cups. A peculiar variety of the oinochoe has a globular body and a small neck – Corinthian Geometric potters always liked plump shapes. The cup, at first deep, grows shallower. The decoration is usually confined to a single reserved field – on the neck of oinochoai and the shoulder of cups – and the rest of the pot is painted dark except for narrow groups of reserved bands. The characteristic ornament is a set of three or four horizontal zigzags, often connected to the frame of the field by short strokes from their apices – a rather clumsy and later example is shown on Plate 8A. The meander is rare.

In *Middle Geometric* the decoration is a little more complex. The single field, which remains normal, is more often stopped at each end by a narrow panel and may be underlined by a subsidiary horizontal strip. On cups and kraters the decorated area, as in contemporary Attic, continues round the pot under the handles. The main field is often filled by the hatched meander and sometimes by cross-hatched triangles. But even there, as well as in the minor horizontal and vertical strips, the favourite ornaments are groups of neat chevrons and zigzags or wavy lines, upright or lying on their sides. Curvilinear ornaments and human or animal figures are not admitted into this simple style.

The *Late Geometric*, in older works sometimes called Linear Geometric or Protocorinthian Geometric, continues the tradition of sober neatness but accelerates the trend to lightness of tone. The main decoration is, as before, at the level of the handles; but below it narrow stripes, alternately painted and reserved, spread well down the vase, and the neck (if the pot has a neck) is similarly striped. A few new ornaments and arrangements are added to the repertory, for instance opposed triangles (as on Plate 7A), the false spiral, and – more significant in that the Geometric tradition of continuous ornament is broken – intermittent groups of zigzag or wavy strokes spaced, sometimes alternately, in a narrow band round the pot. The hatched meander soon proves too cumbrous for the new environment, except in the Thapsos class, which also has a fondness for the running spiral. Of the shapes the ordinary oinochoe remains popular (for the shape only see Plate 8C), the conical oinochoe – like a narrow-necked version of the last sawn off at the shoulder – becomes more frequent, and the kotyle is invented. The kotyle (see Plate 8B) is the most characteristic product of Corinthian Late Geometric, and shows the new style to best advantage. Its popularity was immediate and enduring. The shape, delicate and thin-walled to match the decoration, is derived from the Geometric cup by removing the lip and lifting the body and conformably the earlier examples are more spreading than the later. In contemporary Athens, where the Geometric tradition could not be so boldly denied, there occurs an opposite development of the cup, in which the body becomes shallower and the rim shoots up to equal it in height. Other common shapes are krater, round pyxis, plate and especially in the Thapsos class (where the kotyle is neglected) kantharos and cup. This Thapsos class, which has a distinct but not alien character within the Corinthian Late Geometric style, also tends to a greener tone of clay and a darker colour of paint. It is generally and reasonably considered to be the product of a more conservative workshop or group of workshops in Corinth; but if another home should be wanted, Megara has the advantage of being geographically convenient and ceramically still unknown.

Corinth was the first city to advance beyond Geometric principles. Its own Geometric school had been modest, so that tradition was not too strong to hamper innovation, as happened at Argos and even at Athens, and its characteristic virtue of neatness, as opposed to grandeur, was well suited to the new style that was forming. About this time Corinth's commercial importance seems to have been increasing, at least in the pottery trade, but whether that immediately influenced the style of Corinthian pottery (as some claim) is very doubtful. During the last quarter of the century Orientalizing motives entered Corinth, and though much of the Late Geometric style persisted and indeed continued to develop, it is more conveniently classed with Protocorinthian.

Technically the quality of Corinthian Geometric is good, more so at the end. The clay is fine and in colour lightish brown with a tendency towards pink or green. The surface is well finished and shiny. The paint is at first generally dark-brown, but in the later eighth century a red tone comes to be preferred. In the earlier stages it is not always easy to distinguish Corinthian clay from Attic by eye, but they gradually diverge – Attic towards orange, Corinthian towards yellow. Sometimes, in the later stages, an orange-red paint is used for ornament alongside the usual brown or red, of which perhaps it is a more dilute solution; and occasionally, at the end, white paint (or rather a solution of the pale clay) is used over the dark paint for an ornament normally painted dark on a reserved ground.

The export of Corinthian Geometric was negligible before the eighth century. Then there was progressive expansion. Middle Geometric (though except at Medeon not of the early phase) is fairly frequent at Delphi and in Ithaca and occurs in Aegina, Thera, Cnossus, Smyrna and Thessaly. Late Geometric and its Early Protocorinthian successor appear, often in quantity, throughout the Greek world, from Al Mina in Syria to Etruria. The stylistic relation between the Corinthian and other Geometric schools corresponds. Till the early eighth century some mild influence of Attic and perhaps Argive is visible in Corinthian. In the later eighth century Corinthian Geometric was imitated in varying degrees by most of the other Greek schools, even by Attic.

LACONIA

Knowledge of Laconian Geometric, as of Protogeometric, depends mainly on finds from sanctuaries in Sparta itself and at Amyklae a few miles south. These are generally unstratified, very fragmentary and probably deficient in some of the ordinary shapes. So, apart from the observed testimony that Protogeometric precedes Geometric, classification is by style. The account that follows is tentative.

Since there is very little in the decoration that would not or could not be considered of the Late stage elsewhere nor is there much sign of a transition from Protogeometric, it seems that Laconian Geometric appeared fairly suddenly about 750 BC. At first, perhaps, a band of continuous decoration was regular and the typical ornament was concentric circles, the sets often carelessly spaced and sometimes intersecting. Later, richer decoration and panelling were preferred and the influences of Argos and Corinth are visible, even on the same pot. The step meander, other meanders with hatching at right angles, the big hatched zigzag, the quatrefoil and the occasional human figures are taken from the grandiose Argive style. The contribution of Corinth, increasing during the Early Protocorinthian period, is evident not only in a neat system of narrow fields and fine striping, but also in some linear ornaments and the little silhouette birds. Concentric circles, triangles and lozenges are Protogeometric survivals, and gridded hatching of meanders is a local aberration. The shapes generally lack the logic of the best Geometric schools. Those recovered include cups, a big stemmed bowl (perhaps a local equivalent of the krater), a small bowl, low flat dishes with incurved rim, tall pyxis with doubly curved wall, oinochoai (some with high narrow neck and strutted handle) and the lakaina (a derivative of the cup that remains popular in Laconia but is very rare elsewhere). Fairly soon slip was introduced, but did not drive out the older technique. In the slipped ware the clay is coarser and pink, the slip itself is thin, greyish and friable, and the paint is duller.

Until more is discovered it is impracticable to define the duration of Geometric in Laconia. It seems that from the end of the eighth century onwards there was a gradual infiltration of Orientalizing motifs (such as the broken cable, small solid meander, rays and chequers) but no consistent style was formed for another generation or more. If dates however arbitrary are wanted, then the Laconian Geometric style may be said to finish about 690 BC and Subgeometric (or Transitional) to continue till about 650 BC.

This is a clumsy school. A few pieces have turned up in neighbouring districts, four latish pieces at Tarentum, one in Samos and a cup (so it is said) in Cyrene, and Laconian as well as Argive influence is discernible in Arcadia. From the late eighth century on, Corinthian imports appear, though not frequently, in Sparta.

WESTERN GREECE

Excavation in *Ithaca* has produced a fair quantity of imported Corinthian from the end of Middle Geometric onwards and also of a ware found nowhere else and presumably local. This Ithacan pottery is a mixture of Protogeometric legacies and Corinthian loans, the loans steadily becoming more dominant; some minor influences of Euboean and other schools have been detected, perhaps too hopefully. The typical ornaments, derived from the Protogeometric of the island, are sets of concentric arcs and large pothooks. The commonest shapes are krater, various types of oinochoe, kantharos, deep cups and globular pyxis. The clay is usually reddish to brown or occasionally pale. The paint is dark-brown with a violet tinge. Dating, which depends through stylistic comparisons and contexts on Corinthian, is fairly safe. Ithacan Geometric begins little if at all before 750 BC and continues well down the first quarter of the seventh century, till it shades into what may be called Subgeometric or perhaps rudimentary Orientalizing.

Finds of Geometric have been increasing in *Achaea,* but there is much less from *Acarnania, Aetolia, Elis* and *Messenia.* Again some groups are datable by the import or imitation of Corinthian. Direct connection with Ithaca is hardly apparent, though the looseness of decorative composition is similar. Nor is there any evident connection with Laconian. The chronology seems to be more or less as that of Ithacan.

BOEOTIA

Boeotia is rich in cemeteries, as the peasants know; but archaeologists, contemptuous of its art, prefer to excavate elsewhere. So though there are many Boeotian Geometric pots in museums, of few is the place of finding recorded, let alone the context. It is lucky for classifiers that their style is imitative.

Very few graves of the Early or Middle Geometric phases have been recorded in Boeotia. They contain imported Attic and fairly close Boeotian imitations of Attic. It is not always easy to distinguish the simpler or rougher examples, and perhaps among better Geometric pots some which pass as Attic were made in Boeotia. Attic influence was still dominant in the second half of the eighth century, when the finds become more plentiful. The local painters even attempted ambitious scenes of human figures, but the drawing is usually clumsy and the composition often chaotic. There are also some characteristic ornaments. The Attic band of circles joined by tangents is developed into a high wavy line of thin up-strokes and very thick down-strokes. A spidery swastika with more than four arms appears among the filling motifs. Rows of large concentric circles, a form of decoration too loose for Attic taste, are or become common. Towards the end of the eighth century Corinth was in the ascendant and Corinthian influence is to be seen, especially in alternating groups of upright straight and zigzag lines and in strips or narrow bands of zigzags, horizontal or vertical, which are sometimes joined to the frame by short strokes (as on Plate 8A). This Late Geometric, with or without Orientalizing intrusions and often affected, persists into the seventh century. The important shapes are the tall neck-amphora, the big oinochoe, and towards the end a simple kantharos with high vertical handles. An amphora of Linear Island type, with high foot and broad neck, appears towards the end (see pp. 101–2). In the Atticizing group the clay resembles Attic, though rather coarser, and the paint tends to be duller and less even; the Linear Island group prefers a redder clay and a whitish slip. There is not the evidence to decide in which of the cities of Boeotia Geometric pottery was made, or whether there were local schools. Export was negligible.

EUBOEA

Euboean Geometric is important more for its distribution than its artistic merit. At home the main finds – mostly of sherds – are from Eretria and Lefkandi, and what is available from Chalcis is similar. The clay, which has no mica, looks much like Attic, though often finer and harder. Slip, when used, is creamy in colour and thick. At Lefkandi, but perhaps not at Eretria, the dominant style remained Subprotogeometric till the middle of the eighth century, though for a generation or so a Middle Geometric variant was forming under Attic influence. This influence continued briefly, though vigorously, into the Late Geometric period, as it did in the Cyclades, and it is not always easy to distinguish their products. So experts have disputed whether Euboea or Naxos should have credit for the gifted Cesnola painter, partly perhaps because he was thought too good to be Euboean: his clay appears Euboean, according to analyses, but he could have been an immigrant. About 725 BC, as Attic influence ceased, there was a short vogue for imitations of Corinthian, which left a number of Corinthian motifs and shapes or variations of them in the Euboean repertory. The Euboean Geometric style is not a coherent one: still it has some conveniently recognizable mannerisms. Among these are rows of small concentric circles or cross-hatching round the vertical lips of Atticizing cups, and the careless lozenges with a dot in each quarter that serve as a main or subsidiary ornament in the panels; on Corinthianizing kotylai, besides clumsiness of composition and the coarser drawing of silhouette birds, fine striping is sometimes done in white paint instead of by reservation; and, more originally, slip may be used as a stuffing for the meanders, lozenges and fat crosses which decorate a class of late cups. The Late Geometric shapes – not in order of first appearance – include amphora of Linear Island type (cf. Plate 29A), deep krater with flaring pedestal, oinochoe of normal type, oinochoe with cut-away neck, conical oinochoe, a slim jug with tall narrow neck and round mouth, aryballos, cup, kantharos and kotyle. Of these the amphora probably comes from Cycladic, the jug with cut-away neck is derived from Thessalian, the slim jug has no obvious Greek ancestry, and the others are taken from the Attic and Corinthian repertories. By the early seventh century Euboean Late Geometric is decadent, enough so to be classed as Subgeometric, and in this form it lingered on for another generation.

Export of Euboean Geometric is much the same as that of the PSC cups, which went out of production about 750 BC or not much later. In the Levant it is notably frequent at Al Mina, where by the end of the eighth century there was also some Cypriot Geometric in a partly Euboean manner. In the West some Euboean Geometric pottery appears with Corinthian in the early finds at Pithecusae (Ischia) and Cumae and, to judge by clay, was also imitated there. Elsewhere in South Italy and Sicily a few pieces have been recognized as Euboean, of the time when Greek colonization had begun. There are also imports in Etruria (especially at Veii) which look Euboean – some still Middle Geometric in style – and the local Geometric style which developed there is considered to show specifically Euboean traits. In the older Greek lands, though not the Cyclades, imported Euboean Geometric is very rare.

THE CYCLADES

Travel in the Cyclades has usually been inconvenient, and so students have rather neglected the archaeology of these charming islands. Many Geometric pots have been found in the cemeteries of Thera, Melos and Kimolos and in the Purification enclosure on Rheneia, to which the Athenians transported the contents of graves from nearby Delos. There are also a few pots and some assorted sherds from Naxos, Paros, Delos, Tenos, Andros, Keos, Siphnos, Melos and elsewhere. But most of this material is Late Geometric, stratification and context have been unhelpful – least so in Thera – and Delos, a religious centre, imported catholically.

The Cyclades were not a political unity and it was only natural for particular islands or groups of islands to develop their own schools. For the earlier ninth century finds are still few, but it seems that the dominant influence was Attic, though in the northern chain there were connections with Euboea and Thessaly (see p. 11). The Middle Geometric style, which began about 850 BC and became normal everywhere, was (as clay shows) practised in several places but without much local variation. This is because there was a common dependence on Attic models, from which the Cycladic imitations are often stylistically indistinguishable. Still there are some peculiarities – a preference, for instance, in shapes for the amphora with handles on the belly and in decoration for putting circles in each panel of important tripartite fields. With Late Geometric the material becomes much more varied, so that it has been possible to isolate four main schools and to locate them more or less convincingly according to their frequency in one island or another.

Naxian has a clay which fires from brick-red to dark-brown and contains specks of golden mica. Most often there is a creamy slip. In style it at first leans heavily on Attic and then repeats itself with complacent care. The grander products show an unusual understanding of the Attic system of decoration and generally Naxian is well-mannered. Of the shapes the most typical are neck-handled amphora and oinochoe, both of them narrow and becoming still narrower, till they reach proportions comparable to those of the Protoattic hydria of Plate 14A. This school begins about 750 and ends about 700 BC.

'*Parian*', found also in Siphnos and Tenos but more credibly at home in the more important island of Paros, shows a wayward initiative. The clay is brownish tending often to orange and again has golden mica; on exposed surfaces there may be a thin wash of finer quality. The style starts strongly Atticizing, but gradually emancipates itself. In decoration the trend is to looser and sparser composition, with minor ornaments enlarged and promoted to major positions. The most characteristic motifs, all drawn thickly and used in rows, are tall blobs (or billets), short vertical zigzags and later the broken cable – perhaps here a simplification of the circles joined by tangents (as on Plate 6B); there is also the thick wavy line, again in a band of its own, and circles become commoner. The consummation of 'Parian' Geometric is in the fat, wide-necked amphorae of the Wheel group (Figure 3), where the shoulder has three equal panels, each exhibiting a heavy spoked circle and obliquely across the corners a row of short zigzags or chevrons. Here by orthodox standards the effect is no longer properly Geometric. Favourite 'Parian' shapes are amphorae with vertical or horizontal handles and the hydria – all (in contrast to Naxian) abnormally plump – the krater, the cup, the kantharos and the plate. 'Parian' Late Geometric too seems to have been current from about 750 to about 700 BC.

The *Melian* school, known from finds in Melos and Kimolos, has silver mica and black grit in its clay, which is a little darker than Attic. The style forms under Attic influence but without ambition or exertion, and then quietly declines into a tame Subgeometric. Figures occur, often ingenuous and sometimes grotesque. On large pots the style is passable, but lesser work tends to be mean. Among shapes the fenestrated stand shows some inept originality. Stylistic evidence suggests that this school began about 750 BC, and it may have lasted well into the seventh century.

Theran clay is reddish with coarse volcanic particles of various colours, and needs the yellowish slip that is regular in the Late Geometric school. Once more the origin of the style is in Attic, much transmuted, and though later a few Corinthian and East Greek elements are incorporated development proceeds in sluggish isolation. The characteristic shape is a big funerary amphora with broad flat lip and handles set horizontally on the shoulder, wider in the neck than the normal Geometric types and often about 60 cm high. Development is towards a slimmer body and a narrower foot. The front of the neck and of the shoulder carries the main decoration, which is arranged in broad and narrow bands, on the shoulder usually complicated by panelling; the rest of the body has spare groups of stripes. As can be seen on the smaller and simpler amphora of Plate 6B, the result is affected and arid, partly from loose spacing and partly because the decoration of the main field has a routine precision. The most important ornaments are the meander, heavy zigzags, big circles containing an eight-leaved star or four discs, cross-hatched lozenges and triangles, the quatrefoil, and for minor bands the false spiral (or row of small concentric circles joined by tangents). At first the centre of the main field is

31

Figure 3 Cycladic Geometric amphora.
Ht 42 cm. Wheel group, *c.* 725–700 BC.

occupied by a meander; but later the big circles replace them, the true spiral appears besides the false, and composition tends to be fussier. Of the other frequent shapes a squat pithos (or stamnos), dark-ground in its lower part, is an early alternative to the big amphora, and there are kraters, cups, kantharoi and plates. The Theran school looks as if it began later than other Cycladic schools of Geometric, perhaps about 720. The introduction of big circles into main panels early in the seventh century has been taken as marking its passage into Subgeometric, though stylistically there seems no sufficient change till rather later, and the tradition – reinforced by such simple Orientalizing motifs as tongues and a primitive floral chain, and once even by incised figures – still persists in the middle of the seventh century.

Cycladic Geometric, of the Middle as well as the Late stage, has turned up occasionally in Crete and in respectable quantity at Al Mina; there both Naxian and 'Parian' products have been recognized. There are also Late pieces, certainly including 'Parian', from Cyprus. Elsewhere exports outside the Cyclades are rare and negligible, unless some pots from Veii and Cumae in Italy, of the first half of the eighth century, are Cycladic rather than Euboean. The distribution of cups with pendent semicircles, some of which might be North Cycladic, has been given already (p. 11). There was a modest import of Attic till the third quarter of the eighth century, when Corinthian began to come in, and less often East Greek.

THESSALY

Thessaly does not deserve much notice. Here the local Protogeometric style was tenacious, though some pots add on their necks rectilinear decoration apparently derived from the earliest Attic Geometric. This amalgam, which according to taste may be called Early Geometric or Subprotogeometric, lasted roughly through the ninth century. Around 800 BC Attic influence became much stronger, in shapes as well as decoration, though complex ornaments were avoided. How long this Geometric continued is not known, but so far there is nothing demonstrably later than the eighth century.

THE EAST GREEK REGION

At the beginning of the Iron Age Greeks had settled the west coast of Asia Minor and the islands offshore. Politically – to use the term loosely – this region was divided into the Dorian South, Ionia, and to the north Aeolis, but since in art it is more conveniently treated as a whole it has received the general name of East Greek. In the Roman period many of the East Greek cities were very prosperous and in modern times they were within the empire of the Turkish sultans; but neither of these difficulties, the heavy deposits overlying early remains and official obstruction, excuse the excavators of several important sites for their reluctance to let others know what they found. In Rhodes, after consuls and local inhabitants had looted for half a century, the Danes and Italians have made available a mass of material. The Italians again during their occupation of the Dodecanese published a cemetery in Nisyros and later another on Cos. In Samos the Germans keep excavating methodically and have issued some comprehensive accounts. In Chios and Lesbos small sites have been dug and reported, and the pottery and other finds from the Aeolian site misnamed Larisa have eventually been revealed. For Old Smyrna parts of the publication have appeared. A few sherds are illustrated from Miletus, Ephesus, Clazomenae, Phocaea, Pitane and Lydian Sardis, and there are other sites of which even less is known. So knowledge of East Greek vase-painting is more or less hazy. For Geometric the only fairly complete series is from Rhodes; at Cos the finds stop early in the Late phase; elsewhere what can be studied is mostly or wholly Late.

33

Even so, though local distinctions should become clearer, the Geometric pottery of the Dorian and Ionian settlements has enough common characteristics to be regarded as a loose unity, and this unity continued into the sixth century. There was a radically different standard in Lesbos, which preferred a *Grey ware* (often called *Bucchero*) derived from a tradition already old when the Greeks arrived. Its shapes are sometimes Greek, sometimes Anatolian; the decoration, if there is any, consists of ridges and impressed or incised patterns of which the most elaborate, borrowed probably from the East Greek painted style, are hatched triangles and meanders. Presumably Grey ware was normal or common at other Aeolian sites in the Geometric period, as it was later – in some places at least down to the Hellenistic period.

It is in *Rhodes* and *Cos*, as has been explained, that the painted style can be examined best and for that reason its importance may be overemphasized. Here during the first half of the ninth century, that is while the Early Geometric style was current at Athens, the local workshops accepted some of the new developments in shapes, but not in decoration. The emphasis continued to be on the shoulder of closed pots, though occasionally the neck is allowed a thick zigzag. Concentric circles and even semicircles continue in use, if more coarsely drawn, but the linking of circles is abandoned. As before, cross-hatched triangles, often opposed, and lozenges are quite as frequent. Strictly this stage is a decadent Protogeometric, even if – for convenience – it is described as Early Geometric. A properly Geometric style, the so-called Middle Geometric stage, begins around 850 BC. Though for closed shapes the decoration is still concentrated on the shoulder, the meander appears, both in its simple and battlement form, with hatching (as usual in East Greek) in one direction only. Later, other varieties of meander develop and new ways of stuffing the members. A novelty, presumably of local origin, is the triangle filled with hatched lozenges. The commonest shapes are oinochoai, the lekythos with a protruding ring where the handle joins the long neck, krater with pedestal, kantharos with high handles and cups of various types. The lekythos is the most significant, since though the shape came from Cyprus it was the first recipient of the new decoration and on it – not altogether conveniently – the new style was formed. The Middle Geometric of Rhodes and Cos is unusually composite; it absorbed much from Attic, perhaps indirectly through the Cyclades, but retained much of the older tradition and added a Cypriot ingredient. In the Late Geometric stage, which seems to begin rather after 750 BC, the Rhodian material is richer in both quality and quantity. The dark-ground system continues and the field on the shoulder remains important, but close panelling partly replaces the old system of continuous bands. Of the ornaments the square hooks, which had been invented before the end of Middle Geometric, become very popular: they are used to embellish the free angles of lozenges as well as triangles (Plate 7A) or are joined four pairs together into a cross. Birds, often cross-hatched, are frequent, other figures rare. Some Orientalizing motifs too occur, notably a stylized palm tree and the cable. The shapes include oinochoai of various types (of which that of Plate 7A is a late but long-lived byform), lekythos, pedestalled krater, kantharos, cups and kotyle – this latter sometimes imitating Corinthian in decoration also. Besides the orthodox style there are various minor but distinct classes of Rhodian pottery that imitate Cypriot or Levantine models: some of them continue well into the seventh century. Generally Rhodian Late Geometric seems independent of other schools, at its best it has a dry competence, but its composition is often inconsequent, even on so careful a piece as the oinochoe of Plate 7A. In Cos the local Late Geometric is, anyhow at first, more conservative and seems not to have taken to panelling. Rhodian clay, darkish brown with occasionally some silver mica, is considered distinctive. Exports – mostly Late – have been recognized in Ionia, the Cyclades, Euboea, Aegina and Asine and further afield at Al Mina, Tarsus, Ischia, Megara Hyblaea and Gela. There was some import into Rhodes of Cypriot. The end of the Late Geometric style, partly determined by context with Protocorinthian pottery, may be put about 680 BC, though some Orientalizing experiments are probably earlier. A Subgeometric style lasted some while longer and in one special class – the Bird bowls – till the end of the seventh century.

In *Ionia* the course of development seems generally to have been similar. In the Early stage, which remains basically Protogeometric, circles are more and rectilinear ornaments less common than in Rhodes. In Middle Geometric and at the beginning of Late Geometric Attic influence is evident here too, but goes deeper. In Late Geometric, if not before, some Rhodian peculiarities were adopted – the square hooks, for example, though not the lekythos – and Rhodian products were copied, particularly the kotylai with birds. Of local trends within Ionia not much can yet be said. *Samos* shows some sophistication, especially in the Late stage, when even human figures are attempted, if without much comprehension. A minor idiosyncrasy, shared with Chios, is the stuffing of the meander with dots. Sometimes in the Late Geometric and more often in the Subgeometric stage there is a whitish slip. For *Miletus* the special characteristics of the local Geometric cannot be deduced from finds so far published. In *Chios* the Late Geometric usually has a thick whitish slip, sometimes used inside open shapes as an undercoat to the dark paint. In decoration the panel system is not adopted, and the arrangement tends to be in rows of shallow horizontal strips. The occasional human figures show more spirit than skill. Here, it seems, Subgeometric continued until about 630 BC. From *Smyrna* only a few Geometric pieces have been made known. What there is suggests a sense of composition much like that of Chios, but a more ornate taste. There was little or no export of Ionian Geometric, except perhaps inland to Lydia. The chronology is presumably much as that of Rhodian.

In native Anatolia *Caria* progressed from Protogeometric to a Middle and then a Late Geometric. How much local variation there may be in this school is not yet clear, but evidently it owed much to the Dodecanese and one might expect to Miletus too, but it has its own vagaries, like the single cross-hatched leaf. Shapes as well as decoration tend to be clumsy. It is, though, cautionary to reflect that, if one judged only by style of pottery, Caria might be considered more fully Hellenic than Sparta. Further east in *Lycia* some reflections of Greek Geometric have been discerned, but the tradition there was for Black on Red and Bichrome styles. In *Lydia* scanty finds from Sardis suggest a wayward local Geometric, indebted presumably to Ionian models.

There is also the parochial *G2-3* ware (so named after the area at Troy where it turned up). The technical quality is unexpectedly good, the style anaemically Subgeometric with sparse use of neat, unemphatic ornaments, such as zigzags and brackets (rectangular Zs) and occasionally a spiral hook. At present it is known for certain only from Samothrace, Lemnos, Troy and Antissa in Lesbos; and though excavators of those sites disclaim its manufacture there, presumably the workshop was somewhere in the northeast corner of the Aegean. Contexts support a date in the first half of the seventh century.

CRETE

The pottery of Crete does not fit comfortably into the regular classifications of Greek Geometric. Still there is plenty of it, especially in the museum of Heraklion, and the general development is clear, anyhow in Central Crete. West Crete seems to have had a local version of Protogeometric, but almost nothing is known of what came after it. At the other end of the island East Cretan – or, more tendentiously, Eteocretan – workshops show peculiarities that may be as much independent as provincial. The account which follows is concerned with the products of Central Crete.

Protogeometric B

The nonconformist Protogeometric style, which lasts well down the ninth century, is succeeded by a sudden and precocious experiment with Orientalizing and other motifs named, with justified misgiving, Protogeometric B. Favourite ornaments are loop patterns, either single (Plate 7B on the neck) or opposed and with hatching between, cables, double arcs, the mill-sail pattern, hatched zigzags, cross-hatched lozenges and triangles. Concentric circles and semicircles survive on more traditional pots. The meander is rare and clumsily used. Occasionally figures, animal and human, make an appearance; they are loosely drawn and even in part outlined. The decoration is in general planned and executed with neat facility, and sometimes it covers most of the surface of the pot. The hydria of Plate 7B is typical.

There are innovations in the shapes too. Of these the most distinctive are the pithos with straight sides and angular shoulder, and the low-bellied hydria. The stirrup vase is at last abandoned. Small pots, especially a squat jug, develop. The technique as in the preceding Protogeometric is poor, with coarsish light-brown clay and often a thin whitish slip.

This Protogeometric B style contains some traditional elements, notably the triangles, and some derived from standard Geometric elsewhere, such as the chain of lozenges. Others – particularly the cables and the loop (or spiral) bands – look like borrowings from Oriental art and are paralleled in metalwork which seems to have been made about that time in Cnossus by immigrant Eastern craftsmen. The mill-sail motif and the new shapes may be credited to local inventiveness. For the home of this curious style the evidence points fairly clearly to Cnossus, artistically the principal city of Central Crete, but it spread widely, even into East Crete, though there the painters preferred to hatch the background and not the body of curvilinear ornaments. Outside the island no effect is apparent. A few imports and still fewer imitations of Attic or Atticizing Cycladic wares suggest that the period of Protogeometric B was short, roughly from 850–820 BC according to the current chronology.

Geometric

Towards the end of the ninth century the Attic style at last imposed itself on Cretan vase-painters and there arose a fairly orthodox Middle Geometric school, which quickly rejected most of the innovations of Protogeometric B. After a brief and turbulent initial phase a compact and even ornate style sets in, particularly on the large pithoi which are its most careful products: here the influence of Athens is especially strong. The Late phase, which begins in the 740s, soon dispenses with Attic models and, while borrowing casually from Corinthian and Cypriot, can claim independence, if not creative power. Though an Orientalizing style emerged in Central Crete around the end of the eighth century, for most of the seventh the stock product was aridly Subgeometric.

The decoration is modest in extent. The pithos, for instance, usually has a main field on the shoulder, later supported by a band of ornament below, and the rest of the body has groups of reserved stripes to relieve its dark ground. Of larger motives the meander is the most common, of lesser cross-hatched lozenges and grouped zigzags. More progressive are the free-hand curving ornaments, especially the simple cable and the newly invented tongues. In the Late phase a closer system of panelling is introduced, concentric circles are often set in long bands or used as borders, and birds – sometimes with heads turned back or multiplied – show a wayward originality. Towards the end some use is made of white paint on a dark ground, especially for the rows of concentric circles. In general the smaller vases are decorated more simply and carelessly and for that reason are harder to date.

In the shapes there was some Attic and later a little Corinthian and Cypriot influence, but local tradition and initiative were not swamped. The large pithos some 50-cm high remained the standard ossuary of Central Crete and was probably copied in Thera: its Geometric form has no neck and tends to become narrower, and the lid (which it regularly possessed) is usually conical with a central knob. Several varieties of oinochoe are found, mostly small; among them is the round-mouthed jug that approaches the aryballos. There are also kraters, at first pedestalled, cups and – later – the kotyle. Cretan technique shows an improvement in Geometric. The clay fires light-brown to pink. Usually there is no slip. The paint is dark-brown to coarse red. White is used as already described. Clay and paint have a fair sheen.

There was some export of Cretan to Thera, but very little has been found elsewhere. Imports are rather more numerous – of Attic, Cycladic, Cypriot and finally Corinthian.

ITALY

The Mycenaean Greeks had left their pottery in Italy and Sicily, and it would be odd if in the early Iron Age sailors from the Ionian islands did not sometimes cross the straits. But Greek contacts with the West, to judge as usual by imported pottery, did not become regular and close till the eighth century. The first traces, some probably Euboean cups at Veii in Etruria, seem to precede the earliest Greek settlement – that of the Euboeans at Pithecusae (Ischia), which can hardly be later than the 760s, and a generation later the massive colonization of the coasts of Sicily and South Italy was beginning. The circumstances were fortunate. In the south the native tribes had a weaker organization and a lower culture, and in Central Italy the new Etruscan states, though able to prevent Greek encroachment on their territory, welcomed Greek trade. One result of these contacts was Italian Geometric pottery.

The term Italian Geometric (or Italogeometric) is elastic. It is properly used only if those wares which were made in Italy and Sicily outside the Greek colonies and are in the Greek sense Geometric. But it has often been extended with confusing and absurd results to any subsequent Italian pottery on which the decoration consists of simple lines or nondescript patterns. Generally the earliest Italian Geometric is the purest and liveliest in style – naturally enough, if it was the work of immigrant Greek potters, whose successors whatever their paternity had only local training.

In the *Greek colonies*, anyhow in their early years, there was more local production that used to be credited. At Pithecusae (Ischia) and Cumae close imitations of Euboean and Corinthian Geometric have been found: these imitations, of which the Euboean group ventures on figures, are often distinguishable only by the clay, which is characteristic of Ischia. In Sicily and South Italy, where settlement was later, colonial imitation was only or predominantly of Corinthian and its style generally tame and weak. So far these colonial wares have rarely been studied or even closely defined, but their importance is more for the history of Greek colonization than art.

Of the properly Italian Geometric styles the earliest and most robust is found in Etruria, where the native tradition already had a loosely Geometric character. On present evidence Veii appears as the pioneer, followed quickly by Vulci and Tarquinia and rather later by Caere, and soon lesser places also in Southern Etruria had their own workshops. The earliest products, which go back to the mid-eighth century, are typically Euboean in their decoration and sometimes are recognizable as Etruscan only by their clay: they have the familiar silhouette animals, the hatched birds, meanders, quatrefoils and lozenges, the rows of concentric circles, and thick zigzags and wavy lines, though some of the shapes are indigenous, as for instance the biconical amphora. In the next generation, in spite of the growing influence of Corinthian, the style is becoming sterile or by contamination with the native tradition barbarized: so Tarquinia spins out its Metope style with modest panels containing a lozenge or a pair of horizontal zigzags and at Bisenzio there are clumsy bowls with splayed lip and high, narrow foot and painted with desiccated Geometric motifs in contrasting black and red colours. A kind, or rather various kinds, of Geometric (or perhaps more correctly Subgeometric) continues well down the seventh century, sometimes admitting Orientalizing motifs, but no thoroughly Orientalizing style established itself. Clay varies; in the more orthodox groups the appearance is often not unlike Euboean, but elsewhere it is often coarse and with a pale slip. The paint is often fired red. Export outside Etruria was negligible. The detailed study of Etruscan Geometric began only recently and some workshops have been disentangled, but connections remain uncertain and any general account must still be provisional.

In the extremity of *south-west Italy* a few native cemeteries contained Villanovan amphorae and other pots of impasto together with painted amphorae, oinochoai and cups of simple Geometric style. The important motifs are hatched birds, vertical zigzags, lozenge, quatrefoil and hatched units of meander. Shape, style, clay and paint might often be taken for inferior Greek. Again the Greek models may be Atticizing Euboean. The date looks to be the generation around 700 BC. In *Apulia* and *Lucania* native schools absorbed a few Greek motifs, but remained independent.

In native *Sicily* the Geometric style is looser and less Greek than in Italy. Birds, zigzags, straight and wavy lines, and concentric circles are the staple ornaments. The main shapes are an amphora with broad out-curving neck and handles set vertically on the belly, oinochoe and a one-handled drinking bowl. Clay and paint are fairly good. This Sicilian school, which is Subgeometric rather than Geometric in character, belongs to the southeast of the island, and elsewhere in other native sites the Greek element is more dilute. This phase, which corresponds to what is called Siculan III, begins in the late eighth century and lasts till the late seventh. Its successor, Siculan IV, which is slighter and more sophisticated and has lost almost all trace of Geometric, continues into the fifth. In the main, Siculan Geometric is derived from Corinthian, probably by way of colonial imitations of that style. Not surprisingly, some Euboean traits too have been detected.

CHAPTER IV

THE ORIENTALIZING AND BLACK-FIGURE STYLES

———— ·◆· ————

INTRODUCTION

From the beginning of the Iron Age Greece had been self-satisfied in its economy as well as in its art. During the eighth century this changed. Around 800 BC Greeks, apparently from Euboea, were busy in Syria, most notably at Al Mina near the mouth of the Orontes. Not much later other Euboeans established themselves in Pithecusae (Ischia) on the north of the Gulf of Naples and seem to have been active in Etruria. Towards the end of the century vigorous colonization set in of coastal sites in Sicily and South Italy. This expansion had different objects. In Syria the Greeks were traders, shipping home luxuries, which included small objects of art; in Etruria they were again traders, but offering luxuries for raw metal; in Sicily and South Italy they came to make a living from the land and, as they prospered, could buy manufactures with their surplus corn. For the development of Greek art the Western markets stimulated production, but the imports from the East had more obvious results. This was not simply because the Greeks now first became aware of Oriental art; some imports had filtered in throughout the Early Iron Age, though admittedly in much less quantity, and the Protogeometric B style of Crete shows a premature attraction to it. Nor was the effect of closer contact immediate; the Dipylon painter must have known but ignored Oriental metalwork when he was thinking out his abstract formulas for figures. More important was the growing exhaustion of the Geometric style, which opened the way to new influences, and Oriental models were handy. In vase-painting these influences were indirect, since painted pottery was a minor craft in the Oriental world and the models used by the Greeks were works in metal and ivory, of which we have a fair number of specimens from Greek sites, and perhaps also textiles, which had no chance of survival. The technique of these works is generally competent, their style often a stale and varying medley of the traditional Hittite, Assyrian and Egyptian elements that were currently available in North Syria. Fortunately the Greeks were not overwhelmed by the example of this more finished art, but selected and adapted to suit their needs, after the first experiments only casually. So even the beginner can usually distinguish between what is Greek and what Oriental in manufacture.

The pots reproduced on Plates 8C and 9A illustrate the first stage of the new style. Geometric painting had been abstract in its conception and analytic in its expression. Now there appeared a freer use of curve and a more organic sense of form. New ornaments and a richer fauna were introduced, and there was some stirring of vegetable life. The composition in its turn loosened: here Late Geometric had prepared the way, but the oblique asymmetry of the volutes of Plate 8C shows a new advance. There were experiments in drawing also; reservation and incision enliven the Geometric silhouette. The results are often crude, but they are vigorous and confident.

The phase of Greek art that now began lasted for some two centuries. Its two main branches are concerned (1) with displays of animals, and (2) with scenes of human action; and though men and animals often appear on the same pot, they rarely mix in the same field. The *animal style*, decorative in its intention, did not progress far. Its common fauna was lion, bull, boar, sphinx, griffin, goat, deer, dog, hare, eagle, cock, goose. Of these goat and deer were already familiar in Geometric, and some of the others (borrowed from the East) intrude occasionally at the end of that style. In the second half of the seventh century further species became popular – Corinth at least seems to have admitted some new Oriental influence – and there starts a plague of 'panthers', that is lions or other felines with head drawn in full face, and various hybrids such as the siren (or bird with a woman's head). The arrangement of animals in file, which had been normal in Geometric was continued in Old Greece for dogs chasing and in the Wild Goat style of the East Greeks for the regular procession of goats or deer. Otherwise the animals are more usually assorted and disposed in confronting pairs or less formally in threes. The poses are conventional, as a glance through the Plates in this book will show, and the general absence of aggression or even activity would have satisfied Isaiah: in the sixth century lions or panthers mauling other beasts become commoner but never the rule. Once suitable formulas had been discovered there was little development except towards delicacy and slickness of drawing. It is true that vast-painters had no chance of studying some of their favourites, but the Greeks were not much interested in animals except for the noble horse (which is very rare in the animal style) and less so man's humbler friend the dog.

Progressive artists turned increasingly to depicting the *human figure* in action. Here the debt to Oriental art was small: in Attica indeed one can trace step by step the evolution from Geometric to the new type of man. The layer-wigs of the early figures of Plate 9B come second-hand from Egypt, but this fashion appealed less to vase-painters than to sculptors. The conventional pose of flying figures, such as the Gorgon of Plate 17, is probably Oriental too. But even in early Greek sculpture the foreign contribution to human studies was superficial, and in painting it was smaller still. Battles, races and processions were favourite subjects. To these, as competence increased, were added more particular incidents from mythology, drunken revels, and quieter scenes of domestic life. Horses are common, other animals rare apart from dogs and those monsters which complicated human life in the Heroic Age. Scenes of action made for the overlapping of figures and a considerable freedom of pose; in the orthodox animal style neither was necessary. The view of the figure was similar to that of the Geometric artist – a profile head in which the eye is frontal and profile limbs, but painters soon learnt to draw the human chest in profile as well as frontally and to add and improve anatomical details. There is no background to the scenes and a deliberate avoidance of spatial depth. It is unreasonable to complain of these conventions, which have an artistic justification in the medium; a pot is not a canvas.

The new range of *ornament* includes such abstract motifs as hooks, spirals, cables, rays, crosses; some of these came from the East, others were native inventions. Volutes, palmettes, lotus flowers and buds, and often rosettes still show their vegetable origin: the Oriental models were already stylized, the Greek versions though more stylized in detail have a greater vitality. But generally ornament had a subordinate function in Greek vase-painting.

Roughly the animal style, which constitutes the Orientalizing style (properly defined), was the standard style of the seventh century, went out of favour in the sixth, and lingered on through the Classical period. But it was an interlude rather than a necessary stage in Greek art, and if there had been no Oriental contact in the eighth-century Attic vase-painting of the mature black-figure and the red-figure styles might not have been much different. For the characteristic subject of Hellenic art was the human figure, and this developed out of Geometric in slow but almost complete independence.

Corinth about 720 BC was the first Greek city to develop the Orientalizing style. In Athens, some of the Cyclades and Crete the change began around 700 BC. The East Greek cities were later still, perhaps by half a century. How the Orientalizing impulse reached each area is not known. Corinth presumably had it direct from the Syrian coast, her neighbours perhaps from her. But the influences that formed the Wild Goat style of the East Greeks (Plates 30–31) certainly came separately and perhaps in another medium or from another source. The Mycenaean vestiges that have been detected in Orientalizing art were not local survivals: either they are casual resemblances, or they were repatriated from the Levant where Mycenaean art had in its prime transplanted itself.

The two centuries that followed saw the growth and decay of a rich assortment of local schools. In Greek art as in much of Greek life there were two opposite tendencies, a striving for local independence and the assimilating attraction of some major power. Since Mycenaean times local schools of vase-painting, though based on a common tradition, had on the whole been diverging, and the new movement with its new repertory encouraged further divergence. But the new style required a more accomplished draughtsmanship than had Geometric, and soon lesser schools began to imitate more closely their greater neighbours and gradually to give up the unequal competition. By the end of the sixth century Athens was left in undisputed supremacy.

The history of this period is largely the history of Corinth and then of Athens. Corinth, the pioneer, kept her lead into the sixth century and set a standard for much of the Greek world. The early or Protocorinthian stage established a precise and elegant animal style (Plate 11A), based on the black-figure technique – that is the use of silhouette with incised detail and occasional patches of added colour – and there are a few admirable examples of human scenes (Plate 9C); but pots with Subgeometric, linear or other simple decoration still greatly outnumbered the figured pieces. Then in the third quarter of the seventh century the Corinthians turned over to a popularized version of the animal style (Plate 11B and Figure 6G–I) with which they flooded Greek markets and Greek taste; this Ripe style lasted till the second quarter of the sixth century. Meanwhile some enterprising painters concentrated on human scenes and in the early sixth century formed a gaily handsome school (Plates 12C–13); but Attic competition was growing, and in spite of concessions to the new fashions the Corinthians had by 550 BC succumbed. After this Corinthian vase-painting was reduced to very simple patterns. In Athens the new style pursued grandeur without having learnt discipline or consistency (Plates 14 and 16), till finally in the last third of the seventh century Corinthian example established the black-figure technique and a steadier tradition (Plate 17). But Corinthian influence did not stop at that, and the grand style of late Protoattic declined towards pettiness: some of the Corinthianizing painting of the early sixth century is humiliating (Plate 20A). Other Athenian painters, though they borrowed much from Corinth, kept and refined their standard (Plate 18) and by the 570s the character of the mature Attic black-figure style is becoming clear (Plate 19). It is a style that inherits the old Protoattic interest in human subjects, is tenser and more austere than contemporary Corinthian, and has a more sober balance of colour. Round the middle of the sixth century a generation of able painters, culminating in Exekias, brought the black-figure style to its perfection (Plates 22–23). It was the need for a medium more subtly expressive that about 530 BC created the red-figure technique and style. Though the black-figure style survived into the fifth century, its artistic work was done.

In Boeotia there were some simple original experiments (Plate 28A), but imitation of Athens proved stronger; though there is little artistic merit in the products of Boeotian workshops, at least they continued in production. Eretria till the early sixth century was clumsily dependent on Corinth and Athens. In the Argolid the local Geometric style had been impressive, but no new style followed it. Laconia made timid and sluggish use of the new repertory till about 620 BC (Figures 11–12), when it began to admit from Corinth the black-figure technique and modern ideas; the early sixth century saw the emergence of a vigorous local school (Plate 27), provincial but self-confident, which flourished for fifty years and then rapidly decayed. One or two workshops in Messenia may have attempted an Orientalizing style, there is rather more from Elis but of no better quality, and Ithaca had an undisciplined local version of Protocorinthian; but generally the potters of Western Greece found the new standards beyond their powers. In Crete, where the Geometric tradition remained firm and the Orientalizing spirit fluid, there was a century of futile experiment. In Thera its peculiar adaptation of Geometric survived for a time, accepting little innovation. The Cyclades in the early seventh century possessed some short-lived small workshops (Figures 14–16), skilful but mannered in their individual ways, and providing exemplary definitions of the terms Subgeometric and Early Orientalizing: from one group developed the so-called 'Melian' school which for a generation on either side of 600 BC produced a showy but conventional pottery, heavily indebted to its neighbours to the west and east of the Aegean. To the East Greek cities, where Geometric may have lasted through the first half of the seventh century, the new movement brought the Wild Goat style (Plates 30 and 31A), an animal style executed in slack reserving technique, in Ionia decorative but costive and in Aeolis (where Grey ware or Bucchero also persisted) sliding into barbarism. Rather before 600 BC Corinthian ideas intruded and for some twenty or thirty years the black-figure technique is found alongside that of reservation (Figure 18 and Plate 31B); but by the 560s the Wild Goat style was disappearing on pottery, at least in the southern cities, though it lingered on for another hundred years on Clazomenian sarcophagi. Chios in the early sixth century developed two new schools, one notable for its human subjects, ably drawn in outline and sometimes brightly coloured, the other a miserable perversion of black-figure. Elsewhere the successors of the Wild Goat painters recognized the supremacy of the black-figure style; it was accepted in northern Ionia, which broadly followed Attic models (Plate 32B), and imitated in the more traditional south by the reservation of details within a full silhouette (Plates 32A and 33). But in spite of some excellent and original pieces these later East Greek schools soon declined and did not outlast the sixth century. On the other side of the Greek world Ithaca and Sicily have provided evidence of provincial schools producing Protocorinthian to a local recipe, and rather earlier a more orthodox Protocorinthian was made at Ischia and Cumae in Italy. In Etruria – which had also its own Bucchero – local craftsmen imitated with varying degrees of fidelity Protocorinthian, Ripe

Corinthian, and from about 550 BC Attic black-figure. Most of these imitations were begun presumably by immigrant Greek craftsmen, and in the middle and later years of the sixth century there are also some wares of first-rate and more original quality – notably what is called 'Chalcidian' pottery (Plate 36) and the more eccentric Caeretan hydriai (Plate 35). Further research will no doubt discover still other local schools and perhaps make the history of this period more bewildering. But its end shows Athens triumphant; in Boeotia and Etruria and Campania local workshops turn out indifferent or distorted renderings of Attic; elsewhere there may occur some trivial Atticizing (as in Rhodes and even at Corinth), but vase-painting as a serious art is not even attempted.

CORINTH

Corinth, on whose happy commercial situation Thucydides remarks, was the first Greek city to exploit the Orientalizing style and so established a dominance in vase-painting which she kept till the early sixth century. Most of her rivals at one time or another imitated her, and Corinthian pottery is found on almost every contemporary Greek site both at home and overseas. Fortunately the style of Corinth is easy to classify, since its evolution is generally even and steady.

Early Protocorinthian (*c.* 720–*c.* 690 BC)

The Late Geometric style of Corinth, as was mentioned before (pp. 25–26), had begun to discard the strict Geometric principles. Within a generation Orientalizing elements were welcomed in, and by about 720 BC the so-called Protocorinthian style is apparent. The first phase, the Early Protocorinthian, covers the process of digestion, which was remarkably quick and sure. There is nothing hesitant about the swing of the volutes on the oinochoe of Plate 8C, and nothing Oriental although they are inspired by Oriental flora. The carefree balance of the composition and its invasion of three-quarters of the body of the pot are a manifesto of the new movement which rejected the rigid symmetry and the restrained emphasis of Geometric art. The decoration is conceived as an object of beauty in itself. Equally assured is the ring of rays or solid triangles from which the vase seems to spring. This favourite Protocorinthian use has a subtlety that would have repelled the true Geometric artist who cross-hatched his triangles and disposed of them only as ornament. But when he came to the neck the painter of this pot reverted to his Geometric training (cf. Plate 8B).

The commonest and characteristic Protocorinthian shape is the aryballos, a small flask six or seven centimetres high, intended for oil or scent and so narrow in the neck. The Early type (Plate 9A) has a roundish body with a low ring foot, short neck, simple lip and narrow handle. This is called the 'round' aryballos or the aryballos 'pansu'. It was derived, probably at Corinth, from a simple type of small jug that was common throughout the Geometric period. The shape gradually narrows in body and widens in lip and handle, and the 'ovoid' aryballos is regular for Middle Protocorinthian (Plate 9D). Continued evolution leads to the rather taller 'pointed' or 'piriform' aryballos of the Late Protocorinthian and Transitional periods (Figure 5B). This top-heavy form is then replaced by a new round shape (Plate 10B). Because of their frequency and regular development the aryballoi have become type-fossils for excavators of late eighth- and seventh-century Greek sites.

An aryballos in Naples (Plate 9A) shows again a mixture of Orientalizing novelties and Geometric survivals. Geometric are the row of triangles, cross-hatched and on the shoulder, and the fine banding that contains the lower part of the body. But the strokes round the base of the neck are already turning into tongues, and the main field is wholly Orientalizing. The cock, which had only recently made his entry into Greek art and perhaps backyards, struts with an assurance justified by his substantial build and gay detail; a demure hen awaits him further round the vase. Geometric figures are patterns, abstract and stiff, but here is a creature of flesh and blood, drawn with the same organic curves as the volutes of the oinochoe already discussed (Plate 8C). Behind the cock two of the new ornaments, a cable and a rosette, have been casually added. The inner details are reserved. Incision was still exceptional and, as on the volutes of Plate 8C, tentative.

This phase, which lasts about thirty years, was experimental. The animals and birds, which are rare, vary greatly, partly perhaps because Corinth had had little concern with the regular Geometric fauna. There is more unity in a larger group of aryballoi with spiral hooks or tongues round the shoulder and banding on the body. But the great majority of pots made in the Early Protocorinthian period stayed close to the older Geometric tradition (see p. 60). The commonest shapes were the aryballos and the kotyle, and after them the ordinary oinochoe, the conical oinochoe, and the straight-sided pyxis with flattish knobbed lid. In general only the aryballos and the oinochoe, and they not regularly, carried the new decoration. Even so, Corinth was now the dominant supplier of the growing export trade in Greek pottery.

Middle Protocorinthian (*c.* 690–*c.* 650 BC)

In the early seventh century Corinthian painters settled down into a style of sober correctness. The most important single factor was the invention of the black-figure technique, which became for the best part of two

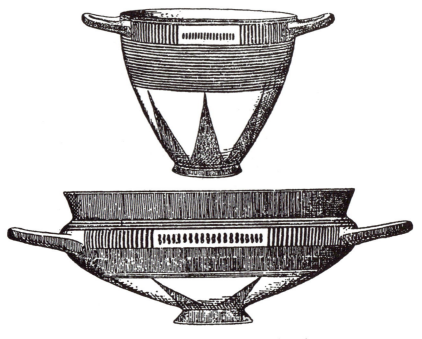

Figure 4 A. Protocorinthian kotyle.
Ht 7.5 cm. Subgeometric style, first half of 7th century BC.
B. Protocorinthian cup.
Ht *c.* 5 cm. Subgeometric style, mid-7th century BC.

centuries the medium of the progressive schools of vase-painting. The technique consisted in making first a silhouette of the chosen subject, and then engraving the details with a sharp point; this was done, of course, before the pot was fired and while its surface was still only leather-hard. It soon became regular to supplement incision with colour, first purple and later white also. Geometric artists had occasionally incised a zigzag line to relieve a dark band, but the systematic use of incision probably came from the engraving of metalwork, a process introduced into Greece from the East; this would account for the unnecessary incising of outlines in earlier black-figure work. Still, whatever the causes, the effects of the new technique were immediate. Incising lends itself to fine sharp lines, which the miniature scale of normal Protocorinthian figures required. Brush strokes can be sketched with fluent ease, but an incised line if it is to be clean must be traced more slowly and carefully. Lastly the dark silhouette to which the details are added discourages an illusionist treatment of the subject, and emphasizes the enclosing contour. So a new conventional style was created, dependent on delicacy of line and balanced masses. The dog

Figure 5 Protocorinthian aryballoi.
A, ht 6.2 cm. B, ht *c.* 8 cm.
Linear style, third quarter of 7th century BC.

on Plate 10A will serve as an example. The animals of the rather later East Greek oinochoe, Plate 30A, which are drawn in a more freehand technique, are by contrast flabby.

On Plate 9D is shown an aryballos in Boston of about 675 BC. It is a small vase, little more than 5 cm high, of the new ovoid shape. Round the lip there are spiral hooks. The shoulder carries a chain of lotus flowers and volutes, a severely stylized version of a favourite Oriental design; the outline technique, abandoned in the drawing of figures, is still used for subsidiary ornament. In the main field, which is less than a thumbnail deep, two black-figure sphinxes confront each other in a now standard grouping. The species sphinx, the wig-like coiffure and the filling rosettes are all of Oriental origin, but the style is entirely Greek. Below there is a file of dogs hunting: such hunts, black-figure or on less elaborate pots in silhouette (as on Figure 5A), are now a stock item of decoration. The inevitable rays surround the base. The exuberance of Early Protocorinthian has been tempered by discipline.

Another ovoid aryballos in Boston has round the mouth tongues, spiral hooks, and short rays pointing outward, and down the handle a complicated triple cable. On its shoulder in black-figure style a lion (Figure 6B) faces a ram and a goat stalks away; the necks of these animals are overpainted in purple. The main scene round the body is drawn out on Plate 9B a little under natural size. On the right a bearded figure wearing a sword and grasping sceptre and thunderbolt, and therefore to be identified as Zeus, is attacking a monster compounded of man and horse. To judge by mythology and later monuments this must be one of the Giants; the man–horse hybrid, already known in Attic Late Geometric art, had not yet been fixed particularly as a centaur. Between the Giant and the armed male who is rushing up there stands a curious object, which is most probably a krater with pedestal. If so, the krater is viewed from above according to a perspective that would be more intelligible in Geometric painting. The figures are drawn boldly with full rounded forms and in postures of extravagant vigour, as if in deliberate defiance of the old Geometric rules. Details are sparingly but effectively marked by incision, and purple is freely added for its decorative value. Four eagles and a variety of the new ornaments are spread generously in the field. Round the base we have again the narrower rays that are well suited to the narrower shape of aryballos. This pot also is of about 675 BC. It is one of the first scenes in Greek art certainly taken from mythology.

On these foundations Corinthian vase-painting in the second quarter of the seventh century reached remarkable heights. The animal style is refined to a delicate vigour (cf. Figure 6A–C). The filling ornament lightens; stalked dot-rosettes become the commonest form, but often even they are omitted. Chains of lotus flowers and palmettes are drawn, still in outline technique, with an elaborate grace that later vase-painters never equalled. The Macmillan aryballos of the British Museum (Plate 9C) shows the achievement in human figures. This frieze, reproduced a little under natural size, comes from an ovoid aryballos with a plastic lion's head for its neck, a lotus and palmette chain round the shoulder, and on the body below the main battle frieze three narrower bands containing a horse race, a hare hunt and double rays. Eighteen soldiers in hoplite armour are engaged: their long trim limbs and easy agility show what full use Corinthian artists had made of the twenty or thirty years since the Boston aryballos of Plate 9B. The admirable composition contrives to keep the figures, if not quite in a single plane, yet in a shallow register, as though on the stage they were acting in front of the curtain. This principle, which obviates the need for perspective, was maintained by vase-painters until towards the middle of the fifth century when some of the bolder Athenians – with unhappy results – tried to emulate the novelties of contemporary murals. Greek relief sculptors resisted the temptation longer.

The Macmillan aryballos is one of a small number of Corinthian pots of about the middle of the seventh century which experiment with a more natural coloration, notably by the use of a warmish brown painted directly on the clay to represent human flesh. But the colour is laid on in a flat wash and details are incised, and the treatment as well as the technique is essentially that of black-figure. Here the rather laboured arrangement of shields and the helmets and greaves leave little flesh exposed. But on other pots, of which the most famous is the slightly later Chigi vase of the Villa Giulia in Rome, the areas of flesh are much larger and give a brilliant air of gaiety. This venture in polychromy, so contrary to the general current, was short-lived. It was probably inspired by free painting, of which we have examples of Corinthian style some fifteen or twenty years later in the painted terracotta metopes from Thermon and Calydon in Aetolia. These metopes, which incidentally are our earliest relics of Doric architecture, have fields around 60 cm square containing single figures or small groups. The figures are drawn in dark outline on the yellowish clay and then filled in with a variety of flat colours, on which anatomical details are marked in dark paint with the same economy as in vase-painting. Till about 500 BC the principles of composition and anatomical drawing were similar for the two arts, which were very closely related. Yet though the Protocorinthian *Polychrome style* (as it is called) is probably indebted to free painting, some large plaques of the sixth century were decorated in the full black-figure technique. But too little of free painting has survived.

The vase-paintings so far discussed have all been of small scale. Protocorinthian was essentially a miniaturist style. There are a few examples of drawing on a larger scale, of which the kotyle in the British Museum (Plate 10A) is one of the best preserved. The height of the main frieze is about 10 cm. The formalized anatomy of the dog has the torsion of a steel spring, and the effect is enhanced by the precise beauty of the incised lines. Yet there are signs that this is not an independent grand style, but an enlargement of something smaller; the double and treble incisions of the head and the large blank area of body and rump suggest perhaps that the artist was not familiar with the decoration of surfaces of this size. The throat of the dog has been picked out in purple and the scruff of its neck in yellow, a colour which now began a short vogue. The filling ornament is restrained. The date of this kotyle should be about 660 BC.

The style now about its zenith depends on the clarity and elegance of its line. Though purple is often used, especially on the necks of animals, it is not indispensable. The animal style, in which action was neglected, was reaching its decorative limits. There was more scope in the human figures, although the engaging polychrome style proved a blind alley. A similar neatness and delicacy refined the floral motifs and reduced and simplified the filling ornament. The aryballos remained the favourite shape. Next come the kotyle, the flat-bottomed oinochoe (with stumpy body and short broad neck), the pyxis with slightly concave sides, and the ordinary oinochoe. But pottery painted with Subgeometric or Linear decoration (see pp. 60–1) is still much more frequent; besides the shapes just listed, cups and conical oinochoai are common in these styles.

Late Protocorinthian (*c.* 650–*c.* 640 BC) and Transitional (*c.* 640–*c.* 625 BC)

The twenty-five years that followed the middle of the seventh century saw a transformation of the black-figure animal pottery, which now became the staple line of the Corinthian industry. The style was cheapened too. The series of lions on Figure 6 illustrates the descent from fine and sensitive quality to pretentious mass production. The total effect is still more striking if one compares, for example, the two pots on Plate 11.

There is first a tendency to bigger, and then to longer animals. This was partly reaction against the miniaturists, partly a deliberate device to cover larger areas more quickly. Inner detail, both incised lines and purple patches, correspondingly increased and coarsened; forms grew lumpy, and postures wooden. New species, flashier or easier to draw, were introduced; so the panther now begins to replace the lion. In long friezes the group of three animals – as for example a bull between a lion and a panther – becomes stereotyped. There is a greater change in the general composition, in the relation of the animals to the field they are set in; the filling ornament is by its density becoming as important as the figures. Protocorinthian paintings are worth detailed study, but the new Ripe style can be appreciated at a glance.

The first stage of this progress improved the Protocorinthian style towards a slightly mannered charm. The well-bred animals have not lost their vigour, and the filling ornament, standardized as dot-rosettes which are usually stalked, is scattered lightly in the field. Hitherto the divisions between friezes had, following the Geometric practice, been composed of two or three narrow lines; now painters prefer a broad band of the dark paint, on which there may be a few narrow stripes of purple and of yellow or white – generally yellow is earlier than white. The subsidiary ornament too is adapted to the black-figure style. The outline floral designs that had been common on the shoulder of aryballoi give way (as on Figure 5B) to tongues, some of which are painted over in purple. More logical still is the *black polychrome* system of decoration, well exhibited in the scale pattern on the olpe of Plate 11A. Here the pattern is incised by compasses and in alternation left dark and filled with purple and yellow or white. The regular motives are scales and, round the shoulder, tongues. On the necks of olpai and oinochoai, which are painted dark, white dot-rosettes are evenly spaced. Some pots are wholly in black polychrome style. This kind of decoration to be effective must be carefully and accurately done, as is painfully evident a generation later. The new fashion for a dark ground also encouraged painters to paint figures in white on dark, and there are one or two examples of what one may call black-figure on a black ground.

In the so-called Transitional phase the new tendencies in the animal style harden. Compare the lions of Figure 6C, E and F, and it is plain that

A

B

C

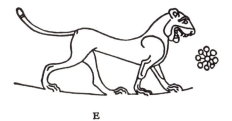

D

E

F

G

H

I

Figure 6 Protocorinthian and Ripe Corinthian lions.
A, beginning of 7th century BC. B, *c.* 675 BC. C, *c.* 660–650 BC.
D, *c.* 650–640 BC. E, *c.* 650–640 BC. F, *c.* 640–625 BC. G. *c.* 625–600 BC.
H, *c.* 615–600 BC. I, *c.* 600–580 BC.

spontaneity is being replaced by a standardized repetition of types. The olpe Plate 11A is a handsome and careful piece, but its line-drawing has not the sensitive precision of the best Protocorinthian. On other pots the Ripe style is more obviously foreshadowed.

The change in style was accompanied by changes in the shapes of pots and by the adoption or invention of new decorative types. The types, which show a renewed artistic contact with the East, will be mentioned in the section on the Ripe style. The commonest shape was still the aryballos, now lengthened and narrowed to the 'pointed' or 'piriform' variety (as Figure 5B). The alabastron (a later example is shown on Plate 10C) appeared just before the middle of the century. The Protocorinthian form is squat with a small bevelled mouth. By the Transitional period the wide flat lip is canonical, the body is slimming, and manufacture increases rapidly. The new round aryballos (see Plate 10B) also begins its career. Among larger vases the olpe is new; as can be seen from Plate 11A its sagging belly shows a kinship with the alabastron, and it too grows narrower. The ordinary oinochoe becomes more popular – a willingness to paint larger pots was another result of the impulse that led to larger figures – and the shape was revised. Till the middle of the seventh century Corinthian painters had been content with the old Geometric shape (see Plate 8C), and though the belly of the pot had shifted slightly upwards a Subgeometric decoration of the neck often emphasized its ancestry. The new shape with broad high-bellied body and squat neck has a certain heaviness of form that suits the new animal style: the example of Plate 11B belongs to the Ripe style, when necks were becoming narrower. Flat-bottomed oinochoai, conical oinochoai, kotylai and concave-sided pyxides continued.

The Ripe Animal style (*c.* 625–*c.* 550 BC)

The general character of the Ripe Animal style has been described in the last section and is more clearly illustrated by Figure 6G–I and Plates 10B–C and 11B. The *Early Ripe* period, which covers the last quarter of the seventh century, was its heyday. The painter's aim was to obtain quickly and easily a rich and immediate decorative effect. So he preferred broad friezes, long careless animals, and thick gaudy detail and filling ornament. His success may be judged by the comparison of Figure 6H and Plate 11B; in its proper environment the lion is inconspicuous. The solid incised rosette had made a modest entry in the Transitional period, but it is now enlarged and fragmented to fill every corner in the background of the frieze. This practice has sometimes been attributed to the imitation of textile models, but weaving has no monopoly of close decoration. Imagination found its outlet more in the introduction of novel creatures, some for variety and others for convenience. The new Assyrian breed of lion had arrived soon after the middle of the century and by the beginning of the Ripe period had driven out the older 'Hittite' (that is Syrian) type – on Figure 6C–E are 'Hittite', F–I, Assyrian: the mane is often cross-hatched in summary rendering of the more laborious flame-like tufts of hair. Common though the lion is, the panther has become commoner. Other traditional animals – boar, bull, goat deer – remain popular. Eagles, geese, hares and snakes are from the Transitional period regular central motifs on alabastra. Owls grow more numerous. Cocks reappear. The sphinx and the griffin survive, but no longer walk. The siren (or human-headed bird) becomes a favourite, as do many other hybrids – the griffin-bird, the panther-bird, the snake-tailed man ('Typhon'), the fish-tailed man ('Triton'), the winged man ('Boread'), the winged woman gripping a pair of birds (the 'Mistress of the Beasts'). The siren and the Boread appear already in Protocorinthian, but are more congenial to the Ripe style, where figures with wings, worn outstretched in the new fashion, one to the front and one to the back, have the merit of filling more space. Whatever the origin or ultimate significance of the half-human creatures, their use was almost always decorative. It is futile to ransack catalogues of Corinthian vases for evidence of obscure cults. The Gorgon, though, may truly be a Gorgon. Its disembodied head, the Gorgoneion, is an ornamental – perhaps also an apotropaic – device from early in the seventh century, but the full-length type in the familiar story of Medusa appears at Athens before and in Corinthian not long after the middle of that century.

Plate 11B is an average specimen of the Early Ripe style. On the alabastron Plate 10C the effect is much lighter. The explanation is probably in the shape. The earliest Corinthian alabastra, which are of about the middle of the seventh century, are naturally decorated in friezes, but the growth in the size of friezes and of animals led to the treatment of the whole body as a single field, carrying either a solitary figure or a small group. These groups are as a rule arranged heraldically, two lions or cocks for instance facing each other over a hare or snake or other suitable marker. The standard was fixed by the Transitional painters, and their light use of filling ornament was continued on the small alabastra, some 7–10 cm high, as well as in the group of round aryballoi which adopted their scheme of the single field. It spread too to the large alabastra of 25 cm or more in height, which were common by the end of the sixth century: earlier examples are usually decorated in friezes.

One embellishment of the black-figure style is not illustrated here – the emphasizing of incised lines by rows of white dots. The practice, said to be borrowed from metalwork, flourished in the early sixth century. This decorative trick takes the animal style even further from nature.

Floral ornaments, now regularly in the black-figure technique, are composed mostly of the lotus and the palmette. In spite of stylization and haste their structure has still an organic clarity. Besides continuous chains there are independent forms, of which the commonest are the doubled lotus (used especially as a central motif on the heraldic alabastra), the quadruple lotus, and the lotus-palmette cross. At the same time a new outline ornament was developed, of four lotus flowers and four buds arranged radially and much cross-hatched; this quatrefoil, which originated in Assyria, became popular on aryballoi in the Middle Ripe period, and simplified and debased lasted out the sixth century.

Mention has been made of Assyrian art as influencing Corinthian. For the quatrefoil and the new lion this is certain, and it is possible for some traits of the horse, the scale pattern and the solid rosette. The influence came during the third quarter of the seventh century, probably by way of Syria. In themselves these borrowings are not important, but if the thick filling of the background also is Assyrian, then this phase of the Corinthian and other Greek schools owes more to the East than is usually thought.

To the taste for new types there was joined a taste for new shapes, particularly in the middle and larger ranges. The commonest Early Ripe vases are however the round aryballos and the alabastron. The kotyle and the olpe continue, and the ordinary, broad-bottomed and conical oinochoai. The concave-sided pyxis becomes more concave, and new types of pyxis are invented. More significant is the appearance of the neck-amphora and the new column-krater (Plate 12C).

The popularity of the Ripe style is striking. Not only was output and export immense – the number of aryballoi and alabastra surviving whole or in fragments must be in the tens of thousands – but imitation by other Greek schools was widespread. The conclusions for Greek taste are of interest.

In the *Middle Ripe* period (*c.* 600–*c.* 575 BC) the Animal style is disintegrating. Generally the figures become clumsier and dispirited and the repertory smaller, while the filling ornament melts into rosettes and little dots. Figure 61 shows the characteristic trend of this period. There was, though, a more delicate style, especially among a group of painters who were interested also in the drawing of the human figure. Here the animals are slender and filling ornament is often omitted. The Gorgoneion group, which will be discussed later (p. 58), specialized in a now important shape, the cup. The Chimera group, which dates to the end of the Middle period, consists mainly of plates handsomely decorated with a large, often heraldic design; their painter, it is plain, owed something to the alabastra. By now the commonest shapes are alabastra, usually large, kotylai, and round aryballoi (some with a very low foot). In the second rank are various types of pyxis with convex sides, the cup (with broader foot and so rounder bowl than the Subgeometric type of Figure 4B), the plate, the phiale, various bowls, ring-vases (shaped like an invalid's rubber cushion), the ordinary and also the broad-bottomed oinochoe, the olpe, the neck-amphora, the amphoriskos and the column-krater (which is now the pre-eminent large vase).

The *Late Ripe* period (*c.* 575–*c.* 550 BC) sees the extinction of the Animal style. The stock has shrunk to sphinx, siren, panther, goat, goose, griffin-bird and cock – emaciated creatures perfunctorily drawn. White is now freely used for broader areas, as in bands along wings. The quatrefoil aryballoi flourish. But artistic interest has passed altogether to human figures and the Red-ground style, and for cheaper ware a development of the Linear style predominates. The Animal style is chiefly found on aryballoi and alabastra, on kotylai, cups, lekythoi and oinochoai and in subsidiary friezes on column-kraters. Floral chains are common on the convex pyxides. For hydriai, amphorae and the main fields of kraters the Red-ground style is normal. This interest in larger vases, general by the middle years of the sixth century, perhaps reflects the influence of Attic, which was now capturing the Corinthian markets. The old Animal style was obsolete.

The Ripe style – human figures (*c.* 625–*c.* 550 BC)

Protocorinthian pots with human figures are rare, and Ripe Corinthian not common. There are two influences discernible. The first is that of the black-figure technique of the Animal style, which was practised by the same painters, though generally they put more originality into their human scenes. The second influence, which is intermittent, comes from free painting. Of this the painted metopes from Thermon and Calydon, works of the Transitional period, are our only direct evidence and there, since the fields are square, the compositions are necessarily simple. The numerous small clay plaques from Penteskouphia, which range in date from the middle of the seventh to the end of the sixth century, belong rather to vase-painting than to free painting. So the influence of free painting must in the main be inferred from tricks and trends in vase-painting that cannot be explained otherwise, as for instance the short-lived polychrome style of the middle of the seventh century, which shows not only a new and more natural range of colour, but also a sudden and assured elaborateness of composition.

During the Early Ripe period there are a good many examples of a humdrum, and sometimes slovenly, style. It is closely related to and often infected by the Animal style, and the protective background of rosettes is equally necessary. But in general proportions are better than in Protocorinthian, particular features less exaggerated, and inner details more extensive. The common subjects are riders, soldiers and the 'padded dancers' whose identity has teased many scholars (for the type see Plate 12B). Most of these human subjects appear on simple aryballoi and the composition too is simple, with figures placed clear of each other, though in battles shields may overlap. Plate 10B is a fair sample.

A few large vases of around the end of the Early Ripe period offer more ambitious scenes in a more independent style. The best is a column-krater in the Louvre (Plate 12C) with conventional animals round the flat of the rim and two zones with human figures on the body. The lower and subsidiary frieze has a rather perfunctory horse-race. The main field contains on one side a battle, on the other the entertainment of Heracles by Eurytos. On this unhackneyed subject the vase-painter exerted himself. Four couches stand in a row, and on them recline Heracles, Eurytos, and his four sons, while his daughter Iole stands coquettishly between a brother and the hero. The composition has a spaciousness due not to the absence of filling ornament (which is indeed partly compensated by the sprawling names painted against each figure) but to the relation of the figures to each other and to the frame. Their anatomy is conventional, but the varied posing – with all the unnatural mobility of early Greek art – has a new and pictorial dignity. Except for the small exposed parts of Iole's person the figures are done in the black-figure technique with plenty of added purple. Their dark masses are balanced by the low tables with food and drink and by the dogs tied under the couches, cheerful accessories which are mostly drawn in outline with painted inner detail. The outline technique is used also for Iole's face and throat, finger and feet, and contrasts strongly with the purple heads and dark bodies of the men. This secondary distinction of sex was now becoming regular in the black-figure styles of the Greek world; it is not certain where it was first established, though Corinth is likely. A certain unevenness in style resulted in the compromise between the techniques of incision and outline in a single scene, but it was an unevenness that vase-painters turned to good account.

The larger scale of drawing – the main panel on the Eurytos krater is over 10 cm high – offered more scope than the aryballoi and other small vases. But during the early sixth century some competent Corinthian vase-painters were content with small figures. The cups and kotylai of the Gorgoneion and Samos groups, though their subjects are often conventional, show a neat and delicate vigour. On Plate 12A–B are details from two of them, reproduced at about two-thirds of their natural size. These groups, which belong to the end of the Middle Ripe period, had a strong influence on Attic, particularly on the Comast cups. But in Corinthian vase-painting the small black-figure tradition wilted, though something of it survived in the Penteskouphia plaques. A bottle by Timonidas, the only Corinthian vase-painter whose name we know, is contemporary with the Gorgoneion and Samos groups, but the composition and contrast of colour in its ambushing of Troilus is more akin to the Grand style.

The broader style of the Eurytos krater was continued in the first quarter of the sixth century in a group of large vases. The compositions are now bolder and more involved, the contrast of incision and outline drawing is more fully employed, and the profiles of figures become milder and more fluent. The favourite subjects are battles, riders and banquets, of which some are not heroic.

About the end of the Middle period a new technique was introduced of using an orange-red slip. This slipping became regular in the second

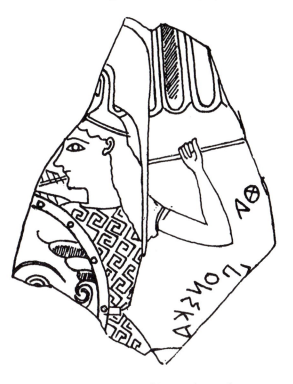

Figure 7 Ripe Corinthian column-krater.
Fragment: scale 1:1. *c.* 565 BC. White for for flesh and
plume of helmet.

quarter of the century for the larger shapes preferred by the few progressive painters, but it is used only for the principal fields, which gain in emphasis by the contrast with the pale yellow surface of other parts of the vase. The cause of this change was presumably the growing competition of Athens and the desire to emulate the redder Attic clay, but its stylistic consequences show an original Corinthian spirit. Attic vase-painting continued to be strongly black-figure in style, and the purple and white embellishments are normally subsidiary. In Corinth the white and purple are used more freely and the picture is conceived in terms of colour, so much so that white (now regular for women) is sometimes used also for the flesh of men, if it is felt that too much black-figure would give a sombre effect. The drawing progresses in accomplishment. Profiles soften, the side view of the chest is better understood, limited facial expression is attempted, but drapery is still painted as flat surfaces without folds. Compositions are often elaborately crowded, sometimes with an architectural setting. The krater of Plate 13 is to be dated about 570 BC, the sherd of Figure 7 a little later. There are also less elaborate pieces, some with sirens or cocks, which are painted with the same enjoyment of colour.

The subjects of this *Red-ground style* are more varied than those of preceding periods. From human life come wedding scenes, banquets, drunken dances, races, the soldier's farewell, and battles, sometimes anonymous, sometimes labelled as heroic. Of the heroes Heracles is most popular, and there are scenes from martial legend. The moment represented is, as in all Archaic art, one of dramatic emphasis, which summarizes the story or incident. It is probable that many of the subjects popular in the sixth century were first invented or adapted for vase-painting in Corinth. But for all its brilliance the Corinthian Red-ground style succumbed about 550 BC: it was technically inferior to Attic. Though a local style persists for a generation or more on the clay plaques from Penteskouphia and the wooden ones from Pitsa, the rare contemporary pots with human figures are straightforward imitations of Attic black-figure.

Subgeometric and Linear styles
(*c.* 720–5th century BC)

The invention of the Protocorinthian style did not kill the Geometric tradition. There was instead an immediate enrichment of the repertory of ornament by borrowing such Oriental novelties as the spiral hook and the four-leaved rosette for contexts that were traditional. Less ambiguous are the net of dotted lozenges, files of puny silhouette birds (as on Plate 14A and Figure 8), and the sinuous snakes or wavy lines with stars and swastikas in their curves. But the most important innovation was the adoption of the new rays or solid triangles, at first still hung round the shoulder (as on Plate 9A), but about 700 BC transferred to the base, where they soon became indispensable. Till the end of the eighth century the new and the old styles run close together, and are often mixed. In the seventh *Subgeometric* drops behind and is content with a poorer repertory of ornament: the kotyle Figure 4A is typical in its neat and simple linear decoration, and a comparison with the Late Geometric example of Plate 8B shows the nature of the change. After 650 BC Subgeometric hardly continued except on the long narrow necks of conical oinochoai. A meagre tradition can be traced in the kotylai and the cups with offset rims, some still close to the Geometric shape and others more developed (Figure 4B), but the fine narrow banding has generally been replaced by solid areas of dark paint often enlivened with thin stripes of purple. These survivals did not outlast the seventh century.

There are many other Corinthian pots which are also called Subgeometric, though there is nothing particularly Geometric about them. A better description is *Linear*. Examples of two common types are shown in Figure 5. The Protocorinthian black-figure style was a luxury style, and the great mass of pottery produced at Corinth in that period was decorated more simply. Plain bands of paint played a big part, but the easier of the black-figure fashions were copied. Rays for instance soon became regular, and about the middle of the century broad bands (often enlivened with purple) replace the older narrow striping. A common motif throughout the seventh century is the simplified hare-hunt, reduced to a row of dogs clumsily drawn in silhouette (Figure 5A). In the sixth-century version we have goats or soldiers, sometimes with closely packed dots as filling ornament. Bands of small chequers are also very common (Figure 5B); these begin early in the seventh century and in the second quarter of the sixth merge into the White style. Broad areas filled with dots were popular in the Early Ripe period. All these forms of decoration, which are most frequent on aryballoi, kotylai and alabastra, were sedulously and closely imitated in Etruria.

Later styles (mid-6th–4th centuries BC)

The *White style* appears in the second quarter of the sixth century. Its characteristic is that broad areas, often decoratively the most important, are left blank, and for the rest there are simple bands of dark and purple paint or meagre linear ornament. Such unambitious but pleasant decoration is found on a wide variety of shapes as the exhausted Animal style recedes. A similar phenomenon is found rather later in Fikellura, the result not of imitation but of a similar weariness with tradition. The *Black Pattern style*, as it has been named, pursues an opposite effect. Its main decoration consists of floral or linear patterns such as palmettes and meanders, purple bands are common, and no large area is left reserved. It begins in the Late Ripe period, in its way develops, and lasts into the fourth century. Towards the middle of the fifth century interest revived a little in animals, but not of any evident Ripe Corinthian ancestry. They are done in dark paint, either in full silhouette or with reserved or unintelligently incised details: the style, though hasty, can be lively. Sometimes too animals and ornaments are painted in white on a dark ground. None of these late wares (which used to be called *Conventionalizing*) achieves or regularly attempts more than a respectable mediocrity. Besides such products of local character we find at one time or another a little straightforward imitation of contemporary Attic (see also pp. 178–9).

Technique

Corinth has deposits of a fine whitish clay which contains very little iron oxide and so fires a pale yellowish colour. It can easily be distinguished from the redder clays used in most schools of Greek pottery, though some Etruscan and Campanian clays have a similar, but generally muddier, appearance. The pale clay was regularly used at Corinth from the second half of the eighth century. At first it often has a pinkish tinge, but by the late seventh century a greenish tinge is common. It does not seem when fired to be as hard as good Attic, and the paint does not adhere to it as firmly. The paint is at first often red or a medium brown, but during the seventh century it becomes darker and red tones are avoided. Both clay and paint have a good sheen. The Red-ground ware of the second quarter of the sixth century and later some of the imitations of Attic employ an orange-red slip for the principal fields. Purple additions are frequent from early in the seventh century. White for ornament on a dark ground is not uncommon from the last quarter of the eighth century. White details on figures appear at the beginning of the sixth century, and in the Red-ground style white is a principal colour. The shaping and the firing of pots are generally competent.

Export and influences

From the last quarter of the eighth century to the last quarter of the seventh Corinthian pottery – figured, Subgeometric and Linear – was exported to all parts of the Greek world and was, except in the East, the only pottery that was at all widely exported. It is especially frequent in the western colonies, since they imported a great part of their painted pottery. The trade reached its peak in the Early Ripe period, although some competition was just appearing. During the sixth century Corinthian exports declined rapidly, but did not entirely disappear.

The popularity of Corinthian naturally provoked imitations. Around the end of the eighth century there was widespread, though mostly trivial copying of the Subgeometric style, particularly on kotylai. But the Protocorinthian style proper, while influential in Greece, the Cyclades and Crete, was only casually imitated except in the West. In Ithaca (cf. pp. 27–8) a wild version of Protocorinthian was current in the first half of the seventh century; it is most interesting for its oinochoai with high shoulder and narrow conical neck, which are decorated with great loops in a bold early Orientalizing style. In Corcyra the Animal style was copied. At Pithecusae (Ischia) and Cumae in Italy the local Protocorinthian of around 700 BC cannot always be clearly distinguished by eye from genuine Corinthian (see p. 138). In Sicily there are kraters of the early seventh century which develop the Protocorinthian style in their provincial way and both there and in South Italy smaller, less ambitious pots were made longer and in some quantity (see pp. 138–9). In Etruria from the end of the eighth century to the middle of the sixth the prolific Etruscocorinthian school copied and adapted with varying fidelity (see pp. 142–4).

The Ripe style was still more effective. It was accepted and modified, not only in Etruria but also in all the surviving Greek schools of the end of the seventh century. During the early sixth century the progressive group of Corinthian, that interested in human figures, was influential so long as it lasted.

There appears to be no influence of other Greek schools on Corinthian till about the second quarter of the sixth century. Then in the red ground of the Red-ground style and perhaps in its preference for larger shapes Attic competition is recognized. Finally, in the later sixth and earlier fifth centuries, a few red-ground and white-ground Corinthian pots are creditable imitations of current Attic black-figure.

ATHENS

The Geometric style of Athens had been distinguished by a strong sense of order, and both collapsed together. During the next two or three generations Attic vase-painters showed a readiness to experiment and a grandiose imagination that was not troubled about scale or balance. But at the end of this period, which is known as Protoattic, discipline and a black-figure system were adopted and a new monumental style emerged. It is all very different from the steady refinement of contemporary Corinth; in the seventh century Corinthian vase-paintings can generally be visualized from a short verbal description, but only illustrations do justice to the unexpectedness of much Protoattic. Students do not agree whether to class the monumental style as Protoattic or Attic black-figure. It has the grandeur of the one and the technical manner of the other. But perhaps it is better to put the division (which is anyhow conventional) after the monumental style, when for a generation closer imitation of Corinthian and a preference for correctness rather than originality shows a more modest and even timid spirit. Then, in the second quarter of the sixth century, the Attic black-figure style found itself and became the standard of the Greek world.

Both Protoattic and Attic black-figure pottery is plentiful, since excavators, mercenary and scientific, have been busy in Attica and Italy. This and the strongly individual quality of the style enable us to see in fair detail the personalities of the artists and their relations to one another. That in the seventh century they were artistically wilful cannot be excused by isolation; a tenth of the contemporary pottery found in the Agora at Athens was imported from Corinth.

Early Protoattic (*c.* 700–*c.* 675 BC)

The hydria from Analatos (Plate 14A and Figure 8) is one of the earliest of Protoattic vases. The lower half of the body is still Geometric, though the deer are a little more supple and the bands of birds and oblique zigzags are borrowed from Corinth. Above we are in the new world. The lions,

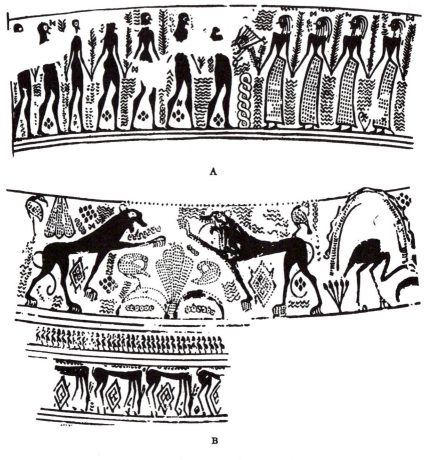

Figure 8   Details to supplement Plate 14A.
A, neck; B, belly.

crick-necked bird and vegetable medley show a delight in curve and vitality that is the antithesis of the Geometric below, and the filling ornament repeats the contrast. Round the shoulder are the solid rays, which as in Protocorinthian replaced the cross-hatched triangles. In the main field of the body we have witnessed a revolution; the neck offers evolution. Between a row of double spirals and a band of lozenge ornament modernized by spiral hooks six men led by a lyre-player are confronting four women; each party has joined hands and carries branches. Compare the men with their ancestors on the Dipylon amphora (Plate 5) – their calves, thighs, buttocks, waists, shoulders, arms, necks, heads, their stance and poise. This is a native development from Geometric, not the adaptation of Oriental models. In shape too this pot belongs to the new era, with its lankiness and more fluid articulation, the panelling-in of the vertical handle, and the plastic snakes that wriggle round lip and handle and mask the junction of shoulder and neck. The date must be near that of the later of the Early Protocorinthian aryballoi, say about 700 BC.

The Analatos painter was brought up in a Geometric school, the progressive Late Geometric school already mentioned (p. 22) and this hydria owes much to his teachers. The proportions and contours of the shape, the decorative scheme, the spiral hooks, even the litheness of his men originate in their work. But his robust individuality went much further. We can trace for a good thirty years the career of this untiring artist, who as much as anyone determined the course that Protoattic took. The bell-krater in Munich (Plate 14B) shows him at a later stage, about 690 BC. One link between krater and hydria is a fragmentary plaque from Cape Sunion, painted with a warship; the marines by their faces are brothers of the women of the hydria, the steersman of the krater's charioteers. The comparison of the lions as well as the men shows the distance and the direction that the Analatos painter has travelled. There is little that is directly Geometric here. Instead we see a new massive style, that is willing to be crude provided it can be powerful. The Analatos hydria is not so different from contemporary Protocorinthian, the Munich krater is.

Besides the men and lions and horses which are illustrated here the sphinx was popular, often with scaly wings. Winged horses had been introduced at the end of Geometric as well as 'centaurs' (their identity is discussed on p. 50). Dogs, cocks, eagles (as on Figure 9) usually decorate smaller pots. The figures are bulkier and more active than before, their structure organic, the details bold. In composition there is less constraint – the Analatos painter did not feel obliged to show how many horses are pulling each chariot on the Munich krater (Plate 14B) – and the balancing of groups is not always symmetrical. Of the new ornaments the most characteristic are the spotted leaves and palmettes and the heart-shaped pair of spirals; the hooks, known in Late Geometric, grow in size and often (as on the Munich krater) perversely substitute for the rays of Corinthian; and the horizontal rows of zigzag filling acquire a new and sometimes overwhelming character. The favourite subjects are processions, gay or sad, parading chariots and horsemen, 'centaurs' hunting, and monsters and animals in file or less often heraldically confronted. The technique is outline drawing and partial silhouette, occasionally and unintelligently broken by incision.

Of the other Early Protoattic painters some followed the Analatos painter and some played with a mannered archaism. Others were more frankly Geometric and continued for a time the tradition of abstract ornament. The new shapes had already begun to evolve at the end of the Geometric period, but there is still variation. The progressives preferred slimness and the slurring of angles, the old-fashioned clung to rotunder forms. The hydria, a new invention, is illustrated on Plate 14A; from it can

Figure 9 Protoattic oinochoe.
Ht 17.3 cm, *c.* 700–675 BC.

be imagined the change in the amphora and the small globular oinochoe (for the new form see Figure 9), and also in the stemmed bowl and the mug. The old stemmed krater (distinct from the low open krater or bowl which also is common) loses its vertical lip and contracts to an oval body. The wide-necked oinochoe disappears. The kotyle replaces the Geometric cup, and round aryballoi also show the influence of Corinth. But the chosen vessels of the new style are hydria, amphora and krater. Outside Attica, Early Protoattic has been found in Boeotia and Aegina. At home it had to contend with Corinthian, which it sometimes imitated, especially on small pots.

The Black and White style (*c.* 675–*c.* 650 BC)

The works of the Analatos group still show their Geometric breeding, but the second generation of Protoattic artists was born free. In the drawing

66

of figures the silhouette had been the basic form, broken by the reservation of heads and sometimes other areas. But to the new school outline drawing came naturally, and light and dark had equal value. The result was a style of broad contrasts, turbulent and impatient. The first stage has been called the Black and White style, from its generous use of white paint, and lasted till about the middle of the seventh century. It was apparently initiated by the Analatos painter.

The New York Nessos amphora (to be distinguished from the later and more celebrated 'Nessos amphora' in Athens) is a fair work of about 660 BC, though not one of the best. Plate 16 shows a side view. In the main field the centaur Nessos collapses in front of Heracles, while Deianira is slumped in her husband's chariot, faint but self-possessed enough to hold the reins; beyond the horses a rubber-legged Iolaos comes running up. The scale of the figures is unequal – Deianira must be a head taller than Heracles. Unequal too are the style and the planning of the figures. To the powerful forms and action of Nessos and his executioner correspond four old-fashioned horses with their heads in a finicky fan and the caricatured manikin Iolaos. Such lopsidedness is common in this period, as if the artist began his picture before he had fully conceived it. Both outline drawing and incision are used, and the flesh of the human figures and other details are painted in a yellowish white, which contrasts more strongly than appears in the photograph with the brown of the clay. The subsidiary frieze of the shoulder contains a couple of grazing horses, old-fashioned hackwork; and on the neck a moon-faced panther mauls a deer. The filling ornament is less obtrusive and less Geometric; it is only natural that the belated bird between the centaur's hindlegs should be wilting. The other ornaments show the new preference for solid forms, and the cable on the shoulder is characteristically painted in alternate strands of dark and white. The back, as of most large Protoattic vases, is very much the back, though the neck has an unusually charming floral pattern.

The fragments of another contemporary amphora shown on Plate 15A reveal a greater artist, the Ram Jug painter, who was busy in the 660s and 650s. His earlier work has a gauche heaviness, particularly in the ill-proportioned human figures; and even in this more elegant scene, where Peleus is carrying Achilles to be tutored by the good centaur Chiron, Achilles has a puny arm (visible on the smallest of the fragments). The big almond eye and heavy brow are normal in the developed Black and White style, but the fleshy nose is more of an idiosyncrasy, as is the palmette sprouting from the forehead of Peleus. Compare this amphora with the contemporary Protocorinthian kotyle of Plate 10A: both have a feeling for line, but the Corinthian painter has refined it with studied precision, the Athenian is more of a dilettante and a humorist.

In composition vase-painters are much bolder. There are comparatively few stock attitudes, and the use of outline or white as well as black-figure silhouette invited the overlapping of figures, the more so since (as in the later Red-ground style of Corinth) dark and light were not distinctive of sex. Though staid processions continue, there is also much varied and violent action – battles for instance, chariot races and even jugglers. Mythological scenes, such as the fate of Nessos, occur from the beginning of the period. In the drawing of figures anatomy progresses and there is an increase in inner detail, sometimes merely decorative as, for example, cables on the naked thigh or circles on a buttock – on Plate 16 Heracles wears a similar device on the tail of his chiton. The black-figure technique is known – it had indeed been known to the Analatos painter – but it remains subordinate to the gayer variety of outline drawing and colour; sometimes, especially about the middle of the century, white lines accompany incision on dark surfaces. The filling of the main fields is sparser, a prudent reform now that the subsidiary areas of the vase carry stronger decoration of their own. In general the ornaments are Orientalizing, but Attic originality adapted and invented. So the spiral hooks are often adorned with birds' beaks, and palmettes may reproduce themselves till they look like bunches of grapes. Many of the more solid ornaments, such as cables, rosettes, rays, rows of leaves, are variegated by painting alternate members in dark and white paint. Altogether it was an era of exuberant and spontaneous creation. Among the shapes the hydria disappears and kraters become more popular. The oval krater grows taller, then about the middle of the century gives way to the kotyle-krater, which evolves from the open bowl. Pottery of the Black and White style has been found in Aegina, which some students prefer – with awkward consequences – as the domicile of leading exponents; there is some too from Boeotia and a little from Megara, Perachora near Corinth and the Argive Heraeum. In this period the effects of Corinthian on Attic were vague or casual.

Later Protoàttic (*c.* 650–*c.* 610 BC)

During the next twenty or thirty years Attic vase-painting settled into a disciplined black-figure style. The planning of the decoration becomes more thoughtful, the execution more precise, the colouring more sober and outline drawing disappears. Vase-painters were learning the virtues of concentration on definite and limited objectives. In all this the influence of Corinth is visible, as also in many details. But there is a scale, physical and imaginative, that is peculiarly Attic.

The Black and White style fell into a decline about 650 BC, when the use of purple first became regular. There was for a time a three-colour school, which produced some admirable effects, as when a near-black wing is feathered alternately purple and white, but gradually white lost ground. For animals the black-figure technique was already in partial use; the new movement met no obstacle here, and purple necks and belly stripes and feathering were soon the rule. Human figures resisted longer, for it was with them that the outline technique was chiefly concerned. The Cynosarges amphora, for example, has on its shoulder dull black-figure animals, but the wrestlers on the neck and the farewell group on the body are painted with white flesh and much purple on their drapery. On some pots there is a more elaborate polychromy – reds, yellow, browns and bluish green have been observed. This short-lived venture was roughly contemporary with the polychrome figure style at Corinth, but the Attic colours are not fast and the pots on which they appear were apparently specialities for graves. By the last quarter of the century a black-figure style was established.

The Nessos vase in Athens (Plate 17) marks the consummation of the process. It is an amphora over a metre high, intended like the big Geometric pots as a marker for a grave. On the neck, once more, Heracles is killing Nessos. Below two Gorgons take off in pursuit of Perseus (wisely out of sight), while their sister Medusa collapses behind them. This is a monumental style, carefully planned and admirably executed. Comparison with the New York vase (Plate 16) shows what Attic art has gained in compactness and unity, and in subtlety too. The Gorgons vanish round the curve of the pot, their speed underlined by the opposite movement of the dolphins below. Purple is used freely, for the faces of Heracles and Nessos, for the drapery, and on other details. The white paint that was added sparingly, as on the teeth of the Gorgons, has peeled off, but cannot have much relieved the dark masses of the figures. The filling ornament is now light and subdued. The back, neglected as usual, is scumbled over with streaky paint. The Nessos vase is much indebted to Corinthian, in its fully black-figure technique, the choice of inner detail, the type of the Gorgon, the purple faces (a trick that became common in Corinth in the thirties and lasted for some sixty years), the filling ornament, the floral chain, the birds on the facings of the handles. Such borrowings are general on Attic pots of this time, which draw freely on the Corinthian repertory. But there is no slavish dependence on Corinth. Athenian vase-painters kept their sense of scale – large pots with large decoration were still favourites – and there is spontaneity, even in the Animal style current on minor works. The same is true of the subsidiary ornaments, the most striking of which are mill-sail patterns and the strip of oblique meanders (as on Figure 10) which is first found on the large Corinthian kotylai that were made just before the middle of the century. The filling ornament of the Nessos vase is typically eclectic, on the body neat dot-rosettes, in the panel on the neck the same rosettes mixed with older Attic motifs, and in the vertical strips that frame the neck and on the handle-plates incised rosettes. Attic vase-painters were critically choosing Corinthian elements and making them their own. So it is not surprising that resemblances to different periods of Corinthian

Figure 10   Attic Bf bowl.
Details of panels, scale *c.* 1:2. By the Nessos painter, *c.* 605 BC.

vase-painting can be detected on a single pot. The Nessos amphora may perhaps be dated about 615 BC.

The favourite shapes were the big amphora; the kotyle-krater, often united with its stand and furnished with a lid; and towards the end of the period the new one-piece amphora, where neck and body make a single unbroken curve and the proper decoration is a panel let into the dark surface (as on Plate 21A). The popularity of Attic pottery is about to begin. A fragment by the Nessos painter has been found at Caere in Etruria, and about the same time there may be some Attic influence in Eretrian and 'Melian'.

Attic Black-figure: the period of Corinthian influence
(*c.* 610–*c.* 550 BC)

Like other leading painters of his day the Nessos painter straddles the uncertain boundary between Protoattic and the Attic black-figure style proper. On one side is the big amphora in Athens (Plate 17), on the other the fragmentary spouted bowl in Berlin (Figure 10). Here the earlier grandeur and freedom are being replaced by correctness and convention. The wide shallow shape is tauter and finer, as it stretches from narrow foot to high belly and then returns quickly to the mouth. Compared with the simple sturdy contours of Protoattic it shows an advance in the potter's skill and delicacy, but to the painter it no longer offers a large unbroken field. This change in aesthetic principles is most obvious in the substitution of the dinos for the kotyle-krater; Plates 18 and 10A will serve to illustrate the relation between shape and decorative system. The Berlin bowl is then decorated in narrow bands. Round its shoulder were four panels, in one Perseus and Athena, in a second the Harpies, while the other two which are lost presumably completed the stories with the Gorgons and the Boreads. Poses, details of the figures, and both the filling and the independent ornament are very much as on the Nessos amphora, but the effect is tamer and more constricted. On the lower part of the bowl came first a band of animals and monsters in confronting pairs, next – below a strip of small chequers – a row of lotus flowers and palmettes, and round the base rays. Attic now is borrowing not only Corinthian motifs, but something too of the Corinthian spirit. If the Nessos vase is of about 615 BC, the Berlin Harpy bowl is perhaps ten years later.

The Nessos painter was followed by the *Gorgon painter*, who has his name from his most elaborate work, a dinos in the Louvre (Plate 18). The main frieze runs around the shoulder – Perseus in flight from the Gorgons with Medusa collapsing behind them and Athena and Hermes looking on, and a duel of two hoplites flanked by their chariots. The two scenes have no connection of subject, but early artists were not pedantic when filling a long frieze. The duel is the better side with its intent men and horses, as neat and well-bred as the band of lotus and palmette below. The Gorgons of the other side have lost the gusto of the Nessos painter; art has found a human level and there is less sympathy for the old monsters. On the lower part of the bowl and on its elaborately turned pedestal tier on tier of animals go through their paces; a couple of uneasy lads have intruded and the drawing is not yet jaded, but it is clear where Attic art has been busy. Yet the Gorgon painter still takes pride in his lions, whose fine square heads and well-combed manes make them the worthy last representatives of the old square-headed Attic breed, and he knew how to pair them heraldically as the principal decoration of a one-piece amphora or an olpe. After him no Attic vase-painter was interested in the Animal style.

Corinth had now for a generation or more been steadily influencing Attica, and the Gorgon painter kept abreast of current Corinthian improvements. The airy spaciousness of the main frieze of his dinos recalls the Eurytos krater (Plate 12C); so too does the achievement of expression without action, as in the charioteers and the soldiers waiting with spears poised. It is in increasing subtlety rather than in violent movement, though there will be plenty of that, that the future of Attic vase-painting lies. Among minor details the artist has at last after a century of experiment ventured to draw the chariot rail in strict profile. The Louvre dinos, a mature work of the Gorgon painter, is about 590 BC.

Sophilos, the first Attic vase-painter whose name we know, was a contemporary of Timonidas of Corinth. His style comes from the same school as the Gorgon painter's, but is clumsier and more laboured. Sophilos was an ambitious but lesser artist. He too followed Corinthian fashions – in shapes as well as in massed compositions and the lavish use of white paint for the near horse of a team, for drapery, and for the flesh of his women (Plate 15B). For horses and drapery the innovation soon failed; but from the 570s Attic women are regularly white and their menfolk are black, even if often at first still purple in the face. Attic vase-painters, though not Sophilos, are now beginning to paint their white over a coat of the blackish paint and much of the detail on it is incised; the black-figure tradition had taken deep roots. On a fragment of a dinos by Sophilos (Plate 15B), found at Lindos and made in the 580s, is one of the earliest appearances of the tribe of good-for-nothing satyrs. If there is doubt about the satyr's origin, there can be none of his intention. The art of the eighth and seventh centuries had been indifferent to sex, the early sixth displayed its urgency, and the middle added its tendernesses. The progress may be inferred by comparing the New York Nessos amphora (Plate 16) with the fragment by Sophilos, and this again with one of the amphorae by Exekias in the Vatican (Plate 22). Other new types that are making their debut are the old man with a fringe of white hair, the athlete, the drunk, and soon the lover and the adolescent. Artistic interest was changing, but at least as important was the increasing ability of the artists.

Three other dinoi of Sophilos, two fragmentary but all signed, show more fully the complex scenes in which his imagination surpassed his execution. One, found at Pharsalus in Thessaly and now in Athens, has perfunctory animals on the rim and the lower part of the body, and round the shoulder, as an ill-spelled title informs us, the games at Patroclus's funeral are being run – what we have are the horses of the winning chariot and a terraced bank on which grotesque little spectators sit cheering. The other two, which are more or less duplicates, have in the principal field the procession of gods and goddesses to the marriage of Peleus and Thetis, an occasion better known from the slightly later François vase. One of the nymphs here has turned her face to the spectator; but frontal heads, though they appear occasionally from about this time, never became normal in black-figure. To his human figures Sophilos gave all he had; witness the painstaking detail of the chitons (as on Plate 15B) and his careful labelling of persons. Such inscriptions, painted on the pot before firing, had occurred at Athens and Corinth from rather before the middle of the seventh century, but suddenly become the fashion in the 570s. Their purpose is less explanatory than ostentatious as on the Tyrrhenian amphorae or decorative as on lip cups, and often enough they are meaningless jumbles of letters.

The *François vase* (Plate 19) found near Chiusi in Etruria and now in Florence, is a volute-krater some 60 cm high. It was, so the signatures say, made by Ergotimos and painted by Clitias. No other black-figure vase so elaborately decorated has survived so complete, and its rich repertory of subjects makes it in itself a compendium of Attic vase-painting around 570 BC, when it was made. Here we see the gay mastery of drawing and composition that Sophilos could not achieve. On the lip Theseus returns from Crete, on the neck Lapiths fight Centaurs: the other side, which is the front if either side can claim precedence, has the Calydonian boat-hunt: and the funeral games for Patroclus. In the main frieze the divine guests are arriving at the marriage of Peleus and Thetis; the procession encircles the vase, passing under the handles as if behind arches. Then the return of Hephaestus, and on the opposite side the ambushing of Troilus. Further below are animals, and at the base rays. The cranes and Pygmies fight it out round the foot. From the handles proper, which are painted black, spring broad volutes, their outer surfaces decorated too – Ajax carrying the dead Achilles, and above him the 'Mistress of the Beasts' ('Potnia theron'), a winged female gripping on one volute a lion in either hand, and on the other a panther and a deer, to the Orientals a deity but to the Greeks (at least of Europe) no more than a decorative type. The inner face of the volutes carries the now decrepit Gorgon. In all there are over two hundred figures, many of them named, and the detail is equally meticulous. White, in larger areas still put directly on the clay and with details usually painted on it, is in the main restricted to the flesh of the women and to the microscopic patterns and animals of dresses. Much of it has perished, but it matters less since Clitias relies for his colouring on the shiny black paint and plenty of purple.

The drawing of the figures is sure and elegant, their poses varied and convincing in spite or perhaps because of the archaic conventions of anatomy. The composition, clear and well-knit, knows how to mass figures in the shallow focus of the pictorial field – eight deep at times in the wedding procession. Men's faces are still purple on occasion – the François krater is one of the last important pots on which they are – and there are several curiosities, typical of the time. Polyxena's hydria, Priam's stool, the fountain are all labelled with their names; Zeus and Hera, welcoming back Hephaestus, sit tandem – the old-fashioned alternative to the overlapping of figures; and two charming little buildings, the house of Thetis and the fountain outside Troy, tease the Classical architect. A rarer detail is the young Athenian swimming ashore from Theseus's ship. Generally the spirit of this vase is lively and cheerful, yet polite. But the pygmies of the foot are comic, if not burlesque; and in the little panels where Ajax staggers under the body of Achilles there is a new and tragic solemnity.

Much on the François vase is derived from Corinthian; but it comes at second hand, incorporated in the Attic tradition that Clitias inherited. Even the Animal style of the lowest figured zone of the body has a new if artificial animation; the sphinxes and griffins pose, the lions and panthers pull down their prey, all with a mechanical elegance that contrasts with the spontaneous life of the other scenes. Compare this krater with any of the more elaborate Red-ground vases of Corinth (as Plate 13); the styles are parallel, but distinct. Attic art has declared its independence, and indeed is threatening Corinth. Not only did Corinthians from the 570s imitate the colour of Attic clay, but about this time Attic painted pottery began to be imported into Corinth itself.

The François vase has long fields, and Clitias chose subjects that could be extended almost indefinitely. His style is therefore often called 'narrative', but the term can be applied to most black-figure pottery that is not merely decorative. Not till Exekias does mood become important. Several of the scenes of the François vase are found elsewhere, on Corinthian Red-ground, the remnants of Sophilos, Siana cups and Tyrrhenian amphorae; and in literature we have the Chest of Cypselus seen by Pausanias at Olympia and the Hesiodic *Shield*, both of them contemporary with the vase-paintings. The resemblances between the different representations are sometimes striking; for instance in the episode of Troilus Polyxena's hydria is regularly there, lying on the ground or falling in mid-air. Details like this perhaps suggest that the source was sometimes the memory of some famous wall-painting. But of course vase-painters regularly borrowed from each other.

The cup appears in Attica in the 580s and from then on remains one of the most popular shapes. The first stage, that of the *Comast cups* (Plate 24A), has a low flaring foot and short offset lip. Both shape and decoration are taken from Corinth, where similar cups become common in the early sixth century (see p. 58). The Attic cups usually have three dancers a side, at first in padded chitons, later naked and undeformed; sometimes a short-skirted wench joins them. Purple faces and chests are common. Under the handle is set a lotus flower with sprawling tendrils – floral ornament is now more cursorily drawn – and the lip carries incised rosettes or a rough net pattern. The inside is painted black. The Comast Group includes other Corinthian shapes, kotyle, column-krater and lekane. The clay tends to be more orange, and the technical standard is improved. The date of this group is from about 580 to the 550s BC.

The Comast cups are followed by the *Siana cups* (Plate 24B), named after the village of Siana in Rhodes near which two were found. The rim has grown higher, the bowl wider, the foot taller, the contours more precise: the average diameter is now about 20 cm. The new elegance reforms the decoration too. The Comast cup has a casual top-heavy look, the Siana is planned for a balance of light and dark. Sometimes the lower part of the bowl is elaborately patterned, usually it is painted black (as is the stemmed foot) except for a narrow striped band two-thirds of the way up. The edge of the foot too is reserved. The distinction of handle frieze and the lip is emphasized by a narrow black line, but more often the figured decoration which has now shifted up the cup ignores the division and awkwardly straddles the two fields. Or else the lip is patterned – an ivy branch for instance or dogs coursing a hare – and half-size figures keep within the narrow handle frieze. The overlapping system of decoration is unhappy, the two-zone cumbersome. The Attic lip cup (see pp. 78–9) that triumph of archaic trimness, was the logical consequence. For the friezes the familiar themes are riders, battles split into duelling pairs and dinner parties. Inside, an elaborate frame – usually of tongues and bands of dots – sets off the large tondo filled with a flying or running figure or some other convenient subject; the surround is black, except for a narrow reserved stripe near the edge of the lip. The greater number of the Siana cups are by the C painter and his followers. He owes much to Corinth – his favourite subjects and his lavish use of white as well as purple – but he is an Attic painter and makes full use of the orange-brown Attic clay and shiny black paint. The Siana cups belong mainly to the second quarter of the sixth century, over-lapping with the later Comast and the earliest Little Master cups, though they linger on until the 520s. They have been found even in Corinth.

There are other groups of vases, where the standard of drawing is lower. The best known are the *Tyrrhenian amphorae* (Plate 20B), so-called because most of them have been found in Etrurira and they were once thought to have been made there. The long egg-shaped body balances on a spreading foot and ends at a squat neck, and the average height is about 40 cm. The shape comes from the larger *SOS amphorae*, a line of utilitarian pottery named from the form of the patterns of the neck, which is the only part of the pot not painted black; this simple ware was made from the late eighth to the early sixth century and widely exported, presumably for its contents. But the Tyrrhenians have more decoration. On the neck a chain of lotus and palmette or animals, on the shoulder human figures, round the belly two or three bands of animals, at the base rays – such is the usual formula. Their interest is in the human subjects – the sacrifice of Polyxena, the departure of Amphiaraus, the battle with the Amazons, to mention a few – and in the representation, sometimes in an architectural setting. The draughtsmanship is careless and rough. It is a pretentious and inferior style, which offers cheaply all the latest improvements of the leading masters of

Athens and Corinth. There is of course plenty of purple and of white, though this is put on in the Attic method; and the inscriptions that litter the field, usually nonsensical and sometimes mere blobs that imitate letters, show painters often too hurried to clean their brushes. The Tyrrhenian amphorae are only part of a wider class of which the most striking are some amphorae which under the influence of the panel style (see p. 77) replace the subsidiary decoration of the belly by a solid area of black paint topped with narrow purple stripes. The period of the whole group is the second quarter of the sixth century, at least according to orthodox opinion; some would like it twenty years later.

So far the discussion of Attic black-figure in the early sixth century has kept mainly to the human figures. But the tradition of the Animal style died hard. We can see the creatures, still lively, on the Nessos painter's bowl in Berlin; newly broken in on the Louvre dinos of the Gorgon painter (Plate 18); cowed and weary in the works of Sophilos and his successors (so on the lower friezes of Plate 20B). The main tradition of the Animal style shows a temperate admiration of Corinth. The listless groups recall the Early and Middle Ripe periods, though details and the popularity of species differ. This is a numerous class, more so indeed than the groups of vases with human figures, but the animals have little artistic merit or religious interest, so that few of them are published or exhibited in museums. The Animal style faded out about 550 BC together with the old system of decoration in several zones.

Two other developments of the Animal style are conspicuous. On one side are the wholehoggers, such as the *Polos painter* and his friends (Plate 20A). If any particular phase of Attic vase-painting should be credited directly to Solon, it is perhaps this uncritical adulation of the Animal style of Corinth, which so abjectly renounces the native tradition. Corinthian too are the shapes of its dumpy amphora and hydria, lekane, kotyle and plate. This Polos style, if style it may be called, lasted perhaps from the 580s to the 560s and somehow found a ready market overseas. The other variation tries to inject elegance if not life into its animals. So Clitias on the François vase (Plate 19); so too the miniaturists of the Little Master cups; and till the end of the sixth century there can be found small friezes of animals supporting the main picture, especially on hydriai, while shield signs carry them still longer.

There is one other strand in the early black-figure of Athens, ultimately as important as any. At the end of Protoattic there had suddenly appeared the one-piece amphora. The prototype is a heavy sagging pot, not unlike the later pelike. Gradually its belly lifts, and by 600 BC is about the middle of the body (Plate 21A). Later changes are to slimness and greater delicacy of contour, and finally to a still higher belly (Plate 22). The shape of the body is in one piece, so too is the decoration; indeed it is plain, if one looks at the illustrations, that it can hardly be otherwise. The same is true of the new olpe that appears at Athens just before 600 BC and is borrowed by the Red-ground school of Corinth. Some of the earlier of these amphorae try to follow the ordinary decorative convention. One of the most determined is a fine piece in the Louvre by the Gorgon painter. On the front two of his magnificent lions with heads turned back sit up on either side of a floral ornament, on the back a pair of sphinxes respond, above is a chain of lotus and palmette and below a band of animals. Yet even here the main picture by its size and position dominates the pot. But from the beginning there was also a new system of a reserved panel let into a dark ground. On this, as if seen through a window, there is generally the head of a horse, or of a man or a woman (Plate 21A). This panel amphora, simple and conservative, was untroubled by the major changes and fashions of the early sixth century; it was not till the 560s that it was caught up in the current of progress.

The shapes preferred during the half century down to the 560s show a general replacement of the older Attic favourites by Corinthian types. The neck-amphora, now that the huge size of Protoattic has been abandoned, loses in interest for artists, but still remains one of the commonest shapes. The one-piece amphora has also established itself. But of the large pots those that most exerted vase-painters were kraters and dinoi. The kotyle-krater survived into the first quarter of the sixth century, when the dinos became popular, a footless bowl which was rare at Corinth but also appeared frequently in East Greek in around 600 BC, though there less ornately decorated and provided with handles. The kantharos and kotyle continued. The olpe was invented at the end of the seventh century. From Corinth came lekane, column-krater, hydria, lekythos, plate, the new cup, and perhaps the tripod cothon, as well as the alabastron, aryballos and pyxis: the greatest borrowing, as in the decoration, was at the beginning of the sixth century.

For the last years of the seventh century Attic pottery is found outside Attica in Aegina and Boeotia, and there are rare fragments from Troy, Naucratis in Egypt and Caere in Etruria. During the first quarter of the sixth century export was increasing rapidly, to the Aegean islands, the Black Sea colonies, Naucratis, Delphi, Ithaca, Etruria and Marseilles; very little has been reported from Greek Italy and Sicily. During the second quarter the advance continued, and Attic black-figure pottery became the favourite painted ware of the whole Greek world.

Attic Black-figure: the Mature style (*c.* 570–*c.* 525 BC)

The François vase (Plate 19 and pp. 73–4) stands at the beginning of the maturity of Attic black-figure, although – as is not surprising on so elaborate a vase – it has some old-fashioned traits. Purple faces and the use of white directly on the clay are details; more significant is the diffusion of the decoration in many shallow zones. The new generation prefers instead a single large design, and if this is framed by bands of minor decoration, they are both in size and emphasis subordinate. So the principal field recovers the importance it had in Protoattic. Its new proportions, higher and relatively narrower, reacted on the drawing and composition. Larger figures gave the artist more scope, and groups became smaller and compacter – the picture replaces the strip.

Something of the old tradition survives in the *Little Master cups*, but remodelled and refined to a new if sterile delicacy. At a time when the scale of figure drawing had enlarged they create a new miniature style. The Little Masters, that is miniaturists, were often also the painters of larger pots; but the style of the cups is distinct and they are best treated separately. There are three chief varieties, all evolved from the Siana cup (Plate 24B and p. 75) – lip cup (Plate 25A), band cup (Plate 25B), and Droop cup – as well as some intermediate forms. Their common features are the tall stemmed foot, the spreading bowl, a clearly marked lip; the sensitive balance of dark and light; the decorative emphasis on the outside, with which goes the careful finish of the bottom of the foot and even of the hollow within the stem – evidently these cups were meant to be seen when hung against a wall. The canonical proportion of height to breadth is about two to three, and there are two common sizes, a larger some 20 cm across and a smaller about 12 cm. The exquisite precision of the shapes has provoked the unnecessary suggestion that they were modelled to a mathematical formula.

The typical *Lip Cup* (Plate 25A) has a slightly outcurved lip, set off sharply from the bowl, and bowl and stem meet at an angle. Outside both lip and handle frieze are reserved, and so are a narrow stripe on the lower part of the bowl, the sharp edge and the underside of the foot, the hollow of the stem, and the inner face of the handles: the rest is black. So two fields are vacant for the painter and the angle that separates them is underlined by a narrow black stripe. The upper field, the lip, concentrates its decoration in a single figure, or less often a small group or even an outlined female head; or else it is left entirely blank. The inscriptions that frame the figure on Plate 25A are abnormal. The lower frieze stresses the handles: from their dark bulk usually spring small palmettes, and the space between carries a neatly lettered inscription or is empty. The inside is most often black, except for a narrow stripe near the rim and small reserved circles inthe middle. A few lipcups have a tondo, but narrower and less elaborately framed than in the Siana group. The commonest subjects on the lip are animals and cocks, drawn with a brittle elegance. There are human figures too – Heracles introduced to Olympus and the Birth of Athena on one of the most famous of these cups. The lip cups begin about 565 BC and were popular for some thirty years. They were imitated in Ionia (see pp. 122–3).

A few early lip cups form a loose group known as *Gordion cups* from the city in Phrygia where one was found. The foot of some is still lowish, the tondo has the Siana's elaboration, and the offset lip is painted black. They belong to the years when the canon was not yet fixed, and may be the stage of transition to the band cup.

The *Band cup* (Plate 25B) differs from the lip cup in its effect even more than in its details. The black concave lip passes into the bowl in a smooth curve, and in correspondence the transition from bowl to stem is often masked by a purple fillet. The decorative accent is on the handle frieze. Usually there are neat palmettes at the sides: between them there may be a figure or small group in the centre as on the lip of lip cups, or an inscription as on the handle frieze of lip cups, or less often the whole space is filled with figures loosely or closely set, or again the field is left empty. Inside, tondos are rare. The band cup runs later than the lip cup, by which its type is influenced. Its popularity is from the 550s to the 520s. The Floral band cups, small tedious pieces with chains of palmettes along the handle frieze, are a late variety which probably lasted longer. Another byform is the *Cassel cup*: the shape is normal, the size small, the outside of the bowl usually entirely covered with bands of simple ornament. The band cup was the model also for a group of low cups (cup-kotylai); the shape is that of the bowl of the cup, but deeper and set on a ring foot, and the decoration is orthodox.

The *Droop cup*, named after its first classifier, is related to the band cup. Its characteristics are generally the broad unpainted channelling of the top of the stem, the convex black edge of the foot, a black border to the inside of the stem and, except in some early specimens, the decoration of all the lower part of the bowl. The handle frieze has most often a chain of buds; then comes a band of silhouette animals upside down (perhaps because they were easier to paint that way) or some not too meticulous ornament; and round the base are rays. These main zones are separated by stripes. There are some good early examples with careful figures in the handle frieze, but much is mediocre and more is shoddy. The Droop cup begins to acquire its separate identity about 560, and is frequent from about 540 to about 510 BC, but trivial pieces were made even later. Its prodigal decoration probably was inspired by some of the Siana cups, and its influence can be seen in Laconian (see pp. 92–5) unless, as some think, influence was the other way. There are also the so-called Black Droop cups, with bowl painted wholly black.

Thanks to the decorative use of inscriptions we know the names of the painters and makers of unusually many lip cups. Fewer band cups are signed, and very few Droop cups. Clitias and Ergotimos of the François vase signed Gordion cups, and a son and perhaps a grandson of Ergotimos were makers of lip cups. Nearchos, another painter of large pots, painted a lip cup; and his son Tleson has left us more than fifty signatures as maker.

Even the great Exekias made lip cups, and two band cups are painted by the Amasis painter. Sakonides painted and Hermogenes made lip cups with outline heads. But the first places belong to Tleson, son of Nearchos, and to Phrynos or whoever painted for them.

There is so much on the François krater that discussion of Attic vase-painting of its generation keeps returning to it. This time it is the groups on the handle-plates of Ajax and the dead Achilles. In *the Painter of Acropolis 606* the new seriousness is dominant. His name-piece, a fragmentary dinos in Athens, has, to be sure, animals on the rim and in the third (and lowest) zone of the body, dull creatures akin to though neater than those of Tyrrhenian amphorae. Beneath, in the centre of the base, the whirligig has been metamorphosed into the foreparts of six leaping lions and horses, and in the middle zone cavalry with javelins attack mounted archers. But what interested the artist was the top zone, a battle scene 15 cm high, which occupies the whole upper part of the body and is conceived too on a larger scale. From left and right chariots are driving up, and beyond the horses hoplites are engaged. There is in these figures a severity and even grimness that comes partly from the solid forms, partly from their workmanlike action; the detail too is plainer. Spruce elegance has given way to a robuster appreciation of anatomy, and the strong full features make the figures look larger than life. For all its purple and white – and there is plenty of both – this is a sombre masterpiece. Another of the painter's works, a one-piece amphora in Berlin, is still more austere. On back and front two mounted hoplites ride abreast, behind them an eagle in flight, below on one side a hare and on the other a dog. These pieces are of about 565 BC. Their style with its deliberate severity and under-emphasis leads to the grandeur of Exekias; in lesser hands it can become rough and meaningless. The Burgon amphora in the British Museum (Plate 21B), one of the very early Panathenaic amphorae, is a second-rate work of this trend and time.

Attic vase-painting in the 560s and 550s was in transition. The Painter of Acropolis 606 pursues the monumental, the Little Masters elegance, the Tyrrhenian group quick returns. Between these extremes were other less single-minded painters. Nearchos, from whose hand we have also an early lip cup, combined on larger pots the delicacy of Clitias with the new enlarged concept of humanity; a fragmentary kantharos in Athens with Achilles standing by his horses' heads has a delicate melancholy that recalls the *Iliad*. Tleson had good reason to advertise himself as 'son of Nearchos' on many of the lip cups he made and there is a kindred nicety of style in the painting. *Lydos* whose career lasted from the 560s to the 530s, has a robuster quality with more of gusto and less of grace: his firm, solid figures suggest more plainly their third dimension. His best work is in scenes of lively action, as on the krater in New York; here his satyrs and maenads show a remarkable and convincing variety of pose, which compensates for the uniformity of their pouting faces. On another vase, a fragmentary dinos in Athens, he experiments with landscape and a crowded procession. Towards the end, on an oinochoe in Berlin, he was tempted into delicacy, but though his workmanship was equal to it the effect is mannered. His name means 'the Lydian', but his art is consistently Attic.

About 550 BC two other masters begin their careers, Exekias and the Amasis painter. The *Amasis painter* was an admirable draughtsman with a strong decorative sense. His early work is conventional and tame, but as he matures he displays a more individual assurance. For the dignified and the sublime he lacked talent, and his best work has a touch of the comic. So he is happiest when portraying the tipsy gaiety of Dionysus and his satyrs and maenads (Plate 23). His heroic scenes have sometimes a cheerful irreverence, but often they are empty of meaning. Throughout his working life he kept abreast of changes in general design and in the details of figure-drawing, but was himself no innovator, though he had a fondness – unusual in his time – for the technique of outlining female flesh instead of overpainting it in white. We have over a hundred pieces that he painted, representing an unusual range of shapes. Besides the one-piece amphora, neck-amphora, oinochoe and olpe he tried his hand on lekythos, band cup, eye cup, cup-kotyle, alabastron, 'Sosian' stand, little bowl and plaque. His potter, if it was not the Amasis painter himself, showed an equal technical dexterity. He introduced for larger shapes the elaboration and refinement of profile that had before been applied to the Little Master cups (compare for instance Plates 20B and 21B with 22 and 23), but his passion for novelty at the expense of harmony lost him his lead. The activity of the Amasis painter is from about 550 to about 525 BC.

The Amasis painter stands apart from the run of Attic vase-painting of his time, which followed Exekias. For that reason he has sometimes been claimed as an immigrant to Athens from Ionia, and his personal peculiarities have been dubbed Ionian. In fact his decorative elegance has its origins in the style of Nearchos and Clitias, and its counterpart in the Little Master cups. From Ionia we have nothing comparable. For all his excellence the Amasis painter founded no lasting school, though a few of his lesser contemporaries admired his obstinacy against the new Exekian spirit. 'Elbows Out', whose neat manikins earn him his name, and the Affecter with his larger gawky figures are both excellent technicians; their styles (and even their shapes) are self-consciously old-fashioned, more concerned with obsolete types, including even starveling animals, than with coherent subjects. The black-figure style has reached the stage where archaism can be engaging.

Exekias is as a draughtsman the equal of the Amasis painter, but in spirit his opposite. His style has a grave inwardness inherited from the Painter of Acropolis 606, to whom he comes nearest in his set battle scenes; but his best work is in quieter figures and groups. It is natural that he preferred to paint amphorae. There are few artists in whose work shape and style progress so harmoniously. Of his earliest amphorae, squat and pot-bellied, the majority are necked and some have subsidiary zones of little animals; later the shape tapers and the one-piece amphora predominates. At first his style is conventional and close to the so-called Group E. But already in the 540s a neck-amphora in Berlin, one of the earliest of his slimmer vases, gives a foretaste of his individual quality. On the front Heracles grappling with a lion is fine drawing though not particularly sensitive, but Iolaos, hands locked in sympathy, is something new. The Athena who completes this scene and the dismounted riders of the back are undistinguished. In the 530s comes the maturity of his style. The one-piece amphora in the Vatican shows on one side (Plate 22) a domestic idyll, full of sober charm; even the horse is thoroughbred. On the other side the incident is trivial, Ajax and Achilles armed and playing backgammon, but their intentness on the game, as they while away their watch, invests the picture with a universal quality. Another one-piece amphora in Boulogne gives a new tragic grandeur to the suicide of Ajax: earlier artists had shown him spitted; here with furrowed brow, quietly and methodically, the hero fixes his sword in the ground. The same reflective dignity reforms even Dionysus on a rather earlier neck-amphora in the British Museum; there is a sacramental feeling as the wine-god takes the cup from his server Oinopion. Dionysus appears again on one of Exekias's latest works, the eye-cup in Munich, reclining in his ship while beside him sprouts a giant vine and dolphins tumble around: this scene fills the whole inside of the bowl – a rare variety of the tondo throughout Attic cup-painting – and on the outside beyond the eyes hoplites fight grimly across the handles (Figure 30A). Exekias was the greatest of black-figure artists, and he brought the style to its limits. It is hardly credible that so much human dignity and pathos can be expressed in so artificial a convention. Besides the amphorae and his one eye cup we have by Exekias a calyx-krater, a dinos and two sets of fine plaques some 40 cm high designed with funeral scenes to adorn a tomb. There are pots of other shapes signed by him as 'maker', but with trifling impersonal decoration. If it is fair to judge by what is known, he painted comparatively little. But his influence on his contemporaries – not only in style of painting and in types, but also for the shape of the amphora – was profound and enduring; and it is from Exekias that the Andocides painter and the main stream of red-figure painting derived. His activity as a painter lasted from about 550 BC into the 520s, but he did not so far as we know himself attempt the red-figure style.

Exekias, the Amasis painter and Lydos are the most considerable black-figure artists of the third quarter of the sixth century, and they had their followers and friends. There are other painters who stand apart, some laggards from an earlier phase, others of slight but original talents. The Swinger, one of the most prolific, will serve as an example, pleasant and uninspired; his composition is careless, his figures simple and without expression, but his drawing is clean and his range of subjects untiring. There were also in the 530s the devotees of the *Eye cup*, which was now replacing the Little Master cup; to a generation that approved the rhythm of the one-piece amphora the lip cup was a *tour de force*· and band and Droop cup trivial. As early as the 560s there had appeared a cup with bowl shaped like the segment of a sphere and a knob standing on each handle (the 'merrythought' cup), but this had not become popular. The new eye cup retains the single curve of the bowl but is generally shallower, and the stemmed foot which is surmounted by a broad purple fillet is stumpier. Progress is towards shorter stem and deeper and more strongly modelled foot, to which Exekias gave a fine concave profile (Figure 30A). The inside of these cups is generally simple – a small reserved circle or a shabby Gorgoneion. The outside is distinguished by a pair of great eyes on each side in black and white and purple, with strong brows above; between them may be a rough nose or a figure, at the sides more figures; and round the base run bands and often rays. The eye cup and its decoration are an Attic invention. At the beginning of the sixth century a group of rough East Greek cups had been decorated with eyes (p. 111), but these probably ceased a generation earlier; and Greek ships were often painted with great eyes, as were other things that had to find their way home. The eye cup was imitated in Italy (see p. 150). There are also other Attic cups of eye-cup shape, but decorated more conventionally with a frieze of human figures.

The character of the Mature style is evident in composition, the drawing of human figures, the subjects and subsidiary ornament, as well as in its choice and remodelling of shapes. The standard amphora offers a field, whether framed in a black ground as on the panel-amphora or supported by minor decoration as usually on the neck-amphora, that is not much broader than high. So the typical scene contains not more than five or six figures and only a single incident; the importance of the action is concentrated. There is no longer room for old favourites like the chariot race, the fight between Lapiths and Centaurs, or the thronged return of Hephaestus; instead we have the soldier waiting to drive off, Heracles strangling the lion, Dionysus with a few intimates. The figures, fewer and larger, have to stand a closer scrutiny. Greek artists, as is often said, did not till much later model from life; but they observed it. Anatomy now becomes more coherent, particularly in the region of the waist and belly, and poses are easier and more natural, though oblique views are still avoided. Drapery too is studied. Earlier artists had been satisfied with a flat surface, varied sometimes by a border or a vertical panel. By the time of the François vase there are three techniques, one for each of the three common garments. The peplos, a thick long dress, is still flat though often elaborately patterned; the chiton, a lightweight shift, has wavy lines running down it; the himation, worn short as a cape, ends often in formally stepped folds. To these fashions a fourth is soon added – diagonal striping of black and purple that follows the lie of the long himation or cloak. Figures so enveloped, 'mantle figures', are often brought in as supers when the central group does not of itself fill the field. The tendency during the Mature period is towards simpler patterning and more natural folds (note the right-hand and central figures of Plate 22). The change in subjects is the result partly of the shape of the normal field – much as in sculpture friezes and metopes are differently designed – partly of greater technical competence and the desire to express mood. Greek artists had never set up a separate hieratic style for the representation of gods and heroes, and they as much as ordinary mortals begin to respond to the natural pleasures and sorrows of life.

The subsidiary ornament has lost in importance. On the one-piece amphora the panel is usually framed above by a narrow band of lotus and palmette, and there are narrow rays round the base. The neck-amphora has most often lotus and palmette on the neck, round the shoulder a chain of buds, or sometimes a small figured scene, bands of simple meander and buds below the main scene, and rays at the base; and after the middle of the century there are often fine volutes springing from the handles (as on Plate 23). The hydria, remodelled in the 550s, has commonly a figured scene on its flat shoulder, on the belly a broad panel bordered at the sides with ivy leaf, and rays round the base. These and other ornaments are generally careless, and sometimes slatternly. It is clearly the day of panel decoration.

The chief shapes are one-piece amphora, neck-amphora and cup. Hydria, olpe, oinochoe, lekythos and column-krater come well behind. The modelling is becoming precise and delicate. Export was vigorous and universal throughout the Greek world, and competition was negligible. Vase-painters in Boeotia, Eretria, Thasos and the East Greek area tried to imitate Attic, and so did a few Greek and Etruscan artists in Italy. If foreign vase-painters emigrated to Athens, they must have been very quickly assimilated into the Attic tradition.

Late Attic Black-figure (*c.* 530–*c.* 450 BC)

The production of black-figure pottery, so far from ceasing at the introduction of the red-figure technique, continued to increase in quantity and for a generation red-figure decoration is comparatively rare. This is still evident in the offerings found at Marathon in the grave-mound of the Athenians who died there fighting the Persians in 490 BC. But it was the red-figure technique that attracted the greater vase-painters, even though for forty years some of them worked in black-figure too; and the red-figure style they created and developed became increasingly the model for the lesser painters who held to the black-figure technique. For a time tradition and even rivalry maintained a competent standard, but by the end of the first quarter of the fifth century competence was lost, and during the second quarter production (now mainly of the small lekythoi) petered out. Only the official Panathenaic amphorae preserved a senile reminiscence of the black-figure achievement.

For a generation the black-figure style continued to develop. Compositions are often fuller, with closer grouping and much foliage (perhaps because leaves and branches are more easily done in the black-figure technique). The relations of the figures are carefully worked out, and supers no longer stand by but have been taught to act – and overact – their byplay; there is plenty of expression in faces, hands and attitudes. This histrionic business is in strong opposition to the simpler movements of contemporary red-figure. The black-figure champions are responding to the challenge. The Andocides painter, the pioneer of the red-figure technique and style, was more prolific of black-figure. Some of his vases conveniently show the same scene on front and back but in different techniques, an illuminating contrast. His red-figure, fittingly for a pupil of Exekias, becomes bold and clear; but his black-figure, though the drawing is neat and expressive, tends to fussiness both in composition and in detail – he does not instinctively know when to leave well alone. But Psiax, another very early red-figure painter, is at his best in black-figure. His is a slighter finicky style, with a gift for the drawing of character; a three-quarter torso, done with conviction, is a sample of his interest in anatomy. Close to Psiax is the Antimenes painter, who seems to have worked only in black-figure. Both pursue charm and humour rather than grandeur, and it is not surprising that the Antimenes painter occasionally puts his figures in a setting that is artistically of equal importance, as on his well-known amphora in the British Museum with a scene of olive picking.

The stronger style has its last flowering in the *Leagros group* in the years around 510–500 BC. The subjects are predominantly heroic, but the harnessing of a racing chariot is popular too, and there are several hydriai with women at the fountain house – an appropriate subject for a water-jar. In the 480s the Cleophrades painter could still paint a worthy Panathenaic amphora. But after him the special character of the black-figure style faded away. For the black-figure style does not stand to the red-figure style in the relation of simple reversal of colour. One is an engraver's, the other a draughtsman's style; and – more important – the optical balance of light and dark is totally different. The last painters of black-figure lekythoi were purblind hacks.

The better of the black-figure recusants asserted their independence in their favourite compositions and subjects, and to some extent in their choice of shapes. But even they could not ignore the inventions of their red-figure rivals. In dress, for instance, the soft chiton is from the beginning normal in red-figure, and the black-figure painters, used to the heavy peplos, followed reluctantly. The drawing of folds is also imitated from red-figure, but when translated into the black-figure technique becomes tiresome or cursory. Anatomical structure and occasionally foreshortenings are also copied. The use of purple decreases. It is easy enough to distinguish black-figure vases painted before and after the establishment of the red-figure style.

Early in the red-figure period specialization increases. One painter generally decorates large pots, another cups and small pieces. In late black-figure the painters of large pots are vastly superior; the cups are mostly trivial and miserable pieces. Eye cups are very numerous till the end of the sixth century, and some amphorae and hydriai borrow the notion of eyes with unhappy effect. Many of these cups combine both styles, black-figure for the tondo and red for the outside. An innovation that was later fruitful (see pp. 168–9) was the introduction near the end of the sixth century of a white ground, principally on lekythoi. The commonest shapes till the early fifth century are neck-amphora and hydria (both these deliberately conservative, and the hydria often provided with a subsidiary animal frieze), one-piece amphora, cup, lekythos, and the small Nikosthenic amphora (a vulgar translation of a metal shape related to the small amphora or amphoriskos of Etruscan bucchero that is mentioned on p. 145). Of the old shapes, next come the column-krater, plate, alabastron, oinochoe; and there are also new shapes invented for the red-figure style, such as stamnos and pelike. Export, even of the poorest black-figure of the decadence, was as wide as ever.

Panathenaic amphorae

In the athletic section of the Panathenaic Games, which (it is said) was inaugurated in 566 BC the prizes were amphorae filled with oil. These amphorae are of special type, though not all the amphorae of this type were prizes: some have no official inscription and others, to judge by the places where they have been found, were or became ordinary articles of trade.

The Burgon amphora (Plate 21B) is one of the earliest Panathenaic amphorae and should be of the 560s. With its fat body and small neck and foot it is a neater version of the old SOS amphora, naturally enough since that too was a container and not table crockery. The shape persisted, though of course revised to suit changing taste. The principal decoration is in the panels of the body, on the front an armed Athena with the legend 'a prize from Athens' and on the back a picture of the event. Early modifications were that a column was placed on each side of Athena, and that a chain of lotus flowers and palmettes became regular on the neck and below them tongues. With minor alterations this scheme continued to the end. So too did the convention that Panathenaic amphorae should be black-figured.

Orders for these amphorae were placed with leading artists. So in the early fifth century the Cleophrades painter and the Berlin painter, two of the great red-figure artists, turned their hand to black-figure Panathenaics. In the next generation understanding of the black-figure style had been lost and the technique becomes little more than red-figure with incision and reversed colouring, at least for the athletic scene. The Athena suffered a more curious fate, since conservatism decided that (as on coins) she should remain archaic or rather archaistic. A fortunate innovation in the early fourth century was the addition of the name of the archon of the year when the amphora was made. Since the archons' dates are known, the pots too can be dated. But towards the end of the century there were substituted the names of lesser magistrates whose dates are mostly unknown. About the same time red-figure came to its end in Athens and there were no more vase-painters worth the name. Though Panathenaic amphorae were made much longer – until the second century BC and perhaps till the fourth century AD – and though in the Hellenistic period some of them were painted in a white-ground style, these later products have little interest of any sort.

Technique

In general early Protoattic, from negligence rather than incompetence, is technically inferior to the preceding Geometric. The clay is paler and coarser, the paint less evenly dark, the sheen duller. There is some improvement in later Protoattic and early black-figure. Then about 580 BC a new standard is set with finer clay of a deeper orange-red colour, paint that may be described as black, and a high sheen. This is first regular in the Comast group, where for the first time since the late eighth century the potters of Athens interested themselves in small fine shapes, and soon becomes characteristic of Attic black-figure. A yellowish slip is correspondingly common in Protoattic, as it had been in Protogeometric and Early Geometric, but very exceptional during most of the sixth century, though at its end a whiter slip becomes popular for lekythoi and some other small pots. White as an accessory colour is used erratically on some Late Geometric pots, becomes important in the Black and White style of the second quarter of the seventh century, and then declines to a minor aid. In the earlier part of the sixth century some Corinthianizing painters are more lavish with their white, but in the mature phase its main purpose is to distinguish female flesh, and in the late phase it becomes rare. Protoattic white is often yellowish. Till the beginning of the second quarter of the sixth century Attic painters put white directly on the clay or over dark paint as was more convenient, and details on white were usually painted. Afterwards the dark undercoat and incision of detail are normal. Purple, regularly over dark paint, is frequent from the middle of the seventh century. Outline drawing is common and reputable in Protoattic, though less so towards its end, and it recurs occasionally in the black-figure of the sixth and fifth centuries.

THE ARGOLID

The Argolid had like Athens a rich and heavy Late Geometric school, but there is no sign of a similar progressive group which by simplifying the current Geometric style cleared the way for new developments. It is likely that this entrenched conservatism of the Argives resisted the Oriental impulses till Protocorinthian, rapidly advancing some thirty easy miles away, had taken too big a lead to be caught up. In the first half of the seventh century some simple Orientalizing ornaments were admitted into the Subgeometric workshops, and later there was a humble use of floral and linear designs. One ambitious but fragmentary krater from Argos recalls Middle Protoattic and another from Mycenae Attic black-figure of about 600 BC but these are exceptional.

It is, no doubt, surprising, till accepted, that in the Argolid no advanced style succeeded Geometric. The lack used to be made good by attributing awkward pieces from other schools. The odd Fusco kraters from Syracuse are still sometimes classed as Argive, whether imported or made by an emigrant from Argos, but the resemblances may be collateral. More remote is a krater from Etruria which from the painted name of the maker is called the Aristonothos krater; this much-illustrated vase has on the front (like the krater from Argos) the blinding of Polyphemus and on the back a naval battle that recalls the Attic Black and White style. Here without much doubt we have provincial Greek products made respectively in Sicily and Italy.

LACONIA

The reserving period: Transitional and Laconian I
(*c.* 690–*c.* 620 BC)

Laconian vase-painters after the Geometric period did not show much enthusiasm for the Orientalizing style and it was not till about 620 BC that the black-figure technique was accepted. In the later eighth century the new trends of Corinthian Geometric had had their effect in Laconia and from Corinth too came specimens of the new art, but though there are some faithful Laconian copies of Early Protocorinthian the impulse soon weakened and the native style proceeded on its leisurely way. Third-rate and unpretentious, but still independent, it escaped the fate of Argive pottery.

Figure 11 Laconian lakaina.
Ht *c.* 7.5 cm. Third quarter of 7th century BC. Restored.

The so-called Transitional style is an assortment of Subgeometric and Early Orientalizing, not yet understood. From this, around 650 BC, emerged a more consistent school, Laconian I. Here the traditional chequers and other solid ornaments presumably continued for some time, and new motifs – broken and unbroken cables, rosettes (sometimes reserved on a dark ground), tongues, rays, rows of pomegranates, spirals, hollow squares with a dot in the centre, and even clumsy palmettes - make modest appearances. A common and characteristic ornament of the finer vases is the row of squares set between two rows of dots that runs round the rim of a pot (see Figure 11: as time goes on these squares are more widely spaced). Broad painted areas and bands of purple have a large part in the decoration (see Figure 11). Animals are not common, and human figures and heads set in panels are rare. They are drawn in the reserving technique with large outlined heads and little body detail (as in Figure 12) and sometimes patches of purple or white are added. There is not much filling ornament. The negligent and extremely simple style often has a liveliness that suggests caricature. Laconian I is divided into a finer and a rougher school, both contemporary. The rougher vases, especially the larger of them, show a clumsy and intermittent taste for experiment. The finer school, which limits itself to small vases, is excellent in technique but conservative and restrained in decoration; it is for long content with linear and abstract patterns, and seems to have admitted the animal frieze only about the end of the period. The lakaina of Figure 11 is a fair example of its unpretentious merit. Slip is now regular, and at least on the finer pots thicker and better. In shapes, which have a strong local individuality, there is a liking

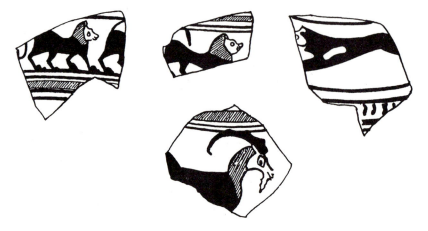

Figure 12 Laconian animals.
Fine style, third quarter of 7th century BC.

for ridges and angles that interrupt the smooth curve of the contour. The commonest are the low cup with shallow ring foot and large offset lip, the cup with high straight lip, small bowls, the chalice or low handleless cup on a high stem, the mug with boldly outcurved wall, the kalathos, the dish, the lakaina (Figure 11: the Geometric type has often a convex, Laconian II a concave lip), a squat jug or olpe, oinochoai, large bowls and pierced stands. Plastic heads are sometimes attached to bowls and oinochoai. There was during this period almost as little export as before, though a fragment has been found in Samos. Some Corinthian was imported.

The early black-figure period: Laconian II
(*c.* 620–*c.* 580 BC)

About 620 BC, to judge by parallels with Corinthian, Laconian pottery took a firm step forward. The black-figure technique was adopted, ornament becomes more assured and varied though still abstract in form, and a more unified and vigorous style developed. These changes coincide with the establishment of the black-figure style in Athens and are in part the result of a similar relation to Corinth, where the new Ripe style with its increased productivity was starting on its commercial triumph. But Laconian vase-painters, content to remain provincial, kept their own character.

Around the end of the eighth century Laconian painters had occasionally imitated the simple incision of Early Protocorinthian, but the experiment was soon abandoned. The black-figure technique was therefore strange to the painters of Laconian II and it took them a generation to master it. At first the incision often does little more than follow the outlines of the figure and border the internal patches of colour, and there are later sherds that show the opposite fault of meaningless detail. But by the beginning of the sixth century a workmanlike black-figure style had been created. From the scanty remains it seems that the Laconian animals and monsters were selected from the simpler of the Corinthian types, but the composition favours files of creatures of the same species and there is little filling ornament. The most original design is that on an early sixth-century cup found at Tarentum, inside which fishes swarm about a central rosette, reserved in a dark circle, and dolphins circle them cf. Plate 26A). Commoner than any incised animals are silhouette birds with drooping purple tails (Plate 26B). Human figures are rare, though there are from the centre of cups a few large Gorgoneia drawn mainly in outline.

The majority of Laconian II pots were more simply decorated with a little ornament to relieve the plain banding. The row of squares between two rows of dots remains common for rims, though the squares are more widely spaced (cf. Plate 26B), and rays are sometimes doubled. Of the new ornament many are variations on the step and hook meanders, often built up, of rectangular units like the patterns on old-fashioned linoleums, and there are also chevrons, tongues, cables, pomegranates and rosettes. Purple is freely used, and there is strong contrast of colour in the ornament and in the plain bands. The shapes include the lakaina, the mug (both these with pronounced ring foot and outcurving wall) the cup which is closely modelled on Corinthian, the chalice, the plate, the stemmed dish, bowls, a primitive bell-krater, the convex pyxis, the squat olpe and various small closed pots with spouts. Ridges, grooves, knobs and plastic heads, strong angles and bold curves are popular. In this period some modest export begins. Examples – mainly cups – come from Olympia (where Laconian artists were active), from Samos which during the sixth century had seemingly intimate relations with Sparta, from Delos, Rhodes, Ephesus, Naucratis, Cyrenaica, Sicily, South Italy and Etruria. Corinthian import continued, and there are some Laconian imitations of East Greek Bird bowls and helmet aryballoi of the Gorgoneion group.

The developed black-figure style: Laconian III–IV
(*c.* 580–*c.* 500 BC)

About 580 BC – the date is fixed by grave groups that include Corinthian – there begins the phase of Laconian pottery that is best known and was once called Cyrenaean. Human figures and vegetable ornament now become common, and, since much has been preserved the work of individual painters can be recognized. The cup which grows a stem appears as the principal shape, partly because of its popularity in overseas markets.

This blossoming of Laconian art, which is visible also in the painted architectural revetments, could not have happened without the fertile contact of Corinth, but the new style has a native character that is to be explained not by incompetence (though there is some of that) but by a restrained and independent judgement which does not strain its limited capacity and perception. From this come the honest, simple charm and liveliness of much Laconian vase-painting at a time when imitation of Corinth was having disastrous effects elsewhere.

The outside of a typical cup of the mid-sixth century is illustrated on Plate 27B. The shape, compared to Plate 26B, shows a development similar to that of Attic and East Greek cups. The lip has grown more important, the bowl shallower and its curve flatter, the stem is taller and often ends in a rounded moulding. The decoration has a richness that is comparable to some of the Siana cups of Athens and to their successors the Droop cups. On other cups the lip is covered with a double network of pomegranates, which has ousted the bands and squares normal there in Laconian II, and in the handle frieze between clumsy palmettes a row of elongated flowers and buds shows a stylization of the lotus that is characteristically Laconian. Purple is freely used on ornaments and for bands, in cheerful contrast with the dark paint and creamy slip. Stem and foot are dark, except that the moulding above and the edge of the foot if sharply profiled, are not only reserved but unslipped. Shuffle the motifs, put animals or birds in the handle frieze – the formula covers most of the more elaborate cups.

On the inside (Plate 27A) the lip is modestly painted over except for a reserved and unslipped stripe at top and bottom, or occasionally it is patterned. The bowl reveals more fully the Laconian artist. Here, as already in the Tarentum cup (p. 91), the full space is used, and it was not till the middle of the century, when Attic influence was growing, that small tondos became common. At Corinth too the whole field of the bowl was sometimes decorated, but in concentric zones. Yet though Laconian vase-painters also used this scheme, they preferred to take advantage of the opportunity for drawing and composing on a larger scale. Composition is perhaps too definite a description of Laconian methods, since the deliberate planning of the picture to fit a round field was to them unnatural and unless they had to hand a ready-made design (such as the Gorgoneion) they tried to square the circle. In this the contrast with Athens is instructive. Attic vase-painters were more interested in the outside of the cup, and the tondo – if there was one – was small and usually contained a single figure; but they took pains to choose poses which fitted that figure to the circular space. At Sparta, on the other hand, the painters of cups – at least till the introduction of the smaller tondo in the mid-century – were not content with just one figure, and in their composition preferred the less exacting method of drawing a horizontal base-line for the main scene, as did the uninspired painters of the plates of the Wild Goat style in the early sixth century. There are some curious experiments – the division of the field into two equal halves with the figures of each group set foot to foot, the breaking of the exergue by another baseline so that it is divided into a narrow frieze above and a smaller segment below, and even the use of two opposite exergues with a narrow frieze between them. But the normal scheme is that of the cup illustrated, with a single exergue containing a lotus member or figures of animals, birds or even fish.

Besides the elaborate cups there is a smaller and simpler version, in which lip and bowl are hardly distinct and the stem has no moulding, and about 550 BC there appear relatives of the Attic Droop cup with lightly concave lip and channelled stem. Some cheaper cups have no decoration inside, or a small medallion. In the later stage simpler decoration becomes more common.

The pioneers of the new style were the Boread–Lane's Hephaestus – painter and the Naucratic painter. The Boread painter, whose figures based on Corinthian models, have a direct vigour that owes much to a firm and careful economy of incised detail, fixed the canonical system for decorating cups. The Naucratis painter, longer-lived, was less austere in the drawing of his figures, which influenced all his successors. Generally, Laconian vase-painters were lavish with purple but made little or no use of white and for female flesh were satisfied with outline drawing on the light ground or else did not distinguish sex by colour. Of other masters, the Arcesilas painter, active around 560 BC, takes his name from the cup in the Bibliothèque Nationale in Paris with – presumably – the second Cyrenaean king of that name superintending the packing of wool. It is a lively scene, full of gesticulation and jabbering and appropriate properties, and notable also for being a topical sketch, but the detail is inferior and rather fussy. The Hunt painter, younger than the Arcesilas painter and at first influenced by him, is a draughtsman of greater technical competence whose solid well-built figures and firm detail give a new realism to Laconian art. Some of his cups have the curious trick of showing a scene as viewed through a porthole, the outer figures being cut through by the frame. Clearly he learnt his composition on friezes, as of that of his hydria in Rhodes, and made no concession to the circular field of the cup. About 550 BC Corinthian vase-painters were abandoning the figure style, and Attic standards proved too much for the Laconians. The decline, visible in the later works of the Hunt painter and his followers, was rapid and, though a few respectable works were still being produced, the native tradition of figure painting did not outlast the sixth century.

Laconian artists of this period gave their best to their human figures. The debt to Corinth is evident, but they took only so much as they were capable of digesting and so their art has for all its awkwardness a homogeneity that raised it to the third place among contemporary Greek schools.

The subjects, drawn from myth and daily life, make a strange collection. Besides such widespread favourites as Heracles with the hydra and men drinking or dancing or wenching there are others that are unique – as Atlas with Prometheus, the building of a temple, Arcesilas at his wool business, soldiers carrying home their dead. But the strangeness of the subjects must not be exaggerated, as it has been by some interpreters; much is due to the Laconian practice of excerpting incidents for their cups from larger scenes – so the ambushing of Troilus is reduced to Achilles lurking behind the well-house. Filling ornament is rare, but winged lads and birds and other creatures are fairly common, and Laconian artists have a weakness for settings – buildings, bushes and once even a creditable pond.

The animals and monsters are of Corinthian stock, but mostly show clumsy drawing and awkward grouping. The most successful are the grubbing cocks, less showy than the Corinthian breed but nearer to life. The chief vegetable ornaments have already been mentioned in the description of Plate 27B. The pomegranate, in the seventh century shaped regularly like a ball with a spike through it, puts out two stamens for the Boread painter, and after him these multiply and often add a cross-bar: on some early cups it is used to fringe a tondo. Buds and flowers with austerely stylized petals grow spindlier still. Tapering 'myrtle' leaves which sprout from each side of a steam are common too ' – at first they have no stalks, and at the end neither stalks nor stem – and in the 530s ivy is creeping in. These are all continuous ornaments. Other floral ornaments are the handle palmettes (at first with volutes and triangular base), the lotus and palmette unit which is used in exergues and sometimes in animal friezes, and small varieties that sphinxes and other figures occasionally wear. The Laconians soon tired of vegetable ornament, and made it even less lifelike than did other archaic Greeks. Of the abstract ornaments the most notable are the bands of squares and dots, of a sort of bracket ($\lrcorner$), and of hook meanders.

The cup is a shape much honoured by Laconian painters. The hydria, a tall handsome pot with high belly and flaring foot, the dinos and the volute-krater also received decoration with human figures. The lakaina, oinochoe, stemmed dish, plate, bell-krater, chalice and flat-bottomed aryballos rarely rise above animal friezes. In his shapes the Laconian potter carries still further his remarkable fondness for technical dexterity; the hydria in particular may repeat a bronze form, and bronze details are imitated by the plastic palmettes and heads on oinochoai at the attachments of the handle as well as by bosses where in metalwork there would be the heads of rivets. These are the more important of the elaborate vases, which are mostly decorated in narrowish bands from rim to foot and even on the underside of the foot, if that is flat. There are also plainer pots, mentioned in the next section. The clay, which is less fine than Corinthian or Attic, is fired to colours ranging from pink to light-brown, pink if the vase is wholly slipped, brown if the clay surface is to show. The slip, at first thick and a pale cream, deteriorates or disappears in later work. The paint has usually a deep sepia tone, but after about 550 BC is sometimes as good a black as Attic. The contrast of cream ground with dark paint and rich purple makes an effect unusually gay for a black-figure style, and the practice of leaving parts of pots (especially cups) unslipped adds to the polychromy.

Export was wide, but declined after the middle of the sixth century. There is remarkably much from Samos, an appreciable amount from Olympia, Taranto, Cyrenaica and Naucratis, and a thin scatter round Greece and the Aegean, and at many colonial and Etruscan sites in the West, and even Carthage. The catholic taste of Etruria drew on Laconian also for its hybrid art, and there was some borrowing by East Greek workshops – Fikellura took the pomegranate, Samian potters reproduced the handleless chalice, and there are one or two forthright copies. In return Laconian vase-painters occasionally show knowledge of East Greek, as in the concentric rings on some of the cups of the Boread group (cf. p. 133) and in the use in the last third of the century of the crescents familiar from Fikellura. Corinthian influence has been mentioned already, and with the Attic Droop cup it is not clear who was the borrower. The rise of Laconian vase-painting is surprising, but no special explanation is needed for its decline, which resulted from Attic competition, not the hauntings of the ghost of Lycurgus. Those who do not like the idea that a commercial industry could flourish in Sparta itself may prefer to find the workshops in Gytheion, the port of Laconia and a town not of Spartiates but Perioeci: Gytheion has not been excavated.

Plain ware

During the sixth century Laconia did a brisker trade overseas in plainer wares, which are not always recognized as Laconian. The numerous column-kraters, usually painted all over or with a simple linear pattern on the reserved and slipped outer face of the lip, deserved their popularity for the excellence of their shape. Aryballoi of Ripe Corinthian shapes are very common. During the first half of the sixth century there are three main groups. Some are flat-bottomed and have all or most of their surface painted dark; but most are of the simpler round type with a little decoration – the upper part dark and the lower left slipped (much like a darning egg), or the whole pot covered with paint and the belly girt with a purple band which is bordered above and below by a pair of white lines enclosing dots. This last group alone survives after the middle of the sixth century, somewhat flattened and with a plain reserved border to the purple. About the same time, ring-footed cups, generally unslipped, come into favour: here the inside is painted over, the outside carries a single or double row of leaves and for the rest is plainly painted or carelessly striped. A few stemmed cups are similarly decorated. Other shapes include amphorae, oinochoai, mugs, kantharos, flat-based cup, bell-mouthed two-handled aryballos and miniature pots, painted dark all over and sometimes enlivened with a stripe or two of purple or white. Miniature pots, which were regularly offered at sanctuaries, seem to have continued till the third century.

BOEOTIA

For Boeotian pottery of the seventh century we rely mainly, as before, on style. A basically Geometric school continued for a while to work in a tradition derived from Attic and Corinthian, but at the same time Orientalizing motifs were becoming acceptable. This is most evident in a class of big amphorac with a high conical foot, which may be fenestrated, and a broad neck passing into a flaring lip. The principal decoration, of Subgeometric or early Orientalizing figures or ornaments, is set – sometimes in wild confusion – in a panel on the shoulder; neck and often the foot and the band round the belly are crudely filled with a row of thick vertical zigzags. The shape, the system of decoration and the zigzags were current too in Euboea and the Cyclades where they belong particularly to the Linear Island group (Plate 29A–B); but the Cycladic decoration is quieter and finer, and Euboea – which is also nearer - was probably the immediate source for Boeotia. Later examples, which are more Orientalizing than Subgeometric in effect, show peculiar forms of plant ornament, have tidier zigzags and add a plastic rim below the lip. There are besides pots of other shapes and more humbly decorated which have similar zigzags and banding. Dating is difficult. Some of the figures and ornaments can be paralleled elsewhere in the first and also the second quarter of the seventh century; but unless there is a gap in the present sequence of Boeotian, this zigzag manner may have lasted through the seventh century and even into the early years of the sixth. The coarsish clay is buff to pink, with a cream slip or wash, and the paint is dull and uneven.

There follows, so it seems, an original product of Boeotian taste, the *Bird cup group*, which takes its name from such pieces as that of Plate 28A, a clumsy sort of dish with or without a high foot and decorated in the manner of modern folk art. On the outside birds or palmettes, zigzags and cross-hatched triangles are the commonest components. The birds and other ornaments are regularly upside down, whether because the cup was meant to be hung high up or that the painter found it easier to work that way. The inside is simply banded. Of other shapes the kantharos is most important. The clay, buff or pink, has a pale slip. At first this slip is cream, and the decoration in the standard dark paint and red or purple; but from about 520 BC the slip becomes whiter, purple and yellow are used liberally, and the surface is powdery. The effect is remarkably colourful. At Rhitsona, the ancient Mycalessus, and at Akraiphia, the only Boeotian sites where a cemetery has been carefully excavated and reported, the series of Bird cups beginning in the 570s and lasts till 500 BC or a little later. Examples, which are numerous, come mostly from eastern Boeotia, where they may well have been made in several places.

During the seventh and for much of the sixth century, Corinthian pottery was imported in great quantity. Some simple Boeotian imitations have been recognized; since recognition depends on the clay, inferior workmanship and place of finding, but not on a coherent local style, they are often disputed. A *black-figure style* was not established till the early sixth century, and then naturally under Attic influence, if not by graduates from Attic workshops. The first models are in the Comast group and the Animal style of the time. Animals, now as in Attic tamer and thinner, remain popular during the middle and third quarter of the century, but the Boeotians surround them with thick filling ornament. Human figures are rarer and lag further behind Attic standards. A large class regularly does without incision and added colour, though the forms and disposition of figures and of ornaments are those of contemporary black-figure. This use of full silhouette is sometimes described as Geometricizing, but there is no need to derive from the Geometric style of a century and more earlier a practice that is readily explained by indolence or the example of Droop cups then being made in Athens. Both silhouette and incising black-figure continued throughout the fifth century, first following the minor tradition in Attic black-figure and when that ended with a new vigour. Even at the end of the fifth century output was large, especially of cups decorated with floral ornament or with a figure or small group, usually in silhouette, between heavy palmettes. Early in the fourth century even the floral style withered away. The notable shapes are at first kantharos and tripod-pyxis, lekane and kotyle; later cups of various types become increasingly common.

This late black-figure is redeemed by the *Cabiran style*, so-called because of its popularity at the Cabiran sanctuary near Thebes. The school begins in the third quarter of the fifth century, decays during the fourth and expires in the second quarter of the third. The drawing, which uses incision and added white, sometimes shows a skilful translation of the manner of Attic red-figure, but much more often it is perfunctory or negligent. Besides Cabirus reclining at the banquet there are less elevated scenes from mythical, human and pygmy life, grotesque in poses and proportions but vivacious and convincing (Figure 13). This is the only truly comic school of Classical Greek art. Some instances of what appears to be actor's costume suggest a connection with farce. These pots with human figures are, especially in the later phase, less common than those decorated with a band of ivy or other floral ornament; and sometimes a floral ornament surmounts

Figure 13   Boeotian kantharos.
Detail: scale *c.* 2:5. Cabiran style, by the Mystae painter,
early 4th century BC.

a figure scene. The characteristic shape is a kantharos like a deep mug, narrowing towards the rim: it has a low foot and a pair of vertical ring-handles, to which one or two spurs are attached. The lower part of the pot is often left unpainted.

The clay of Boeotian black-figure is normally a pale brown. Sometimes the surface or part of it given a reddish wash to imitate Attic or to contrast with the main field. The paint is often rather dull and streaky. A few pieces resemble Attic very closely. Thebes was perhaps the chief place of manufacture; it was accessible to Athens, the largest Boeotian city and probably the home of the Cabiran workshops. Inferior contemporary groups seem to come from northern Boeotia and perhaps Euboea. A few Boeotian pots have been found in Attica and other parts of Greece, but there was no regular export, unless to more backward neighbours.

EUBOEA

The two big cities of Euboea, Chalcis and Eretria, were only a dozen miles apart. From Eretria we have enough pottery to judge the school current there, from Chalcis nothing of importance. But it is not likely that if pottery was painted in Chalcis it differed much from what may be called Eretrian. The admirable ware known as 'Chalcidian', which many think was made at Chalcis, is here assigned to Italy for the reasons set out on p. 151.

A largish amphora with broad neck and high conical foot appears at Eretria (as in Boeotia and the Cyclades) about the beginning of the seventh century, soon becomes the principal shape – at least for infant burial – and with modifications lasts well down the sixth century. Dating, though by stylistic analogies, is fairly secure. The earliest of these amphorae, of the groups A and B, make much of vertical zigzags, big and little, in a close row or more often spaced in groups: the main panel, between the handles, has sometimes Subgeometric animals and sometimes simple Orientalizing ornament. Corinthian influence is evident, though the effect is nearer Boeotian. Later the decorative bands grow fewer and much of the pot is covered with dark paint, relieved by stripes of purple and white: a peculiar ornament is an upright bar, shaped like a sausage, which repeated in the centre and singly at the sides gives weight to the main panel. In group C (Plate 28B) a new kind of decoration is introduced. Usually the front of the amphora has women on the neck and a lone animal or monster on the upper part of the body, while the back is filled in with heavy loops. The figures are drawn in partial outline, white and not incision is normally used for details on dark areas, and purple is added freely. The helpless style and the repertory of filling ornament most resemble 'Melian', but may rather be debased from Attic. In spite of old fashioned traits this group is probably of the last quarter of the seventh century. In contrast group D attempts a regular black-figure technique with incision, though still allowing itself outlined heads. The model, as elsewhere in the early sixth century, is the Corinthian Animal style, but mixed with other elements, some local and others paralleled in Attic or 'Melian'. Probably the Corinthianizing style came through one or other of these schools. The result anyhow is singularly uncouth. Here the strictly Eretrian school ends. Its style had been costively provincial, moving – when it moved – by sudden jerks. Groups A and B (and for that matter D) show some resemblances to contemporary Etruscan: either Eretrian was imported to Italy – and for this there is no evidence – or, more credibly, both Eretrian and Etruscan sometimes made similar use of their Corinthian models.

A few amphorae found at Eretria, of the same type but more finely modelled, are elaborately and competently painted in a black-figure style that in large part is pure Attic of the middle of the sixth century. The painters must have trained in Attic workshops; but some of the details of the decoration are foreign to Attic, and shape, use and place of finding are Eretrian. Some smaller pots with similar un-Attic details may also have been made in Eretria, but attributions of this kind are dangerous. Finally, in the late fifth and early fourth centuries a sort of black-figure that indulges in palmettery shows Euboean paying homage to Boeotian depravity.

Clay and paint cannot regularly by distinguished by eye from Attic. There was hardly more export of Eretrian than of Boeotian pottery, though odd Atticizing pieces of the late sixth century have been noticed at Megara Hyblaea in Sicily and Olbia in South Russia.

THE CYCLADES

The Orientalizing movement reached the Cyclades early, and more or less independent workshops concocted different mixtures of Subgeometric and Orientalizing. Some clung to a looser version of the old style, admitting a few new motifs. Others innovated more frankly, but with a tendency to mannerism which was refined and exaggerated by their successors in the middle of the seventh century. The black-figure style with its regular use of incision was not accepted. The general impression is that there were scattered round the islands a few progressive painters, gifted but isolated, who could not establish a living tradition of their own and though casually imitating would not adopt the tradition of others. The one exception is the showy 'Melian' school, which through the later part of the seventh century and the early part of the sixth drew what can hardly be called inspiration from the major schools of its time.

The study of Cycladic Orientalizing is confused. Many more or less complete pots, among which amphorae have a probably unrepresentative importance, have been found in the Purification enclosure on Rheneia (to which were transferred the contents of graves on Delos) and in the cemeteries of Thera. There are also sherds from Siphnos, some pots from Melos and Kimolos, and a few oddments from elsewhere. These finds give some idea where particular groups were or were not current, and in Thera a few early pots were noted in useful contexts. A better knowledge of the Late Geometric of the Cyclades has helped to locate some of the schools that developed from it, but there remains much for which specialists rely mainly on intuition. The opinions that follow are possibly too sceptical, but a short concordance of other opinions is added on pp. 340–1. The dating of Cycladic has often been too early, and perhaps the dates proposed here have not all been lowered enough; for if (as is likely) the deposit on Rheneia conceals a steady series of Cycladic pottery, some of the earlier Orientalizing groups must continue beyond the middle of the seventh century to link with 'Melian'.

Several groups had some general currency within the Cyclades, but only 'Melian' was at all regularly exported beyond them. In the seventh century there was much import and some imitation of Corinthian, less import but perhaps more imitation of East Greek. In the early sixth century Attic became dominant, and its simpler forms were occasionally copied.

The Linear Island group

Linear Island is the least prejudiced name that has been proposed for this group of pots, mainly neck-amphorae around 50 cm high; Plate 29 offers an example typical in shape and system of decoration. The vertical zigzags on the neck are standard. In the three panels of the shoulder, the principal field of decoration, various motifs occur. Some, not necessarily confined to the earliest stage of the group, are of Geometric origin, such as the heavy concentric circles (often flanked by four dots), the quatrefoil, the big lozenge that sprouts extra corners from its sides, and opposed or boxed triangles. Others are Orientalizing – rudimentary florals or simple curvilinear patterns, birds of various forms and structure, and the lion. The style has a simple but studied elegance which relies on line. This is obvious in the narrow stripes surrounding neck, shoulder and foot, and in the groups of thin uprights, stopped by thicker, which separate the panels. It appears more subtly in the fauna, wiry and boneless, and unencumbered by filling ornament: the lion of the illustration is treated as a linear pattern, its body lightly sprinkled with dots except on the shoulder (which, as often in Cycladic, is defined with inorganic emphasis) and its pose adapted to the panel rather than for action. With these amphorae go a few kraters of the low Geometric shape. Many cups and other simply decorated pots have also been connected, without much more reason than general similarity of clay. This in Linear Island is fine, varies in colour from reddish to yellowy brown and contains some mica. There is usually a yellowish slip or wash. The paint is normally dark-brown.

The origin of this group is disputed. There is nothing distinctive about its Geometric components, its Orientalizing forms seem to be independently received or adapted (though some of the birds have relatives in Cretan), and the shape of the amphora was evolved in Cycladic Late Geometric. Nor is its distribution decisive. The humbler candidates for the group appear in Thera, Delos (including Rheneia) and Paros, which is often accepted as its home. But almost all the important amphorae and kraters have been found in Thera, though their style is very different from the contemporary Theran Subgeometric.

The end of Linear Island is also obscure. Its only recognizable descendant is a close group of three amphorae in Leyden, Stockholm and Paris. Their shape is tauter and more subtly proportioned, their decoration simpler and bolder with the central panel extended to take a crouching lion or grazing deer. In some details they resemble the Protome group, but not more closely than might be expected from two workshops of much the same time and region.

On style and the contexts of Theran graves the date of the Linear Island group should be the early part of the seventh century, though what looks like a fragment of this ware has turned up at Aziris in Cyrenaica in a context not earlier than the 630s. The shape of the amphora and some elements of the style were probably borrowed and debased in Eretria and Boeotia. The Leyden group appears to be of the middle of the seventh century.

The Ad group

The Linear Island group is calligraphic and primly modern. The contemporary Ad group prefers crude contrast of dark and light and an antique manner. Here the whole surface of the pot is decorated with coarse but effective brushwork. On the broad neck-amphora, a standard shape, the full width of neck and shoulder is taken for the field; the neck usually has an elongated horse and the shoulder two or more animals, grouped or in file. Below come two, three or four bands of ornament, and at the base heavy rays. A few close stripes bound each field and band. The favourite animals (sometimes reduced to protomes) are horse, with or without wings, deer, griffin and lion. Of these the lion is Orientalizing in build and in its technique of reserved head and dotted – and even chequered – body.

Figure 14 Cycladic oinochoe.
Detail of shoulder: ht of field 7 cm. Ad group, first quarter of
7th century BC.

The other creatures are typically Subgeometric in their exaggeration of Geometric traits: note on Figure 14 the overgrown hindquarters and the extensible body, which is sometimes broken by sections reserved and filled with dots. Columns of horizontal zigzags and compositions of lozenges fill the vacant spaces. These ornaments also appear together in the bands on the lower part of the body, as do flattened chequers, the open cable, tall blobs and short vertical zigzags. Other shapes are hydria, krater, oinochoe and skyphos; and from Siphnos came a terracotta figure, originally about 30 cm high. The clay is fine and brown. There may be a creamy slip. The paint is dark and dull.

Pots or sherds of the Ad group have been found on Rheneia (in the Purification deposit), Siphnos, Kimolos and Paros, and at Al Mina, but not on Thera. In decorative details the closest parallels are in 'Parian' Geometric and, since the clays are similar, 'Paros' may be considered the home of the Ad group too. It is, though, a compact group of very personal character – many of our pieces are evidently by one painter – so that purely stylistic argument is less secure. The date, by the look of the animals, which have some affinity with Protoattic, is in the first thirty years of the seventh century.

The Heraldic group

The Heraldic group, of much the same date, uses a similar repertory in yet another mode (Figure 15). The principal shape is a slim neck-amphora with handles on the shoulder up to 50 cm high, an exaggeration of a standard Late Geometric type. The lower half of the pot is striped. The back of the upper part has sprawling lozenges, loops, cables or grotesques. The front of neck and shoulder receives elaborate decoration. On each there is a main field, bordered above and below by one or two bands of simple ornament, and divided into a narrowish central panel and flanking strips or subsidiary panels. The panels contain a couple of dancing lions, a solitary lion or horse (winged or wingless), a sphinx, or the head and neck of a horse – all these in a rubbery Orientalizing style and with reserved heads – or else simple curvilinear or even floral designs, or step-pattern. In narrower strips a simple cable and latticing are frequent. For the horizontal bands the favourite ornaments are lozenges, void or cross-hatched, and S-shaped blobs: sometimes there are simple tongues or floral chains at the top of the shoulder. The sphinxes are notable for the three-leaved drape over their forelegs, a misunderstanding of the ultimately Egyptian skirt. The drawing is cursory, with more attention to a general effect of vertical elaboration than to detailed accuracy of line or anatomy or to grand composition. Of shapes other than the amphora the most remarkable is a large figure from Siphnos. The clay is reddish brown, with a creamy slip, and the paint is dark and shiny.

Figure 15 Cycladic amphora.
Detail of neck: scale *c.* 3:7. Heraldic group, first or perhaps
second quarter of 7th century BC.

Most of these amphorae are by one painter, a decorative mannerist who
had some knowledge of Geometric but was familiar with the early
Orientalizing style. Similarities in shape and the use of striping suggest a
connection with Naxian Late Geometric, and the clay and slip agree; but
stylistically the Heraldic group looks invented rather than evolved. One
example has been found on Thera, one on Siphnos and more on Naxos;
the rest are from the Purification deposit of Rheneia and from Delos itself.
Style suggests a date early in the seventh century, though the context of
the amphora from Thera is later.

The Protome group

The consummation of Cycladic mannerism is reached in a small group of
neck-amphorae, hydriai and one cup, which has been named the Protome
group. The decoration is disposed and designed in harmony with the full
but simple shapes. The amphora is especially successful. Here the lip has
a band of simple ornament – trios of S-blobs separated by grouped strokes.
On the neck a central panel usually displays the head and neck of a horse
or the forepart of a lion, and the narrow flanking panels some simple linear
or floral motif. The shoulder is decorated like the neck, but on a larger
scale, and below comes a border of ornament as on the lip. The lower half
of the pot makes a good setting with its deep band of dark paint, relieved
by two thin purple stripes, and the thick rays round the base. The sophisticated simplicity of the style may be inspected in Figure 16. The balance
of light and dark is carefully studied, most obviously in the structure of

Figure 16 Cycladic amphora.
Details of shoulder (front and back): scale 2:3.
Protome group, mid-7th century BC.

the lion; and, as the horse's jaw shows, line is developed for its own sake in defiance of anatomy, something very different from Corinthian calligraphy (of which Figure 6C and E gives mature examples). This is a style complete in itself; it can advance no further. Some students assign the Protome group to Paros, others to Naxos. But the painter of the amphorae was an individualist rather than an adherent of a school. The clay is brown and micaceous, the slip cream, the paint dark and usually dullish. The date should be about the middle of the seventh century, if only because of the teeth of the lion: till the second quarter of that century Greek lions are fitted only with incisors. So far this group is recorded only from the Purification deposit on Rheneia.

Other Orientalizing groups

Many Orientalizing pots and fragments, especially from the Rheneia deposit, do not fit into any of the groups already described, though place of finding and various stylistic connections argue that they are Cycladic. A group consisting in the main of miserable one-piece amphorae and hydriai and of big cups – *group D* (or the *Big Bird group*) – is decorated in an execrable style, probably of the first half of the seventh century. The upper part of the body has a row of birds or lions' heads or a whole animal, supported by such ornaments as simple florals, lozenges, thick vertical zigzags and open cable. On the lower part are stripes and rays. If the Ad group is Parian, then because of its similar lions' heads group D might be too, though so far it has not been observed outside Rheneia and Delos. The clay is fine and brown, with a dirty slip, the paint dark and shiny.

Theran Subgeometric, as has been said (p. 32), flourished well into the seventh century and some pots show Orientalizing motifs, though it would be supererogatory to separate them into a Theran Orientalizing style.

Imitations of Corinthian, not always close, occur sporadically in the first half and middle of the seventh century. *Imitations of the Wild Goat style*, rather more frequent, are mostly of the later part of that century. Where the style does not betray them, these imitations are recognized by their rougher clay and yellowish slip. Other pots show a style *related to 'Melian'*, if not an early stage of that school. The most remarkable are some pieces from Naxos, of the mid-seventh century, which use a light-brown for male flesh and other parts of the decoration. A number of *ring-vases* (shaped like a bloated lifebelt with a vertical spout) are on their distribution probably Cycladic; they are palely slipped and are decorated simply with cross-hatched triangles, tongues or floral forms. Finally, there is an assortment of pieces, a few reputable but more inept, which display Orientalizing patterns, vegetation or figures.

'Melian'

The 'Melian' school takes its name from a series of big amphorae found on Melos and published as long ago as 1862. At that time they were the largest and gaudiest of known Greek pots, and their importance and age were and still sometimes are exaggerated. But the school is sluggishly imitative, not pioneering.

The decoration is by monotonous formula. The big amphora (or krater), which runs about a metre high, is a modernization of the Linear Island type. The neck is broader and taller, the body more elegantly ovoid, the foot higher and slit by vents. The decoration, as always in 'Melian', covers the whole pot. On the neck there are usually a human or divine pair in the central panel and double volutes at the sides and back. On the body

Figure 17 'Melian' amphora.
Ht (without lid) 45.5 cm. Early 6th century BC.

a grand scene is exhibited in front, confronting horses or other unimportant figures at the back, and below them come a band of double spirals or other large ornament and a deeper band of volutes. On the foot female heads or more volutes occupy the panels between the vents, with a band of ornament above and below. Round the moulding at the bottom reversed rays are normal. The subjects of the main field are sometimes mythological. A smaller and more simply decorated version of this type of amphora is illustrated on Figure 17. The ordinary neck-amphorae and hydriai, which are very frequent, are of course less ambitious, but again the whole surface is decorated. The shapes are not well defined: some are tallish with ovoid body, others (perhaps later) more squat. The familiar motifs are on the neck a female head, double volutes, or occasionally a complete figure, on the shoulder, volutes or animals; on the body, in the main field animals, and below it meander or chevrons and then rays or even tongues. The shallow dishes (or deep plates with two handles) are usually surrounded with volutes on the outside and banded or plain inside. Other shapes include the one-piece amphora, the plate and the phiale mesomphalos.

The drawing is unequal and rather coarse. The human figures and still more the female heads are often gawky and angular, and the detail is stupidly excessive: there is much resemblance, and presumably indebtedness, to Corinthian (as on the neck of Figure 17). The animals are more varied: on some earlier pots the horses have a Cycladic look, but soon the fauna of the Wild Goat style is copied, and that is succeeded by Corinthianizing birds and beasts. The filling ornament changes in harmony, though it too keeps its own flavour. Of the larger ornaments volutes in one form or another occur on almost every 'Melian' pot and with their latticed appendages make identification easy. Also common are double spirals and lotus chains with flowers of an undeveloped type known earlier in Cycladic. Samples of volutes and flowers are shown on Figures 17 and 24. For minor bands there are tongues, meanders, chevrons and other angular patterns, big round dots, and spiked dots that are perhaps derived from the Laconian pomegranate. Latticing is frequent for the side frames of panels. Under handles set horizontally eyes often peep out, as in some earlier Cycladic groups. The technique of figures is at first reserving, that is heads and other appropriate parts are outlined, but in time a little unsystematic incision is attempted, and for Corinthianizing animals there is especially in the late stage a sort of black-figure method which substitutes white lines for incision. Purple is used freely throughout, and on the big amphorae a light-brown denotes male flesh. The coarse clay is a greyish brown ranging to pink and contains mica. The slip is yellowish. The paint varies from brown to blackish and is rather dull. The general effect is loud.

The 'Melian' school, as at present defined, is compact and not of long duration. Imitation of Corinthian, which appears early, is of the last quarter of the seventh century and the first of the sixth. Even if some disputed pieces are included, it seems to me hard to date the beginning before 650 BC, though some experts put it twenty years earlier. The main finds are from Rheneia (where over three hundred pots were recovered in the Purification deposit), from Delos itself, and from Melos; there is a fair amount from Thasos and Tocra in Cyrenaica; other examples are recorded from Siphnos, Paros, Naxos and Kavalla (the Thracian Neapolis), and isolated fragments from Icaria, Samos and Lindos.

Where 'Melian' was made is still uncertain, but opinion now favours Paros. There appears to be a connection with the Ad group, which may be Parian, and clay analysis gives some support. Also, for what it's worth, a 'Melian' amphora or hydria was for a while a standard show-piece in graves on Delos, which is not far from Paros, and Paros was the mother-city of Thasos, where 'Melian' was imported.

Polychrome plates

A few plates of the early sixth century pose in a field of blue human figures or animals done in white, red and the usual dark-brown. The style is not specifically Cycladic, but finding places point strongly to the Cyclades: there is one each from Thera and Tocra, the others come from Delos (including Rheneia) and from Paros.

THE EAST GREEK REGION

Ionia and Aeolis were pioneers of Greek literature, but in their barren vase-painting rare spurts of energy were followed by long spells of stagnation. East Greek Geometric was irresolute, the Orientalizing style tame, the black-figure without roots. A little isolated imitation comprised East Greek influence in European Greece, though there was naturally more in the Cyclades but Corinthian and then Attic models dominated much of East Greek in the sixth century. Exports tell the same story: from the later seventh century the pottery of Corinth and then of Attica becomes common on East Greek sites and even Laconian not unknown, while East Greek pottery was rarely carried across the Aegean except perhaps to such East Greek foundations as Gela in Sicily. It is often said that there is much that is East Greek in the art of Etruria. The claim is exaggerated, for part of their similarity is that neither is Attic.

It was probably not till the second quarter of the seventh century that East Greek vase-painters began to reject the Geometric tradition. From Smyrna some tantalizing fragments suggest a mood of uncoordinated experiment: but the successful Orientalizing style, which first established itself in South Ionia, was an Animal style, from its commonest species best called the *Wild Goat style*. In no part of the Greek world is the contrast stronger between old and new – in decoration, shapes and technique – and the intermediate stage is less a transition than an uncompounded mixture of the two styles. Here the influence of Oriental models is more persistent and if the source was the same as that on which the Greeks of Europe drew, the vehicle was not. Protocorinthian has a fine precision of line that suggests engraving, the Wild Goat style with its thick careless brushwork and dependence on mass and colour has more of a textile look. In Greek vase-painting of the seventh century it was the human figure that more and more attracted the progressive artists; there were no progressive artists on the east of the Aegean and once established the Wild Goat style steadily declined. A little before 600 BC a North Ionian workshop attempted to graft on to its old reserving tradition the black-figure Animal style of Ripe Corinthian, with commercial success: the rejuvenated version lasted some fifty years. The Wild Goat style had been universal in the East Greek region, except that in Aeolis its provincial schools could not oust the older Grey ware (or, as it has misleadingly been called, Bucchero), but in the sixth century there was more divergence. In the south the *Fikellura* style continued some of the Wild Goat tradition, at first with revived delicacy, then more carelessly till it petered out in clumsy linear and vegetable patterns: its period is from near the middle to the end of the century. *Chios* during the first half of the century developed both a polychrome style, sometimes elegant, and a cursory black-figure style. There were also groups inspired by or imitating Attic black-figure, notably the *Ionian Little Master cups* of the years round 550 BC, and in the north the slightly later *Clazomenian* ware. Yet another establishment produced the *Situlae*, mostly found at Tell Defenneh in Egypt and posing a curious problem. But by 500 BC East Greek vase-painting was deservedly dead. Only the *Clazomenian sarcophagi*, tedious monuments of painted terracotta, show that from the 540s to the 460s BC there were still one or two workshops which not only imitated contemporary Attic but remembered the old tradition of the Wild Goat style. Disappointing as the admission may be, the Persian conquest in the 540s had no visible effect on East Greek vase-painting.

Knowledge of East Greek pottery in this period is patchy, for reasons mentioned on pp. 33–4. What is available is a fair amount from Rhodes, Samos, Smyrna (though here not yet of the seventh century) and 'Larisa', a modicum from Chios, Pitane and Nisyros, and a growing assortment from the looting of graves in Caria. Further, much has been excavated overseas, at Naucratis and Tell Defenneh in Egypt, Tocra in Cyrenaica, Istria in Romania, and Olbia and Berezan in Ukraine, though little or nothing at these sites is earlier than the last quarter of the seventh century. Unhappily there are few useful contexts except on Rhodes, where graves have been recorded, and even there the series is good for the main schools only for the last thirty years of the seventh century and the later part of the sixth. Still, there has been one notable advance in recent years: clay analysis has found probable homes for several of the East Greek styles.

Subgeometric and Bird bowls

In the early part of the Orientalizing period there was much Subgeometric pottery, though hardly a Subgeometric style. The best-known examples are round-mouthed oinochoai decorated wildly with Geometric ornaments and birds, with which simple Orientalizing motifs may be mixed. Such Subgeometric occurs on most East Greek sites which have deposits of the mid-seventh century.

A peculiar East Greek byform is the *Bird bowl* of which Plate 29D offers a sample: the inside is covered with dark paint. The Bird bowl evolves in shape and decoration from a Late Geometric kotyle and once established shows little variation, even in the placing and forms of the filling ornament. Generally nicked rim, ring foot and the painting over of all the lower part of the bowl are signs of an early date; and smooth rim, moulded foot, rays round the lower bowl and bands of white–red–white on the painted inside are late. The clay, usually light-brown and unslipped is, like much of the ornament, Geometric, but the mannered style betrays its later date. The period of the Bird bowls is roughly the whole seventh century. Some examples have a pale slip, and a few display Orientalizing fauna. The more orthodox are mostly North Ionian, but local imitations or variants appear throughout the East Greek region and at some colonial sites. Export of Bird bowls was rather wider than that of the Wild Goat pottery to which they are complementary. A few examples have been found as far west as Etruria and Malta, and some local imitations occur at Sparta.

In the later seventh century the Bird bowls were being succeeded by cups of similar shape but more modern decoration. The rigid compartments of the handle frieze disappear, the ornament turns to large dot-rosettes or a lotus flower or even a roughly sketched nose and pair of eyes set loosely in the field, and the use of a slip is perhaps rather less exceptional. These *Rosette bowls* and *Lotus bowls* are still common in the second half of the sixth century; the *Eye bowls*, less frequent, may not have lasted so long. They are all rare outside East Greek settlements and imitations are rarer still.

The Wild Goat style

The Wild Goat style, still sometimes described generically as Rhodian, began little, if at all, before the middle of the seventh century and for some three generations was the principal style of East Greek vase-painting. It is easy to recognize even in its later Corinthianizing products (for examples see Plates 30–31 and Figure 18). The clay is coarser than that of the preceding Geometric, and the exposed surface (except of some Late pieces) has a pale slip or wash. The draughtsmanship has a careless facility which might be thought spontaneous if there were not so many examples of it. It is a style without ambitions.

Early Orientalizing experiments evident at Smyrna and elsewhere came to nothing. More of a transition may be divined in the Subgeometric round-mouthed oinochoai. Here there may appear on the broad shoulder a fish or tentative goats, in silhouette relieved by a little reservation, and on the neck a simple cable. Slip is not yet regular. There are, besides, sherds on which panels with animals and ornament in a developed Wild Goat style adjoin bands of purely Geometric meander. The Wild Goat style, ornaments and animals, seems to have been introduced very nearly in the form that became canonical and not to have passed through a long evolution. A few sherds show abortive experiments in incision. The date of the transitional phase is probably well on in the second quarter of the seventh century.

The Wild Goat style proper begins about the middle of the seventh century and in South Ionia, principally perhaps at Miletus, which clay analysis indicates was the principal exporter in the last quarter. So far there is no sign of its adoption in North Ionia or Aeolis before the end of its Middle I stage: at Emporio on Chios, the only site for which contexts have been published, Subgeometric was still dominant in the third quarter of the seventh century. For Chios and Aeolis the South Ionian Middle II style remained more or less the model; but on the North Ionian mainland, particularly at Clazomenae, there was soon, if not immediately, innovation, and what is here called the Late Wild Goat style was concocted.

South Ionia. The Early Wild Goat style was still erratic and, to judge by its present rarity did not last long, perhaps only from *c.* 650 to *c.* 640 BC. The staider Middle style, roughly the old style 'A', may be subdivided into I and II about 625 BC, when ornament and poses become stereotyped. The round-mouthed oinochoe of Plate 30A exhibits the Middle I style. The shoulder as usual carries the principal subject, a neat but stiff composition of two griffins posing across a lotus ornament and flanked by a bull and a goat. But there is a refreshing liveliness in the two friezes round the belly, with their broken groups of dogs coursing goats and deer. The light filling ornaments are deftly scattered in the field, the independent bands of ornament nicely judged not to overweight the figure scenes. This vase, made about 630 BC, plainly shows the strength and weakness of the Wild Goat style. It is admirably decorative in its design and in the gay contrast of cream ground and dark paint, but it aims at nothing more than being decorative and an ideal so easily satisfied does not stimulate a progressive tradition. The result can be seen in the trefoil-mouthed oinochoe of Plate 30B, of the last quarter of the seventh century. Oinochoai like this, some neater and some more negligent, are to be seen in most sizeable collections of Greek vases, and their cumulative effect is monotonous. On the dark lip eyes and rosettes are often painted in white; the neck carries a ribbon of simple cable or meander and square; the shoulder is still emphasized by the animals and geese which beneath tongues strike prescribed attitudes, sometimes across a floral ornament; round the belly goats follow one another grazing, each kind of filling ornament having its appointed place; and the base is encircled by a chain of lotus flowers and buds or long rays. There are variations: the goats on better pieces sometimes run, there may be more rows of figures on the belly, an occasional creature forgets its drill, or the decoration may be simplified – for the shoulder frieze a lotus chain, for the belly frieze a broad dark band enlivened by purple stripes and enclosing some simple ornament such as the hook meander. The general tendency is towards rougher draughtsmanship, a narrower repertory, heavier and coarser filling ornament, a more lavish use of purple, and the labour-saving elongation of animals already noticed in the Ripe Animal style of Corinth.

Much the commonest species in the fauna is the goat, which in the Middle II phase has almost a monopoly of the belly of the pot. Spotted deer, lion, griffin and bull occur throughout the Middle phase; dog and hare are usually early, sphinx and goose mostly later, panther and boar rare. Occasionally around the 620s there is the pretty conceit of swallows perching on tails and rosettes. The characteristic lotus (drawn on Figure 19A) remains closer to its Oriental model than do its relations in European Greece. At first it is small and delicate and is used in subsidiary bands, but soon it grows large and bold. This type, in a chain of alternate flowers and buds (the two ends often carelessly united), is familiar round the base of trefoil-mouthed oinochoai; but units are also made up into compact ornaments – surmounting a pair of volutes in the middle of the shoulder, or joined in a cross in the centre of dishes; and sometimes a flower or bud stands alone in a panel. Compared with the Corinthian lotus (Plate 12C) the East Greek type is both truer to nature and less convincing: at Corinth the stylization is more abstract, but the vigorous play of the connecting tendrils suggests organic life. Towards the end of the century a simpler and smaller variety of lotus (Figure 19B) was invented for shoulder friezes and dishes. Other continuous ornaments are few – the cable (on fine pieces two or more courses deep) and the meander and square are needed on necks, but subsidiary bands are rare after the Middle I phase. The character and general progress of the filling ornament can be seen in the illustrations. Of the shapes the oinochoe is the most frequent. The broad round-mouthed type of Plate 30A was perhaps the only shape that survived from Geometric to Orientalizing, gradually assuming a wider and lower body: it began at the end of Geometric, had its popularity, and fell out of favour after the Middle I phase. The canonical trefoil-mouthed oinochoe (Plate 30B), though it occurs in the third quarter of the seventh century, is characteristically a Middle II shape: its development seems to be towards a higher and narrower body and a feebler neck. A squat variety too appears near the end of the Middle II phase: the shoulder usually has a panel with a figure or head, the belly has bands of paint striped with purple. The stemmed dishes, which become common in the Middle II phase, have a conventional charm: the decoration, on the inside, is usually a central rosette or lotus cross, then bands of dark paint enlivened by narrow purple stripes and inset hook meanders, and round the edge between groups of wedge-shaped leaves or rays six or seven panels framing rosettes, heads of goose, goat or sphinx, or curious stylized sets of a nose and a pair of eyes. Contemporary with these but without figure decoration are other dishes with ring foot and heavy flat rim. Further shapes include krater, dinos and probably the plate, though its heyday was later. The accident that so many of the pots of this period come from graves in Rhodes may give a wrong idea of the frequency of various shapes; but there is no doubt of the rarity of the amphora, the place of which as in contemporary Corinthian was filled by the oinochoe, and of the cup and other drinking pots – here probably for the technical reason that the Wild Goat fabric was coarse to the lips.

Pottery of Middle II style is not found in the graves of Rhodes after about 600 BC, and finds in the Black Sea colonies suggest that its importation ended at that time too. There are, though, some indications that for a while a degenerate Middle style survived at Miletus, serving home customers and some Carian neighbours: besides a few likely pieces from the excavation of Miletus itself, there are Carian pots of the mid-sixth century from Mylasa (30 miles inland) which still offer a recognizable version of the Middle Wild Goat style, and the Fikellura style, invented at Miletus at much the same date, makes some use of the Middle tradition.

North Ionia. The Late Wild Goat style (the old style 'B'), which began shortly before 600 BC was and remained a North Ionian speciality Clay analysis makes Clazeomenae a (perhaps the main) producer. In spite of heavy import of Corinthian pottery into the East Greek region, the conservative manner of the Middle style had remained pure-bred; now there appeared an uncritical imitation of Corinthian black-figure (see Figure 18), especially of the dense fauna and (though less wholeheartedly) of the filling ornament of the Ripe Animal style. The black-figure style of the Wild Goat painters is coarse and blotchy, but they thought so highly of the novelty as to give it the place of honour on the shoulder and sometimes the neck of important pots, relegating the reserving style to the lower field or fields. The reserving style soon finds new formulas. The ubiquitous goat, for instance, increasingly becomes a chubby creature, running with buttocks raised and head turned back, and the filling ornament too is revised. One of the more careful Late goats is illustrated on Plate 31B below a deer of the end of Middle I (Plate 31A): the new laxity is evident. Though much Late work is tedious, it sold well to East Greeks overseas. How long the style lasted is still uncertain, perhaps till the 550s.

In the black-figure style the regular fauna includes lion, boar, bull, goat, deer, sphinx, griffin, goose (or swan) in the usual Corinthian groups. In the reserving style goats, grazing or running, are normal for friezes. The lotus takes the lumpy form of Figure 19C–D and loses in size and importance, long bunches of leaves sprout from corners, cables exude drops at their angles, the filling ornament solidifies, new continuous ornaments develop, and dividing bands are heavier and now often variegated with stripes of white, purple and white. There are new shapes too. The oinochoe is long and narrow, with oval body and high neck: it shares its popularity with an amphora of similar build. Other common shapes are kraters (including column-krater), dinos, stemmed dish and ring-footed dish (both now less carefully modelled and more simply decorated), and little plates.

Figure 18 Wild Goat style oinochoe.
Details of shoulder: scale 2:3. Late Bf style, first quarter of
6th century BC.

In the second quarter of the sixth century the reserving ware seems largely content with simple floral decoration. There is, though, clumsy development in the black-figure which now makes some use of human figures: examples are known from Smyrna and Naucratis. Clazomenian is the most familiar descendant of this indeterminate East Greek black-figure.

Besides these two main schools was, it appears, Miletus and Clazomenae, but there were others, all – so it seems – derived from the Middle II style. The earliest, perhaps, is that of *Chios*, described on pp. 119–22. It was exported widely, though except to Naucratis not in much quantity.

Aeolis continued with its Grey ware (or Bucchero). This was, coarse ware apart, the normal pottery at Antissa in Lesbos, about equal in quantity to that of Wild Goat style at 'Larisa', and common at Troy. But in some place or places the Wild Goat style was practised too. The

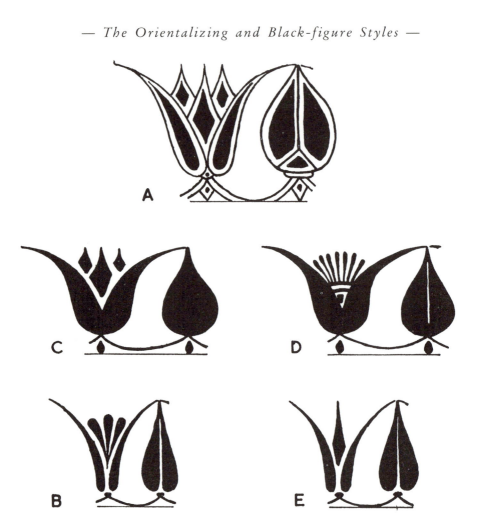

Figure 19   East Greek lotus flowers and buds.
A, Middle Wild Goat style, *c.* 630–600 BC. B, Middle Wild Goat style,
c. 615–600 BC. C–D, Late Wild Goat style, early 6th century BC.
E, Fikellura, middle and later 6th century BC.

best-known examples are from 'Larisa', a minor, and inland, Aeolian city. Here the style of drawing is angular and uncertain, and there is a lack of proportion and restraint. Lotus flowers for example may reach 17 cm high and grow extra petals; roundels and triangles often make a continuous fringe to a frieze; the loop pattern (a South Ionian specimen appears on Plate 31A) becomes rectilinear. The favourite shapes are oinochoe, kotyle-krater (popular elsewhere only in Attica in the second half of the seventh century), dinos, stemmed dish, ring-footed dish. In technique a character-istic is the use together of two shiny paints, dark-brown and red, as well as purple retouches: the two paints are sometimes found at Corinth in the later eighth century and the method of producing them may have been widely known to Greek painters, though some think that the Aeolians were indebted to inner Anatolia. There is better work from Pitane, where an informative cemetery has been excavated and, though that has not yet been published, some of the choicer pieces are exhibited (but without context). These show a wayward but more orthodox style, which sometimes achieves a spindly elegance; the amphora seems to be the leading shape, with flaring neck and the handles on the shoulder, where the decoration is concentrated. A few similar pieces come from Myrina. All this is in a Middle style, though much may be of the early sixth century. There are Late Wild Goat pots too from Pitane, but these look North Ionian imports. This Aeolian painted pottery is rare outside Aeolis, and the similar appearance of some fragments from Sardis and Amisos may only mean that other places too were independently imitating the canonical Wild Goat style.

Clay analysis has also assigned a commercially more successful reserving school to Aeolis – that of the London Dinos. Here the style, based generally (though perhaps not directly) on South Ionian Middle II, is neat and unadventurous. Goats are the favourite animals, filling ornament tends to be heavy and big triangles replace roundels. Of the continuous ornaments a band of big tongues, doubly outlined, is notable and the loop pattern appears in its rectilinear version. There are also borrowings from the reserving style of North Ionia – the running goat with rump raised and head turned back, the double spiral below an animal's belly, and the rows of short strokes attached to the upper border of a field. Purple, often put directly on the surface of the pot, is used freely. The commonest shape, so far, is the dinos, followed by plates. This school was flourishing in the first quarter of the sixth century, but may have begun earlier and lasted later. Its products were exported to Naucratis and the Black Sea. There may be yet another school for Aeolis, if what from clay analysis had been dubbed 'South Ionian 3' should find its clay matched there: this is more orthodoxly South Ionian in style – Middle II of course – and was exported in respectable quantity.

Samos, so clay analysis suggests, made little for export and was not or did not remain a major producer. A few unusually fine sherds from *Ephesus* may well be local, the product of a single exceptional workshop. *Rhodes*, after all, contributed little or nothing.

There is also the *Nisyros group*, mainly of plates, for which distribution argues strongly for manufacture in Doris, the most southerly part of the East Greek region. Here the usual formula is a single animal in reserving technique – the favourites are striding sphinx and dog – posed amid heavy filling ornaments, above a large exergue, usually filled with a fan of tongues. The execrable style derives more from South than North Ionian. Graves on Rhodes give a date of about the first quarter of the sixth century. Where in Doris they were made is uncertain, but a single clay analysis suggests that it was not on Rhodes. Export was negligible.

In the adjacent territories of Anatolia there was fumbling imitation of the Middle style at Mylasa and perhaps other pieces in *Caria*, and in Lydia some potters adopted it with cheerful freedom. On Thasos, it seems, one workshop experimented with it competently.

There are other reconstructions of the Wild Goat style, of which the most considerable is the division – popular in Germany – into Camirus and Euphorbos groups, the former corresponding roughly to what is here called Early and Middle, the latter to Late. But instead of one proceeding from the other, the two groups are considered to be contemporary (or at least widely overlapping) and largely independent. A refinement of this system detaches a Vlastos group from the Euphorbos group, which is left with little but the Dorian plates: the three groups so constituted are again contemporary, the Euphorbos group flourishing in Rhodes and the Dodecanese, the Camirus and Vlastos groups both there and elsewhere.

The clay used for Wild Goat pottery is generally coarse and gritty (and often described as micaceous); when fired it has a wide range of colours, but typically is sandy brown to pink. The slip of the Early and Middle styles is thick and ranges from yellow through cream to a near white. In the Late style the slip is often only a streaky whitish wash or omitted altogether. The paint aims at dark-brown, but has the usual transformations to red; it has little sheen. From the start of the Middle II phase purple retouches are common, white except on the lips of oinochoai is mostly Late, when too there was some use of the black polychrome technique. Efforts have been made to distinguish local schools by the look of clay and slip; but though admittedly Chiot slip is unusually white, I doubt if the naked eye will do much in this field.

Wild Goat pottery was not much exported except to East Greek settlements. It is plentiful at Al Mina in Syria, Mersin in Cilicia, Naucratis in Egypt, Berezan and Olbia in Ukraine, Istria in Rumania, Apollonia Pontica in Bulgaria, perhaps at Ak Alan near Samsun in northern Turkey, and there are isolated finds from native sites in Syria and Palestine, Egypt and the interior of Ukraine; it has been recovered from Kavalla and Thasos; some pieces have been found at Gela (traditionally a Rhodian foundation), Selinus, Megara Hyblaea and Syracuse in Sicily, and in South France; and in its Late phase it is relatively frequent at Tocra in Cyrenaica. In Crete and Cyprus and mainland Greece, and generally in Etruria, it is very rare. More went to the Cyclades, where the influence of the Wild Goat style is plain in 'Melian' vase-painting, and there were imports and (as has been said) imitations or adaptations in Lydia and Caria and perhaps even in Pamphylia and adjacent regions. One Wild Goat painter of the Middle II phase appears to have emigrated to Etruria, where he picked up some Etruscocorinthian habits. Except at Al Mina, where the Wild Goat style succeeds Geometric, Tarsus and perhaps Mersin, the finds are generally not before the Middle II phase; but this is evidence not so much of a change of taste in many East Greek colonies, as of the lateness of their foundation.

The Chiot styles

The island of Chios long maintained some artistic independence. Its Late Geometric pottery differs a little from that of other East Greek cities, its Wild Goat style shows individual traits, and in the sixth century it took an original course. Since the first important finds were made at Naucratis, the later Chiot style used to be called Naucratite. Now there is a fair quantity from Chios town and Emporio.

A Subgeometric style seems to have lasted well down the seventh century, till eventually a Wild Goat style became established. Of this, whether or not by chance, we have little or nothing that is certainly earlier than the Middle II phase. Here the decoration seems to have been fairly orthodox, though with some minor peculiarities. Roundels of horseshoe shape become common and sometimes (as in Aeolian) they form with pendent triangles a continuous border to a figure frieze; dots along the reserved belly stripe of animals and on volutes are more usual than in the southern school, the slip is rather whiter. Generally the Chiot Middle II school looks less considered and less hackneyed, but it may only be that there is less of it. The goat is not so prominent as in the south, perhaps because so few of our fragments are from pots with secondary friezes of animals. Bull, lion, boar, dog, goose and sphinx are also common. The essentially decorative character of the Wild Goat style is very evident in the unnatural but ornamental patterns and patches reserved on many of these creatures. Plate 31C gives a fair example.

The Chiot Wild Goat style, still of Middle II type, continues into the sixth century, but divides into two groups – the so-called Animal Chalice and Chalice styles. The first retains the groups and files of animals, set among thick filling ornament. The second is less traditional, preferring a single figure, sometimes human, set in an empty field, and the subsidiary decoration too becomes lighter (Figure 20). In both these groups, which probably last through the first quarter of the sixth century, there is a decline in quality of drawing, though the Chalice style often has an engaging effect.

Another innovation of the beginning of the sixth century was the Chiot Black-figure style. This (like the Polos style of Athens) is a careless small-scale adaptation of Corinthian, of the Middle rather than the Early Ripe phase, but retains a little East Greek in its details: general resemblances to Laconian are probably the outcome of a similar ineptitude. The favourite subjects are rows of crouching sphinxes or lions (these usually wearing a ham frill), and alternatively drunken male dancers with protruding rumps and clothing reduced to a band across the chest and a cap on the buttocks. The thick filling ornament consists of Corinthian rosettes and half-rosettes used as roundels, and purple lavishly supplements incision. There is not much variety, sirens and bulls occur among the animals, and there is one fragment with centaurs. All this is trivial hackwork, but a few sherds with larger and more careful human figures show that there were Chiot artists who understood and were interested in the black-figure technique. The Chiot Black-figure style probably lasted till about the middle of the sixth century, and perhaps beyond. One late group does without the white slip.

Much more remarkable is what is dubbed the Grand style, known regrettably from little more than small fragments. Here there are elaborate compositions of battles, horse-racing, drinking parties, women's dances, processions and even mythological scenes. The common facial type, at least of the men, is taken from Corinthian of the early sixth century, as perhaps are the riders and the general inspiration of this class. But there are other faces with fleshy profile and receding forehead inherited from Middle Wild Goat sphinxes; the favourite dress is the full-length sleeved chiton; the filling ornament, which is sometimes retained, is Chiot; and the mythology includes besides the popular Heracles such rarities (it seems) as the Danaids with their husbands' severed heads. The quality of the work varies from a wooden angularity to a flowing draughtsmanship that makes good use of colour. The whitish slip makes an admirable background to the brownish-black paint, which for details is often diluted to a golden brown, and there is much purple and even a purer white. The finest group adds a buff to yellow wash for male flesh, so coming closer to the polychromy of free painting. For this appreciation of colour the nearest contemporary parallel is again in Corinthian, where too the distinction of dark men and light women is not rigid. The life of the Grand style is perhaps from the 580s till near the middle of the sixth century.

The inside of Chiot chalices and other small open vases is distinctive. The surface is first slipped and then covered with dark paint, and on this after the end of the seventh century bands of ornament are often boldly painted in white and purple. In the centre there is usually a cross or a rosette; round the edge lotus flowers are common (especially of the types of Figure 19D), alternating with buds or rosettes; and there is a selection of linear ornaments. A few sherds show white human figures floundering uncertainly on a dark ground, and on a chalice in Oxford this technique is used for a pair of riders on the outside.

The shapes that are known are in the Wild Goat style dinos, open bowl (with out-turned sides), chalice, dish, jug and – a curiosity at this stage of East Greek art – the phallus-cup; in the Black-figure Sphinx and Lion style pyxis with lid, ring-vase, stemmed dish, oinochoe and bowl; in the other styles pre-eminently the chalice and after it the phiale. Plastic heads,

Figure 20   Chiot chalice.
Ht 14 cm. Chalice style, late in first quarter of 6th century BC.

of which several survive, were sometimes attached to handles or in other places. Pots without painted ornament include amphora, hydria and kantharos besides the inevitable chalice of which some late examples from Chios are very clumsy. But in all the chalice is much the commonest among the existing material, as it was in the sixth century, to judge by the finds overseas, the most admired. The earliest complete examples are the two from Vulci in Würzburg of the end of the seventh century, and here the lip is of only moderate height, the bowl sharply distinct, the foot low. The origin is plain; the chalice arose from a cup of the general type of Figure 4B by the exaggeration of lip and foot, a process which is paralleled in the kantharos and the Laconian lakaina. In the early sixth century the lip grew still taller, the transition to the bowl was slurred, and the foot – concave or conical in profile – became higher (so on Figure 20). The lip carries the main decorative field. In the Wild Goat style it is heavily framed, often with a meander, the bowl is emphasized by such patterns as double cable or meander, and the low foot is painted over. In the Black-figure and Chalice styles the subsidiary decoration becomes much lighter or disappears. The usual formula is now at the edge of the lip a narrow strip of simple ornament, between the handles the characteristic saw-pattern or something as slight, and round the base of the bowl a couple of plain bands instead of the former rays. The chalice was a long-lived shape and continued, debased and decorated at most with banding, till the fourth or even the third century.

It was once widely supposed that the pottery of these styles was made in Naucratis, and so it was regularly called Naucratite pottery. That was reasonable on the evidence then available; so little had been found in Chios and so much at Naucratis, where also many inscriptions painted on kantharoi or chalices before they were fired were dedications to Naucratite deities. But later excavation on Chios showed that the Chiot Wild Goat style and its successors had their origins in a local Geometric and must themselves be local. Some diehards have compromised on a dual style with workshops both in Chios and at Naucratis, but clay and slip are uniform and painted dedications have been found not only in Chios and Naucratis but in Aegina. Chiot pots were fashionable for dedications, and evidently vase-painters in Chios were willing to oblige the whim of a customer who travelled. A newer theory, that at least the polychrome style was Naucratite, is more plausible but hardly convincing.

The clay is sandy in texture and fires usually from lightish to reddish brown. The slip is rather hard and white: its use inside open pots has been mentioned. The paint is normally dark brown, often with an olive tinge. Purple additions are common. White (except for decoration on a dark ground) is limited to more elaborate work. The walls of chalices and phialai are often very thin, and the firing as well as the shaping is competent.

The later styles of Chiot pottery are easily recognized and exports have been widely reported. It is common, of course, in Chios, and not uncommon at Erythrae, Smyrna, Pitane, Phocaea and perhaps Clazomenae. In southern parts of the East Greek homeland it is rare. Overseas there is much from Naucratis, Tocra and Cyrene, Thasos and the neighbouring Greek colonies, and Berezan and Olbia, and some from Istria and Catania. At Aegina it seems relatively common in the sixth century. Isolated pieces have turned up in most parts of the Greek world. But the influence of Chiot does not correspond to the quality of its best work. Some inferior imitations were made at Erythrae on the mainland opposite – again according to clay analysis – and there were better ones on Thasos; an Attic chalice of about 580 BC is like an earlyish form of the Chiot shape; some later East Greek styles which used human figures were probably influenced by Chiot types; and there are reminiscences of the reserving Animal style on a few early Clazomenian sarcophagi.

Ionian Little Masters

In Ionia as elsewhere the influence of Attic black-figure succeeded Corinthian during the second quarter of the sixth century, and though it did not generally go deep it inspired a few cups of exquisite quality. Clay and paint are close to Attic and the shapes follow the Siana and the lip cup, but the arrangement of the decoration is freer and the style eclectic. The cup was already long established in East Greek pottery (see p. 133) and from that tradition the Ionian Little Masters took their usual practice of reserving both sides of the lip, often decorating the outside with a row of doubled myrtle or ivy leaves and the inside even with birds or animals. From the Wild Goat repertory came some of its fauna, but now planned in silhouette without the outline drawing of the head, and as on the plates of the early sixth century the tondo is sometimes filled by a single large figure placed on a broad exergue. Much too is original. Tradition and originality make a useful basis for a style, but here we have virtuosity. Detail is marked sometimes by reservation that equals incision in its fineness, sometimes by incision which may be so minutely elaborated that it is finicky. Individual figures are often admirable, but the composition tends to be loose and careless. The most remarkable effect is that of the Vineyard cup in the Louvre (Plate 33B) an archaic Greek version of the arabesque to which there is an apt contrast in Exekias's rather later cup of Dionysus at sea. In the Ionian cup the ordinary rules of top and bottom are confounded and the subject has no particular content: instead we have a brilliant exercise in decoration, which even manages to enclose in its pattern a little running man – a concession to the Greek sense of artistic propriety. The shape of this cup is that of the early lip cup, and the outside decoration differs only in the doubled ivy leaves of the lip; details are reserved; the date is about 550 BC. There are not many of these Ionian cups and only two or three are complete, but their variety is bewildering. The impression they give is of artists of great ability and little direction, and so their promise came to nothing.

The places where these cups have been found are first Samos and Naucratis; isolated examples come from Miletus, Smyrna, Apollonia Pontica, Aegina, Perachora perhaps, and Italy; and there must be fragments not yet identified from other sites. Their home is generally thought to be Samos though connections with Fikellura then need explaining. Comparison with Attic and Fikellura shows that the date of the group is around the middle and third quarter of the sixth century.

Fikellura

The Fikellura style, named after a modern place in Rhodes, is the last genuinely East Greek style of vase-painting. Its home was in South Ionia, at Miletus, and its life from around 560 to the end of the sixth century. Its basis was the old Wild Goat style, particularly of the Middle phase, but modernized. Some of its new types and methods are shared with the Ionian Little Masters – for instance the man on the Vineyard cup (Plate 33B) is in pure Fikellura style – but its spirit is less volatile and so it succeeded in fixing a tradition. But though Fikellura kept its independence and had

Figure 21 Fikellura amphora.
Ht 29 cm, *c.* 540 BC.

also a shrewd originality, Attic competition was always too strong for it: in Rhodes graves of this time contain more Attic than Fikellura.

The characteristic shape is a squat amphora about 30 cm high of the shape of Figure 21. In the decoration there are some constants – on the lip rough strokes, on the neck double cable (a simplification of the Middle Wild Goat form and usually early) or meander and square or meander cross, on the three-reeded handle coarse blobs, and the low foot is painted over. Variety comes in the decoration of the body. In those groups which form the core of the style it is arranged in zones, at first numerous and with the emphasis on the shoulder, then in sympathy with Attic fashion giving more size and importance to the top field of the belly. On early vases groups of animals and men are common, but gradually such figures become perfunctory and are replaced by vegetable or linear ornaments. An amphora (Figure 21) of about 540 BC in the British Museum represents the turn of the style: here the main field is on the belly and contains a partridge between large and spreading volutes, but the composition is compact and the draughtsmanship for Fikellura conscientious. The last stage is slapdash, with continuous sprawling volutes between roughly drawn tongues and crescents.

The other important system of Fikellura decoration is that of the free field, of which Plate 32A is an admirable example. This anticipates an effect of Attic red-figure of the early fifth century, but here the boldness of the conception does not need delicacy in execution. To balance the central figure the artist has sketched under each handle an ornament of about the same height. Free field decoration had been tried around the beginning of the Fikellura style in a group of oinochoai which make do with neat ornament at the top of the shoulder and short rays round the base and a blank between. But there is a gap between the oinochoai and our amphora, which was painted not before 540 and perhaps as late as 520 BC, and though in Cyprus a similar idea had been current it is best to honour the Running Man painter as an original creator. His influence survived on some later amphorae on which volutes are the sole decoration of the belly; and perhaps a group with animals on the shoulder and a blank zone below profited by this demonstration of the value of empty space.

Another original but this time unsuccessful experiment was made on some early oinochoai. The front of the body is treated as a single panel, filled in the main with scales; and from this panel broad bands, generally barred, sweep back and up towards the line of the handle. The effect is so irregular that it is hard to believe that this was an exercise in pure invention, and perhaps it was prompted by a plastic bird with feathered breast and wings laid back. This group had no successors.

Animals and birds are common at the beginning of the Fikellura style. They are drawn, as on the Ionian Little Master cups, in full silhouette with reserved detail. In the earlier groups the work is delicate and the species numerous. Lion, panther, bull, boar, deer, goat, sphinx and griffin appear in the conventional groupings; dogs chase hares; ducks or partridges waddle in file. By the 530s little more is left than dogs and hares and unspecified birds, larger and summarily sketched but not necessarily feeble; and by 520 BC even these were extinct. Human figures fared better. Neat small figures were succeeded by larger and clumsier, but even in the fourth quarter of the sixth century there were painters capable of such exquisite draughtsmanship as the Dionysus of Figure 22. The commonest subject is the drunken revel round the winebowl, and there are pygmies fighting cranes, satyrs (once chasing maenads) and Busiris. Isolated figures begin after the middle of the century, such as the hare of Plate 32A or a solitary reveller or the Dionysus of Figure 22 who is matched by·Ares on the other side of the vase. There are also fanciful creations – winged man, hare-headed man, even a winged dog-headed man. Fikellura had a taste for comic and whimsical subjects.

Volutes of the type of Figure 21 are the principal decoration of later amphorae: in the 540s, when they first appeared it was as sidepieces to a central figure. Other ornaments used to fill the wide belly field are net pattern (often of dotted lines) and sometimes scale pattern. For minor

Figure 22 Fikellura amphoriskos.
Details of body: scale *c.* 2:3. *c.* 520 BC.

zones the commonest and most characteristic ornaments are crescent and
lotus (of the type of Figure 19E, at first sometimes with two extra petals
inserted); often there are several rows of crescents, one above the other
and facing in alternate direction, and the lotus band is occasionally doubled.
A chain of buds is common on the shoulder, and on some earlier pieces
a band of simple cable marks the transition from shoulder to belly. Besides
these are rows of ivy or doubled myrtle leaves and of enclosed palmettes,
and an effective pattern made up of overlapping leaf rosettes. Filling ornament, often sprinkled in figure-scenes, is light.

The commonest shape is the amphora. The oinochoe, a smaller version
of the Middle Wild Goat type but with strong upright neck, is early. So
too is a little simple cup some 13 or 14 cm across with short offset rim
and ring foot. The amphoriskos, a small very slender byform of the
amphora, is common later: it often has net pattern on the belly. Of the
rare shapes the most remarkable is a large cup from Samos with offset rim;
its elaborate decoration, with a Gorgoneion in the centre, is exceptional.

The technique is that of the Middle Wild Goat style. The clay which
fires from buff to pink is gritty, the slip creamy yellow to white, the paint
dark-brown to red. Details are reserved. Purple is used on early pieces,
white very rarely except for eyes and rosettes on the lip of oinochoai. There
is no distinction of colour between men and women. The workmanship is
often very careless; note the lip on Plate 32A.

The Fikellura painters drew heavily on the Wild Goat style, particularly of its Middle phase, for fauna, ornaments, shapes and technique. They have much in common with the Ionian Little Masters; which borrowed from the other is not clear, but perhaps they were sometimes the same individuals. Attic (or Corinthian) influence is remotely visible in the abandonment of outline drawing, directly in the change of emphasis in the decorative scheme and in some details. But generally the Fikellura style kept to itself. The crescent, the development of the volutes, the use of the free field are original. In execution the Fikellura painters were economical and even on their most careful pieces the minor detail is rapid and negligent. The Birmingham amphora (Plate 32A) shows the spontaneity that this freehand style can achieve, but in later and less imaginative pieces it degenerates into boorishness.

Much Fikellura pottery has been found in Samos, Rhodes and especially Miletus. It is common at Naucratis and Tell Defenneh in Egypt; a few pieces have been found in Cyprus. A fair amount comes from Olbia, Berezan and Istria on the western coast of the Black Sea. There are several examples from Delos and a few from Aegina. In mainland Greece and further west it is very rare. This is a normal distribution for an East Greek style. The influence of Fikellura was alight; Clazomenian probably took over the crescent, Attic perhaps adapted the big handle volutes, and free renderings are rife in Caria. For the principal home of Fikellura analysis of clay insists on Miletus, where also it seems, there is a greater variety of shapes. Samos, so long a favourite, had at most a minor part.

There was also some petty copying overseas. At Istria, the only site where clay analysis of pottery has been extensive, 13 out of 62 Fikellura sherds proved to be of local clay – 'local', that is, to a region probably stretching as far north as Olbia. Except for one piece with inept human figures this local Fikellura attempted only routine ornament. There was also a very small local imitation of simple Wild Goat style and Chiot. How widespread such invisible imitation was is at present beyond useful speculation.

Clazomenian and other East Greek Black-figure

The black-figure technique was not used regularly on East Greek pottery till the early sixth century. Then there was perhaps a little imitation of Attic and in the Late Wild Goat style much emulation of Corinthian. From this in the second quarter of the century some North Ionian workshops developed more independent if not very distinguished lines of their own. Of various small schools that called Clazomenian is the best known, since it was occasionally shipped overseas. Most of the others were exported even less, so that we depend on local finds, of which only those from

Smyrna have yet been published conscientiously. Towards the end of the sixth century there was again some imitation, more or less pawky, of current Attic.

Clazomenian, to judge by places of finding and analysis of clay, was in fact made at Clazomenae and perhaps elsewhere nearby. It is a school which took more note than others of the technique and types of Attic, but was usually content to be decorative. The earliest recognizable group, the Tübingen group of the mid-sixth century, is showy and in character traditionally East Greek with an admixture of Attic. The Petrie group, which follows and was flourishing in the 530s, is both more Attic and more original. The Urla group, more or less contemporary, is their drab and degenerate heir.

The arrangement of the decorative fields follows Attic. In the principal frieze or panel human figures are regular, animals usually occupy secondary fields, vegetable and abstract ornament is less important. The commonest theme is a file of women, each gripping her neighbour's wrist or modestly holding her cloak. Besides these there are satyrs, revellers, sacrificial processions, riders, chariots and occasional excerpts from mythology. There is little interest in anatomy – witness the favourite distortion of the shoulder (as on the boy of Plate 32B) – or in composition. The fauna comes from the ordinary repertory of black-figure and is generally drawn with a scratchy carelessness, suitable to its inferior position. But more pains are taken when a bird or animal appears on the neck or strays into the main field. The large long-necked birds, feeding in line and occasionally white, are characteristically Clazomenian. Of the ornaments scales containing a large white drop, which may have a dark centre, sometimes fill the main panel; white, or alternately white and purple, crescents on a dark band are normal below the shoulder of the early amphorae; a big palmette with matted incised fringe may occupy the neck, or a lotus and palmette cross take the centre of a field. The quality of the work varies greatly, even on the same pot, and the school has little active character. Of the old Wild Goat style almost nothing remains, there are connections with Chiot, some of the female heads have the shelving East Greek profile, crescents and perhaps scales seem modified from Fikellura. But for the present we cannot define closely the sources of the East Greek idiom of this adaptation of Attic.

The common shapes are various neck-amphorae and a hydria with a flat shoulder that sometimes makes a sharp angle with the belly. Other shapes are a very large low pyxis (reminiscent of an Aeolian Wild Goat form, but with a large domed lid) and some kind of krater or dinos. The typical amphora of the Tübingen group has a general likeness to Fikellura, but with some moulding and handles set on the shoulder; this type is elaborately decorated and often embellished with plastic female heads at the bases of the handles. The amphora illustrated on Plate 32B which should be completed with vertical handles and a lowish spreading foot, is the speciality of the Petrie painter, the most robust and able of the Clazomenian vase-painters. The broader amphora of the Urla group follows Attic models of the third quarter of the sixth century.

The clay, which varies in purity, is leathery brown, generally lighter than contemporary Attic. The paint is not far from the Attic standard of blackness and sheen. Purple and white (which is often put directly on the clay) are disposed much as in Attic, except that white is permitted for male flesh (as on Plate 32B) and is popular for small ornaments like little stars on dresses and rows of dots between a pair of incised lines. This last trick, which goes back indirectly to Corinthian of the beginning of the sixth century, is habitual in Clazomenian. Details on white are usually drawn in dark paint. Incision is careless, if not stupid, more concerned with the creases of the belly than the musculature of the chest.

A fair quantity of Clazomenian has been found at Clazomenae and at Smyrna, and very little elsewhere in the East Greek region. Much comes from Tell Defenneh and Naucratis and some from native sites in Egypt. We have a little from Istria, more from Berezan and much from Panticapaeum. In European Greece it is extremely rare, and there is no certain example from the West. To judge by its style and its association with Attic black-figure and Fikellura at Tell Defenneh, most of the pottery defined above as Clazomenian belongs to the third quarter of the sixth century.

Related to this Clazomenian but more subdued is the *Camel* group, notable for the earliest known Greek depiction of a camel. So far it has been recognized only at Smyrna, but it could have been imported from Clazomenae. This is less likely for the amphorae and askoi of the miscellaneous *Enmann class* and the more homogeneous *Knipovitch class*. Both use scales with white drops, and the Knipovitch amphorae are fond of the forepart of a winged horse to fill the panel on their sagging bodies. These classes have a rather different distribution, being relatively rare at Clazomenae and Smyrna, but not uncommon in Delos, Ukraine and Egypt. Besides these more or less coherent groups there are various isolated pieces, a few with drawing of high quality. Some of these are legitimately, if loosely, connected, but the term 'Clazomenian' is still sometimes extended to shelter miscellaneous black-figure work that looks even vaguely East Greek; some are earlier East Greek experiments in black-figure, some are feeble imitations of Attic made in other East Greek workshops, and some are Etruscan or Italian Greek. Among these last are the Campana and Northampton groups (mentioned again on p. 151).

Clazomenian sarcophagi

Coffins of fired clay were used widely in the East Greek region during the sixth century. Many were simple in shape and undecorated, but some were given a rather wider rim on which such unexacting motifs as wavy lines were painted. These led about the middle of the century (according to a preliminary excavation report) to an improved version for the better-off. A heavier box was now (like an old-fashioned panelled bath) surmounted by a flat rectangular or trapezoidal frame, the top and edges of which were slipped and decorated. The strips at head and foot were usually painted with figures, the long sidepieces with cable and palmette, and panels at each end of the sidepieces with figures or ornaments. These sarcophagi are pretentious monuments, at best inoffensive but more often vulgar, and their interest is in their retention of a style we should other-wise suppose extinct. For much of the figure decoration – such groups as a lion and a panther posed stiffly about a boar or bull or goat – is in the Wild Goat style, not the modified version of Fikellura but a further degra-dation of the Late Wild Goat style of the earlier sixth century (Plate 31D). Often also, especially on headpieces, a laborious black-figure style imitates Attic of the last years of the sixth century, but with painted white lines in place of incision; an old-fashioned trait is the rich use of purple and white, without which the individual figures in the sometimes crowded groups are hard to separate. The favourite black-figure subjects, often symmetrically incoherent assemblages of stock types, refer to warfare and chariot racing. In style there are resemblances at first to Clazomenian black-figure and then to Attic, but some details are faithful to East Greek traditions – a salutary reminder that the influence of Attic painting was not all-perva-sive. A few sarcophagi of the early fifth century experiment clumsily with the red-figure technique. Since we have a fragmentary pot decorated by the earliest recognizable painter of sarcophagi, he must have learnt his trade as a vase-painter; but there is no style of vase-painting that corresponds as closely with those of his successors.

Because of their distribution Clazomenae is fairly certainly the home of these sarcophagi. Many have been found in its territory, a respectable number at Smyrna, some thirty kilometres away, and a few in other neigh-bouring places. Not surprisingly, when one considers their weight, distant export was rare. One richly decorated specimen comes from Abdera (a colony first of Clazomenae and then of Teos) and of the seven more modest works attributed to the latest of the painters five are from Rhodes and one from Acanthus, so he may have travelled or even emigrated. A few simpler sarcophagi from Ephesus and Pitane may well be local work, as related sarcophagi from Sardis certainly are, and at Abdera some unorthodox frag-ments look local too. Useful contexts are very few, not as much because so many of our sarcophagi have been unearthed by private enterprise as that grave goods are abnormal with them; evidently the provision of a painted coffin was thought to show sufficient respect to the dead. So dating has to be by stylistic comparisons, some more imprecise than others. But it is unlikely that the series of elaborately decorated sarcophagi begins before the middle of the sixth century or lasts much beyond the first quarter of the next. The clay is reddish and of the texture of brick, the slip thick and creamy, the paint very dark brown; the white and purple used in the black-figure style have almost always perished.

The Situlae

Tell Defenneh lies at the east of the Egyptian Delta on a caravan route to Asia and was probably the ancient fortress of Daphnae. There in 1886 Flinders Petrie found with about equal amounts of Attic black-figure, Fikellura and Clazomenian about thirty of what he called *Situlae*. The shape is a tall narrow tube, swelling gradually towards the base and then curving quickly in to a low foot: the lip is flat and wide, and below it, separated by a narrow ridge, are two small but sturdy handles. The outside is painted dark except for an oblong panel on each side between the handles and for groups of narrow reserved bands which divide the body into three parts.

On most of these situlae the two lower zones are decorated with large pendent lotus flowers or buds and palmettes, incised and picked out in purple (as in Vroulian), and a black-figure subject is put in the panels. The composition usually fits the space – a single kneeling animal, an interlocking group, a symmetrical pair facing across a central ornament. The clay fires from light-brown to greyish, and splits badly; the paint is a dark-brown with little sheen; purple is used but not white; the wall of the pot is thin. The drawing has an extraordinary range from childish crudity to a vigorous assurance and there is no stylistic unity. Two poor situlae decorated in the same way and of similar fabric have been found at Ialysus in Rhodes. These come from contexts of 500–490 BC while those of Tell Defenneh because of the associated pottery should belong to the third quarter of the sixth century. Fragments have been reported also at Migdol, not far from Tell Defenneh, but interestingly there are none from Naucratis. Preliminary tests by clay analysis suggest Rhodes as a place of manufacture.

A few pieces belong to a stylistically earlier group of situlae, which seem to be the product of a single workshop or painter (Plate 33A). These are heavier pots, made of a better and browner clay and painted in a neat style which frames its figure panels with affected Subgeometric ornament. Here the lower part of the pot is dark with sparse groups of reserved bands. The places of finding are Rhodes, Tell Defenneh and Memphis. Their date, by comparison with more advanced wares, should be the second quarter or middle of the sixth century. So far Rhodes has the best claim as the home of this group,

The later of these two groups may reasonably be derived by adaptation from the earlier, but their styles cannot generally be traced further back.

For the shape there are older models in East Greek pottery, though the series is not yet continuous. From Vroulia in the south of Rhodes there are from contexts of around 600 BC a few squat situlae, decorated only with bands and large splashes of paint. Others found on Samos are rather earlier and not much more ornate, except for one which exhibits a competent sample of the Middle II Wild Goat style in the fields between the handles.

Vroulian

Decoration on a dark instead of a light ground is an obvious though uncommon technique that recurs throughout Greek vase-painting. In the East Greek region it had some popularity from the end of the seventh century, probably in emulation of Corinthian black polychrome. A few Late Wild Goat pots have on the shoulder a lotus chain incised on the dark paint and enlivened with purple and white additions, and Chiot vase-painters made much use of white and purple ornaments painted without incision on the dark inside of chalices and phialai. But the fullest exploitation of dark-ground effects is on a group of cups, which are known as *Vroulian* from the discovery of specimens at Vroulia in Rhodes.

On these cups (Figure 23) the whole surface is painted over except sometimes for a reserved band at handle level, and the outside – and often the inside too – is covered with large ornaments boldly incised and variegated with purple. The typical ornament is the enclosed palmette, but unenclosed palmettes, lotus flowers, buds and rosettes are common; usually there is a zigzag on the lip and attenuated sets of opposed triangles in the handle frieze (if it is reserved). The shape, still near the cup of Rhodian Late Geometric, has a low offset rim and a narrow conical foot. The clay is fine, firing from yellowish to reddish brown, and the paint near black and shiny. With their thin walls and trim decoration these cups are among the most charming products of East Greek pottery.

A few clumsy amphorae and stamnoi go with the cups. The body is divided into two or three zones by reserved bands and the ornaments are limited to lotus flower and bud and palmette, as on the situlae which probably copied them.

Vroulian pottery has been found throughout Rhodes, where clay analysis confirms it was made, but there was little export except to Naucratis. Grave groups suggest that the cups continued from the beginning till the third quarter of the sixth century and that there was no development in the style.

East Greek cups

The cup is very rare in the major East Greek styles – Chiot developed its chalice and the others stuck to large shapes – but drinking vessels were

Figure 23 Vroulian cup.
Ht 7 cm. Early or middle 6th century BC.

needed and were made in large numbers. Two types had evolved by the end of Geometric, the wide kotyle without a separate lip (from which the popular Bird bowl developed) and the lower cup with short out-turned rim and narrow foot. During the rest of the seventh century this cup continued with little change in shape except for a tendency to a rather higher conical foot, and the type survived till the middle of the sixth century as is shown by the Vroulian cups and by the still more old-fashioned Fikellura cups with ring foot. But in the first half of the sixth century there begins a development parallel to Attic which leads to the canonical lip cup. In the later sixth century the finer East Greek cups disappear.

The decoration consists principally of reserved bands, usually one at handle level (occasionally with hour-glass ornament) and often another below it or on the lip. A small fine group of the late seventh century uses instead white–red–white bands on a dark ground. On the progressive shapes of the early sixth century the decoration too advances until eventually the inside of the lip or even the whole of the bowl is ringed with groups of very fine bands in dilute paint alternating with broader, darker stripes; on the outside of the enlarged lip a garland of doubled myrtle leaves is common. A special class of these cups, the Ionian Little Master cups, has already been discussed (see p. 123). There are also a few cups and bowls with plastic ornament in low relief in the handle frieze – hands, knuckle-bones, garlands and suchlike.

The clay varies from a sandy texture and colour, to a clear light-brown that is close to Attic and the paint ranges similarly from dark-brown to near black. Manufacture was general throughout the southern part of the East Greek region, Samos being particularly prolific according to clay analysis and frequency of finds. But cups of this general type were made at Athens too, Corinth and in the West (where misfired examples have been found at Metapontum). The fabrics are not often distinguished and there is a misleading practice of claiming all for East Greek.

Banded wares

Many other pots besides cups were simply decorated with bands of paint. Most are of coarse clay firing from pink to pale-brown and very rarely slipped, but some are of shiny orange-brown clay with good near-black paint. Their export has been greatly exaggerated, since there is an inclination to describe as East Greek almost any pot of brownish clay and banded decoration that is found on a colonial site: in fact most of these banded wares have no particular character. It is anyhow unlikely that the plainer East Greek wares were imported where the fancy wares were not.

THASOS

Thasos, founded by Parians early in the seventh century, was the oldest and for long the most important Greek city along the southern coast of Thrace. Excavation has been intensive only at Thasos, a sizeable deposit of painted pottery has been discovered at Kavalla (an ancient Neapolis), there is some material from Abdera, and from other sites we have little more than casual finds. Not much has been published, but it is clear that there was considerable local imitation of imported wares, presumably at Thasos, though for the versions of Chiot, Maroneia, as a colony of Chios, has its backers.

First, there is a class of Subgeometric pottery, especially cups with sets of concentric circles ringed often by dots and separated by vertical strokes. These cups are of a type which evolve from 'Parian' Late Geometric, and in the south as well as in the northern Aegean seem to have persisted till the late sixth century. Still it is easy to believe that most of those found in Thasos and on the Thracian coast were made locally.

For the late seventh and early sixth centuries much pottery of the 'Melian', Wild Goat and Chiot styles has been discovered in Thasos and on the mainland opposite. Some of this is evidently imported, but there are other pieces of high and even superior quality for which local manufacture has justifiably been claimed. It seems then that distinct and competing styles were practised without serious contamination in a single place, though the practitioners may have been immigrant craftsmen who arrived with their style already formed. Clay analysis so far rejects local production of 'Melian'.

Further, through much of the sixth and into the early fifth century we have a black-figure style based in the main on Attic but on pots not of Attic clay, and this must be local. Though there is some careful work, more is clumsily debased. The frequency among the shapes of lekane and plate is notable.

CRETE

When towards the end of the eighth century the new Orientalizing movement was felt in Crete, the local Geometric was still strong and healthy
and already possessed some of the freehand ornaments – tongues and
cables – which were favourites of early Orientalizing elsewhere. So for a
time the two styles ran together, combining rather than in competition,
and differing not so much in the syntax as in the units of the decoration.
Older traditions had delayed the establishment of Geometric in Crete, and
now the persistence of Geometric hampered the growth of an original
Orientalizing style.

In the first stage of Cretan Orientalizing the decoration is compact and
tight. The commonest ornaments are cable patterns, often elaborate; heavy
close-set tongues, both leaf and star rosettes; rudimentary volutes and
palmettes; lotus flowers and buds, drawn with unusually inorganic abstrac-
tion (examples on Figure 24) and sometimes flowers are even transformed
into bees. Birds are many and varied: the strangest, already known in Late
Geometric, are freaks with two or more heads, or bodies split into a 'U'
and a forked tail floating loose in the gap. Animal and human figures are
few and clumsy. All these are combined readily with such old favourites
as concentric circles, and since the old Geometric division into narrow
zones and panels is maintained the effect is less of a new independent style
than of well-mannered variation on the old theme.

The most curious product of the early Orientalizing style is a group of
polychrome pithoi found so far only at Cnossus. They have a thick white
slip and are painted, sometimes over the whole surface, in bright red and
indigo. Slip and paints, which are matt, are very friable and may have been
intended for use only in burials. There are instances where pithoi painted
in the ordinary Geometric manner were then slipped and repainted in polychrome. The decoration, painted with a sure but thick brush, appears more
consistently Orientalizing than on the unslipped pottery, partly because of
the freer use of new ornaments and partly because solid colour often
replaces Geometric hatching. In composition the most remarkable experiment is a scene of birds perching in a thicket; the detail is conventional,
but there is an appreciation of nature very rare in Greek art. The idea of
such polychrome decoration, where the two colours have about equal value,
is new to the Greek world and possibly came from Cyprus, to which
Orientalizing Crete had other debts.

During the seventh century the Geometric tradition weakened and the
Orientalizing style becomes looser and its vegetable ornament more
exuberant. Figures, especially sphinxes, are commoner and there are such
decorative fancies as long slanting volutes that end in a panther's head.
Bees are popular as ornaments; and the row of ➥ solid or in outline,
is characteristic. The drawing occasionally has a delicate charm and a few

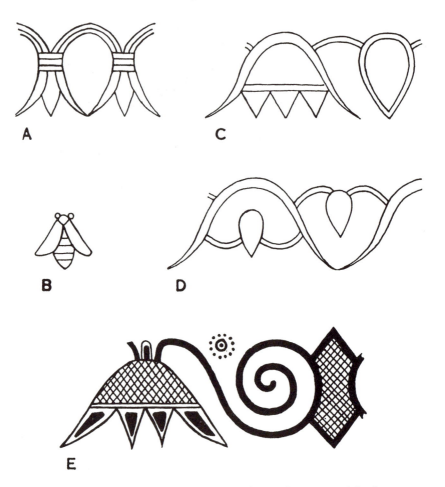

Figure 24 Cretan and 'Melian' lotus flowers and buds.
A–D, Cretan, early 7th century BC. E, 'Melian', late 7th to
early 6th century BC.

pieces show something more, but though some Cretan vase-painters were versatile and receptive, they lacked direction. So it is difficult to define a Cretan standard, more so even than to define a Protoattic standard; for Attic eccentricity comes largely from its search for a grandeur beyond its powers, but the Cretans spent themselves on novel or curious detail. There is experiment in technique too. Besides the usual dark on light there is much use, especially for Subgeometric decoration, of white paint on a background of dark paint, and the two methods are sometimes combined on one pot. Both the incising technique of black-figure and outline drawing are mastered. Occasionally (anticipating by a century or so Attic red-figure) there is reservation in a dark ground. At the same time an unambitious Subgeometric continued to decorate pots, mostly small, with sparse concentric circles which are now usually reduced to two or three rings. The few bucchero pots mostly belong to this period. But Cretan vase-painting, like East Greek in the sixth century, was too capricious and uneven, and the style – or the attempts to form a style – petered out in the early sixth century.

The principal large shape remains, at first anyhow, the pithos; its body tends to lengthen and ends often in three looped feet, occasionally in a pedestal. A dinos with rings through the handles and a sort of hat-box (decorated with figures in white) occur in graves at Arkades. Of the oinochoai, many and various, the commonest is the old small jug with round mouth, still wearing its garland of cross-hatched triangles or instead small concentric circles. The round aryballos, a smarter relative of this jug, is also popular; circles are similarly its usual decoration, but sometimes it Orientalizes. Later there appear ovoid aryballoi, imitating Corinthian. Alabastra, often sagging and with plastic rings round the neck, look nearer Cypriot than Corinthian in shape; they mostly have simple Orientalizing patterns. Kotylai ape Corinthian; and there are the usual cups, mostly Subgeometric in style. Dish and plate are not common. Finally, there are many plastic vases and pots with plastic attachments. In general, Cretan shapes like Cretan decoration often differ from Greek norms. The technique ordinarily continues that of Geometric. Occasionally there is a yellowish slip. The peculiarities of the polychrome group have already been described.

The impulses that aroused the Orientalizing style of Cretan pottery came in part from Cyprus, where there are precedents for some of the ornaments (for instance the form of the lotus), various shapes and the polychrome technique; and some of the plump flasks with a great set of circles on each side are frank copies of Cypriot. Later, and increasingly, Cretan imitated Corinthian. The doctrine, once widely held, that the Greek Orientalizing style was established first in Crete and from there transmitted to Corinth is for painted pottery untenable, even though some of the Orientalizing forms appear less Hellenized in Cretan than in other schools: the chronology of the ending of Geometric, now worked out in fair detail, is decisive. For metalwork and perhaps for sculpture Crete was more important, but its vase-painting in spite of some engaging originality was not progressive.

Cretan exports, almost all Subgeometric, have a limited range. They are least infrequent in the neighbouring islands of Thera and Rhodes, and there are a few pieces from Gela, founded by Cretans and Rhodians about 690 BC, Ischia, Cumae and Tocra. Reports of finds in the Peloponnese and Etruria need to be checked. There was a little connection between Cretan and Cycladic. Resemblances in the Italocorinthian of Etruria, as in the shape of one type of alabastron, are probably accidental. A fair amount of Corinthian and some Cypriot were imported and had their effects.

ITALY

After the Geometric period first Corinth and then Athens dominated the market for Greek pottery. This appears more clearly in the West than round the Aegean, where there was more competition from established local schools. Some Cretan Subgeometric and rather more East Greek of the southern Wild Goat style have turned up at Gela, a joint colony of Cretans and Rhodians, a little East Greek occurs at Catania, Syracuse and Selinus, and in sixth-century Italy there is a sprinkling of Laconian; but other exceptions to the rule of Corinthian and Attic are very rare, unless of course 'Chalcidian' came from Chalcis. In general for their better-painted pottery the Greeks of the colonies imported, those natives who had adopted a Geometric style continued it, and the Etruscans both imported and imitated.

Ischia and *Cumae*, just north of the bay of Naples, are the earliest and most distant of the Greek colonies known in Italy. In their cemeteries have been found not only much imported Protocorinthian but also imitations of Protocorinthian of the late eighth and the seventh centuries. These imitations (now usually called Pithecusan and formerly Cumaean) can often be distinguished by a wilder or clumsier style and by a coarser clay which is sometimes disguised by a yellowish slip. But the distinction is not always clear to the eye. At Pithecusae (Ischia) the local school appears to have persisted through the seventh century; the evidence for Cumae needs to be examined afresh.

At *Megara Hyblaea, Syracuse, Gela* and other sites in Sicily and South Italy local workshops tried the Orientalizing as well as the Subgeometric style. Their models were generally Corinthian. Most of this local pottery is unassuming, though recognizable by the clay and sometimes by the presence of a slip, but it is only at Megara Hyblaea that – thanks to conscientious excavators – we know much about it. Here manufacture of decorated ware decreased rapidly in quantity after the first quarter of the seventh century, when Subgeometric was becoming unfashionable, and had finished by its end. For the earlier part of this period Sicilian workshops exploited the Orientalizing style most eagerly on larger pots, in which the parent Corinthian school was deficient, and during the generation around 650 BC they produced some figured polychrome work of erratic grandeur. The character of this polychrome decoration is much less dependent on Corinthian, but other sources are no more evident and polychromy – that is the addition of a light-brown to the range of colours – occurred in several schools of that time. Perhaps we should give most credit to local originality, but anyhow production was too small to allow a coherent style to develop. After this experiment we have nothing better than straight-forward and sometimes competent imitation of the Animal style of Corinth. On the present evidence it is reasonable to suppose that the bulk of the colonial wares found at Megara Hyblaea were made there, but we do not know how many other Greek colonies in the West engaged in local production of decorated pottery. The kraters of the Fusco group suggest something similar at Syracuse, where they were found. One of them has on it a couple of tolerable figures, but most are tamely Subgeometric or develop simple Orientalizing motifs with heavy-handed incomprehension. Before colonial vase-painting was considered credible, the Fusco kraters were often attributed to Argos – improbably, if only because of clay and slip; they may though be due to an emigrant Argive potter. Their date should be in the second quarter of the seventh century. In the late sixth and early fifth centuries a little poor imitation of Attic black-figure seems to have been attempted here and there in South Italy and Sicily, most notably in Campania. But unless 'Chalcidian' was made in one of the Western colonies, no important local school took root there until after the middle of the fifth century.

The *native Sicilians*, so long as they were not submerged by the Greeks, continued even into the fifth century a weakening Geometric tradition, varied occasionally by more modern borrowings. In Southern Italy the native style of *Apulia* and *Lucania* split up into distinct local schools in the eighth and seventh centuries; but though some Greek motifs were copied where there was contact with Greeks, the old Geometric tradition persisted. Central Italy belonged to the Etruscans.

The *Etruscans* in the seventh and sixth centuries were expanding their dominion, and in spite of local divergences and survivals the culture they imposed was fairly uniform. In art they had a taste for sophisticated imports, but also a tenacious local tradition. The primitive pots of the native Italians had been made of coarse gritty clay, shaped by hand, and uncertainly fired. Acquaintance with Greek processes – and presumably immigrant craftsmen – introduced better levigation, use of the potter's wheel and control of firing; but the older tradition was not discarded and Etruscan pottery (or pottery made in Etruscan territory) has a remarkable range of technical quality. In the shapes some old favourites continued, often refined under Greek influence, Greek imports were directly imitated or adapted, and there was much unmistakable reproduction of metal forms. For decoration the models were mainly Greek, since though the early Etruscans welcomed objects of Oriental as well as of Greek art the pottery was Greek: even so, such ornaments as the 'Phoenician' palmette (Figure 25) may not have come to them from Greek artists. This Etruscan pottery, which varies from more or less close copies of Greek to clumsy barbarisms, can be roughly divided into fabrics with a light ground (whether produced

Figure 25 'Phoenician' palmette.
Scale 1:2. Etruscocorinthian, late 7th century BC. Black polychrome technique: the pattern is incised on a dark ground and embellished with added purple (here hatched) and white (here black).

by a slip or of a ware that is light throughout) and those with a dark ground: the former are decorated by painting which is often careful and sometimes ambitious, on the latter incised and relief ornament is more common and painted decoration is generally rough and unskilled. Both techniques might be practised in the same workshops, or at least some painters practised both. Though our concern is with the finer of the light-ground groups, it would be unkind to pass over the finest of the dark-ground; for the Etruscans were not at their best in pottery, and their one excellence is in their bucchero.

Light-ground painted pottery first appears in Etruria decorated in the Geometric style and was presumably borrowed with it. This *Etruscan Geometric* (mentioned already on p. 39) continued with declining vigour throughout the first half of the seventh century, and offshoots (often degenerate) survived longer in remote districts. There were also Orientalizing experiments, which came in at the end of the eighth century, but were desultory or feeble till around 630 BC the Etruscocorinthian style began its prolific copies and adaptations of Corinthian imports. Rather before the middle of the sixth century this in turn gave way under Attic influence to *Etruscan Black-figure*, which lasted to the middle of the fifth century. But Etruscan vase-painting was not yet done, and turned to a *Red-figure* style that even outlived its Attic parent. Remoteness in space, which made Greek imports expensive, and the size of the home market rather than artistic or patriotic appeal are reasons for this remarkable persistence of what is one of the lesser schools of Greek painted pottery. As for *Bucchero*, the most original product of Etruscan workshops, its heyday was from the second quarter of the seventh to the middle of the sixth century. There remain two notable classes of painted pots, 'Chalcidian' and the *Caeretan hydriai*, one the product of a school, the other of a single workshop: their styles are unmistakably Greek and so many scholars have believed their makers worked in Greek lands, but distribution makes it more likely that we have here Greek vase-painters who were settled in

Italy and more precisely – anyhow for the hydriai – in Etruria. There are signs of a few other such settlers.

Although the Etruscans imported a great quantity of Greek pottery, their own wares were exported to Campania and had some market overseas. Etruscocorinthian has turned up in Carthaginian territories and Greek colonies in the far West. Bucchero deservedly had a wider range and finds – mainly of kantharoi – are known also from Greek Sicily and occasionally even from Greece and the Aegean. 'Chalcidian' (if it was made in Etruria) appealed more directly to Greek taste; it was popular in South Italy and reached the western Mediterranean. But it is easy to exaggerate the scale of the Etruscan industry; for though its products are numerous in the museums of Western Europe, that is because so large a part of their contents have come from the prolific cemeteries of Etruria. Unfortunately, useful contexts have not always been recorded, and so the dating of all these wares depends too much on stylistic comparisons with Corinthian and Attic. There may sometimes be more lag in the chronology than is suspected.

Earlier Orientalizing

In comparison with Subgeometric and more traditional wares Etruscan Orientalizing is not common before the explosion of Etruscocorinthian about 630 BC. At present we have a couple of close groups and some more or less isolated experiments. At Tarquinia, where the Subgeometric Metope style was prevalent, the first half of the seventh century is enlivened by *local versions of the Protocorinthian Cumae group*, though after a brave beginning – one piece recalls the Corinthian oinochoe of Plate 8C – they content themselves with the simpler Orientalizing ornaments, not always used canonically. Rays for instance (as elsewhere in Etruscan) are not restricted to the base, but occur on any part of a pot, either way up and sometimes in rows two or more deep. In South Etruria, and especially at Caere, the *Heron style* becomes standard at the start of the century and seems to linger on till its end. Here the characteristic feature is the file of sinuously elongated birds, painted in full silhouette and too simplified to justify speculation about their paternity; for supplementary decoration there may be bands of ornament, usually simple, or more often – especially on the popular plates – plain bands. This banal recipe, neither properly Subgeometric nor Orientalizing, was remarkably successful; export to Latium and Campania was considerable, though more northerly Etruria with its Metope style remained immune. Caere also harboured a few more ambitious painters, who in the first half of the seventh century decorated clumsy shapes with human and animal subjects, rendered with inept but refreshing abandon. More soberly impressive is a krater of the 650s, signed in Greek by Aristonothos as maker and displaying on one side the blinding of Polyphemus and on the other a naval encounter; because of the language of the signature Aristonothos was presumably an immigrant, but where he learnt his style is still a puzzle. He had no following.

Etruscocorinthian

The term 'Etruscocorinthian', now replacing the less precise 'Italocorinthian' is in practice restricted to the imitations and adaptations of Transitional and Ripe Corinthian. These began about 630 BC, to judge by the models used and by grave groups, and continued till the 540s, when Corinthian models were no longer available and black-figure workshops were being established in Etruria. Etruscocorinthian was a universal Etruscan style, with its main centres at Vulci, Caere and Tarquinia, and at present thirty or so painters have been identified credibly. The largest output was in the Linear style, but that in the Animal style was large enough; human figures occur, but are not common. Generally the Etruscocorinthian workshops followed Corinthian developments, though sometimes retaining outmoded forms and misunderstanding others. They also showed more fervour for the black polychrome technique, which they often used for figures as well as for ornaments. Figure 26 shows an olpe by an early and fairly attentive exponent of the Etruscocorinthian Animal style; compare its lion with the contemporary Corinthian one of Figure 6G. Elsewhere the difference is much greater. So in Etruscocorinthian we often find figures grotesquely proportioned, shoulder markings converted into meaningless circles, creatures with three wings, stridently particoloured animals and human legs dangling from a lion's mouth. Greek figures are credibly constructed, Etruscan more often not.

Most of the Corinthian shapes were copied more or less faithfully, but Etruscocorinthian was inventive too. An amphora some 50 cm high, apparently a speciality of Caere, looks like a refined version of the Attic SOS type with its narrow neck and foot; decoration is regularly in black polychrome. Also popular is the olpe, usually with Animal or black polychrome decoration; in the latter group big overlapping semicircles or 'Phoenician' palmettes (Figure 25) often replace the more orthodox scales, which themselves are larger than in Corinthian. Oinochoai, with animals or simple bands and tongue pattern, are also common. Plates are mostly of the sixth century. The cup is rather deeper than the Corinthian shape; a popular sixth-century group has on the lip the Laconian squares and dots (as Plate 26B) and in the handle frieze a row of balloon-bodied birds. The pointed aryballos with its heavy foot is succeeded before 600 by an ordinary round aryballos; another variety has a round body drawn out below into a point, much like a lemon. The common alabastron is of Corinthian shape, often rather flatter at the base. There is also a very long alabastron with flat bottom, as if it had been sawn off near the middle. Many of the alabastra

Figure 26 Etruscocorinthian olpe.
Ht 26.8 cm. By the Bearded Sphinx painter, late 7th century BC.

are embellished with a bolster round the neck, and bodies are sometimes channelled or ridged. On these small pots Linear decoration remains common: the effect is sometimes indistinguishable from Corinthian, sometimes remote with clumsy banding and (especially on the pointed shapes) a prominent band of herring-bone ornament. Usually the clay is fine, firing from a light cream (which differs from Corinthian in a slightly muddier tone) to a dull medium-brown. The dark paint tends to be duller and thinner than Corinthian; and purple and white are rather more freely applied. Dating is uncertain, since it is mostly by style. This allows a rough estimate of when a foreign model was first imitated, not how long imitation continued. But it does not seem that Italocorinthian, strictly defined, much outlasted the middle of the sixth century.

The dominant factor in Etruscocorinthian is always Corinthian, but there is some borrowing from other styles at home in Etruria and a little from Laconian. Though sometimes robustly exotic, the effect is usually trivial. So though finds are frequent in Central Italy as far south as Campania, not much went overseas – a little to Carthage and Sardinia and even to

Provence and to Emporion in Spain. It could not compete on equal terms with Corinthian.

A curious intrusion, but without any significant effect, is that of the Swallow painter, whose work ranges from a fairly straight Middle II Wild Goat style, though with Etruscocorinthian filling ornament and on pots of Etruscocorinthian shape and clay, to a much more contaminated idiom. From this it is reasonable to infer that he had trained in an East Greek workshop before settling in Etruria, it seems at Vulci, where he soon picked up local habits. This is relevant for the pioneers of Etruscocorinthian, whom one might expect to have been emigrant craftsmen from Corinth. Yet, if so, their earliest work in Etruria should still be fairly pure Corinthian, and so far in the diagnostic Animal style no such work has been recognised.

Etruscan Bucchero

Bucchero (or Grey ware) had long been popular in Aeolis when Etruscan Bucchero emerged. There seems no direct connection in shape or decoration, nor yet in technique. Anyhow in Etruria development can be traced from traditional Italian wares; the clay is refined and reduction in firing, previously perhaps accidental, is in the end deliberate and complete. Good specimens are in this way fired throughout to a dark-grey with a blackish surface (perhaps improved by adding carbon to the clay) but the colour ranges to a light and sometimes yellowish grey. Though there are, especially in the seventh century, many partially reduced pots (mostly with brown surface and pale core) which differ from bucchero only in the degree of reduction – a difference that is not obvious in photographs – it is fair to speak of a Bucchero style, compounded for this fine variety of Etruscan dark-ground ware. In spite of the great quantity of this bucchero its history was till recently neglected and still is only partly clear.

Bucchero, so defined, appears to have begun at Caere in Southern Etruria. The earliest stage, of the second quarter of the seventh century, is the finest and perhaps the product of a single workshop. Here walls may be as thin as in Protocorinthian and the surface deep black with a high sheen. Origins for shapes and decoration, which can be extensive, are varied; some are Greek (more precisely Corinthian), some directly Oriental and some indigenous. The success of this Caeretan novelty led soon after 650 BC to manufacture in other South Etruscan cities too, but as output increased quality declined; the surface becomes lighter and duller, walls thicken, new shapes are borrowed from Corinthian, and decoration is rarer and less elaborate. Later, around the end of the seventh century, new Bucchero workshops grew up in Central and Northern Etruria and also in Latium and Etruscan Campania, but with a heavier and clumsier character; and though Caere kept its primacy, there, too, technical and artistic standards continued to fall so that by the middle of the sixth century little vitality was left. Still, some production went on into the fourth century, after about 500 BC mostly of unpretentious little bowls and plates.

The most important shapes are amphorae, oinochoai, olpe, cup, kotyle, kantharos, kyathos, handleless chalice. The typical 'amphora, often quite small, has a high neck wide at the base but contracting towards the top and ribbon handles which reach from shoulder to lip, while the body, set on a rudimentary foot, at first is globular, but in time tautens and becomes egg-shaped; this amphora is common from the beginning of Bucchero till the first quarter of the sixth century, finally evolving into the Nikosthenis type (cf. Figure 38). A small jug (or 'olpe'), like the typical amphora except that it has a single high handle, starts as early but lasts rather longer. An orthodox larger neck-amphora becomes current, especially in Northern Etruria, during the sixth century. Oinochoai with trefoil mouth are numerous; the earliest variety, which lingers on till near the end of the seventh century, has a narrow neck that tapers upward, and more canonical forms, with wide neck and piriform or later globular or barrel-shaped body, begin in the late seventh century and persist well down the sixth. An olpe of Corinthian type has a short run in the late seventh century. The cup, much of the type of Figure 4B, is another of the first Bucchero shapes; it disappears in the early sixth century from South Etruria, rather later further north. The kotyle is an initial favourite, but hardly outlives the seventh century. The kantharos with tall upright handles and highish splayed foot (Figure 27) is popular from the last quarter of the seventh century till the middle of the sixth, when it is ousted by a dumpy ring-footed version. The kyathos, current from the mid-seventh to the early fifth century, has many forms. There is also the chalice, a thick-walled handleless pot with high lip and shallow bowl like the kantharos and supported usually by a high pedestal, a splayed foot or a ring foot; its period is from the third quarter of the seventh century to the beginning of the fifth. Some of these Bucchero shapes have obvious prototypes in Greek pottery, for instance the kotyle and the cup. Others, particularly the standard amphora and the jug, refine native Italian types. The kantharos has a Greek look, but no Greek kantharos of fired clay and so elegant a form is as early and its ancestry seems again to be Italian. The pedestalled chalice evidently copies an Oriental ivory shape of which examples have been found in Etruria. The tapering oinochoe originates in Phoenicia or Syria. Generally there appears to be considerable imitation of metalwork and a few early Bucchero pots are said to have been covered with silver leaf; but it is going too far to claim that the black surface itself imitates metal, unless of course the Etruscans had a perverted taste for tarnish.

No reputable seventh century ware relies for its effect so much on shape as does Etruscan Bucchero, though some of it has decoration. In the early stage and continuing more feebly into the sixth century the normal medium for this is incision, supplemented by rouletting, and the commonest motifs

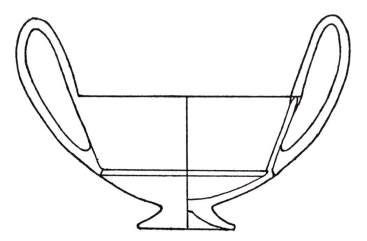

Figure 27   Etruscan Bucchero kantharos.
Ht 11.6 cm. Later 7th or early 6th century BC.

are a bold double spiral (on the belly of the amphora), open or closed fans (usually pricked with a notched tool), vertical striations and rays; figures are relatively rare. Simple stamped designs, such as rosettes and animals, are less important; they appear on early Bucchero, are least uncommon in the third quarter of the seventh century and disappear before its end. Other stamped decoration, repeated with a roller and equally trivial, encircles chalices at Tarquinia and has a wider use further north. There too, especially at Orvieto and Chiusi, and at about the same time, there was a vogue for relief embellishment, often heavy and negligent – thick tongues for instance on the shoulder of an oinochoe and round the belly Orientalizing beasts. In general the models for Bucchero decoration, incised or in relief, were Greek, particularly Corinthian, though at the beginning (as for shapes) mixed with direct Oriental influence, presumably from metalwork, and of course there were some inheritances from the native style. Lastly, in Etruria, as in the East Greek region, a few pieces of coloured bucchero have turned up – that is, with ornaments painted on the dark ground in white, purple and sometimes blue or green (which implies that painting was done after firing): their date seems to be the third quarter of the sixth century.

Some South Etruscan Bucchero was exported outside the Etruscan area, mainly in the late seventh and earlier sixth centuries, the favourite shape being the kantharos of the type of Figure 27. It has been found, sometimes in appreciable quantity, at Greek, Carthaginian and even native sites in the western Mediterranean and less frequently in the Greek colonies of Sicily and South Italy. In Greece and the Aegean it is very rare, less so perhaps at Corinth; but it is widely distributed, more so than the Greek Bucchero of Aeolis. Further afield odd pieces have been noticed at Istria and at Naucratis and in Syria. In the older Greek world, it seems, Etruscan Bucchero pots were curios rather than objects of ordinary trade.

Etruscan black-figure

In the second quarter of the sixth century Attic imports replaced Corinthian in the Etruscan market and set a new standard for local imitation. The first Etruscan workshop which regularly produced Atticizing ware seems by comparison with Attic to have begun around 550 BC. In general Etruscan black-figure painters were careless draughtsmen and did not fully comprehend the style of their models, nor always the subjects. Floral ornaments are disintegrated and reformed in a more abstract spirit, sometimes (as on Plate 34) with pleasing results. Inner detail tends to be inorganic. Groups are often made up of stock figures in meaningless relations, and Greek mythology – naturally enough – is sometimes mixed. What we have in the earlier phase of Etruscan black-figure is not so much copying as adaptation.

Pontic is the most attractive and probably the earliest school. The name, given in the hope that the place of making was some Greek colony of the Black Sea, has survived for want of a better and because there is no genuinely Pontic vase-painting to dispute it. The style is based on Attic, as exhibited in Etruria by the Tyrrhenian amphorae. So in Pontic too the staple shape is the neck-amphora, with its principal field on the shoulder. Two more fields on the belly and another on the neck display rows of animals or ornaments. The decoration is completed by long rays round the base and sometimes a band of pattern on the lip. Distinctive motifs are single or doubled band of meander and star, net pattern (especially on the lip), partridges, sea-horses and Tritons, and panthers with blank white eyes like headlamps. The drawing of outline and detail is weak, and the effect depends on diffusing the decoration and enlivening it with much purple and white. At its best Pontic has a cheerful gaiety, more often it is passably decorative, and towards the end it reverts to more native forms. Plate 34 shows a fair specimen.

Though Attic is the basis of Pontic, there are other constituents. The neck-amphora is derived from Attic of the second quarter of the sixth century, but hydriai follow Red-ground Corinthian in shape and also decoration, and the chalice and some oinochoai take their shape from Etruscan bucchero. Etruscan too are the pointed coifs worn by some female figures, the motley animals with legs of different colours and (though not exclusively) such details as boots with up-turned toes. The lanky birds that often attend human figures have a Laconian look, and the partridges apparently come from East Greek. Other motifs that are not Attic, as for instance pomegranates, may not be directly imported, since they occur already in native Etruscocorinthian. The rejection of the Attic male eye could be the painters' whim or indolence, and general resemblances to East Greek are so vague that they may well be accidental; the often lavish use of red and white is more likely to come from Corinth. The plants, natural or abstract, that sprout in figure scenes, perhaps reflect Etruscan taste. Towards the end the Caeretan hydriai had a little influence. In short there is very little direct foreign influence besides Attic.

The Pontic workshop was at Vulci and under the Paris painter and his followers flourished for perhaps forty years. So far as is known, none of its pots has been found outside Etruscan lands. Whether by origin the painters were Greek or Etruscan is unimportant; as painters they were Etruscan. Some of their details are at the time characteristic of Etruria, no intimate stylistic relation has been discovered to any Greek school, and technical proficiency is too low for craftsmen trained in a reputable Greek workshop. The rather muddy clay varies from dirty yellow to pink. Often there is a yellowish slip. The paint, brownish black with some sheen, is applied unevenly and for that reason or because of bad firing is often discoloured.

Other Etruscan exponents of black-figure are more progressive and usually less successful. They prefer large fields, and any subsidiary decoration is modest. Their figures are in consequence large and few and exposed to undistracted inspection: the animals are more passable than the human types. The *Ivy* or *Ivy-Leaf group*, apparently of the third quarter of the sixth century and perhaps made at Vulci, specializes in the one-piece amphora with a mythological excerpt in the panel or a straddling lay-figure swinging monstrous ivy leaves, or just an animal. The painter follows the Attic style with some care and even attempts the Attic form of the male eye. His lumbering short-legged men have a likeness to those of the Affecter. The shapes of oinochoai and some small pots belong to Etruria, but in the drawing it is the general flavour that is Etruscan rather than specific details. The unassuming style, which makes some use of white and purple, has a dry merit. At Caere the *La Tolfa group*, which runs rather later, prefers a neck-amphora with simple ornament on the neck and a single human or animal figure spreadeagled across the panel on the body. Here the Attic influence is more remote, though the painters advance to a more plastic representation of folds. The last quarter of the sixth century is dominated by the *Micali painter*, who worked at Vulci. Prolific and usually negligent, he owes a little to Pontic, but much more to his own lively and original talents. Inner detail is inconsequent and sometimes omitted, or white lines may replace incision. White and purple additions are scanty. His favourite shape is the neck-amphora, with a main field on the belly and a minor on the shoulder, or with a single field covering both; often the rest of the pot is covered with dark paint. His late work shows awareness of Attic experiments with the three-quarter view. The contemporary *Orvieto group*, made apparently at Orvieto, is a parallel but coarser product; its technique is uncertain, its decoration – with free versions of Attic black-figure – has a quality of its own. Of other contemporaries and the followers of the Micali painter some show competence or occasionally more, but after him there was a general decline. Late Etruscan black-figure, which continues into the second quarter of the fifth century, becomes more and more abject. Generally it apes the black-figure and even red-figure fashions current in Athens, so far as that can be done in a technique dependent on silhouette with or without inner detail of white lines: few ancient pots are more miserable than the small neck-amphorae with a single sloppy figure between rank palmettes.

The technical and artistic skill of Etruscan painted pottery is not high. The shapes are often badly proportioned and the painting and firing uneven. The clay ranges in colour from yellowish grey to pink and is not always well refined. Sometimes there is a slip, normally yellowish, but in the Micali group reddish brown. The paint varies in darkness and is rather dull. Though much Etruscan black-figure has been preserved, the painters were relatively few. It is not surprising that their products are very rarely found outside Etruria.

'Chalcidian'

The school known as 'Chalcidian' appears suddenly about the middle and continues till the end of the sixth century. Its dating depends on stylistic comparisons with Attic, which are close enough to be reliable to a few years. The founder of the school, the Inscription painter, was an artist with an unusual and decorative sense of mass as opposed to line. The contours of his figures are less important than the areas they contain, inner detail is restricted and overlapping is unwelcome. In composition there is a conscious balance of dark painted and light unpainted surface. Shape and decoration are carefully related. It is not surprising that this painter is more at ease in conversation pieces, of which Plate 36 gives a good example, adapted to serve as Hector's farewell. The shapes of his pots, their large fields, and the repertory of figures and ornaments come generally from Attic, but he impressed them with his own character. His younger contemporaries and followers observed his standard as best they could, adding from time to time new borrowings from Attic. In the second generation the Phineus painter, who adopted the relief line, retained a feeling for mass in his figures, but combined it with calligraphy in his ornament, especially on the outside of his admirable eye-cups. His repetitive types have a uniform elegance with their chirpy poses, weak profiles and, if female, rouged cheeks. Charming but mannered, he did not inspire successors.

The system of decoration, as was normal in the modern schools of mature black-figure, displays large figures in a deep field, sometimes bordered by narrower bands of ornament, sometimes panelled in a dark ground. Scenes of heroic and mythical action are less frequent than groups of stock male and female figures, and on lesser works of all painters the animal style often recurs. Two typical subjects are the frontal quadriga (or four-horse chariot) and lions or panthers mauling a deer. In the drawing of the figures detail is usually scanty and sometimes mean. Draped figures tend to reveal their back contour, like the Helen of Plate 36. The shape of the head exaggerates a widespread trend towards receding foreheads and longer skulls. Female eyeballs are often purple. Of ornaments the most characteristic is the great square of interlaced lotus (or ivy) and palmette, erected in the centre of a main field. The chain of lotus flowers and buds, of the plump type shown on Plate 36, is popular for subsidiary bands or to fill the neck of smaller neck-amphorae.

The principal shapes are the large neck-amphora, the hydria, the column-krater and later the cup. Of less artistic importance are the smaller neck-amphora and oinochoe. Among other shapes are one-piece amphora, kotyle, pyxis and even the psykter. The modelling of the finer pieces is excellent and corresponds to the best Attic of the third quarter of the sixth century. The clay is fine and its colour ranges from yellowish orange towards a reddish brown. The paint is shiny, and near-black or golden brown according to its density. The use of purple and white conforms more or less to Attic custom. In all this the effect is, deliberately, very like Attic, though the firing is less sure. But there are also differences of technique. In painting figures the 'Chalcidian' practice, at least on more careful works, was first to apply a thinnish coat and then to daub over it a thicker, which does not reach the edges. Sometimes, when a dark neck was wanted, the pot was dipped upside down in a bowl of paint: such dark necks were often embellished with a wavy line of purple.

'Chalcidian' borrows heavily from Attic, but the borrowing was intermittent: this is particularly clear in the folds of drapery, which show no development but jump from one Attic stage to another. In the early phase Corinthian legacies are visible, though most of these probably came through Attic. As the style develops a few details suggest a flavouring of East Greek or Etruscan. But 'Chalcidian' has a positive character of its own, less disciplined and precise than the Attic standard, but more fluent and more decorative. It is the only properly black-figure school of the second half of the sixth century which stands comparison with that of Athens.

The distribution of 'Chalcidian' is unusual. It is relatively frequent in Etruria, a large find of sherds was made at Rhegion, and there are several other pieces from South Italy and Sicily. A very little comes from Marseilles and Emporion in Spain. But in spite of false alarms from Chalcis no example has certainly been discovered east of the Adriatic. Two dependents of

'Chalcidian', the Memnon and the Polyphemus groups, occur in Etruria and, more rarely, in South Italy and Sicily. There is no other plainly discernible influence of 'Chalcidian'.

The home of 'Chalcidian' is disputed. The relevant facts are its style, influence and distribution, and its painted inscriptions which by alphabet and dialect effectively limit the candidates to Chalcis in Euboea (which has been explored only casually), to some Chalcidian colony in the West, or to a Chalcidian or colonial workshop in Etruria. The more valid arguments are for Chalcis that the quality is too good for Western manufacture, for the West the absence of specimens in Greece and of influence on the receptive schools of Eretria and Boeotia. The Western claim seems to me the stronger, but a closer localization is difficult. Numerically Rhegion has the advantage, but the frequency of 'Chalcidian' there – most of it from a single deposit – may be accidental and its extreme rarity at the well-excavated site of Megara Hyblaea suggests a more distant place of manufacture. Perhaps, in spite of its quality, the school was settled in Etruria; still, Rhegion is a safer bet.

There are similar doubts about some other groups of pottery so far found only in Etruria. The very small *Northampton group* aims at Attic standards, but has a few resemblances to East Greek as well as some kinship with the art of Etruria. Its quality is good, and its date apparently in the 530s. The related *Campana group*, clumsier and lasting longer, has stronger connections both with East Greek and Etruscan. Both these groups and the Caeretan hydriai (discussed in the next pages) are by some assigned to the east Aegean, though it is difficult to find a place for them there. The opinion seems more credible that their makers were Greek settlers in Etruria.

Caeretan Hydriai

A group of some forty hydriai and fragments of hydriai, most of them found at Caere in Etruria, are known as Caeretan Hydriai. Their painter (or painters, if there were two of them) must be counted among the great archaic masters. An adequate draughtsman with a good eye for colour, he excels by his flair for comic expression: when his subject is conventional, he is often mediocre.

The standard hydria, a sturdy well-balanced pot 40 or so centimetres high, shows some influence of metal vases. Its shape and system of decoration appear clearly on Plate 35; inside the lip there is usually a deep band of thick purple and white tongues. The emphasis is on the belly with its large field in front and two shorter fields behind on either side of the vertical handle. On one piece the secondary frieze below also contains figures. The most famous of these hydriai is the Busiris vase in Vienna; Heracles, a hefty nude of little intrinsic interest, massacres the puny white-shirted Egyptians, who are drawn with a venomous ridicule that contrasts with the stolid dignity of the Negro slaves coming to their aid on the other side. Other good pieces have Heracles bringing Cerberus to the terrified Eurystheus, griffin and Arimaspian, the battle with the hydra. Besides mythology there are hunts, battles and conventional groups. Generally the figures are solid and fleshy, and their motions rather jerky. The ornaments are drawn broadly but surely, with a gay reliance on added purple and white. No artist better exploits the narrow formulas of Archaic vase-painting.

The clay varies from a light yellowish brown to a warm brown and even to orange-red; such a range is more usual in Etruscan than Greek pottery. Besides the shiny dark paint, purple and white are used freely and arbitrarily; a light-buff also occurs on the Busiris hydria for the flesh of some of the Egyptians. The bright colours and ample figures suggest, perhaps wrongly, a connection with free painting.

The Caeretan master (or masters, if there were two of them) was an individualist who belongs to no known school but his own. So it is hard to place him or to date him exactly. The style of his drapery suggests that he was active in the last third of the sixth century. Opinions differ on where he worked. None of his pieces (so far as can be proved) has been found outside Caere and perhaps Vulci, so that some think his workshop was there; others who find it unthinkable that such masterpieces of Greek art could be painted in Etruria settle him on the coast of Asia Minor – at unknown Phocaea, for example – or compromise on a Greek city of South Italy. The argument for Caere is to me convincing. But the Caeretan master was a Greek (though perhaps a second-generation immigrant); if his style and subjects are not proof enough, there is also an erudite Greek inscription painted by him on a hydria rescued from the cellars of the Louvre. The common view is that he was an Ionian (as his lettering suggests) though for the figures at least there are parallels on the contemporary terracotta altars of a Corinthian painter; it is anyhow safe to say that the Caeretan master was not trained in Athens, but we know too little of later sixth-century painting elsewhere to define his connections exactly. The only certain signs of his influence are on some Etruscan black-figure pots, and there are a few connections with wall-paintings in Etruscan tombs.

Campanian Black-figure

A number of black-figure works have been recognized as Campanian, though attributions are not always agreed. The earlier class, of the late sixth and the first half of the fifth century, is related to and in part dependent on Etruscan black-figure – not surprisingly since the Etruscans then held Campania. Though sometimes lively in its effect, the quality of the draughtsmanship is very provincial. There is no continuity to the later Pagenstecher group of Paestan and Campanian black-figure, which was made in the same workshops as red-figure pottery or at least was sometimes painted by known red-figure painters. Here the stock shape is a kind of lekythos or bottle, often decorated with a clumsy, plump bird, but sometimes using red-figure types with fair elegance. Its period should be the middle and third quarter of the fourth century. Manufacture probably extended to Sicily.

THE EASTERN FRINGES

Some of the eastern neighbours of the Greeks were influenced by their art. For *Caria*, unhappily from illicit exhumations, there are a fair number of imitations of East Greek pottery from Subgeometric through the Wild Goat style to Fikellura. The shapes tend to be clumsy and the decoration deranged. How far Carian vagaries are random or more positive constituents of a local school or schools is not yet clear. In *Lydia*, at Sardis, specimens have turned up of a confidently deviant version of the Wild Goat style, mixed sometimes with other ingredients, such as the use of streaky paint for arcs or wavy lines and occasionally of a shiny red paint in conjunction with a matt black but there is not enough yet for generalization. *Phrygia*, further inland, had what might be called an Orientalizing Animal style with some resemblances to East Greek, but it is distinctly earlier and the connection, if there is one, should be collateral, though odd instances of Greek borrowing from Phrygia had occurred in the late eighth century. *Lemnos*, an island in the north-east Aegean which probably did not become Greek till the sixth century, drew eclectically on Greek sources for its earlier painted pottery and occasionally developed them adventurously.

CHAPTER V

THE RED-FIGURE STYLE

—— ·◆· ——

INTRODUCTION

In the mature work of Exekias the black-figure technique reached – and perhaps passed – its limits, and artists interested in the new problems of a more natural anatomy and the expression of mood needed a freer medium. They found it in the red-figure technique, by which the figure was drawn in outline on a light ground, inner detail marked by the brush instead of the burin, and the background filled in with solid black. Something of the sort was inevitable. Outline drawing with painted linear detail was a common practice in free painting and an occasional variation on contemporary black-figure pottery; black-figure artists were used to dark detail on figures painted in white; and the black background, desirable in itself to give the drawing prominence on the retreating surfaces of a pot, had parallels in relief sculpture (where the background was coloured red or blue) as well as on some painted slabs. The important question is not how, but why artists came to choose the red-figure technique; for it was a choice made by artists to suit themselves and not to satisfy the market, where for another generation or more black-figure was as popular as ever.

The red-figure style was founded on line drawing, independent of colour or shading, but (what is not always evident in the familiar black-and-white reproductions) two kinds of line were very quickly distinguished. One is the flat line, which may be diluted to a light-brown. But to emphasize major details vase-painters preferred a fine ridge of shiny black that can be felt by the finger – the 'relief line' (see Plate 37A). This was not a new invention, since for a generation it had been popular in black-figure in such humble places as the divisions in bands of tongue pattern; but its importance is new and gives a peculiar precision to the earlier red-figure work. Incision was not at once entirely renounced; for about thirty years it was commonly used to outline black hair against the black background, and it occurs even later. Accessory colour was for a century very modestly applied. Purple was convenient for such things as fillets and for the inscriptions in the field where reserving the letters would have been tiresome; but white is rare, even for the hair of old men. In the late fifth century an ornate taste erupted into white and gold embellishments, and later still white was used freely for flesh. Occasionally a brown wash of the diluted paint picks out a small area. Other colours appeared now and then, particularly in works influenced by free painting, and became regular on the white-ground pottery of the middle and later fifth century.

The red-figure technique was invented about 530 BC in Athens. The earliest exponents had of course been trained in the black-figure style, and their first red-figure ventures are not much more than translations from black-figure. But within ten years the character of the new style is clear, even though many of the red-figure painters of the first generation were working in black-figure too, sometimes – especially for the inside and outside of cups – using both techniques on the same pot. The black-figure technique is an admirable medium for puppets, whose jerky movements and (for white men) unnatural colouring set them apart in a conventional world of their own. The red-figure technique permits a rounder illusion of humanity and the human figure becomes a subject to be studied for itself, not as a component of some scene of action or decorative grouping. The formula inherited from black-figure was that head and limbs should be in profile and the upper part of the body either in profile or frontal, the waist there acting as a simple pivot By the end of the sixth century the leading artists could show the twisting of the waist and of other parts of the body; so we get three-quarter chests and backs, frontal legs and feet, and in kneeling figures the masking of the lower leg by the thigh. But in spite of the interest in foreshortening and complicated poses the general direction and grouping of figures remains in the plane of the picture. At the same time the details of ribs and musculature were being more closely studied. The next generation of vase-painters, brought up to the new views, was less aggressive in displaying them; their figures have an easy suppleness and grace, and still are at home on the surface of a pot. In this period, the first thirty years of the fifth century, the art of painted pottery reaches its highest level, judged by the accepted standard of Greek beauty. Further development – and Greek art had a long tradition of development – could only be towards fuller modelling of the figure, subtler expression of mood and composition in three dimensions, in fact towards free painting which was at last advancing rapidly. Great artists might perhaps have adapted this new pictorial vision to the requirements of pottery, but vase-painting was sinking to a minor art and soon it no longer produced or attracted great artists. So in the mid-fifth century Attic vase-painters range from mannerists trying to perpetuate the style of their predecessors to the admirers of free painting with their grandiose figures and sometimes grandiose compositions; the best work of this period, calm and refined, tends to be academic. The innovators of the late fifth century are content with prettiness or ape the florid, of which the culmination is the Midian school with its lavish display of white and gold. But a soberer classicism survived, till in the middle years of the fourth century a more loose and pictorial style brought a new spirit to Attic workshops. Even so, by 300 BC the red-figure style had come to its end in Athens. It did not adapt itself to being one of the humbler graphic arts.

Another response to free painting was made in the White-ground pottery. From the late sixth century some black-figure vase-painters had had a liking for a white slip as a background to their figures or designs, and by the second quarter of the fifth a few red-figure artists were adopting the white ground for their outline drawings, supplemented – to give contrast to the figures – by washes of colour. The result is a style softer and more pictorial than red-figure, and soon in their white-ground work – for at first white-ground and red-figure were often practised by the same man – painters abandoned the emphatic relief line. Most of the white-ground pots are slim lekythoi which were used especially as offerings to the dead and so did not have to stand ordinary wear; their purpose allowed the use of delicate fugitive colours, their narrow fields encouraged quiet compositions of a pair of figures. The earlier of these lekythoi with their simple schemes have often a classical grace and pathos, which later decline into emotion and clumsiness. The white-ground style did not outlast the fifth century.

Attic red-figure pottery was universal in the Greek world and popular beyond until the later part of the fifth century, when it began to lose its Italian markets to local competitors. Elsewhere Attic was still appreciated, but even before its collapse customers generally preferred the black-painted wares to the largely degenerate survivors of the red-figure tradition.

In time Attic red-figure had its imitators and rivals. A few Clazomenian sarcophagi borrow the technique soon after 500 BC, though the ground is not red but the normal cream of the slip. At Corinth sherds of the outgoing fifth and earlier fourth centuries show a style very like Attic, but the red ground – as in some black-figure Corinthian – is provided by a slip or a thin wash over the yellowish local clay. There is more from Boeotia, where contemporary Attic was followed from the second quarter of the fifth century to the middle of the fourth: the earlier examples were a sideline to black-figure and have a character of their own, the later are little more than travesties of red-figure. Elsewhere in Greece and even in Ukraine local craftsmen occasionally tried their hand at red-figure. But it was in the West that independent schools developed. In the third quarter of the fifth century painters fully trained in the Attic tradition appeared in South Italy and from them there gradually developed local standards, influenced by Attic but also more susceptible to the innovations in free painting. By the second quarter of the fourth century South Italian had split into five recognized schools, of which the Apulian was the largest and most important. It is best known for its elaborate volute-kraters, gaudily but competently decorated with pretentious set-pieces. Etruria too – earlier even than Greek Italy – had its red-figure painters: during the fifth century they were content to follow Attic, generally in simplified techniques, but in the fourth century output increased and more homebred Etruscan schools were modestly successful. Both South Italian and Etruscan survived into the early third century. But these competitors, in Italy too, could not exclude imported Attic, which even in its decline still kept some classical dignity. Compared with the well-bred red-figure of Athens, South Italian is parvenu, Etruscan provincial and Boeotian rustic.

ATTICA

Early Red-figure (*c.* 530–*c.* 500 BC)

The Attic red-figure technique was invented, not evolved. The pioneer of the style (and so far as we know of the technique too) was a painter who worked with the 'maker' Andocides and so has been christened the Andocides painter. He was appropriately a pupil of Exekias and had been trained in the black-figure style, in which (if he is also the Lysippides painter) he continued to work while he was teaching himself red-figure. His work is uneven, varying from a mannered elegance and elaborate patterning to a bold but cheerful simplicity. An amphora in Munich (Plate 38) shows the red-figure maturity of this painter: Athena is still posed and dressed with a black-figure stiffness, but Heracles is a large and limber figure and the folds of his drapery have a plastic quality. In spite of the scanty anatomical detail (though the collar-bones already show a movement towards an oblique view) the sure outline gives this Heracles some appearance of being in the round. On the other side of the same pot is a similar scene in black-figure, competent but petty; our painter was by now out of sympathy with the old style.

The Andocides painter was an artist of the first rank and he impressed his personality on his successors. Though he himself did not exploit the relief line regularly and a stricter canon rejected the plant life he was fond of, his strong plastic forms and simple expressive groups and his understanding of the new balance of light and dark determined the direction of Attic red-figure. Figure 28 gives a specimen of the new standard of the human figure, sturdy and supple. Here there is very little inner detail to distract the eye from the compelling clarity of the outline; but often the markings of the belly, ribs and the muscles of arms and legs are added (some of these details appear on Figure 29). In general the red-figure style of the 520s was experimental, in the 510s the new types were consolidated, and in the next ten years the problems of oblique views and of foreshortening were seriously considered. The greater realism admitted by the red-figure technique had already made the more sensitive artists uncomfortable at the abrupt swivel from profile hips and belly to frontal chest and they had tried various devices to make the transition more organic. Often the markings of the full belly appear, but pushed away towards the

Figure 28   Attic Rf cup.
Inside: diameter of field 10.7 cm. By Oltos, 520–510 BC.

further side of the body and sometimes also set at an angle; or the muscles of the chest or the collar-bones might be shifted (as on Plate 38) to make the torsion appear less violent; but in general the old principle still held that the body is the sum of its parts, all of which must be represented in a typical view. Now in the last ten years of the sixth century two great masters, Euphronios and Euthymides, proved that other views of the human body were artistically possible. A model though unusually thorough exercise in the treatment of the torso is given by Euthymides on one side of an amphora in Munich (Plate 39) and a new view of the leg has been adopted by Epictetus for the satyr on a cup in Boston (Figure 29); frontal legs and feet seen from above or below are equally successful. Less happy is the full view of the female breasts, which usually project like a pair of lemons one below each armpit, though occasionally the nearer breast points inwards: female anatomy is still distinguished from male only by its accessories. The eye continues to be drawn full though in a side face, but the almond shape inherited from the light-ground heads of black-figure has been modified and the pupil set further forward. With greater versatility in drawing goes greater freedom of pose; to the satyr of Figure 29 corresponds for instance the crouching archer seen from behind, and reclining or fallen figures have a wider and more graceful range of movement. Pride in their new achievements tempted artists at first to display them a little

Figure 29 Attic Rf cup
Inside: diameter of field 9.8 cm. By Epictetus, *c.* 500 BC.

incongruously, sometimes even clumsily; but their good sense kept them faithful to the sound principle that the figures should appear to be and move in the plane of the surface of the pot.

A similar interest in the twisting and foreshortening of the human body appears in relief sculpture of the end of the sixth century and in free painting also, to judge by unambitious painted plaques of terracotta and by the common interpretation of Pliny's remark that Cimon of Cleonae invented 'catagrapha'. What precisely 'catagrapha' may mean we do not know, even if Pliny did; but if Cimon was active at this time – and Pliny puts him much earlier – the invention attributed to him was probably in the field of foreshortening. But Pliny is untrustworthy as well as obscure and there is no reason to suppose that all advances were made in a single one of these three branches of art, which were still closely connected, and that the others only imitated. At least the great red-figure painters had the ability and assurance to invent for themselves, and it is likely that they took their part in solving problems common to all two-dimensional art of that time.

Drapery, as well as anatomy, interested artists. The heavy, sleeveless peplos was already in the 530s being replaced by the chiton, a short-sleeved garment of lighter weight. The regular red-figure dress is chiton and the thicker cloak or himation, worn singly or together. Various schemes were inherited from black-figure. The peplos was decorated, if at all, with a pattern of small chequers; for the chiton a set of vertical lines, straight or wavy, was usual; wider oblique lines marked the transverse folds of the long himation, and often the ends were sharply folded back or the hem stepped in series. The red-figure artists with their more fluent lines developed the use of folds, parallel or diverging, and ending in steps; for soft materials the lines are dilute and close together, for heavy in relief and further apart. By the last decade of the sixth century the single set of stepped edges had been replaced by series of steps going alternately up and down with a wider space left between each group of folds, the ends are no longer rectilinear but curved, and the further side of the skirt is shown as a long loop below the nearer. The elegant fall of drapery is becoming a subject that can be represented for itself.

Mythological events and battles are still common subjects, but, scenes of more ordinary human and subhuman life are rapidly increasing – youths exercising in the palaestra or before or after their exercise, evening parties, soldiers arming, and so on. The subtler composition that red-figure encouraged in place of the strongly vertical accent of black-figure brought a renewed interest in the circular field of the inside of the cup, and now it is the outside which often is undecorated: Figure 29 shows how admirably the new freedom can be employed.

Ornament in the Early phase is still largely black-figure, except for the palmettes, enclosed or free, that are large enough to be conveniently drawn in outline. This elastic and often graceful form is sometimes used as part of the standard frame to the panels of large pots, though such arid black-figure relics as the single or doubled chain of lotus and palmette are throughout more common, but it reaches its richest development where it sprouts about the handles of kraters or stamnoi. In contrast to the elaborate framing on large pots the cup is severely simple. Inside the tondo has no surround of ornament; outside a large palmette springing from each handle often flanks the central decoration, particularly on the eye cups which remained popular till near the end of this period.

Shapes are in general simply but rhythmically designed and finely executed. Already in the black-figure work of the mid-sixth century a reaction against angularity had begun; so the one-piece amphora had been rising in favour and was more delicately modelled (cf. Plates 21A and 22) and in the 530s a new standard was established for the cup in which the profile of the bowl makes a single shallow curve from rim to rim. In the red-figure style this tendency grew stronger in harmony with the subtler lines of its composition. The one-piece amphora is the most frequent of the larger pots, and the pelike with sagging belly and the squat-necked stamnos make their appearance. The old hydria is gradually replaced for red-figure by a more fluent form, where the shoulder is rounded and the neck low; but most of the hydriai of this time, as also the neck-amphorae and lekythoi, are still black-figure in decoration. The calyx-krater, used by

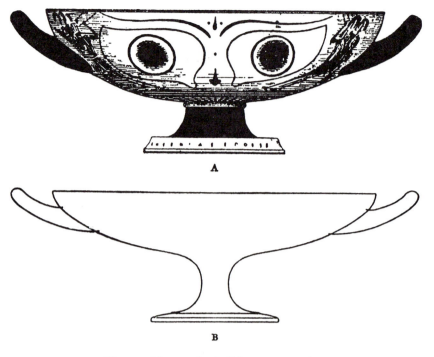

Figure 30   A, Attic Bf cup, type A.
Ht 13 cm, *c.* 530 BC.
B, Attic Rf cup, type B.
Ht 11.7 cm, 490–480 BC.

Exekias, becomes more usual. But the commonest of all shapes is the cup, the early type of which is shown in Figure 30A: the trend is towards a shallower bowl, taller and narrower stem, and a curving transition between which ousts the masking fillet (Figure 30B).

The output of red-figure pottery was growing steadily and very soon painters concentrated either on large pots or on cups. Of the painters of the former - 'pot-painters' as opposed to 'cup-painters' – the Andocides painter (Plate 38), who was active in the first half of this period, had the virtues and faults of the pioneer. His junior contemporary Psiax had a greater delicacy and observation of detail, but lacked his robustness and gusto. Both worked in black-figure too. In the last ten years of the century Euphronios and Euthymides were great and original artists: Euphronios had a grandeur that is not always controlled, Euthymides (Plate 39) a smoother assurance with a spice of malice. The best of the cup-painters are Oltos, Epictetus and Skythes. Oltos, an early pupil of the Andocides painter, shows a sturdy competence (Figure 28), but Epictetus (Figure 29) has an effortless economy of line and a graceful vitality that make him one of the greatest of draughtsmen. Skythes, towards the end of the century, adds to a precise style a taste for the unheroic, but there is no need for that or his name to suppose he was trained outside Athens. In general the work of this period, even when mediocre, is vigorous and cleanly drawn.

The normal technique of red-figure is described elsewhere (pp. 233–4). At the beginning there was some experiment. On a few pots figures were painted in colour over the black background and the detail is incised; there are one or two instances of outline drawing where the background is not filled in; occasionally incision marks not only the outline of hair (as remained normal throughout this period) but also a few other details. Purple – for beards, hair, exceptionally even for outlines – was used more freely than later. The combination on one pot of black-figure and red-figure scenes continued for some fifteen or twenty years, and is most common on eye cups, many of which have a black-figure tondo but red-figure decoration outside. But the superiority, technical or artistic, of the red-figure method easily asserted itself.

Late Archaic Red-figure (*c.* 500–*c.* 480 BC)

The successors of Euthymides and Euphronios refined their inheritance and where the earlier painters had aimed at strength they preferred grace. There is little innovation in the drawing of anatomy but greater facility, so that though poses are more varied and sometimes more acrobatic than before they do not appear forced. Artists – at least the better among them – had now so thorough a control of their medium of line drawing that they could turn their figures as they wished and view them from any angle, but they did not misuse their control; so though the three-quarter torso is a commonplace, the three-quarter face is extremely rare and even the full face unusual. But there was much improvement in the natural and delicate representation of details: the eye, for instance, becomes less symmetrical and is often opened at its front end, and the female breasts can be convincingly outlined (Plate 40). A subtler expression of mood in face or gesture ranges from the ecstasy of the two contrasted maenads of Plate 42 to the momentary impulses of the carousers of Plate 43. The isolated figure can (as on Plate 41) justify itself by grace of body or the manifestation of feeling and, since a group no longer requires a physical connection, composition becomes less formal. On the amphora of Plate 42 the arrangement is centrifugal – in earlier vase-painting that would hardly have been tolerable – and on the outside of the cup of Plate 43 the loosely radial composition is in large part held together by the personal relations between the figures. Dangers to which such a style is liable are on the one side prettiness and posturing, on the other a statuesque inanity and indifference to formal composition. Already the cup interior of Plate 40 for all its charm is less attentive to the circular field than the earlier tondo of Figure 29, and soon a favourite group is two standing figures tilted slightly away from each other: the border of meander which occurs at the very end of the sixth century is becoming a necessary frame.

A parallel change appears in drapery. At first a decorative but artificial elaboration of folds was fashionable, but soon the leading artists were studying the hang of dress to make it conform to the body inside. Contrast Plate 42 of the beginning of this period with the slightly later Plate 43: here is a keener perception of the texture of material.

In the sculpture of the first quarter of the fifth century the cheerful and decorative formalism of the Archaic style was being transformed into the severer but more natural discipline of the Classical. Vase-painting, being essentially decorative, admitted the change with more reluctance; the arts were beginning to diverge. Of contemporary free painting we have little idea. Some of the grander vase-paintings may reflect its themes and the occasional use of shading and such rare tricks of foreshortening as the three-quarter face and the oinochoe tilted towards the spectator were very likely borrowed from pictorial art, but vase-painters stuck resolutely to their old rules of linear drawing and two-dimensional space.

The repertory of subjects is enlarged. Mythology keeps a place but with a wider range of incidents; many of the old favourites were not suited to the new more intimate style of drawing. Among scenes of human life battle-pieces are less common, drinking parties and youths at exercise very numerous: a typical new choice is the school-room. In general the treatment becomes more refined; passion is often there, but it is human and not bestial, and even satyrs are sometimes gentlemen (Plate 41) or fond parents.

The typical ornament is now a simple meander, usually of the type of Plate 40; it is often interrupted by squares containing crosses (so on Plate 42). Some of the more old-fashioned painters continued the black-figure patterns, and the delicate red-figure palmette – sometimes set obliquely in a band – is used when required. But ornament has a small part in Late Archaic red-figure, smaller than before or after. Inside cups there is usually a border of meander, outside more often there are not even palmettes at the handles. On amphorae the advanced artists normally do without a frame; their figures stand on a band or strip of meander or even, if solitary, float in space. Much the same happens on other shapes, with variations according to their needs.

The one-piece amphora is losing in popularity to various forms of the neck-amphora, particularly those with twisted handles, of Panathenaic shape and of the small kind called 'Nolan'. The pelike, introduced at the end of the sixth century, and the stamnos become very frequent. The new rounded hydria has not quite ousted the old angular shape. Kraters are numerous; the greater masters prefer the calyx-krater, the lesser the column-krater, and the volute-krater survives. The lekythos comes into favour with red-figure painters, and one workshop specialized in long white-ground alabastra which are mostly decorated with a lanky Negro in striped trousers. The cup, with low spreading bowl and an unbroken sweep from top to graceful foot, is now at the summit of its glory and its outside decoration is adjusted to the shape as never before. The average standard of execution is extraordinarily high, partly because so many inferior painters still stuck to black-figure.

The division between painters of large pots and of cups continues, and the painting of small closed pots is becoming a separate trade. Of the painters of large pots, two are pre-eminent. The Cleophrades painter, whose name turns out not to have been Epictetus (the signature on the Berlin pelike is modern), was a pupil of Euthymides whom he resembles closely in his earliest work. His own style, grand and expressive, was mature in the 490s (Plate 42), in the 480s there is less fire but more dignity, and afterwards his powers waned. From his hand are also several Panathenaic amphorae in the black-figure style which the Cleophrades painter was one of the last Attic vase-painters to understand. His contemporary the Berlin painter, in his delicacy reminiscent of the same Euthymides, was a rather mannered draughtsman of unusual grace, particularly successful in the single figures he delighted to put in the unframed fields of slim pots (Plate 41). His long career lasted into the 460s, but though his later work is less careful there is little development in his style. His decorative elegance had a wide influence. Myson, an old-fashioned mediocrity whose taste was for column-kraters decorated with large figures, had a following in the Early Classical mannerists. Among cup-painters Onesimos (the Panaitios painter), already active in the closing years of the sixth century, kept up with the times (Plate 40); his drawing is usually vigorous and always fresh. His pupil the Brygos painter refines on his model and at the best combines delicacy with passion (Plate 43), but later he grew tamer and more correct. Duris, another long-lived artist, began as a colleague of the young Onesimos, who both influenced and was influenced by him; his style has a youthful affected charm till he settled into an academic propriety, receptive of the new classicism. Makron was a lesser artist, remarkable for the flow of his women's clothes. The most influential of these cup-painters was the Brygos painter, and next to him Duris. The end of the period sees the growth of an academic trend and other signs of flagging imagination.

In red-figure technique there is little change. The outline of hair is now commonly reserved and not incised. Purple is used very modestly. Dilute washes appear a little less rarely, sometimes applied unevenly to suggest an object's texture. A few red-figure painters still did passable work in black-figure too. The white-ground technique of outline drawing against a light background had yet hardly interested red-figure artists outside the workshop that turned out the Negro alabastra, and their thick summary style cannot be reckoned as true red-figure.

Early Classical Red-figure (*c.* 480–*c.* 450 BC)

In the second quarter of the fifth century the Attic red-figure style splits into schools that aim at different ideals. The reasons lie in the gradual establishment of the classical standard with its emphasis on a calm and reflective humanity and in the related advance of free painting towards pictorial art, for neither classical figures nor spatial depth could easily be suited to the scale and scope of vase-painting. So red-figure vase-painters divide according to the degree and manner in which they reject or accept the old and the new. There are the frank imitators of the grandeur of free painting (Figures 32–33), the moderate classicists who thoughtfully adapt the new types and groupings (Plate 45), miniaturists preferring charm and prettiness (Figure 31) and mannerists who continue or reinterpret archaic forms (Plate 44). There is about much of the work of this period an air of study rather than of spontaneity and a feebler sense of the relation between shape and decoration so that it is easy to enjoy the drawing and forget the pot. Admirable individual figures are often set in casual, static compositions, for which the high fields of tall pots offer the best chance of success: the decoration of cups, especially of the long narrow frieze of the exterior, becomes less attractive. Though its technical tradition of line drawing saved it from collapse, the art of painted pottery is beginning to decay and sink gradually to a minor rank.

Greek free painting has been mentioned several times in this book, but now its influence becomes more evident. Little is known of its early history. Murals and large wooden panels, presumably its main forms, have vanished completely in Greece though some works painted by or for colonists at Paestum, Etruscans and Lycians survive in their tombs and there are (or were) the little wooden plaques from Pitsa. Besides these we have a

Figure 31 Attic Rf cup.
Outside: ht of field 9.5 cm. By the Penthesilea painter, 470–460 BC.

Figure 32   Attic Rf calyx-krater.
Detail: scale *c.* 2:5. By the Niobid painter, *c.* 460 BC.

few painted slabs of terracotta and marble which served as architectural decoration, gravestones or dedications, with uncertain statements of ancient writers, and with the reflections to be glimpsed or guessed in vase-painting and sculpture in relief. Probably free painting began in the seventh century, since the Geometric style as we know it can hardly bear enlargement. Our earliest examples are the painted terracotta metopes from Thermon and Calydon, coloured drawings in the Corinthian style of around 630 BC; the technique is outline drawing with simple linear detail and the enclosed surfaces filled with flat washes of various colours, but the style, poses and types resemble contemporary vase-painting. The square field of the metope forbids elaborate composition, but that there were more ambitious paintings is deduced from some polychrome Corinthian pots of the mid-seventh century (such as that of Plate 9C, discussed on pp. 50–1); here the composition is more largely conceived and colours are used freely though incision is retained. So far as can be inferred, free painting continued the technique and general standards of the Thermon metopes till the end of the sixth century; its scope may have been wider than that of vase-painting, but both were governed by the same ideals and perhaps often practised by the same artist. The difference in technique was not important, for though the black-figure style of vase-painting was conventional, so too was the outline and wash of free painting. It is tempting to imagine in the more monumental or elaborate of black-figure vase-paintings the influence of free painting, but there were among the vase-painters artists of the first rank who could themselves be original, and on the other hand the influence of vase-painting is seen on some sizeable clay plaques which are decorated in the black-figure technique. Later, when vase-painters needed a more expressive medium than black-figure and turned to line drawing, they did not adopt the colour schemes of free painting. Vase-painting, free painting and relief sculpture were parallel but independent manifestations of the two-dimensional archaic art, and their differences were the differences that come from the medium used, not from the status of their artists. It was not till the end of the sixth century, when the archaic restrictions were being broken, that free painting started on its pictorial development. The first step, the mastery of foreshortened views of the human figure, was perhaps not – or anyhow not wholly – its invention; intimations of obliquity (though rare and unsystematic) had begun to appear in sculpture and vase-painting some fifty years before their general acceptance. There is more reason to suspect the influence of free painting in certain novelties that occur in a few vase-paintings but were generally rejected. So in the pretentious tondo of a cup by the Sosias painter, where Achilles bandages Patroclus's arm, the eyes of the two heroes are drawn in profile, a rendering that does not become regular in vase-painting for another generation, and the teeth of Patroclus are clenched in pain; and on the slightly later Vivenzio hydria of the Cleophrades painter the sack of Troy is depicted with a grandness of composition that is very rare in contemporary vase-painting. But though the cup with Patroclus may owe details it does not simply copy free painting, since the scene has been specially composed to fit a circular field. In fact the earlier red-figure masters were self-confident and original, the equals in all probability of the free painters of their day, and if they borrowed it was with discrimination. But in the second quarter of the fifth century the position changed. Red-figure vase-painting in its turn was reaching its proper limits and there was little more even to refine. So it ceased to attract or breed artists of the first quality and the achievements of free painting, which now under Polygnotus and Mikon was attempting in earnest the problems of three-dimensional figures and space, set a higher standard for lesser craftsmen to admire and for the imprudent to copy.

Some influence of free painting may be suspected also on the white-ground vases where outline drawing – later regularly supplemented by colour – is set against a background of white or whitish slip (Plate 49A). A pale slip, yellowish to cream, had been used on some Attic pots from Protogeometric to Early Geometric, and again in Protoattic, but was probably not connected with the whiter coating which towards the end of the sixth century became popular in some black-figure workshops for their lekythoi. But red-figure artists made very rare use of this technique till the Early Classical period. Their earliest ventures in white-ground work – by a sensible convention the term excludes black-figure pottery with a white ground – are in effect red-figure drawings the background to which has not been blacked in; now a distinct manner begins to establish itself, though for a generation most painters of white-ground pots painted orthodox red-figure pottery too. The sharp clarity of red-figure line drawing tends to give way to softer effects, as the flush line of dilute paint replaces the strong relief line, even for the outline, and the flat washes of purple, browny red and yellow that often cover the drapery, take a bigger part in the design. The finest of the early white-ground paintings are on the inside of cups and there are also white-ground alabastra and pyxides, but by the middle of the fifth century the lekythos has become the normal shape. The reason is hardly the example of the miserable black-figure lekythoi, even though these sometimes offer drawings that are partly in outline; the lekythos is not at first the white-ground shape most preferred in red-figure work-shops. More important was the demand for lekythoi to deposit in graves, where they had not to stand daily use. So white-ground painters could indulge in new and perishable colours and a whiter friable slip – on some earlier pieces, though the slip is whitish, a purer white paint was thought necessary for the flesh of women – and the white-ground technique became unsuitable for anything except funerary ware. But the full development does not come till after the Early Classical period.

Though the red-figure style declines in artistic quality, there is no decline in skill. The drawing of the human figure is more accomplished than before and drapery more accurately studied. Archaic artists had made clear the structure and working of the body, their classical successors were interested in its surface and bearing. Detail follows nature more care-fully: the profile eye is now regularly drawn in profile, and the separate strands of hair are sometimes suggested by a streaky use of dilute paint. With this more sensuous anatomy appear more graceful or dignified poses and gestures, subtly expressive of purpose or feeling; so the tempting of Eriphyle with the necklace (Plate 45) has a well-bred reticence that is fully classical and even the sentimental boys and pony of Figure 31 palely reflect the same spirit. As drawings the best of these works are admirable, but it is less certain that they are in place as the decoration of pottery. Even so the plane of the surface of the pot is still generally respected, though three-quarter faces are rather less uncommon, inanimate objects are occasionally modelled by shading, and feet may be planted above the baseline. A few ambitious pieces go further and exhibit figures tiered in a sort of Oriental perspective or partly concealed by cardboard hillocks, and there are battle scenes where combatants seem to be bursting out of the picture (Figure 33).

Figure 33 Attic Rf volute-krater.
Detail: ht of field 21.5 cm. By the painter of the Woolly Satyrs,
c. 460 BC.

Drapery, except in mannerist works, abandons the old formal systems of decorative folds. Instead we find sketchier impressions of the fall and pull of material across body or limbs (Plate 45) or dry close-set corrugations as on the half-concealed Amazon of Figure 33. The uncompromising clarity of the traditional line drawing is being surrendered. In the 460s the peplos again becomes fashionable. Ornament is rather less restricted than in Late Archaic. Some painters repeat older – even black-figure – patterns, others try to improve the plant forms: so lotus and palmette are in borders contorted into novel elaborations, and when used independently break into rank, straggly growth.

Shapes continue in general to become slimmer and as in the drawing of human anatomy the transition from one part to another is less sharply defined. The one-piece amphora is now very rare; neck-amphorae, both large and the small Nolan, are common, as are the pelike, the stamnos and the hydria. The column-krater is the favourite of the mannerists; other painters prefer the bell, calyx and volute forms. Oinochoai are fairly numerous. The stemmed cup is losing popularity, the stemless cup and the kotyle gaining. Besides the regular lekythos, red-figure or white-ground, the squat lekythos and the alabastron are frequent.

Most of the greater artists of Late Archaic, though past their best, were still working in the Early Classical period. Their now old-fashioned style was continued more or less faithfully by many lesser painters. Among these mannerists the Pan painter stands out, an original artist with an individual taste for elegance and oddity, who knew to a nicety how to put new wine in old bottles (Plate 44). The Pistoxenos painter is a pioneer of the new classical style; his sharply drawn, staring figures have a dramatic quality. More fully classical is a younger artist, the Villa Giulia painter, whose subtle harmony does not need vigorous or sensational movement: his school is represented here by the work of a pupil, softer but equally correct (Plate 45). The Achilles painter, in the third quarter of the century the greatest painter of white lekythoi, resembles them in character. A more watered classicism is evident in much of the work of the Penthesilea painter – in his day capable of grandeur – and of his colleagues: Figure 31 offers a mediocre specimen, sketchily pretty and sugared. The Sotades painter also belittles his human figures, but is redeemed by an unusual sense of space and even of nature; the white-ground inside of a cup in the British Museum with a girl picking apples is one of the most surprising masterpieces of classical art. Of the adherents of the grand style, who went far in their imitation of free painting, the most notable is the Niobid painter: Figure 32 shows one of his competent but frigid figures, Figure 33 – from a krater painted by a member of his group – a section of one of the elaborate compositions to which he aspired.

Classical Red-figure (*c.* 450–*c.* 425 BC)

The full classical ideal of effortless human dignity now became dominant and in the third quarter of the fifth century permeated Attic vase-painting. The red-figure style, based on emphatic line drawing, found it difficult to translate into its traditional technique the easy harmonious poses in which organic unity of the figure was attained by subtle transitions between its parts, and the result often looks strained or inappropriate. But white-ground was already less dependent on line and perhaps still offered artists the attraction of novelty, and it is in this period that it reaches its finest achievement. There is now a spirit in some vase-painting that recalls the sculptured decoration of the Parthenon, the greatest work of this period and the best preserved; but it is hard to judge what direct influence it had on the painters of pottery.

In their drawing of figures vase-painters had at their service a sound knowledge of the appearance of the human body in a wide range of views and positions, but this knowledge is used with classical restraint. Quiet standing or sitting poses are typical, subtly varied to prevent monotony, and scenes of action, even battles, are for decency toned down: the drunken return of Hephaestus, for example, becomes a respectable procession, and satyrs finding sleeping maenads think first of not disturbing them. Groups are often unified solely by bearing or glance, which some painters make more expressive by shortening the lower lid of the profile eye. So the musical tableau becomes popular, with performer and hearers fixed in varied attitudes of rapture (Plates 46A and 48B). Careful scenes are now usually kept for the front of the pot, while the back – for economy or contrast – is summarily filled with a few stock figures standing aimlessly by. Perspective, of which painters are now more conscious, is confined generally to the legs of tables and chairs (Plate 46A), though some ambitious sets have also half-open doors. In advanced workshops rocks and a variable standing line are used freely but discreetly (Plate 48B). This restraint in representing depth suggests that vase-painting was influenced as much by relief sculpture as by free painting. The relation of shape to decoration is no longer given much thought, and the principles for the composition of groups tend to be based on a rectangular field. The body of the lekythos happily provides such a field; the inside of the cup does not, but the composition is rarely planned to suit the tondo. The effect now is not so much painted pottery as pottery with painting on it.

The repertory of ornament remains much as in Early Classical. Where there is room, the tendency to abstract elasticity increases. By now most shapes have their characteristic ornaments, as for instance the double row of leaves below the lip of bell-kraters (Plate 48A). In technique the relief line is less regularly used and for outlines is by now largely abandoned. Washes of dilute paint, for shading or modelling minor objects, are no longer so rare.

In red-figure the Achilles painter, whose finest work is on white-ground lekythoi (Plate 49A) is the most important of the painters who develop the quiet classicism of the period just past. Polygnotus, a master with a still larger following, who shares his name with two other contemporary vase-painters besides the famous mural painter, is the heir to the grand style, though his forms are fleshier and more rounded and his spirit is fully classical: the amphora of Plate 46A and the kraters of Plates 37B and 48D were painted by his companions. But now that the admirers of free painting had outgrown their early wildness the schools of this generation differ less in their ideals than in the way they express them. Of other vase-painters the Eretria painter had most influence: his style, mature about 430 BC, rejects classical severity for a finicky prettiness, tricked out with ornaments raised in gilded clay (Plate 47). A comparable lowering of ideals appears on the white-ground lekythoi. Red-figure is a declining art; good work is becoming rarer, trivial or bungling more common.

The white-ground style was now almost confined to the very numerous lekythoi. Here the standard was set by the Achilles painter, the last of the great Attic vase-painters. This artist began his career about 460 BC spent ten years or so in finding his idiom and then changed very little. His slender, fine-boned men and women stand or sit with easy dignity, looking at one another in silent, often melancholy understanding. There is no purer expression of classical art than the mature white-ground work of this master (Plate 49A). His followers in the 430s and 420s preferred something more tender or unreserved. Characteristic of the new human touch are children, now pathetically childish. The tall narrow field of the lekythos was admirably fitted for classical figures, at first usually two, later often three. Funerary subjects had become common during the second quarter of the fifth century and now they are regular: the favourites are the lady and her maid, the soldier's farewell to his wife, the visit to the grave where often the dead man or woman appears, and sometimes such scenes are conflated; or, especially later, there are incidents from the other world – Charon and his boat, Hermes guiding the dead, two winged attendants carrying the body away. The progress of the white-ground style was helped by changes in technique. Already by the 460s the relief line had been generally replaced by a flat line of shiny dilute paint, and now this gives way to matt paint, black or red. The staring 'second white' used for female flesh does not last long into this period. To the purple, browny red and yellow pigments that were moderately fast, there are gradually added less stable shades – rose, vermilion, sky-blue and a light purple. The present nakedness of many figures on white-ground lekythoi is a consequence; the flat washes of colour that clothed them have perished.

The shapes of this period often show a new, but mistaken sense of curve. So the amphora of Plate 46A slurs the transition from neck to shoulder and develops an unpleasant concavity at the base of the body. Of neck-amphorae the Nolan is most common, but the pelike is commoner still. The krater remains in favour; first comes the bell-krater, then the calyx and column forms. Stamnos and hydria keep, oinochoai increase their popularity. The stemmed cup is still frequent enough, the stemless cup comes a respectable second to it, the kotyle a poor third. Squat lekythoi are fairly, tall lekythoi (mostly white-ground) very numerous. There are a good few loutrophoroi of one kind or another; these were ritual vases, specially designed for weddings or funerals.

In the earlier part of this period the red-figure style was transplanted to South Italy. The Polygnotan group and less so the Achilles painter were the earliest models of this new school.

Late Classical Red-figure (*c.* 425–*c.* 400 BC)

During the last quarter of the fifth century some painters of Attic red-figure were again attracted to the ideal of pictorial depth and volume. In the past the figures had generally in their direction and arrangement conformed to the surface of the pot. Now they may emerge or recede obliquely from the field or be set at different levels: the decoration no longer needs to have regard to the shape. Similarly the drawing is more diligent in the modelling of rounded forms, on naked bodies by subtler curves of the contour and of the sparse anatomical lines, on drapery by series of folds, often hooked, which cross a thrusting limb. The emphatic relief line and the lucid outline are correspondingly neglected. For hair a curly mass of separate strands is regular. Accessories of white and gold become more common. Dresses are often spangled with crosses or other simple patterns. At the same time poses tend to be theatrical and expressions – partly because of the shortening of the profile eye – vapidly intense. Some of these novelties were probably prompted by free painting, but the tradition of red-figure was too strong for any systematic imitation.

The use of ornament is discreet. Floral forms are drawn out more finely. The acanthus leaf becomes common on the last white-ground lekythoi.

The Polygnotan school, now in its second generation, remained dominant; and its most influential artist, the Dinos painter, was a cautious pioneer of the new style (Plate 48A). His figures, plumper and sinuous but still solid, are economically modelled by firm lines. Though he knows the new tricks – such as the shadowing of a fold by a streak of dilute paint – he uses them discreetly. The work of his prime has sometimes a touch of fire and normally a dignity and sober grace above the average of the school; there are other members, equally competent, who achieve no more than a classicizing elegance.

A different spirit is exuded by a celebrated contemporary, the Midias painter, who developed the style of the Eretria painter. Here is the world of the boudoir, respectably sensual, peopled by feminine women and effeminate cupids. The Midias painter is a delicate draughtsman who lovingly analyses draped forms into a multitude of fine lines. He had also a taste for the florid and indulges in white and gilded details. There is great charm in his smaller scenes (Plate 46B); the larger, heavily ornate and weakly composed, have been admired. Though he had his imitators and some wider influence, his style was in its way too exquisite to leave a lasting tradition.

In minor works the standard falls. The drawing is often negligent and perfunctory, and the effect though plain deplorable. Some unambitious classes of small pots have a whimsical charm – for instance the flat askos with a conventional animal and the small jug called the chous on which a favourite figure is a chubby child.

White-ground lekythoi were turned out in great quantity. Though the medium was more suited to the style of free painting, the field gave little scope; anyhow, decay is rapid (Plate 49B). The white-ground specialists – for white-ground and red-figure were no longer painted by the same man – went their own way. In the standard scene of mourning at the tomb classical restraint often gives way to passionate grief, or what the painter intended for it. Lines are often sketchy, and the choice of colours now includes green and mauve. A few lekythoi of group R come from a draughtsman of exceptional quality, whose sensitive contour needs little inner detail to show how volume can be suggested by pure line. He had no following, and the white-ground style was dead by the end of the fifth century.

The shapes of large vases become more swelling, and mouldings of foot and lip grow richer. The neck-amphora is following the one-piece amphora into disuse. The pelike flourishes. The bell-krater is very popular, the calyx-krater moderately popular. The stamnos is obsolescent. The hydria is temporarily less important. Oinochoai, especially of the small chous variety, are numerous: the body is now nearly globular. The common form of cup is stemmed. Squat lekythoi (Plate 46B) are frequent, as are tall lekythoi, some of which reach a height of 45 cm. Loutrophoroi continue. A shape new to favour is the lekanis of the Midian school.

Fourth-century Red-figure (*c.* 400–*c.* 300 BC)

Red-figure had by now become a minor art of a special character. The gap had widened decisively between vase-painting and free painting, which was at last progressing beyond line drawing towards a systematic use of shading. From early in the fifth century, to judge by occasional examples in red-figure, such minor details as metal objects, pelts and rocks were sometimes shaded; but at its end the revolutionary innovation was made of shading drapery and the male body – the white female body remained unshaded for two generations longer. This new aid to illusion was after a little experiment rejected by vase-painters, whether because the new technique was difficult or the old seemed more pleasing. Even so, new ideas seeped in and in late red-figure works there is often an uneasy compromise between modern expression and traditional style.

Attic vase-painting of the fourth century is less well explored than of the fifth. But the classical tradition, transmitted by the Dinos painter and his colleagues, persisted with modifications for fifty years or more. Shortly before 400 BC it had put out an offshoot, the so-called Ornate style, ambitious and short-lived. Later, in the 370s, some workshops succeeded in harmonizing composition in depth with line drawing and respect for the surface of the pot. Though this new style at its best is skilful and effective, it did not long outlast the classical tradition which it denied. Red-figure had ended at Athens by 300 BC.

The novelties of the Late Classical painters have become commonplaces to the next generation. The silhouette of the figure is no longer studied. Modelling by curving lines is regular, and fully profile figures are rare. Though shading is exceptional, the quality of lines is softer or weaker and some painters vary the breadth of their strokes. Patterning of drapery becomes heavier. Whole figures, especially in the centre of the composition, may be painted white for emphasis or to distinguish the layers of a group or just from habit: details on these white figures are done in the yellowy brown of dilute paint. Buildings, when they are put in, may be tilted or recede in a sort of perspective. These characteristics are more dominant in the Ornate school; the classical wing is more restrained and modest; and the growing mass of hackwork, on cheap pots or the backs of expensive ones, has the simple but irredeemable badness that comes when sophistication is hurried and careless.

The Ornate style begins about 420 BC and trails on for some forty years. Here we meet again after a generation of disuse grandiose compositions in which the figures are tiered above each other to mark their distance from the spectator or (since free painting had discarded that form of perspective) as a device to fill a high field. In the often crowded scenes one or two figures are marked out by their white flesh, white and yellow accessories are spattered around, and drapery is loaded with borders of large hooks, stars, stripes and even little animals, some of them still Orientalizing. One of the most successful of the Ornate confections is the name-piece of the Talos painter, a volute-krater in Ruvo, on which the bronze giant Talos falls back limply into a throng of bystanders. His white flesh, exceptionally modelled by shading in dilute paint, contrasts significantly with the red of the other figures. The small Bacchic scenes on the neck of this krater are more conservative.

At the other extreme the Jena painter is perhaps the best and – through the excavation of his workshop – certainly the best-known of the classicists of the early fourth century. He is in the tradition of the Dinos painter, but quieter and more refined. His composition – at least on cups – is uncrowded and avoids depth; his heads are regularly in profile; and he is attentive to the silhouettes and to the balance of light and dark in his pictures. For inner detail he makes sparing and skilful use of thin lines, which effectively suggest the plastic forms of the body: on Plate 50 may be noted the doubling of the lines across the naked belly and the blank surfaces and cross folds which neatly express the thrust of draped breast or thigh. So lucid a draughtsman had little use for patterns on his dresses and less for added colours, except in the garland of leaves and berries round the inside of cups. At his best the Jena painter is graceful; but sometimes, especially in his later cups, he is as bad as the contemporary hacks who turned out work that for its lack of other character may be called traditional.

Between the Ornate masters and the classicists there stretches a row of intermediate painters with more pretensions than perception. The standard of Attic red-figure is low in the first quarter of the fourth century, and it deservedly lost ground everywhere to black-painted ware and in Italy also to the local red-figure.

From about 380 BC a few competent artists gave a new twist to red-figure. In their line drawing they followed the Jena painter, though they preferred softer and weaker strokes, abandoned the relief line (which is rare after the middle of the century), and made free use of white to give prominence or contrast to particular figures. But their major innovations were in composition. Although on examination the picture often proves to have considerable depth, its depth does not appear obtrusively. This effect is obtained partly by the rejection of perspective tricks, but more by the poses of individual figures, which seem to lean against the curving wall of the pot and so to be on its surface. The grouping too is loose, with the outer figures often turning away from the central action, and the poses have the grace and languor that were then fashionable in sculpture and – no doubt – in other arts. The pelike of Plate 51, about 350 BC shows the new red-figure at its best. Peleus surprises Thetis: Aphrodite seated on the left and the fugitive nymph to the right each in her way exploit the curvature of the pot. The new style is at home on the pelike, hydria and calyx-krater; the bell-krater generally has rougher or less modern decoration. The final generation of red-figure painters grows clumsy and fumbling: figures are often elongated, lines become sketchier or harsh, experiments in colour and relief (which had begun in the first half of the century) are abandoned.

By the beginning of this period Dionysus and Aphrodite were the favourite gods of the vase-painters, and where other immortals appear the setting is likely to be Dionysiac. There is too a growing taste for Oriental costumes; and by the middle of the century Amazons, Arimaspians and griffins are familiar. The backs of bell-kraters and pelikai are throughout disfigured by the inevitable trio or pair of cloaked youths, always (if possible) more degenerate than before (Figure 34). On smaller pots there is a fondness for heads.

The use and forms of the ornaments are much as in Late Classical. Palmettes trimmed almost beyond recognition to make a low triangle fill the lower border on some late calyx-kraters. The band of spiral hooks is common.

The principal shapes are kraters of the bell and also of the calyx variety, the hydria and – commonest of all – the pelike. They suffer a continual elongation of neck, body and stem. The lekanis is frequent in the first half of the fourth century. The cup, stemmed and stemless, disappears in the second quarter. The heavy cup-kotyle has a vogue from the end of the fifth century till about 380 BC. The kotyle continues popular. The squat lekythos, small jugs and askos do not last much beyond 350 BC.

This dwindling range of shapes was supplemented by black-painted ware (or, as it is usually but wrongly called, black-glazed ware). There had always been some pottery of fair quality that was decorated simply by a coat of dark paint, and about the middle of the sixth century Attic workshops began to produce admirably finished black pots. Before the middle of the

Figure 34 Attic Rf bell-krater.
Detail of back (three-draped youths): scale 1:2.
By the Filottrano painter, mid-4th century BC. The upper part
of the figure on the left is uncertain.

fifth century impressed decoration had been admitted, particularly for rosettes and soon for bands of short strokes and small palmettes in the centre of cups, some of which have red-figure decoration outside; and from the later years of the century the bodies of pots are sometimes ribbed. It is difficult to estimate the relative outputs of red-figure and black wares, but by the fourth century black ware – plain, impressed and ribbed – must have been the staple product of Attic workshops.

The end of Attic red-figure came not later than 300 BC. Why it ended is not obvious. The style till the 330s had vitality and inventiveness, the market for Attic pottery was still large, the taste of customers did not jib at decorated wares. Perhaps artists accomplished enough to reach and maintain the standard of the Thetis pelike (Plate 51) could find more congenial and profitable employment than painting pots.

CORINTH

Corinthian clays were pale in colour and did not yield a black paint of Attic quality. So when eventually local potters attempted red-figure, they applied a wash of red ochre to the reserved areas, sometimes over a reddish slip. The style is modestly respectable, imitating Attic but not slavishly. Output was not large, with perhaps not more than ten painters regularly active during a period which lasted – to judge by contexts and stylistic parallels – from about 425 to about 350 BC: presumably the Peloponnesian War, though not preventing the import – indirectly – of Attic red-figure, sent up its price, so that in spite of technical inferiority the Corinthian substitute could compete and afterwards was well enough established to continue. An interesting and possibly significant discovery is that two earlyish pieces in Corinthian technique were decorated by the Attic Suessula painter. The commonest shape is the bell-krater. Corinth is the principal place of finding, but some exported pieces have been observed in the Argolid and at Aegosthena, Medeon, Sicyon and Olympia; more may well turn up west of Corinth, though Corinthian red-figure is not always recognized by those who look at decoration but not clay. There was also much Corinthian imitation of the cheap Attic white-ground leythoi ornamented with patterns, especially of ivy: these begin about the same time as the red-figure, completely replace their Attic models in Corinth, and fade out about 400 BC.

There are also, rather earlier, a few examples of outline drawing on a light ground. The best known, though not the finest, are those of the Sam Wide group of small cups, plates and pyxides, which used to be thought Boeotian and were referred to as Haloa pottery. They exhibit figures of irreverent charm and simplicity in a style well suited to samplers. Contexts give a date around the middle of the fifth century.

BOEOTIA

Boeotian vase-painters remained faithful to black-figure into the fourth century, but there was a little red-figure too. It begins slowly in the second quarter of the fifth century. The style is current Attic in intention; but the drawing of inner details, which often misunderstands the folds of drapery and even the human anatomy, tends to flat and inconsequent patterns of lines without a suggestion of modelling. Perhaps the painters, some of whom certainly worked in black-figure workshops, were themselves primarily black-figure painters and had not enough practice in red-figure. Boeotian taste is to be seen in some of the subjects, for instance the banqueting hero, and among the shapes in the importance of the kantharos. In the years around 400 BC one group shows a little independence: its typical product is a smallish bell-krater with a large female head on the front, a large palmette on the back and another female head on the lid. But the formula is arid and grows clumsy with repetition. During the fourth century such other painters as there are turn out work of more distinctive incompetence. Boeotian red-figure at its best has a dry and simple merit, the worst is inept. It ends probably about the middle of the fourth century.

The colour of the fired clay is usually paler than Attic and the paint is less even. According to the distribution Thebes was the place of manufacture, at least of the better groups. Occasionally a piece of Boeotian red-figure found its way to some other part of Greece, but even at home it was less frequent than imported Attic.

ETRURIA

In Etruria the red-figure style of Athens was at once admired and after a while imitated. Apart from the Praxias group the earlier imitations are more or less isolated. It was not till the fourth century, when production increased and the influence of South Italian (particularly Campanian) was added, that positively Etruscan schools developed. This sluggishness in style is matched by uncertainty in technique: more or less continually painting in applied colour competes with the true red-figure process of reservation, and where reservation is preferred the painters did not consistently use the relief line. The cemeteries of Etruria have been ransacked vigorously, but though the place of finding is often recorded the context usually is not: so dating depends mainly on stylistic comparison with Attic and increasingly South Italian. For the location of the Etruscan workshops our evidence is mainly distribution. There is also some variety in the clay, which is generally fired to a lightish brown, noticeably paler than Attic.

Most of the earliest Etruscan essays in red-figure belong to the Praxias group, which with its successors lasts from the second quarter till near the end of the fifth century. Here the decoration is done in red paint over a background of the ordinary dark paint and at first details are incised through the red so that they show in the colour of the background; the effect resembles that of true red-figure, especially in reproductions. This technique of applied colour had already been tried in Athens and found wanting, but its simplicity recommended it to Etruscan craftsmen. Initially, it seems, the Praxias group owes something to the tradition of the Micali painter, but both for style and subjects it looked to Attic models and the deviations from Attic standards have no common quality except incompetence. But though one of the later painters of this group wrote Greek – in the Euboean alphabet – there is no reason to suppose that it was in a Greek city that he learnt to paint. The home of the group was probably Vulci, where so much of their work has been found.

A properly red-figure technique was becoming established by the end of the fifth century, though at first its practitioners show no coherent style but copy indiscriminately, in part or in whole, models mostly Attic of various trends. Vulci seems again to be the chief place of finding, and a

cup in the Musée Rodin in Paris offers another argument for Vulcian manufacture, since it evidently copies an Attic cup found there.

In the early fourth century, as Etruscan red-figure was growing more
confident, a new school appears suddenly at Falerii, an inland town in the
south-east corner of Etruria, though not properly Etruscan, since its
language was a sort of Latin. This Faliscan school is at first so purely Attic
in style that its founders may well have been emigrant craftsmen from
Athens. But fairly soon, as now at Vulci, the painters become more eclectic
and independent. South Italian red-figure, and particularly the school of
Campania, provides forms of floral ornaments, of which the flower seen
in perspective is the most obvious (Figure 35), and less regularly other
notions; themes, in a few instances brutal, are taken from Etruscan tradition or chosen for Etruscan taste; workshops cultivate their own
mannerisms, and in the second half of the century give up the relief line.
There is also much use of applied colour especially for routine pieces. The
Faliscan school, in its prime graceful and refined, preserves a flaccid
elegance, still Greek in style though Greek with a South Italian flavour.
Minor but convenient peculiarities of Faliscan are, on large pots, the band
of full tongues, each in its rounded compartment, and – though less
constantly – the trefoil leaf. Cup, stamnos and calyx-krater are the important shapes. At Caere too, so finds there suggest, there was busy production
in the Faliscan manner from about 340 BC till the end of the century: the
credit (if that is the word for it) is usually given to Faliscan immigrants.
The school of Vulci (if Vulci it is) has a clumsier vigour and is less self-
effacingly Greek: its favourite shapes are calyx-krater and stamnos. In the
later fourth century both these schools add to their repertory scenes from
the Etruscan netherworld with demons hideous or grotesque. The third
main division of later Etruscan, which occurs in Northern Etruria, is more
conventional in its themes. This is the school which, rightly or wrongly
has been called in its first phase the school of Clusium, in its second of
Volterra. At the beginning there seems to be a connection with Faliscan,
but it soon goes its own way. Its period is from the third quarter of the
fourth century to the first quarter of the third. A characteristic of this
school is the form of the palmette, in which the leaves have decayed into
a simple fringe. The drawing of figures is at first weak, but modest; then,
as the relief line is forgotten, the painters tend to use broader brush strokes,
hatching and shading. These devices of free painting are known in the late
school of Vulci – the purer Faliscan school was more resistant – but the
Volterrans exploited them more boldly. The typical shapes in the early
phase are the cup, the head-kantharos (a sort of Toby jug) and the askos
in the form of a duck; and in the later phase a high-necked kind of column-
krater. these kraters are notable for the large heads painted on them,
especially cowled women in three-quarter view and profiles sketched in
clever caricature. Ordinary profile heads of women in a frame of spiral

hooks decorate many of the miserable Genucilia dishes and plates, one of the later red-figure groups of Caere and the Faliscan district, where they are common in the second half of the fourth century. There is also in the fourth century a reversion to a sort of black-figure, especially in the chain of scraggy palmettes and flowers drawn in silhouette. These simpler techniques are most often used on smallish pots, such as the particularly Etruscan beaked oinochoe, a narrow jug with high neck that ends in a long scoop.

Though the Etruscan versions of red-figure were made for fully two centuries, the output was not very great. Vulci appears to have been the first place of manufacture, and after it Falerii and Volterra. Caere and Tarquinia, more open to Greek trade and taste, did not fancy the local product as long as there was anything better, though Caere at least seems to have been prolific in the later fourth century. At its best Etruscan red-figure is provincial with the merits of good provincial art and while not aspiring to the magnificence that spoils much South Italian, takes an interest in the innovations of free painting. There was a little export beyond Etruscan lands to coastal settlements in the western Mediterranean (Sicily excluded).

SOUTH ITALY

Since the first big finds of painted Greek pottery were made in Campania and the Basilicata, most of the older museums have a surfeit of the South Italian version of red-figure. Its availability, the many theatrical scenes it exhibits, and perhaps their stronger stomachs made it popular with an earlier generation of scholars. Now it is neglected, except by a few specialists.

The Greek cities along the coasts of Sicily and South Italy had for up to three hundred years regularly imported their better painted pottery, first from Corinth and then from Athens. But in the middle and later fifth century a few craftsmen, presumably (except in the Owl-Pillar workshop) trained immigrants from Athens, began to manufacture red-figure ware in South Italy and Sicily. Their products are known generically as South Italian (or Italiot) since, though in Greek history the two regions were distinct, the name South Italian was fortunately too firmly established to be changed when the Sicilian workshops were recognized. Perhaps less fortunate is the established division, based on places of finding, into regional schools – Apulian, Lucanian, Campanian and Paestan (to which Sicilian has now been added): painters seem to have moved about much more freely here than in other parts of the Greek world, so that differences between schools are often blurred. Apulian, the largest and most influential grouping, has some unity and so for a time has its provincial neighbour Lucanian: but Sicilian,

Campanian and Paestan, if a fresh start was made, might be lumped together or divided in some other way. A more serious trouble is the unsteady or sluggish development of personal styles, so that it is sometimes difficult to determine the relationship of one painter to another. New finds are still liable to upset some currently accepted propositions.

The first venture, apparently in Campania, is the so-called *Owl-Pillar group*, which apes Attic of the second and third quarters of the fifth century, though with a strong Etruscan flavour. The commonest shape is the neck-amphora, decorated with a couple of figures on each side. These figures are robustly ill-proportioned, their feet often sink into the frame below the picture, and their interpretation is sometimes curious or obscure. The technique is adequate, and the style though clumsy is clean. Its ingenuous assurance recalls good peasant craftsmanship. The Owl-Pillar workshop, which (like the Campanian black-figure of its time) is perhaps better classed with Etruscan than Greek, was short-lived and had no following or influence.

More successful were two establishments on the southern coast of Italy, the progenitors one of the Lucanian and the other of the Apulian school, and formerly designated as group A and group B of Early South Italian. Early Lucanian (Plate 52B), domiciled – so finds suggest – somewhere west of Tarentum, began about 440 BC, the time when the Athenians colonized Thurii, and perhaps the two events are connected. Early Apulian (Plate 52A), which became much more important, appeared in the 420s and probably had its home in Tarentum, the principal city of south-eastern Italy. Early Sicilian starts a little later, but before the end of the fifth century, and on a smaller scale. These three schools were based, independently of each other, on Attic models and their resemblances in style to particular Attic workshops make it probable that the founders of the new schools had trained in those workshops. Sicilian, being geographically remote, remained apart from the other two, but Lucanian was affected by Apulian; and all diverged from Attic. The painters, few and often isolated, were able to indulge personal mannerisms, which their pupils copied; here, in contrast to Athens, there was not a vigorous and critical standard. Even so, local manufacture increased, whether this was an effect or a cause of diminishing Attic imports, and by the 370s (when the Early stage of South Italian ends) four or five regional schools are recognized. The largest, showiest and most influential is Apulian (Plate 53). Lucanian (Plate 54) was now becoming provincial. As for Sicily, some enterprising painters left about this time to set up workshops in Campania and Paestum; of the three schools, which keep up some connection with each other, Campanian (Plate 55A) is the most varied and prolific, Paestan (Plate 55B) more steadily compact and Sicilian – the smallest – shows greater originality towards its end. South Italian red-figure outlived Attic and a few workshops may have survived into the early years of the third century.

Figure 35   Apulian Rf volute-krater.
Detail of neck: scale *c.* 1:2. By the Darius painter, *c.* 330 BC.
Black areas represent white paint.

It is not easy to describe in words the peculiarities of South Italian red-figure. The technical competence of the best work is equal to Attic, of the poor work generally inferior: the paint, for example, tends to flake away or – in Campanian – to blister. The fired clay varies in colour and texture. Sometimes it looks like Attic; more often it is duller or paler, ranging as far as a yellow which may be mistaken for Corinthian; and in some Campanian examples it is chocolate. But where the colour is far from the Attic standard, the visible surfaces are usually improved by a reddish wash. The paint often appears muddy or greenish, with a sheen that suggests a metallic harshness rather than the glassy transparence of Attic.

The style, starting as second-rate Attic, soon takes its own road or rut. The ordinary work becomes monotonous and impoverished, and in the fourth century repeatedly lapses towards barbarity. Pretentious pieces attain a self-conscious and uncomfortable classicism, often admirable in detail but heavy or stupid in composition. the more original essays in parody or the subhuman are much happier. The red-figure of South Italy is often as accomplished, rarely as successful as that of Athens, where even in the fourth century the classical tradition was supply tenacious. There was not the same restraint on South Italian painters, who continued practices considered freakish by the Athenians and also were more susceptible to the novelties of free painting. In Attic vase-painting towards the middle and again around the end of the fifth century there was a limited vogue for grandiose compositions where depth is indicated by tiering and the remoter – that is higher – figures may be partly concealed by conventional hillocks: this device remained acceptable in South Italy. A bolder perspective is freely used in architecture (especially for ornate structures viewed obliquely from below) and even in floral ornament (Figure 35); and, as the style progresses, forms – except those of the female body – are sometimes modelled by shading and even highlights. Minor aids that become popular are the lines of white dots on which figures stand and the filling ornament – rosettes, bunches of grapes 'and the like – which bestrew the field. Judged by Attic standards – and their work shows a recurrent though remote awareness of Attic standards – the South Italians are heavy or vulgar or dull.

The stock subjects are Dionysiac incidents and increasingly Eros attending women. The perfunctory draped youths are of course normal on the backs of bell-kraters. On more ambitious pieces mythology is illustrated, and there is a persistent taste for tragic scenes, chosen perhaps from a love less of the theatre than of the theatrical. More lively are the so-called Phlyax vases (Plate 55B), with their stubby burlesque actors and stage scenery: the South Italian series begins about 400 BC, apparently developing an experiment made in Athens where similar figures occur very rarely but earlier. From the mid-fourth century on female heads embowered in gross palmettes too often bedizen small pots or in more careful settings the necks of large ones.

The early shapes come from the Attic repertory; but some flourish in South Italy when discarded in Athens, some develop on their own, and there are a few local or native inventions. The bell-krater remains the commonest of the larger shapes. The column-krater is restricted to the Apulian and Lucanian schools, which also exploit the volute-krater for their ornate efforts. The neck-amphora, rare in late Attic, continues popular in Campania and Paestum; and in Campania a new variety – the bail-amphora – substituted an arched handle across the lip. The pelike is mainly Apulian and Lucanian. Hydria and oinochoai are fairly numerous. The so-called nestoris, a jar with high, knobbed handles above ordinary side handles, is characteristic of Lucanian. Smaller vases multiply in the fourth century; notable are the askos (shaped rather like a toy duck), the squat lekythos, the handleless bottle and a clumsy kantharos. The cup is rare, but not the kotyle. A curious speciality of later Apulian and Campanian is the fish-plate, a large saucer with a hollow in the middle and a turned-down rim: it comes from Attic, though there the decoration with edible fishes is not usual. In general the shapes gradually become longer and more angular, and towards the end the ornatest of them are liable to break out into plastic ornament.

On some Apulian works of the second quarter of the fourth century subsidiary ornaments or even figures are not reserved, but painted in colour on the dark ground. This technique becomes commoner in later South Italian red-figure, and is also extended to be the sole decoration of the so-called Gnathian ware (Plate 56B), which begins around 360 BC and lasts for perhaps a hundred years. The Gnathian formula, usually consisting of simple decoration and applied to small pots, remained most popular in Apulia but was adopted in other regions too.

Although so many South Italian pots survive, very often complete, the records of finding and of context are not yet sufficient, except for Sicilian from around 340 BC. For the rest we still have to rely on stylistic criteria – sequences within schools, connections of one school with another and parallels with Attic. This last criterion, on which our absolute dating depends, has the extra hazard that the intermittent Atticisms in South Italian may well be retarded. The early stage is safe enough, but after that the accepted chronology could prove too high.

The South Italian workshops produced mainly for their local markets, and indeed the definition of the local schools depends partly on distribution. Elsewhere a little export has been noticed along the Mediterranean fringes of France and Spain and at coastal sites in Albania and Dalmatia, and a few Sicilian pieces have turned up at Carthage and curiously some Apulian ones at Sidon. Further, during the fourth century Campanian and, perhaps indirectly, Apulian influences are evident in Etruria, and in Spain some ornaments of the native Iberian pottery seem to come from South Italian.

Apulian

The founders of the Early Apulian school settled in the 420s at Tarentum, to judge by the distribution of their products, the importance of that city, and the wasters (admittedly of later date) that have been found there. They started with a version of Attic of the Polygnotan school and followed Attic developments closely for the first generation, then intermittently. But they quickly formed a standard of their own, classical and grandiose; individual figures are well drawn in statuesque poses, but the composition is tiresomely clumsy. This inability to compose large groups continues throughout Apulian, so that its more ambitious pieces look better in fragments than complete. Of the pioneers the Sisyphus painter (Plate 52A), active through the last quarter of the fifth century, was a decisive personality: the two classes of the subsequent Apulian school, the Ornate and the Plain, both descend from him. His competent figures have a studied nobility, and on large volute-kraters pose self-sufficiently in two or three registers. The successors of the Sisyphus painter specialize as Ornate or Plain painters, but do not reach his level.

For the Plain manner bell-krater, column-krater, amphora, pelike and of course smaller shapes were preferred. The normal repertory of subjects is limited – Dionysiac groups or women at their toilet (some-times attended by Eros), and on the backs of kraters the familiar young men in cloaks. Towards the middle of the fourth century this Plain manner began to merge with the Ornate, adopting its richer colouring and ornament; and though some of the old austerity persisted for a time on column-krater and pelike, the term 'Plain' ceases to have much meaning.

The Ornate manner, exhibited first on such large pots as volute-krater, amphora and hydria, reaches its full bloom after the middle of the fourth century. An earlier example is shown on Plate 53. For ambitious pieces the regular subjects are scenes from mythology, notably that of tragedy, and gatherings around a funerary shrine, often one on the front and the other on the back of the pot; the cast is deployed at as many as three levels round the central feature, and vacant spaces are filled with sashes, flowers or rosettes. The abundant subsidiary decoration is notable for the rank vegetable ornament, which is developed with a metallic crispness and displays flowers in three-quarter view – a trick found very rarely (though earlier) in Attic; and there are even meanders modelled by shading. White and yellow – sometimes one denoting marble and the other metal – had been growing popular since the second quarter of the fourth century. In the fully Ornate style they, and purple, are used generously and broadly, and sometimes applied over the dark paint: the effect is gaudily over-whelming in spite of the fluent competence of the draughtsmanship. On lesser works, particularly after the decline of the Plain manner, the subjects are more trivial and the style often more effeminate, and in the second half of the fourth century there is a glut of small vases with palmettes and large female heads. The style, simpler and more negligent than that of the more important productions, is generally of a dreary uniformity. The output was correspondingly immense.

The Apulian school lasted perhaps into the first years of the third century. Its headquarters probably remained at Tarentum; but there may have been workshops in some of the native towns, for instance at Canosa, seventy-five miles to the north-west. There was some export to other parts of South Italy, to Sicily and to the Dalmatian coast. Apulian influence became strong in Lucanian, and both Campanian and Paestan had a late Apulianizing phase. Canosa ware, it seems clear, is derived from Late Apulian.

Lucanian

Lucanian, though the oldest, is the worst of the four South Italian schools. It begins as a respectable second-rate offshoot of Attic – of the school of

Polygnotus and the followers of the Achilles painter – but with more stiffness and angularity in draughtsmanship and less expression (Plate 52B). Contact with Athens is weaker than in Early Apulian and the painters, isolated and unaspiring, grow mannered and provincial. The ideal nobility of Attic eludes this school, but it is sometimes amusing in conscious or unconscious parody. Subjects and types are monotonous. On bell-kraters, the commonest shape, the stock formula for the front is a three-figure group – especially women pursued or satyrs with maenads – and for the back two or three draped youths. During the fourth century Lucanian tags more or less wearily behind Apulian till in the third quarter a stronger dose of that style is injected by the Primato painter (Plate 54), who had been trained in one of its Ornate workshops, and by the Roccanova painter, who had studied what was then its Plain manner. But they in turn succumb to the environment, and the style of their successors can at last hardly be described as Greek. Characteristic of developed Lucanian, apart from clumsy distortions and simplifications of Apulian, are a doubled dark stripe down women's skirts, palmettes with serrated edges, Z pattern, and an old-fashioned taste for thick rays. Next to the bell-krater the hydria has some importance; and there is the nestoris, an unpleasant shape of native Messapian origin but in red-figure almost confined to Lucanian. The school shambles to its end rather before 300 BC.

It is likely that at first the workshops were in some Greek city on the southern coast of Lucania, Thurii for instance or Heraclea, though a kiln used by the principal workshop of the early fourth century has been unearthed at Metapontum. Later, according to the distribution of the finds, they shifted into the barbarian interior, to Armento and perhaps Anzi and other towns. In the earliest generation there is export to Apulia and even influence there, but by 380 BC both have become negligible.

Sicilian

In eastern Sicily, so it appears from the presence and absence of finds there and in Campania, a local manufacture of red-figure began near the end of the fifth century. Initially it followed Attic models of the time, particularly of the style of the Pothos painter (a rather florid and second-rate artist), and then continued on its own. Though in the 370s leading painters of this small school moved off to Campania and Paestum, a few lesser colleagues continued at work in Sicily. Then around 340 BC, presumably as a consequence of the prosperity imposed by Timoleon, the output of red-figure pottery increased and for some forty years several workshops were active, influenced by Campanian models and perhaps immigrants and also showing acquaintance with Apulian, but independent enough to develop (especially in the Lipari group) an unusually polychrome technique.

The style of Early Sicilian, the product perhaps of only one workshop, is floridly tame. In subjects there is a preference for draped women and satyrs; and the favourite shapes are bell-krater and calyx-krater, but amphorae are not yet known. The middle period, between 370 and 340 BC, is still obscure, but later workshops show a more sensuous taste. Their commonest subjects are now half-naked women, indolently posed and often inspected by an effeminate Eros, and – even more than in other South Italian schools – solitary female heads; there are also some Dionysiac and even a few phlyax scenes. Composition is simple. Among frequent shapes are the krater of the calyx (but not the bell) variety, the skyphoid pyxis (like a kotyle with a lid) and the bottle. More remarkable is the trend to polychromy; to the traditional white and yellow are added, first, various gradations of red, then blue, and towards the end green, pink and mauve as well, so that if it was not for the dark background the more colourful pieces would not be recognized as red-figure. From here it was a logical step to the more fully pictorial style of Centuripae ware.

Campanian

After the false start of the Owl-Pillar group no red-figure was made in Campania till the 370s, when followers of the Dirce painter and perhaps that painter himself moved across from Sicily. Campania was mixed in its population and by now under Samnite rule, but affluent enough to appreciate Greek civilization, and the venture flourished. By the 350s the new Campanian school had three branches, located – according to distribution – one at Greek Cumae and one or perhaps two at Italian Capua. Though there continued to be relations between these branches, their development differed. In particular, Apulian influence was much stronger at Cumae, where it looks as if one or two of the earlier painters had trained in Apulia; and one of the Capuan painters may have worked at Paestum and certainly left his mark on its later style. By the end of the fourth century all branches of Campanian were in decay and the school petered out around 300 BC.

The quality of Campanian is rather provincial but has, compared with Apulian and Lucanian, the merit of modesty. There is great play – especially at Cumae – with white and yellow both on figures and to model floral ornament, which is usually stiff and often unduly straight. Palmettes tend to hatched stems or white-rimmed leaves. Women, whose flesh is often white (in contrast to Apulian practice), may have capes fastened at the neck. Soldiers sometimes wear armour of an Oscan type (Plate 55A). The shapes, mostly smallish, include bell-krater, neck-amophra, the peculiar bail-amphora with its one handle arched across the mouth, hydria, kotyle and squat lekythos.

Figure 36 Paestan Rf bell-krater.
Handle ornament. Later 4th century BC.

Paestan

Paestum, another Greek city under Italian rule, lies at the north-west corner of Lucanian territory but has better access to Campania. It too has been given its red-figure school. The founder, Asteas, whose activity began in the 360s, came from an Early Campanian (and ultimately Sicilian) workshop and, if he had not signed some of his works, perhaps Paestan would now be counted as another branch of Campanian. His personal style has a stodgy dignity with its solid figures and compact but heavy composition – for this Plate 55B is not a good example – and his followers remembered his style though they coarsened it. Other late Paestans, from about 330 BC on, turned to Campanian for their models; and before the end, which came about the end of the fourth century, there was much imitation of decadent Apulian.

The school of Paestum, small and concentrated, has till the last quarter of the fourth century an unusual unity. The typical product is the bell-krater, from the time of Asteas straight-sided and decorated with a square picture framed at the sides by a reserved line or the characteristic Paestan volute and palmettes (Figure 36). Dionysiac subjects are popular, and there are showier scenes from Phlyax plays and mythology: the back normally carries a couple of cloaked youths. Drapery often has the so-called embattled border, a row of squares or dots that follow an edge. There is no Ornate manner, though the more elaborate pictures are richly coloured. Besides the bell-krater the main shapes are neck-amphora, hydria and squat lekythos.

Gnathian

Gnathian, which may eventually have been made at Gnathia as well as other places, is a style which for its decoration uses applied colour on a dark ground. The technique had occurred intermittently in one Greek school or another since the late eighth century, but here the main impulse probably came from its subsidiary employment in Ornate Apulian red-figure, which by the second quarter of the fourth century was extravagant with white and yellow colour, not only to embellish its red figures, but also on some elaborate pieces for adding laurel wreaths or, later, heads and foliage on lip or neck. It was an easy step to make this secondary decoration in added colour the sole decoration of smaller pots.

Besides white and yellow there is some purple, and in ambitious early work other colours may appear. Incision is common at first, especially for stems of leaves and, though soon given up in Apulian, persists in Campanian and one of the Etruscan branches. Typical ornaments are wreaths and scrolls of ivy and of vine, horizontal or vertical, bands of laurel, necklaces and ribbons. More pretentious are the female head, the full figure of a woman or Eros, an actor's mask, and as fillers musical instruments, votive tablets, birds and various properties. The decoration is spread often over much and sometimes over all of the available surface. Some early works in Gnathian technique, for instance those of the Konnakis painter, display more important scenes or studies of human figures, but stylistically they are better reckoned with red-figure. The Gnathian style proper (Plate 56B), though it occasionally employs advanced tricks of shading, is deliberately restricted in scope. Its ideal was decorative prettiness, and its course inevitably downhill.

The shapes, many and varied, come mostly from the red-figure tradition of South Italy, but tend to be more elegant: they have some development of their own. Among them are kraters (especially the bell-krater), pelike, oinochoai of several types and sizes, kotyle, kantharos, squat lekythos, a still squatter lekythos, bottle, and small bowls and cups. Ribbing of the body becomes common in the last quarter of the fourth century. A narrowish reserved band is usual near the junction of body and foot.

Gnathian pots are very numerous, especially in the middle phase, and some have useful contexts. Comparison of shapes shows that the style was established by the 360s. It was probably over by the 270s though outlying workshops may have lasted another generation. Early connections with Apulian red-figure argue that Gnathian began in Apulia, presumably – since it was then the dominant city of the region – at Tarentum. But to judge by wasters at Metapontum and by differences in clay and sometimes differences in style, manufacture was diffused over Apulia and as far as Paestum and Campania, where the dark paint and the white are duller and ribbed decoration was more popular. In Sicily in the late fourth and early third centuries a local variety is distinguished by its use of blue and fondness for vine sprays. Related wares, using white or yellow on a dark ground, appear in Latium and Etruria, which had also its own tradition of painting in added colour. Gnathian is most frequent in Apulia, but is found throughout Greek Italy and Sicily, in Etruscan and Latin lands, and even in the Mediterranean settlements of France and Spain. In the eastern half of the ancient world it seems to be very rare in Greece, but not uncommon in Cyrenaica, Alexandria and perhaps Rhodes.

CHAPTER VI

HELLENISTIC POTTERY WITH PAINTED DECORATION

———— •◆• ————

INTRODUCTION

By the late fourth century the red-figure style was dead or dying, and with it ended the main tradition of Greek vase-painting. In the period that followed, the ordinary pottery with painted decoration was for the most part content with a few simple ornaments, simply arranged and drawn either in light paint on a dark ground or in dark paint on a light ground. Whatever the reason, painted decoration was no longer important, and even the more numerous and often more elaborate wares that have designs in relief or impressed are rarely original works of art. The Hellenstic standard of pottery was set by metalwork.

The favourite ornaments of Hellenistic vase-painting are wreaths and festoons of ivy and laurel (in which are included myrtle and olive if they can be distinguished) and also vine. These are supplemented by a few abstract patterns, dolphins and such oddments as round garlands (as on Figure 37), ribbons and musical instruments. It is a limited repertory, taken mostly from established convention, and the forms have no positive development. The effect too is trivial. The decoration appears no longer to be a considered part of the finished pot, but rather to be applied to its surface, as very obviously in the festoon of ivy of Plate 56A. The new vase-painting needed neither the skill nor the imagination of an artist.

The *dark-ground* class divides into two principal schools, West Slope ware in Greece and Gnathian in Italy. Each spawned local varieties. Gnathian (Plate 56B and pp. 191–2), established by the middle of the fourth century, is a byproduct of Apulian red-figure and tends to a similar extravagance. This confectioner's style was arguably extinct by the middle of the third century. The West Slope school (Plate 56A) was more restrained and sturdy. It appears in Athens about 300 BC as a humble successor of Attic red-figure, and persisted in much of the Greek East till the second or even the first century BC.

In the *light-ground* class, though hardly of it, are the veteran Panathenaic amphorae, which till the late second century or even longer exhibit on one side a current interpretation of the Archaic style and on the other modern anatomical drawing painfully executed in the black-figure technique. This black-figure manner was during the third century echoed in Rhodes and on some of the Hadra hydriai of Crete. But the light-ground class proper consists of various groups of pottery decorated with the common Hellenistic ornaments in a brown to blackish paint on a white or pale slip or surface. The most widespread group – east of the Adriatic – is that of the Lagynoi (Figure 37), squat jugs with tall thin necks and a modicum of ornament: their home is uncertain, their date probably from the late third to the middle of the first century BC. More imposing are the Hadra hydriai of Crete, with which a modest Ukrainian group has some affinity. In Rhodes, where a provincial light-ground (though unslipped) ware had survived in the Classical period, a few local pots have a sometimes delusively Hellenistic look. Cyprus pursued its own deviations, yielding reluctantly to the fashions of the times; and central Anatolia had its 'Galatian' ware, with a desiccated version of the familiar flora. In Italy the native tradition of Apulia incorporated contemporary motifs in its spidery late style. Across the sea Carthage, Hellenistic though not Greek, produced modish oinochoai that have a charmingly casual air, and in eastern Spain the decoration of some Iberian pottery would not have looked strange to Greek visitors. In general the light-ground method belongs to the fringes and backwaters of the Hellenistic world, in metropolitan Greece the taste for a dark ground was ingrained.

Hellenistic pottery has been neglected, and deservedly, though now some canny students are sorting it out. The dated Panathenaic amphorae are occasionally useful by way of comparison for the chronology of higher arts. But there were now few intrinsic merits in the painting of pottery, and as time went on production became sparser and feebler. None of the groups mentioned outlasted at latest the first century BC. But the technical methods of this vase-painting were invitingly easy and the stock of conventional motifs simple enough, so that unpretentious essays in dark on light or light on dark decoration were liable to recur in one place or another throughout antiquity, as for example on some poor Athenian bowls of the third century AD and the Yorkshire Crambeck ware of the late fourth.

Hellenistic shapes range from the clumsy to the elegant. The general tendency of careful pieces is to flowing curves and arbitrary angles. There is much more imitation of metal than in the past, and plastic ornament is applied more freely. Since the manufacture of painted pottery, though small, was less concentrated than in the preceding centuries, variation in clay is more marked. The paint is less regularly black and shiny on the dark-ground ware, and on the light-ground is more often streaky and dilute.

Besides these useful wares there are a few Hellenistic groups of *polychrome* pots. At various times since the end of the Geometric period some pottery intended for funerals had been painted with colours that did not and did not need to wear. Examples have already been mentioned in the early Orientalizing of Crete (p. 135) and in Protoattic of the third quarter of the seventh century (p. 69), and there are the sometimes more durably coloured Attic white lekythoi. In the Hellenistic groups the normal procedure was to coat a fired pot with a chalky white solution and to paint on it in tempera. Largish hydriai and amphorae decorated with heavy coloured festoons are known in the Hadra ware of Alexandria and its more modest relative in Rhodes; a few similar urns have come to light elsewhere, perhaps imported. Figures are more usual in the West – at Canosa in Apulia, where their flat treatment recalls the red-figure tradition, and at Centuripae in Sicily, where the style exploits the illusionist tricks of free painting. But these curiosities, which are mostly of the third century, can hardly be reckoned as vase-painting. That art was dead.

WEST SLOPE WARE

West Slope ware, which takes its name from a site facing the Acropolis at Athens, may be defined as pottery made during the Hellenistic period east of the Adriatic and decorated with simple ornaments painted in white and yellow over a dark ground. Painting in colour over a dark ground had been tested in both early and late red-figure, but a more important precedent are the wreaths and festoons of added white and yellow (or gold) that before the end of the fifth century sometimes encircle the field inside cups or modestly embellish the necks of hydriai and other pots. Though this last class survives into the third century and merges into the West Slope style, there is a distinction between them. In one the ornament is subsidiary, in the other it occupies a principal place.

The character of the West Slope style is exhibited most clearly on its amphorae, such as that of Plate 56A. The decoration is limited to the upper part of the pot, and other shapes have similar restrictions. The repertory of ornament is small and impoverished. Of naturalistic patterns the favourites are ivy and hanging buds, and there are also laurel and vine, necklaces with pendants, and the row of spiral hooks. The stock abstract patterns are chequers, alternately plain and coloured, and boxed rectangles; later there appear cross-hatched rectangles. A rosette or rough star is usual in the centre of bowls and other open pots. Animal and human figures are rare, except for dolphins and these hardly rank as more than curvilinear ornaments. A few early pots include in their decoration the painted names of deities. The style degenerates rather than develops, with at Athens a growing preference for abstract ornaments; the drawing steadily coarsens and is supplemented and increasingly replaced by incision.

Though some kantharoi have the excessive refinement of the more elaborate black-painted ware, the typical West Slope shapes are uncompromisingly solid. They include the squat neck-amphora with twisted handles, kantharoi (some resembling the Cabiran type), saucer, plate, small bowls or cups of various kinds, lids, kraters, and oinochoai with broad or narrow neck. There is some use of plastic ornament – for instance, the heads at the base of the handles on Plate 56A; and sometimes a band of moulding is borrowed or the lower part of the body is ribbed or knobbed. In general the shapes grow clumsier and worse proportioned. The amphora, for example, starts with a cylindrical neck and rounded shoulder: that of Plate 56A, of the first half of the second century, has an angular shoulder and flaring neck.

The clay varies from place to place, but is rarely as fine as in red-figure pottery. The dark paint is from the first duller and muddier, and to these faults are added streaky application and careless firing. The thick yellow often stands out in relief. The white, thick or thin, is flush. At first white is subordinate to yellow, but gradually it becomes at least as important.

At Athens West Slope ware appeared about 300 BC. The formula was easy and very soon imitations were being produced in other places too. These local versions vary in standard and to some degree in style (if the term may be so debased). So far only the schools of Athens, Corinth, Pergamum and Crete (or perhaps more specifically Cnossus) have been studied in any detail, though certainly they were not the only ones. In general development was similar, towards clumsier ornaments and greater use of incision; but in the mid-second century Pergamene began to diverge with an increasing preference for a red surface and wholly incised decoration, so evolving into Sigillata. Elsewhere, except where destruction occurred (as at Corinth in 146 BC), the West Slope style seems to have survived till the middle or third quarter of the first century BC. Though nowhere very frequent, West Slope pottery is found throughout the Greek East. There was some export of Attic and of Pergamene (this particularly to the Pontic settlements), but probably local needs were more often supplied locally.

THE LAGYNOS GROUP

The most widespread and, not only for that reason, the most characteristic of the Hellenistic wares with decoration on a light ground is the Lagynos group, named after its favourite small jug (though such jugs occur also in dark-ground and relief-wares). The normal shape and system of decoration is shown in Figure 37. The ornaments, restricted to the shoulder, are sometimes continuous – ivy, laurel or less often festoons looped across the field – and sometimes such isolated objects as wreaths, musical instruments, lagynoi, dolphins and even fighting cocks. Occasionally some convivial word is added as a motto. The style is hasty but adequate; sometimes by streaky application of the paint it seems to hint at modelling.

Besides lagynoi there are also thymiateria with cloche lids, as well as plates and cups, small oinochoai and even column-kraters. The clay, often

Figure 37 Light-ground lagynos.
Ht 19 cm. Later 2nd or early 1st century BC.

micaceous, is moderately fine and in colour varies from light-brown to reddish. The slip is normally hard and white. The paint is sometimes fairly black, but more often diluted to brown and even yellow-brown. There is some sheen. The wall of the pot is often very thin. Fragments of lagynoi are sometimes mistaken for Chiot of the sixth century.

The Lagynos group is thought to continue, but not develop, from the mid-second till some time in the first century BC. Though the style is generally uniform, the clay is said to vary significantly. Finds occur in Greek lands east of the Adriatic, but principally in Western Asia Minor, Delos, Alexandria and the Crimea. So the main factories are likely to have been in or near Ionia.

HADRA WARE

The name Hadra was given to two schools of hydriai which came to light in the Hadra and other cemeteries of Alexandria, where they were used to contain ashes. One school is light-ground in the normal way, the other has polychrome decoration on a white ground. For the light-ground ware the name Hadra is now established firmly, but to avoid confusion 'Alexandrine' would be better for the polychrome ware.

Hadra ware, that is the light-ground ware, is a product of Central Crete. It used to be thought because of the finds there that it was made in Alexandria; but painters of Hadra pots also painted West Slope pots of what is evidently the Cretan school, analysis of clay suits Crete, the dropped bottom of many of the big hydriai is a peculiarly Cretan trait, and smaller pots of Hadra style are frequent in Crete but not elsewhere.

The common shapes are hydria, large or small, krater, oinochoe and bowl. Of these the large hydria is the most important, a slimmish pot around 40 cm high with neck more or less distinct from the body, rounded shoulder and splaying foot, within which the bottom is set very low. The decoration, in general sober and at its best neat, is normally in two minor fields on the neck and shoulder and in a major field (interrupted by the handles) at the top of the belly; the rest of the body is reserved; the foot is dark. The commonest ornaments are laurel and ivy wreaths, and there are also volutes, scrolls, wilting palmettes, garlands, dolphins, long-necked birds and simple abstract patterns. Often a rosette is inserted in the middle of foliage on the neck and on the body the front field is bounded by narrow panels with rough cross-hatching or even opposed triangles. Occasionally this field contains figures – confronting animals or monsters – or such ambitious scenes as Erotes hunting, Nike between tripods, and a race in armour. For these figures the more careful and probably earlier pieces use a niggling black-figure technique, presumably emulating Panathenaic amphorae – and indeed one figured hydria, so an inscription on it says, was painted by Python 'for the games'; there is also the lazy substitution of painted white lines for incised detail; and eventually simple silhouette was thought sufficient. The ornaments generally follow Hellenistic fashions in the minor arts, so far as these can be discerned in the progressive decay of the style. Even so, ornaments as well as figures allow individual painters to be recognized.

The dating of this Hadra ware is fairly clear. Correlation of ornaments with those in other arts offers a general framework; two fixed points have been found in the destruction of the Cretan cities of Lyttos in 220 and Apollonia in 171 BC; and some thirty of the hydriai used for burials in Alexandria are inscribed in ink not only with the name of the dead but also the day, month and regnal year of the reigning Ptolemy and, though the particular Ptolemy is not specified, the likely range is from 269 to 197 BC. From all this it appears that Hadra ware had hardly begun before the second quarter of the third century, was at its most flourishing towards the end of that century and at the beginning of the next (though output never rivalled that of West Slope), and in an attenuated form lingered on into the first century BC. Export was only of the big hydriai and its pattern is curious. Finds have been numerous in Alexandria, all from cemeteries, but elsewhere are very rare, if widespread – in Athens, Eretria, Thera, Rhodes, Cyprus and Ukraine, though some of these could be local imitations. Hadra clay, which is fairly fine, is light-brown to reddish. The dark paint varies from brown to black according to its thickness. A little white is used to pick out details.

The polychrome 'Hadra' ware found at Alexandria is beyond reasonable doubt Alexandrine. Its only shape, the hydria, resembles and presumably copies the Cretan form, though the foot may be fancier; but the coarse red clay matches Egyptian and the chalky white coating (daubed on when the pot was already fired) was too friable to encourage export. The decoration, done in tempera, consists usually of thick festoons slung across neck or belly. Sometimes the belly displays insignia of sex, arms for the man and articles of toilet for the woman. The painting is rather crude, except for a skilfully executed head of Medusa. The colours, which are not fast, are principally reds and blues and also yellow and green, besides of course brown and black. There is one curious hybrid, a normal light-ground hydria converted by a white coat into an Alexandrine. Besides showing that the white-ground painters were aware of the Cretan products this gives a synchronism, but the general dating of the group is insecure, though one may suppose it belongs to the third and early second centuries. A parallel group has turned up in cemeteries on Rhodes, locally made (as clay analysis confirms) and rather less adventurous in decoration, which very rarely is more than floral. Contexts date it to the third and first half of the second century, but it is not clear whether the Alexandrine or the Rhodian series starts the earlier. A few other polychrome hydriai, whether imported or home-made, have been recorded from Thera, Tanagra, Myrina and Ukraine.

CANOSA WARE

Canosa (or Canusium) in northern Apulia has given its name to a well-known group of pots which also displays decoration in colours put on after firing. Here the favourite motifs of the vase-painter were human and animal figures, especially winged or wingless horses, and vegetable patterns are subordinate. Often there are rosettes as filling ornaments in the field. Outlines are drawn in dark paint and filled – at least sometimes – with a yellowish wash; inner detail is done partly by a few dark lines, partly by modest touches of colour. The white background is usually painted over in pink or blue. The style, flat and without modelling, resembles red-figure in its linear draughtmanship and some of its motifs. It develops out of the later Apulian school, and some therefore call it Apulian Polychrome.

The best Canosa vase-painting has a decent charm. This is more than can be said of the shapes. The *chef d'œuvre* is the old Daunian askos, now crowded with figurines and other plastic ornaments, between which there is sometimes space for a little quiet vase-painting. Other, less eruptive, shapes are oinochoe with long, slender neck, and kantharos. The clay is fairly fine and light-brown. The white slip, added after firing, does not always reach to the base of the pot. The colours used are yellow, pink, red and blue.

The connection with red-figure and some vague contexts suggest that this group of pots begins in the very late fourth and perhaps lasts into the second century. They are found throughout Apulia. A few pieces in the same or a very similar style come from Cumae.

CENTURIPAE WARE

Centuripae, a native town in the interior of Sicily, remained independent of the Greeks politically, but admitted their culture. Indeed the polychrome pottery that from time to time is found in its graves offers what in their say are the most accomplished of Greek vase-paintings or, to be more exact, paintings on vases. The favourite shape is a sort of pyxis or bell-krater with high lid and pedestal but no handles. On the deep field of the bell large figures, mostly women at bridal tasks, are spaced in studied poses that usually avoid fully frontal or fully profile views. The figures are modelled by shading and highlights, the colours simulate nature. The background is a flat pink or, on some early pieces, black. The style appears familiar from wall-paintings at Pompeii and elsewhere.

The shapes show a heavy good taste in profiles and even in the plastic ornament which, genteelly florid, on some pots of this group leaves no space for painted decoration. Besides the pyxis a lidded lekanis and a lebes gamikos are fairly frequent. These are all big pots, not intended for ordinary use; for sometimes the lid is fired in one piece with its pot and the colours are very friable. The clay, red to brown, is not fine and, after firing, a white undercoat was applied to take the paint. At the beginning the figures were first outlined in black and then filled in from a wide choice of colours – yellows, browns, reds, blues and black; but fairly soon the technique became more pictorial with fine brushwork and gradation of colour.

This group of pots was probably made at or near Centuripae, since they have been found only there and at Morgantina and are unhandy to transport. They begin probably early in the third century, since fragments have been found at Morgantina in a deposit of the fourth and third centuries and style and shape suggest a connection with Sicilian red-figure (and particularly the Lipari painter). How long they were made has not been determined, though it is unlikely that so compact a group flourished for more than a generation or two. The resemblances to Pompeian and other murals of late Hellenstic or Roman date may be deceptive; these often follow older models.

CHAPTER VII

BLACK-PAINTED
AND RELIEF WARES

——— ·◆· ———

GENERAL COMMENTS

The pottery described in the preceding chapters is characterized by its painted decoration. At the same time there was also much pottery of comparable quality which was simply covered with the standard dark paint. Such pottery has little artistic merit till near the middle of the sixth century, when Attic workshops were refining their standards of shape, paint and finish. For the next century and a half the new Attic *Black-painted* ware (or, as it is often miscalled, Black-glazed ware) is often technically and aesthetically excellent. There follows a steady fall in quality, but not in output. Meanwhile the less exacting requirements of black-painted pottery had encouraged local imitations in many, if not most, Greek cities and in Etruria. But the Attic product, because of its better clay or tradition, was still exported widely, even in the Hellenistic period, though by the mid-fourth century it had lost its Western markets to black-painted Campanian and to Gnathian. At last, apparently in the middle of the second century, a needed revolution began. The native peoples of parts of nearer Asia had been used to pottery with a red surface, and perhaps for that reason as much as technical convenience some potters of the Hellenistic East chose to fire their paint to an even, slightly shiny red. This kind of red-painted pottery is generically and imprecisely classed as *Sigillata*, of which the Hellenistic version is – or used to be – particularized as '*Pergamene*', and there is also a newer term – *Red-gloss* ware. Though Red wares became normal in Greek Asia by the end of the second century, a degenerate black-painted ware persisted at Athens and perhaps in the rest of European Greece till at least the beginning of the first century BC and in Italy about its end. Italian Sigillata, of which *Arretine* is the principal representative, began in the third quarter of that century, and its universal success justified imitation throughout the Roman empire. During the next two centuries, which were the heyday of Sigillata, the manufacture of *Early Roman* wares spread as far as Syria and Britain. The later Sigillata of the eastern or Greek half of the ancient world, the so-called *Late Roman* wares, prolonged their decline from the second to the seventh or eighth century AD when a true glaze was at last adopted generally. So the last flicker of the tradition of Greek vase-painting was snuffed out.

From the middle of the fifth century BC these black-painted and, later, red-painted wares become very frequent and so are most useful to excavators for dating their sites. Knowledge of Western Sigillata is well advanced, thanks in part to the many makers' stamps. For the East progress has been slower, but now there are good (if sometimes preliminary) studies of the Attic, Corinthian, Boeotien, Cretan and Campanian black-painted products, of the Attic, Corinthian, Peloponnesian, Ephesian and Pergamene Megarian bowls, and of the Sigillata.

The shapes of Attic black-painted pottery of the sixth and fifth centuries have the elegance to be expected of their period. In the fourth century hydriai and kraters and oinochoai still show a considered refinement, sometimes (as already in the later fifth century) enhanced by ribbing of the body, but cups and kantharoi and kotylai often suffer clumsy distortions, and the many little bowls are trivial. Later the regular shapes grow fewer and mostly small – bowls, saucers, plates, and for a while kantharoi and dumpy jugs with round or trefoil mouth – and though the imitation of metal forms at times produced an angular or brittle precision, the modelling is more often careless as well as inert. 'Pergamene' invents or introduces new profiles, cleaner though looking more mechanical, but the repertory of Sigillata remains in general limited to plates, saucers and open bowls.

The clay and paint vary from one place and time to another. At Athens the deep and rich black of fifth-century paint tends later to become thinner and duller, and the Hellenistic ideal is a glassy bluish grey though the average approaches a muddy brown. Misfiring is increasingly frequent, so that on many pieces the paint is partly or wholly oxidized to red. At Athens this red comes through negligence, but in 'Pergamene' the darkish and not very shiny red is deliberate. The red of Arretine and its successors is more vivid, and so is its sheen: occasionally a yellow of equal quality is preferred. But gradually decay sets in, and Late Roman paint is usually matt with a pink or even a brown tone. The clay much more than the paint depends on the place of manufacture. Attic in the Hellenistic period is generally a little browner and coarser than before, Campanian is a rather lighter brown, and Corinthian is of course very pale. The typical 'Pergamene' clay is yellowish, Arretine redder and Late Roman generally more pink.

Few of these monochrome wares are regularly plain. The most characteristic decoration was impressed, the most imposing in moulded relief, and especially during the earlier periods there was a modest allowance of reserved or painted ornament.

RESERVED AND PAINTED DECORATION

Much of the dark-painted ware that was current before the black-painted canon was established relieved its monotony by reserving or by adding in white or purple one or two narrow stripes in some emphatic position, for instance on the lip of cups or round the belly of taller pots. Some examples of this banding have been mentioned earlier, and indeed it is not always easy to distinguish logically between decorated and dark-painted pottery. The black-painted practice was stricter. At Athens there are sometimes ovules of red-figure type on the deep lips of pelikai and hydriai, and a group of squat aryballoi of poorish quality and later fifth-century date have a band of paltry ornament round their middle. In the late fifth and the early fourth century a slight wreath or festoon in added white or yellow often crosses the neck or shoulder of hydriai and other careful pots; but this discreet usage soon coarsens and merges with the related West Slope style. The Hellenistic black-painted and the Sigillata wares only rarely indulge in added colour.

IMPRESSED DECORATION

In the seventh and sixth centuries simple incision or impressed stamping was commonly used in Etruria on Bucchero and some coarse wares. In Greek lands at that time the main use of these techniques was for stamped bands of repeated patterns on large rough-surfaced pots, of which the best-known is a group of great amphorae found in and near the island of Rhodes. But such predecessors have no relevance to the new system of impressed decoration which developed in classical Athens and lasted for over a thousand years.

This new system first appears just before the middle of the fifth century as a modest embellishment of the black insides of some Attic stemless cups, a few of which have mediocre red-figure decoration outside. The Sotades painter, as might be expected, was among the pioneers. The units of ornament, incised or impressed before the surface was painted, were and remained small and simple. In the earliest examples a familiar arrangement is a rosette of tongues surcharged with a star and enclosed in concentric circles: these ornaments are incised freehand (with some aid of the potter's wheel and perhaps of a ruler), though the stamped palmette was in use about the middle of the fifth century. During its third quarter the style was fresh and inventive and the effect often rich; but before its end Attic workshops accepted for the various shapes of drinking vessels easier formulas, based on the chain of linked palmettes, ovules and also tongues. They now abandoned the more elaborate motifs, such as the meander regular on a group of miniature pointed amphorae, and made the detail of stamps coarser and more durable. Even so, the Attic standard is superior in design and execution to its new competitors in Boeotia, Campania and elsewhere. Early in the fourth century impoverishment and deterioration were accelerated by the introduction of chains of strokes produced by rouletting or rather chattering – since the impressions come not from a cutting wheel but by the jumping of a thin metal strip held against the rotating surface of the pot – and with this easier technique the stock decoration for most shapes soon became the chain of palmettes with links drawn out into long points and the serried band of chattered strokes. On Hellenistic black-painted plates and saucers impressed decoration became less frequent and more feeble – careless chattering and scattered palmettes, usually not linked and often without volutes at their base. This tradition was taken over in 'Pergamene', but there seems to be no connection to the Sigillata wares of three hundred years later, when we still recognize vestigial palmettes, shaped like fans and ferns, among the more popular stamped rosettes and sets of little concentric circles.

RELIEF DECORATION

There are a few good examples of decoration in relief on coarse Greek pottery from the late eighth to the sixth centuries, and many poor examples in the late bucchero of Etruria. During the later fifth and the fourth centuries at Athens figures in relief occasionally supplement or replace the normal red figures. But a regular use of moulds to decorate and even to shape what may be called fine pottery was an innovation of the Hellenistic period, when vase-painting had decayed and metal ware set the ideal.

The so-called '*Megarian*' *bowls* were not a speciality of Megara and so purists fancy such names as 'Hellenistic mouldmade relief bowls', though the old name is shorter and by now hardly misleading. Commercially this was the most successful relief ware of the Greeks, extending over most of the Hellenistic world and age. The shape is roughly hemispherical with or without a low ring foot. The decoration, which covers all the outside except the lip, ranges from abstract and vegetable ornaments to animals and human figures, usually arranged more or less symmetrically. The finer and more elaborate examples are mostly early. The process of manufacture was first to make a mould and – normally – to impress the patterns in it by stamps. Next, after firing, the mould was centred on the potter's wheel, the bowl of the pot thrown inside the mould and the lip modelled freehand. Then the pot was left to dry and shrink enough for removal from the mould, coated with the ordinary dark paint, and fired or misfired in the same way as the plainer black-painted wares. 'Megarian' bowls were made in many Greek cities, though it is likely that the stamps were often imported. They appear first at Athens, probably in the 220s, but Corinth and Argos adopted the new technique almost immediately and during the second century other cities followed. They continue, anyhow at Athens, till early in the first century BC and in a dubious form at Antioch even longer. The local schools vary both in shape and decoration. For instance the Attic type, which generally is the finest in quality, has a deep bowl and outcurving lip; across the Aegean the bowl is shallower and the lip turned in, and in Macedonia – so distribution suggests – scenes from Homer were a speciality. Some authorities have claimed that the 'Megarian' bowls originated in Egypt, though no suitable clay progenitors have been found there; but since the first Attic examples evidently imitate metalwork and metalwork has poor chances of survival, the models might have been Alexandrine bowls of metal. A heavier form of moulded relief, popular for appliqué medallions in the centre of cups and open bowls, is best-known from the *Calene* ware of Campania, made at about the same time in Campania and perhaps other parts of Italy. Here impressions were taken from older metalwork, and some of the potters had Latin names.

The 'Megarian' technique of moulded decoration was taken over into Sigillata. 'Pergamene' examples are few and mostly undistinguished, but in Arretine the neoclassical groups are often of surprising and delicate excellence. Its successors of the first two centuries AD continued the use of moulds, more commonly in the West than in the East, but standards of design and execution were increasingly neglected.

CHAPTER VIII

SHAPES

——— •◆• ———

GENERAL COMMENTS

Most Greek pots were made for domestic use, even those which were dedicated to the gods or deposited in graves. The chief exceptions are the great
amphorae and kraters of later Geometric, the Attic white-ground lekythoi,
the volute-kraters of red-figure Apulian, the Hellenistic polychrome wares
– all of which were made specially for burials – and the innumerable miniature pots turned out for dedication at sanctuaries. But though these differ
in scale or the fastness of the decoration, their shapes generally follow those
current in useful pottery.

The principal uses for which Greek fine pottery was designed did not
vary much in time or place. They were first drinking and secondly toilet.
In drinking the Greeks mixed their wine with water; so there were wine
jars and water jars, bowls for mixing, jugs for pouring and cups. Toilet oil
and perfume needed flasks with narrow necks. But though the main cate-
gories of shapes remained fairly constant, there was room for variety in
proportions and details. Generally the shapes of any one time or school
are in harmony with each other. In Protogeometric they are loose and full,
in Geometric more sharply defined and tautly compressed. In the
succeeding period the local schools differ in shape as in style, but the trend
is to higher, generous bellies with more taper below, and at Corinth a new
refinement appears, especially for smaller pots. A rapid advance was made
at Athens rather before the middle of the sixth century; shapes, large and
small, are modelled with precision and elegance, and foot and lip receive
increasing attention. With red-figure comes a wider appreciation of rhyth-
mical, uninterrupted curves, already practised in the one-piece amphora.
During the later fifth and the fourth centuries subtlety degenerated into
cleverness or is replaced by a clumsy solidity; the worst excesses are in
South Italian. Hellenistic pottery, which has lesser pretensions to art, is
mostly dull or lifeless in its profile. This evolution can be followed in
details too, most obviously in the horizontal handles of cups and hydriai:
for long they are simple loops, in the later sixth century the crook
grows squarer and begins to turn up, by the end of the fifth century handles
are fanning out and the upward curve is bending over and back, and in
the fourth century these contortions are sometimes exaggerated for their
own sake.

The most distinctive quality of Greek shapes, when compared with those of other civilizations, is the conscious articulation of the parts of the pot, even though precise symmetry may be neglected. This articulation often offends modern critics, who prefer a more fluent use of the plastic character of clay. The Greeks might have retorted that the potter's wheel also invites turnery. There was certainly influence from metalwork, rarer and more expensive than pottery of clay. It is for instance demonstrable for the later seventh century in the attachments of some handles, for the later fifth in the ribbing of some black-painted ware, and for the Hellenistic period in both shape and decoration of Megarian bowls. How much further this influence went is disputed. An extreme view has potters doing little more than slavish copying of metal models – for decoration as well as shape – though one might expect that such expert technicians would sometimes have had ideas of their own and, working in a much quicker, cheaper and more fluent medium, could have afforded to modify or experiment. Indeed it is obvious that they did so with the rotelles of handles which in metalwork clip onto the lip, but in pottery ride clear (Plate 30B), and a stand like that of Plate 18 was more easily shaped in clay than metal. The degree of indebtedness of one craft to the other is unlikely ever to be agreed, but it seems safer generally to talk of influence rather than imitation. There was also some borrowing from woodwork, as of the pyxis, and from basketry, as of the kalathos.

The exquisite forms of the best Attic pots have lured some students to believe in a construction calculated according to geometrical rules of proportion, and they have broken down selected shapes into complex systems of two-dimensional rectangles. That the shapes show a sense of proportion is evident. It is also evident that their makers did not bother about exact symmetry. But the modern investigators must be thanked for the best set of measured drawings of fine Greek shapes.

The names now given to the various Greek shapes are mostly conventional. For many of these shapes there are no modern equivalents, so that it is natural to look for ancient names, of which the largest assortment is offered by the late miscellanists and encyclopedists. Unfortunately literary contexts and dictionary definitions are usually ambiguous, even if the writer knows the shape he is describing. A few names explain themselves or are explained by being inscribed on or against the shape to which they refer, but even these names were not all applied uniformly at every time and place, and besides, it is possible that the vocabulary of the trade and of the public differed. So, for example, in the inventories of the Mycenaean tablets the names of vessels are sometimes accompanied by a sketch of the shape, but of these names only 'amphoreus' can be said to have been currently used in historical times of a pot of similar shape. More significantly, Aristophanes uses 'hydria' and 'calpis' of the same water pot. Again, 'poterion' is written as a description both on a deep cup of Geometric type and on a lip cup, 'cylix' on both lip cup and Chiot chalice. There are other names, such as 'pelike', which are currently used without and even in contradiction of ancient authority. Earlier archaeologists were very ready to adopt Greek names, but in the course of time their more extravagant or unnecessary foundlings have been abandoned and when new definitions are needed the general practice is to invent (as for instance 'lip cup'), to use symbols (such as 'kantharos type B'), or more whimsically and, because of the difficulty of translation into other languages, inconsiderately too – to revive vernacular archaisms such as 'pitcher' and 'chalice'. Though usage has not yet been completely standardized – witness the confusion between 'kotyle' and 'skyphos' – it is unlikely that radical changes in nomenclature will be accepted: utility and habit are more compelling than pedantry. So the student must still remember that where an ancient author names some shape there is no presumption that he means the shape so named by modern archaeologists.

For convenience in sorting sherds, shapes are divided into 'closed', that is with a narrowish mouth, and 'open', if the inside of the pot can easily be seen. Normally, except at the mouth, the inside of closed pots is rough and unpainted. Of large closed shapes the principal are amphora (including pelike), oinochoe and hydria; of large open shapes the krater, and well after it the dinos. The commonest of the smaller closed shapes are oinochoe, lekythos, aryballos and alabastron. Of the smaller open shapes the cup in its many forms is pre-eminent; and from the end of the fifth century black-painted plates and small bowls become numerous.

The paragraphs that follow attempt a summary account only of the more important shapes of the more important schools. So rarities like the psykter are left to the *Glossary*, the peculiar shapes of Laconian and Cretan are neglected, and black -painted pottery – as much from ignorance as contempt – does not receive its archaeological due. Coarse pottery, which has a different and sometimes more fluent range of shapes, is outside the scope of this book. Two more limitations must be emphasized. First, since knowledge of shapes is still based largely on complete pots, complete pots come mostly from graves, and graves have their own fashions in offerings, the shapes with which we are familiar are not always a fair sample of the shapes current in any school: if, for example, our knowledge of Attic pottery in the sixth century came only from graves in Attica the amphora would rank lower than it does and the phormiskos would have more fame. Secondly, a shape may disappear or be absent from the repertory of fine pottery, but flourish in humbler wares. The study of Greek shapes has been laggard.

AMPHORAE

The amphora is a high two-handled pot with a neck that is considerably narrower than the body. Coarse amphorae were the standard containers for transporting oil and wine, and they survive in great numbers. Fine painted amphorae, which have mouths too wide to be easily plugged, were used as decanters. Between these two classes comes the Panathenaic amphora, of fine quality because it was presented at a public festival and narrow-necked because it contained oil. Outsize amphorae were at times made for funeral use, and a special narrow amphora – the loutrophoros – had a place in the ritual of weddings. Amphorae are very frequent. A normal height is about 45 cm, but some are larger and many are not more than 30 cm high.

The name 'amphora' or rather, since that is Latin, the Greek form 'amphoreus' was certainly applied to this shape, though two Attic black-figure amphorae are inscribed 'kados' and a Nolan amphora and a pelike 'kadiskos'.

There are two main classes, the neck-amphora (Plate 23) in which neck meets body at a sharp angle and the one-piece amphora (Plate 22) in which neck and body merge in an unbroken curve. Some authorities choose to limit the simple term 'amphora' to the one-piece shape, although it does not appear till the late seventh century and is never more common than the neck-amphora. The Etruscan Bucchero and Nikosthenic amphorae form a class apart. The pelike, though a derivative of the one-piece amphora, is regarded as a distinct shape. The stamnos is similarly distinguished from the neck-amphora. Very small amphorae are sometimes called amphoriskoi.

Neck-amphora

Protogeometric. The neck-amphora is inherited from Mycenaean (Plate 2A), but is now remodelled to become a leading shape. Of the two main types one has a plump body, concave flaring neck and handles set horizontally on the belly (Plate 2B); the other, with vertical handles, is the more spreading ancestor of the common Geometric type.

Geometric. The shape is narrower and straighter, with a taller neck and higher belly (Plate 3A and B show the development): the handles usually reach vertically up to the neck, except on very large works such as that of Plate 4A. At the end of Attic Geometric the progressive group produces still narrower amphora in defiance of the contemporary tendency to spread. Notable examples of this spreading are in Theran, where the neck too is very wide, and still more in the Cycladic Wheel group (Figure 3).

Orientalizing and black-figure to c. 550 BC. Several forms of amphora are current. (1) A more spreading version of the Geometric standard continues in Attic and appears in 'Melian' and the Pontic group of Etruscan: many amphorae towards the middle of the sixth century have an almost ovoid body (Plate 20B). (2) Still wider amphorae are found in the Cycladic Ad group, and the much later Fikellura amphora is very wide (Figure 21).

(3) The narrow form of Late Geometric is adapted by the Heraldic group of the Cyclades, and recurs in the Attic Polos group of the early sixth century and later in the loutrophoros. (4) The amphorae of the Linear Island group of Cycladic (Plate 29A) and of Boeotian, Eretrian and 'Melian' begin at the end of Geometric, but are much commoner in the seventh century. The amphora was very rare in this period in Corinthian and, it seems, in Laconian.

Mature Black-figure and Red-figure. About the middle of the sixth century the old neck-amphora of form (1) is remodelled and refined at Athens, especially in the workshop of Amasis; and later there are further innovations. (1) The new standard amphora of black-figure, which lasts till the first quarter of the fifth century, has an egg-shaped body with a flat-tish shoulder (Plate 23, though that, like many early examples, is wider and more elaborately modelled than the norm): the shape is adopted in 'Chalcidian', in Clazomenian, where also a very narrow form is derived from it, and in Etruscan black-figure. (2) A smaller version, with simple foot and usually about 30 cm high, is known – after a prolific site – as the Nolan amphora; this is a red-figure shape, common in the first half of the fifth century and a little after. (3) The characteristic neck-amphora of red-figure is a much slimmer pot, which at first often has twisted handles (Plate 46A); it begins at the end of the sixth century and continues in Attic till the early fourth century, in South Italian red-figure till its end. (4) The so-called pointed amphora, with wide belly and knob-like foot, is a large and rare shape of red-figure of the early fifth century, and narrow miniature versions with impressed decoration became common in the black-painted ware of the third quarter of the fifth century.

Amphorae of this period were sometimes provided with flattish, knobbed lids.

Hellenistic. The neck-amphora is important only in West Slope ware, where it is from the beginning squat (Plate 56A). Development is towards an angular profile.

Panathenaic amphora

The purpose of this variety of amphora is explained by its familiar legend, painted before firing, 'τῶυ Ἀθήνηθεν ἄθλων'. Examples stretch from about 560 BC to the second century BC or later, and are conservative in shape as well as in their black-figure decoration. Characteristic are the large body and narrow neck and foot (Plate 21B): gradually neck and stem grow attenuated and concave, till by the fourth century the shape is no longer strictly a neck-amphora. Many full-sized amphorae of Panathenaic shape, and of course all the miniatures, were souvenirs rather than prizes. The shape was borrowed for red-figure by some Attic painters of the fifth century and was elaborated by many South Italians of the fourth (Plate 54).

One-piece amphora

This shape, hardly known outside Attic, appears humbly in painted pottery in the earlier part of the seventh century, but is very rare till its last quarter (Plate 21A). It is remodelled and becomes important about the middle of the sixth century (Plate 22) and is a favourite of the Archaic red-figure painters. It dies out in the last quarter of the fifth century. Three types are distinguished by certain details. In type B, which continues the early shape, the lip is straight or slightly concave, the handles are round in section, the foot is simple (Plate 21A); in type A the lip is again concave, the handles are flanged, the foot is complex (Plate 22); in type C the lip is convex, the handles and foot vary.

Etruscan Bucchero and Nikosthenic amphora

The standard amphora of Etruscan Bucchero, inherited from the native impacto, is characterized by the conical neck, which at the base is nearly as wide as the body, and by the vertical handles that join on to the lip. In the late sixth century an unhappily improved version with black-figure decoration was produced at Athens in the workshop of Nikosthenes, presumably as a speciality for the Etruscan market (Figure 38).

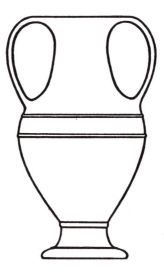

Figure 38 Attic Bf Nikosthenic amphora.
Ht 31 cm, *c.* 530 BC.

Loutrophoros

This is a necked pot, tall and very narrow, reminiscent of the progressive Late Geometric amphora. It was used in the ritual of weddings and at the funerals of unmarried persons.

The name 'loutrophoros' is rightly used, to judge by the references in ancient literature, representations in vase-paintings and the subjects of the decoration of many loutrophoroi.

There are two varieties, which differ only in their handles. The commoner, a neck-amphora, is called simply loutrophoros; the other is the loutrophoros-hydria. A steady series of loutrophoroi continue from the late sixth century, when the special form is first distinctly recognized, until the later fourth century. The shape, which becomes very spindly, is confined to Attic and to South Italian red-figure.

Pelike

The pelike is a one-piece amphora with a sagging belly (Plate 45).

A Greek word 'pelike' exists, but was not applied to this shape.

It appears first as a decorated shape in Attic red-figure rather after 520 BC and remains very popular till the end of red-figure. Small pelikai are common in Gnathian. The tendency is for the mouth to grow broader, till in the fourth century it is wider than the belly (Plate 51). Gnathian pelikai are slimmer and more fanciful.

HYDRIA

The hydria is primarily a pot for fetching water. It has a vertical handle at the back for dipping and two horizontal handles at the sides for lifting. In size hydriai correspond to amphorae.

The name 'hydria' is satisfactorily attested for this shape. So too is 'kalpis'. Some modern writers conventionally use 'kalpis' for the rounded hydria of Attic red-figure.

Most hydriai are broad pots with a character of their own. But in wares in which the hydria is exceptional the shape is often that of the amphora with a different set of handles (for example Plate 14A, which is one of a short-lived group of Attic hydriai around the end of the Geometric period). Similarly the loutrophoros-hydria is only a three-handled loutrophoros. There are also, especially later, many small and miniature hydria.

Outside Cretan, where the form is mean and peculiar, the hydria rarely appears in fine pottery till the end of the eighth century, and then only in some schools. There are in succession three or four main forms. (1) The typical early hydria has a wide belly, broadly rounded shoulder and offset

Figure 39   Attic Rf hydria ('kalpis').
Ht 27.75 cm, 450–440 BC.

neck. It is common in Cycladic from Subgeometric to 'Melian', and a
stumpy variety appears in Ripe Corinthian and the Polos group of Attic.
(2) Rather before the middle of the sixth century the shape is modernized
in the same sort of way as the neck-amphora; the new standard (Plate 35)
has a flatter shoulder that joins the belly in a sharp curve or even at an
angle. This form appears in Corinthian, Laconian, Attic, 'Chalcidian',
Clazomenian, Caeretan and Etruscan. (3) In Attic a modified version,
slimmer and with a more angular shoulder, becomes normal for black-
figure in the last quarter of the sixth century and continues into the second
quarter of the fifth. (4) Another shape (Figure 39), which seems to have
antecedents in coarse pottery, is discovered and immediately preferred by
red-figure painters towards the end of the sixth century. Here the neck is
small, and belly passes into shoulder and shoulder into neck in a continuous curve. The new hydria (which is sometimes called the 'kalpis') is a
broad pot, but gradually it contracts, and in the red-figure and black-
painted wares of the fourth century achieves a slim elegance. A less sensitive
version of this shape, which usually has an offset neck, survives in the
Hadra ware of Hellenistic.

OINOCHOAI

The oinochoe is a jug. It is one of the commonest and the most variable
of Greek shapes. Larger sizes are 30 cm or more high, and till the early

sixth century there are many oinochoai that in scale are comparable to amphorae and in some schools seem to have taken their place. But smaller oinochoai are always numerous. The artistic importance of the shape is roughly proportionate to its size.

The name 'oinochoe' which means 'wine-pourer' fits a frequent use of this shape. The name 'chous' (plural 'choes') is also well attested, but now at lest is confined to the Attic one-piece oinochoe of Beazley's shape 3.

The range of shape is wide. For instance, the mouth may be trefoil, round or beaked; the neck broad or narrow, straight or curved; the body slim, squat, truncated or angular. In Attic red-figure alone ten varieties have been classified. Here only a rough distinction of major forms is attempted. Three varieties – conical oinochoe, olpe and lagynos – are generally classed apart.

Standard oinochoe

This has a more or less ovoid body, widish neck and trefoil mouth. The Protogeometric norm is represented by Plate 1D. With Geometric the body becomes stumpy, at least in the metropolitan schools; later there is a tendency to lengthen it again. This shape is taken over by Protocorinthian (Plate 8C), where the belly grows steadily broader. In the second half of the seventh century the Corinthian belly spreads yet wider, the neck becomes meaner and concave, and the handle is high (Plate 11B). A compacter version of this shape is inherited by Attic about the middle of the sixth century. This necked shape continues with modifications throughout the fifth century, and a sturdier relative with a broader base remains popular in the fourth. This is the main line of development, but some other forms deserve notice. In Etruscan bucchero an early Protocorinthian shape persists till the end of the seventh century, gradually giving way to a heavier oinochoe with barrel-shaped or oval body. Attic in the first half of the seventh century is fond of a miniature jug, with narrow body and neck tapering upwards (Figure 9). In East Greek an ovoid oinochoe with trefoil mouth is a favourite shape of the Middle Wild Goat style (Plate 30B): the oinochoai of the Late Wild Goat style and of Fikellura are more solid.

One-piece oinochoe

This type, which has its predecessor and perhaps ancestor in the Attic olpe, has a generously curving belly, a short neck that merges into the body and a trefoil mouth. It takes form in Attic (where it is known as oinochoe shape 3 or 'chous') during the third quarter of the sixth century, becomes popular in red-figure in the fifth and, ousting its rivals continues till the later fourth, though by then black-painted versions are commoner. Small choes were used in the festival of the Anthesteria at Athens and are frequent in children's graves there. A tallish variant, which is not called 'chous', remains common in Gnathian, where there is also a slimmer, sagging alternative.

Bell-mouthed oinochoe

(1) A peculiar shape (Plate 4B), sometimes called 'pitcher', is popular in Attic Late Geometric. It can be very large. A reduced model of medium or small size and with a lower body persists in Protoattic till the middle of the seventh century, but is usually described as a mug (or sometimes, if the lip is very high, as a tankard). (2) Another and distinct oinochoe with wide neck (the 'round-mouthed oinochoe') is frequent in East Greek from Late Geometric (Plate 7A) till the end of the Middle I phase of the Wild Goat style (Plate 30A). The few examples elsewhere are probably imitative.

Broad-bottomed oinochoe

This is a low, broad oinochoe with nearly vertical sides, a lowish and soon narrow neck, and a trefoil mouth. It becomes common in Corinthian in the first half of the seventh century and outlasts the Animal style. It appears to have Geometric antecedents, and in the later fifth century there is a trivial oinochoe that is perhaps its descendant. This new type, which prefers a concave profile to the belly, an angular shoulder and a beaked lip, persists into Hellenistic and presumably influenced the lagynos.

Small globular oinochoe

A humble but common type of Geometric is a small pot with short, narrow neck and globular or even depressed body. The mouth is trefoil or, less often, round. This is the ancestor of the aryballos and perhaps of the conical oinochoe.

Oinochoe with cut-away neck

This is a jug with a widish neck, cut away deeply at the back to leave a vertical spout. (1) A shape of this type with broadish body is traditional Thessalian Protogeometric and Geometric and is borrowed by Euboean, in which it persists till the sixth century. (2) A narrow, footless version 'Oinochoe, Shape 7', or 'beaked jug' (though this latter term is sometimes used for another form), appears rarely in Attic during the fifth century, and with an inward curve to the lower part of the body is a great favourite of Etruscan throughout the fourth century.

Conical oinochoe

A minor Geometric shape is a little oinochoe with trefoil mouth, narrow neck and a body that consists of little more than a broad shoulder. In Early Protocorinthian the contour of the body is straightened till it approaches a more or less shallow cone, and the neck becomes taller: this conical oinochoe remains popular in Corinthian till the early sixth century. Later there are some slight black-painted oinochoai of truncated type, though the slope of the body is curved.

Olpe

This name is given to some tall jugs with sagging belly.

The Greek word 'olpe' is used of jugs or flasks, and is inscribed on a Ripe Corinthian round aryballos and perhaps also on a Protocorinthian pointed aryballos. There is no authority for its restricted modern use.

Two main forms go by the name of olpe, and a few oddments are sometimes lumped in. (i) The olpe of Plate 11A (which does not show the handle) is frequent in Corinthian from the middle of the seventh to the first quarter of the sixth century and, often debased, for rather longer in Etrascocorinthian (Figure 26); the shape occurs also in Etruscan Bucchero. (2) A shorter pot, in contour something like a pelike, has lip and body continuous, high handle, and often trefoil mouth. This appears in decorated Attic ware early in the seventh century and is common throughout the sixth. Etruscan imitations run later. The oinochoe 'shape 5' of Attic red-figure is a descendant of this olpe.

Lagynos

This is a Hellenistic form of broad-bottomed oinochoe with a sharp or, less often, curving shoulder and a round mouth (Figure 37).

The use of the word 'lagynos' is well supported. It was a kind of wine-flask.

The shape is best known in the light-ground Lagynos group, and appears also in contemporary black-painted and relief ware.

KRATERS

Big deep bowls with a wide mouth were used for mixing wine. A frequent range of size is from 30 to 45 cm high, the stem (if there is one) excluded, but generally the earlier shapes are broader and more capacious than the later. Very large kraters were sometimes made for funerary use, and a special variety – the lebes gamikos – for marriage ceremonial.

The ordinary Greek word for these mixing-bowls was 'krater'. 'Lebes' sometimes, 'dinos' perhaps never has that sense. The restriction of 'krater' to the footed shapes is a modern convention. The application of 'dinos' to the less common bowl with rounded bottom is unreasonable, though there is some evidence for using the alternative 'lebes'.

Mixing-bowls are frequent and important pots from Protogeometric till the fourth century. The varieties are readily distinguished. In all the trend is to narrower forms.

Simple krater

The Protogeometric shape is sturdy and wide, with low belly and modest or later conical foot. The handles, as is regular in this type, sit horizontally on the belly and often are doubled. The ordinary Geometric shape is tenser and curves in strongly to the simple lip, its foot is either low or stems into a flaring pedestal, and the handles are often joined to the lip by a sort of strap. This shape, which with some modification survived humbly well down the seventh century, appears to be the ancestor of the column-krater. A byform of Attic Late Geometric and earlier Protoattic is the egg-shaped krater, in which the body is taller and narrower. The very big funerary kraters of later Geometric add a short vertical neck to the ordinary shape, and consequently the handles do not reach up to the lip.

Kotyle-krater

The kotyle-krater, a giant kotyle usually attached to a high flaring pedestal and covered by a lid, is an Attic invention. Its period is the middle and second half of the seventh century. A kotyle-krater without a pedestal appears also in the Acolian Wild Goat style.

Column-krater

The column-krater is a Corinthian novelty of the last quarter of the seventh century (Plate 12c), and there is some evidence that it was known as the 'Corinthian krater'. The shape appears to be adapted from the simple krater of ordinary Geometric type with the strap from handle to lip. Now the lip is broader and extends at each side in a rectangular plate supported by the handles: their columnar effect gives the shape its modern name. A more advanced form is shown on Plate 36. Widely adopted, the column-krater reaches its greatest popularity in inferior Attic of the first half of the fifth century. In Attic red-figure it dies out early in the fourth century, but continues in the ordinary style of Apulian and has a curious revival in the latest red-figure of Etruria. Development is to a narrower body and higher neck.

Volute-krater

The volute-krater Plate (19A), so called from the form of its handles, comes from the column-krater. Though not very common, it is an important shape. It appears perhaps before the end of the seventh century and continues till the late fourth. The example illustrated is early, before the canon was fixed. Soon the volutes are tightly rolled and the lip is capped with a moulding, and gradually the whole pot becomes narrower. Very big and elaborate volute-kraters, with scenes suggesting a funerary purpose, are the most ornate confections of Apulian red-figure. Possibly the ancient name 'Laconian krater' belonged to this shape.

Calyx-krater

The krater which by a modern conceit is called the calyx-krater is in its structure not unlike the Chiot chalice (Figure 20). It appears in Attic black-figure soon after the middle of the sixth century and becomes a favoured shape till the end of red-figure. It grows steadily narrower, more concave in its upper part and more stemmed at the base. Small calyx-kraters continue for a short time in Hellenistic black-painted and West Slope wares.

Bell-krater

The bell-krater (Plates 44, 48A and 56B) is established in the repertory of fine pottery by the beginning of the fifth century, rises in frequency till the early part of the fourth century and though rejected by the progressive painters of red-figure remains the most common type of krater till its end. It too in the fourth century often grows an incurving stem. Sometimes, especially in early red-figure and in Gnathian, lugs take the place of handles (Plate 44). The shape recalls that of a Protogeometric krater, but if there is a connection it must be through coarse ware, unless perhaps – because of the lugs – the prototype was of wood. A sort of bell-krater, usually described as a pyxis, survives in Centuripae ware.

Stamnos

The stamnos is a wide-mouthed pot with the neck reduced to a collar and the handles consequently set horizontally on the belly (Figure 40). Sometimes at least it was used as a krater.

In Greek 'stamnos' seems to be more or less equivalent to 'amphora'. The modern distinction is arbitrary.

The shape, which properly belongs to red-figure, establishes itself during the last quarter of the sixth century and in Attic is popular throughout the

Figure 40 Attic Rf stamnos.
Ht 33.1 cm, *c.* 450 BC.

fifth, in Etruscan throughout the fourth. It grows taller and thinner, especially towards the base. The name is sometimes loosely and unwisely applied (as on p. 132) to plainer pots of roughly similar body ending in a low rim.

Dinos

This shape, probably misnamed, is a big round-bottomed bowl that curves in to a more or less emphatic mouth (Plate 18). It is normally handleless. Sometimes there is a matching stand, which may be elaborately turned (Plate 18). The dinos occurs in fine pottery from the middle of the seventh till the late fifth century, but is frequent only in the later Wild Goat style.

Lebes gamikos

The lebes gamikos or nuptial lebes, which is probably correctly named and is certainly connected with weddings, has the shape of a small, deep dinos with two high handles, a lid and a simple attached stand (or, more commonly later, a short foot). It first appears early in the sixth century. In Attic red-figure it lasts beyond the middle of the fourth century, in South Italian till its end. Perhaps the kotyle-krater, which also has a lid and an attached stand, is its predecessor.

LEKYTHOI ETC.

Flasks for toilet oil and perfume, and also for some condiments, are distinguished by their narrow aperture and are normally small or smallish. The Attic white-ground lekythoi are larger, but they are pots made specially for the ritual of the grave. Many small oinochoai and the miniature pointed amphorae also served as toilet flasks, but it is convenient to classify them by shape rather than function.

The Greek word 'lekythos' could describe several kinds of flask; there is evidence that it was used for what are now called the ovoid aryballos, the round aryballos, the lekythos of white-ground shape and the squat lekythos, and also for a smallish plump jug with narrow neck and rounded mouth. 'Aryballos' (or rather 'aryballis') is defined by Hesychius, rightly or wrongly, as a Doric equivalent of 'lekythos'. The painter of one Ripe Corinthian round aryballos called his pot an 'olpe', as perhaps did the painter of an earlier Corinthian pointed aryballos. 'Alabastron' is presumably valid for the second and third of the types that now go under that name, since there are alabaster pots of the same shape. But there is no evidence that 'askos' was ever used by Greeks of a pot. The current distinctions between these words are conventional.

Lekythos

Two main types are given the simple name of lekythos: (1) The Protogeometric lekythos (Plate 1C), normally about 12 to 20 cm high, replaces the Mycenaean stirrup vase (except in Cretan) and is itself replaced by the small globular oinochoe of Geometric. (2) A new shape of Attic and Corinthian in the early sixth century is a pot about 15 cm high with oval body, plastic ring round the short neck, narrow round mouth and one handle. This lekythos soon develops an angular shoulder and a stronger lip, loses its ring, and grows narrower. By the end of the sixth century the canonical proportions have been reached and the shape is very popular with lesser black-figure painters. During the second quarter of the fifth century red-figure painters adopt the lekythos and it becomes the characteristic vehicle of the white-ground style (Plates 49A–B). Since the white-ground lekythoi were made for funerary use, their decoration could be in evanescent colours and their size was not limited by handiness. A fair number of them have thriftily a small inner container attached to the neck, so that they could appear full without much expenditure of oil. The shape disappears at the end of the fifth century.

Squat lekythos

This shape (Plate 46B), familiar in red-figure and black-painted wares, appears at the end of the sixth century and is popular in the later part of the fifth and the early part of the fourth. The shape gradually becomes narrower and more elongated. The usual range of height is 8 to 15 cm.

Aryballos

The ancestor of the aryballos is the small globular oinochoe that appears in Geometric and continues after, and indeed one variety of this shape has been called 'jug-aryballos'. But the first true aryballos (according to the conventional definition of the term) is in Early Protocorinthian. The Corinthian evolution from 'round' through 'ovoid' to 'pointed' can be followed on Plate 9A and D and Figure 5A–B: these forms are sometimes confusingly named 'lekythoi'. At the end of the third quarter of the seventh century a new round form (Plate 10B) becomes regular, and there is also a flat-bottomed version: the round shape continues till the fifth century. These aryballoi are very common in Corinthian and in Etruscocorinthian, which adds some original variants, and round aryballoi are fairly common in Laconian of the sixth century. A new type develops in Attic in the last quarter of the sixth century and lasts till the early fourth: this has a bell-shaped mouth rather like the contemporary lekythos, two handles or later no handle, and a flat or rounded bottom. A common height for aryballoi is around 7 or 8 cm, but in Ripe Corinthian there are larger sizes too.

Alabastron

Of three types of alabastron the second and third have justification for their name. (I) The Corinthian alabastron (Plate 10C) comes in about the middle of the seventh century, is enormously popular in the last quarter and dies out about a generation later. A usual height is 7 to 10 cm, though from the end of the seventh century larger sizes are common enough. Etruscocorinthian imitations are numerous and include flat-bottomed variants. (2) A long, pointed alabastron without handles occurs about the same time in East Greek Bucchero, Etruscan Bucchero and Etruscocorinthian. (3) Another alabastron with rounded base and sometimes two small lugs has exact parallels in alabaster. This type, usually from 10 to 20 cm long, is fairly common in Attic from the late sixth to the early fourth century.

Askos

The name is given to various flasks wider than high, with a narrow orifice set at one side of the top, and a handle reaching across to the other side. Four types can be reckoned as fine pottery. (1) In East Greek related to Clazomenian there is a lumpy flat-bottomed askos as much as 15 cm across. (2) A very low neat askos, with flat bottom and about 10 cm wide, is popular in Attic red-figure and black-painted wares of the fifth and early fourth centuries. (3) The bulky 'deep askos', with a body like a brooding hen, flourishes in later Apulian red-figure and other Italian wares, but is known earlier in plainer pottery. (4) A still larger askos with round bottom is a staple shape of the Daunian school of native Apulian and is elaborated in Canosa ware.

PYXIDES

Round, mostly handleless boxes with lids were used by women to hold cosmetics or trinkets. This is evident from the favourite subjects of their decoration, their occurrence in graves and the rare survival of their contents. The commonest size is perhaps 10 cm across.

The Greek 'pyxis' (which gives the English 'box') may or may not have been extended in our period to boxes not of boxwood. But the modern usage is fair enough.

Shapes vary without much logic. Some (agreeably to etymology) seem to show the influence of the wood-turner. Here only the principal types are mentioned. The Protogeometric fashion is for a globular body with out-turned lip and low foot. In Early Geometric (at least in Athens) this gives way to two derivatives: the pointed pyxis (which ends below in a point) hardly outlives the ninth century, but the flat pyxis (which begins later) flourishes till the end of Geometric, growing still flatter and larger and soon elaborating the knob of its lid (Plate 6A). In Corinth a straight-sided pyxis of more modest proportions is at home from the late eighth century; during the seventh century the modish profile is increasingly concave, and in the sixth century convexity is favoured. Attic from the mid-sixth century prefers concave types, with flat bottom or low recessed base. But the simple round box persists and in the fourth century is left as the normal pyxis of Greece, though Apulian red-figure preferred a hemispherical bowl with moulded foot completed by a hemispherical lid with big knob.

CUPS

In fine Greek pottery cups usually have two handles. The normal size varies according to the shape. Cups of one sort or another are very common in all periods.

Of the many Greek words for cups four are now in fairly common use. These are 'skyphos', 'kotyle', 'cylix' and 'kantharos'. The names 'kotyle' and 'kotylos' are written on shapes that we call cup, and kantharos, 'skyphos' on a stemmed cup, and 'cylix' on cups of shapes ranging from

Geometric type to lip cup, on the kotyle (as defined below), the cup-kotyle and also the Chiot chalice. 'Kotyle' was too a standard measure of volume. But there is no ancient authority for limiting any of these words to a particular shape of cup. Nor is the modern terminology consistent. What some call 'skyphos' others call 'kotyle', and their 'skyphos' is the 'kotyle' of the contrary faction: fortunately one of the disputed shapes can be called simply 'cup'. With 'kantharos' the uncertainty is whether or not to include some unassuming types. As for 'cylix', the current fashion is to replace it by 'cup', variously qualified. The special forms known as lakaina and phiale have respectively vaguely plausible and good title to their names.

Cup

The cup in its restricted sense may be defined as a drinking pot with lowish bowl and handles set horizontally. It remains popular till the fourth century, when the kantharos overtakes it. Sizes vary. In Protogeometric a diameter of 15 cm at the lip is fairly normal, by the mid-sixth century the standard cup is about 20 cm across, and some of the red-figure show-pieces are much wider. But there are always many smaller cups. Of the types listed below (1) and (2) are often called 'skyphos' (or 'kotyle'), and (3) and (8)–(11) 'cylix'.

(1) The typical Protogeometric cup is unmistakable (Plate 1A). (2) Its Geometric successor (Plate 8A) renounces the high foot and is squatter in the body: at the end of Attic Geometric an improved version occurs with an oblique and longer lip, but the old shape persists through the seventh century. (3) In Corinthian of the seventh century a modernized cup also is current, neater in proportions and more definite in its narrow foot (Figure 4B): this type of cup continues on the Greek mainland into the second quarter of the sixth century (cf. Plate 24A), and rather longer in East Greek and Etruscocorinthian. (4) Another innovation of Attic Late Geometric has a wider but shallow body and a vertical lip of about equal height, flat instead of rounded handles and often a tall stem ('stemmed bowl' or 'standed bowl'): its descendants last into Middle Protoattic. (5) In Laconian before the end of Geometric a similar glorification of the lip led to the lakaina (Figure 11): this shape, peculiar to Laconian, survived (anyhow in miniatures) till the Hellenistic period. (6) The Chiot chalice (Figure 20), which appears in the late seventh century and lasts at least till the fourth, develops a conical foot as well as a high lip. (7) The East Greek Bird bowl (Plate 29D), which with its descendants is popular throughout the seventh and long into the sixth century, is a back formation from a broad kotyle current in East Greek Late Geometric. (8) To return to the main course of development, the standard shape (3) is during the second quarter of the sixth century refined by Attic potters through the Siana cup (Plate 24B) into the lip cup (Plate 25A) and into the band cup (Plate 25B) and Droop

cup: the lip cup flourishes from the 560s to the 530s, the band cup rather longer. (9) In the 530s Attic masters were turning to another shape, the eye cup: here the lip is abolished, as in the rarish merrythought cups of the previous generation, and the stem quickly shrinks to a heavy flaring member surmounted by a broad fillet (Figure 30A). This, the type A of Attic red-figure is old-fashioned by the end of the sixth century. (10) In type B (Figure 30B) which is the most exquisite accomplishment of Greek pot-making, the curve from rim to edge of base is checked only by a low step on the foot, the stem grows tall and slender, and the bowl is shallower still: its period is from the last quarter of the sixth century to the middle of the fourth. (11) Type C is a humbler cup, which prefers a concave offset lip and interposes a fillet to mark off foot from stem: it too begins in the late sixth century, but continues – especially popular in black-painted wares – till the second quarter of the fourth century. (12) The 'stemless cup', in which foot is separated from bowl by no more than a groove, appears in Attic red-figure at the beginning of the fifth century, becomes very frequent in black-painted wares and dies out in the fourth century. (13) The so-called bolsal is a small shallow bowl with low foot and horizontal handles, frequent in less pretentious black-painted pottery: in the fifth century its profile is usually a simple curve and the foot light, in the fourth century the foot is heavier and often the rim curves outwards.

Cup-kotyle

This is in effect a much narrowed and deeper form of the cup, with foot directly joining bowl. It is common in inferior Attic during the fifth and fourth centuries.

'Tea cup'

A small deepish cup with one vertical handle and 7 to 10 cm in diameter may for convenience be called a 'tea cup', though those who use 'skyphos' for what here is called 'cup', use 'cup' for this one-handled shape. In Protogeometric this 'tea cup' has a high conical foot and is often decorated (Plate 1B). Afterwards it loses its foot and the decoration is restricted to reserved stripes on the lip, but it is unobtrusively frequent in Geometric and Protoattic.

Kotyle

The kotyle (or, according to the opposite terminology, the skyphos) is a deep two-handled cup with no distinct lip (Figure 4A). Though there are earlier Geometric cups with little or no lip, the evolution is not completed till the Late Geometric phase of Corinthian. Often at first the bowl is wide

(Plate 8B) – and it is from such a kotyle that the East Greek Bird bowl diverges – but in Corinthian a standard is soon fixed and the kotyle with its remarkably thin wall becomes the finest of Protocorinthian shapes. In Corinthian the kotyle remains very common into the Hellenistic period, in Attic its popularity begins in the fifth century. Two principal types of kotyle, conventionally distinguished as Corinthian and Attic, now compete. The Corinthian type is truer to tradition, but curves in more at the top. The Attic type curves outward at the rim and has a heavier foot. A byform of the fifth century has one of its handles set vertically and is called owl-kotyle or 'glaux' from the owls that decorate many red-figure examples. During the fourth century both types, the Attic since it lasts longer more so than the Corinthian, grow narrower and more concave in the lower part of the pot. The kotyle does not survive long into the Hellenistic period.

Kantharos

The kantharos, which in its early stages is closely related to the cup, has its two handles set vertically. Except in Etruscan bucchero and after the seventh century in Boeotian it does not become a widely frequent shape of pottery until the fourth century, when it is supplanting the cup. In the Hellenistic period it loses importance to the 'Megarian' bowl. A normal size is 10 to 15 cm across, but there are very many smaller kantharoi and some larger.

The Protogeometric kantharos has low handles and of course a conical foot. In Geometric this foot is rejected, soon the handles may rise high above the rim and sometimes there is no distinct lip. A modified version, narrower in the body and higher in the lip, is fairly common in minor Protoattic and later in the Boeotian Bird-cup group. Comparable deep-bowled kantharoi with high or low handles occur in the contemporary black-painted ware of Boeotia.

What may be considered the characteristic and perhaps the finest form of the kantharos appears in pottery in Etruscan bucchero (Figure 27). Here the bowl is subordinated to the lip and the foot is emphatic. In the sixth century this type is adopted by Attic and Boeotian. It soon develops an inward curl of the top of the handles and taller and more upright stem and lip (Plate 38 – the kantharos grasped by Heracles). The final stage, familiar in later Apulian red-figure as well as in black-painted ware, is much higher and narrower, with a concave profile to the lip, often a strut and a spur to each handle, and a plastic ring half-way up the stem. Smaller versions of the high-lipped kantharos, with low handles and little or no stem, are very common in black-painted pottery of the fourth and third centuries.

The opposite principle of deepening the bowl and suppressing the lip may be recognized in some little Corinthian pots of the late eighth and early seventh centuries: this shape, which has low handles and no foot, is by some confusingly designated 'kyathos'. Something similar but without decoration recurs in Chiot of the sixth century. More significant is the favourite kantharos of the Cabiran style of Boeotian, a sturdy pot about as wide as high, with rotund body, wide low foot and a spur projecting outwards from the ring handles. A closely related shape popular in black-painted and West Slope wares has a narrower, often moulded foot, and tends to be slightly concave in the upper part of the bowl (so giving a vestigial appearance of a lip). This type of kantharos is still found at the end of the Hellenistic period.

Mug

The name, though not in regular use, is sometimes given to small pots with a wide round mouth and one vertical handle, for example the small bell-mouthed oinochoai of Attic Late Geometric and Protoattic and the squatter oinochoai of shape 8 of red-figure and black-painted wares.

Hemispherical bowl

Roughly hemispherical bowls without handles and with or without a ring foot are common in Hellenistic black-painted ware. The most elaborate of them are the so-called 'Megarian' bowls, which have a good lip and some-times a small ring foot. A normal diameter is 12 to 15 cm. The shape may have been called 'hemitomos' in Athens.

Phiale

A phiale is a wide, shallow saucer, often with a hollow boss rising in the centre (the phiale mesomphalos). 'Phiale' was applied by the Greeks to pots for pouring libations and vase-paintings show this shape so used, and a silver specimen is inscribed 'phiale'; but the name was given to the rhyton too. The phiale appears in Chiot and Corinthian at the beginning of the sixth century and afterwards in Attic too, but in pottery is not common except in miniature. To judge by finds the shape is taken from Oriental metalwork.

PLATES AND DISHES

Plates and dishes to hold food are unusual in pottery of good or moderate quality till the late fifth century. Presumably the ordinary platter was of wood, as the Greek name 'pinax' suggests.

'Pinax' evidently could describe a plate, but is ambiguous and unnecessary and happily obsolete. The authority for 'lekane' and 'lekanis' is not conclusive.

The distinction between plate and dish and lekane and saucer must be arbitrary, but what is called the lekanis has a lid.

Plate

The plate is a flat or flattish disc with a rim and often a low ring foot. It is fairly common in the latest Corinthian and Laconian Geometric: the Corinthian shape has a straightish oblique rim which may be prolonged below into a low foot, the Laconian a more horizontal lip from under which extends a pair of handles. In the early sixth century a footless plate is a main shape (at least in graves of the Nisyros group of the Late Wild Goat style): here the disc rises slightly to the centre and the short lip curls outwards. About the same time plates become more frequent again in Corinthian, and appear also in Attic and in Etruscocorinthian: their lip curls out and over, and the ring foot under it is sometimes double. A flatter lip and foot is usual in the next considerable batch of plates, which are Attic of the late sixth century. From this form develop the black-painted plates that become frequent from the late fifth century, though the subsequent variations of the lip are perhaps prompted by metalware: the trend is to a more centrally placed foot and a more curving section. Large plates, as much as 35 cm across, are frequent in the earlier groups; later plates are mostly much smaller.

Fish-plate

The fish-plate, which takes its name from the fishes that so often decorate its surface, is a sort of plate with downturned rim, disc sloping inwards to a central hollow and a ring foot. A normal size is 20 to 25 cm across. The shape appears in black-painted Attic at the end of the fifth century and lasts there till the middle of the fourth. By then it was established – via Sicilian – in South Italian red-figure, where except in Lucanian its popularity was excessive. There are occasional imitations elsewhere.

Dish

The name of dish is given to almost any sizeable shallow bowl. A few groups have some importance. (1) In the Wild Goat style around 600 BC there are many large dishes, some with simple rim and high stem, others with flat wide rim and high stem or ring foot. (2) A large shallow basin with narrow ring foot, flattened vertical lip and two recurving handles is fairly common in poor Attic and in Boeotian black-figure around the middle of the sixth century, and with the lip more and more assimilated to the bowl is popular again in later red-figure: it is to this shape that the name 'lekane' is confusingly assigned.

Lekanis

The lekanis is much like the lekane (or second type of dish) except that its rim has a ledge to receive the lid. Though it has predecessors, the lekanis proper comes in during the second half of the sixth century and flourishes in the red-figure and black-painted wares of the late fifth and fourth. In Sicily it may have been called 'sipyis'.

LIDS

Some shapes – pyxis, lekanis, lebes gamikos, the large Geometric bell-mouthed oinochoe and the kotyle-krater – regularly had a lid which was made to fit. Other shapes sometimes had careful lids – in Attic, for example, many fine amphorae of mature black-figure and earlier red-figure – and rough lids for trefoil-mouthed oinochoai are very common in the Orientalizing stage of Corinthian pottery. But there is no reason to suppose that most pots of closed shape had their own lids.

CHAPTER IX

TECHNIQUE

—— ·◆· ——

THE STANDARD PROCESSES

There is of course no ancient account of how Greek pots were made. What we have are the remains of several kilns, some terracotta plaques and vase-paintings with brief illustrations of potters at work, comparative technology and the pots themselves. But most of the processes are obvious enough, and for those that are not explanations have been proposed that are at least generally probable. Since Greek pottery reached its highest technical refinement in Attic workshops of the later sixth and earlier fifth centuries, it is convenient to take for summary description the making of a typical red-figure pot.

Presumably the potter dug his clay locally, piled it in his yard and left it to weather. Next he washed – or levigated – it; that is he mixed it with water, let it stand till the coarser and heavier particles had sunk to the bottom and the finer were still in suspension, and ran off this refined solution. In the Greek climate it was not long before evaporation left a paste of the right stiffness for kneading. After kneading the clay was ready to be worked. Like most Greek potters' clays, it contained ferric oxide (Fe_2O_3) and so was reddish in colour. It was also, as can be judged from such shapes as that of Figure 30B, very plastic. How regularly the Greeks mixed their clays is unknown.

The potter next took a lump of his prepared clay and centred it on his wheel, which was spun directly, often by an assistant. Most sizeable pots were made in sections; sometimes neck and body were thrown separately, the body (if large) might be in two parts, and the foot was often attached later. Such sections were put aside to dry to a leather hardness. When they had dried the potter assembled them and luted the joins with a thin solution of clay, and then, turning the pot on the wheel, pared down the surface with a knife, cut mouldings and hollowed out or trimmed the foot. Lastly he added the handles. Greek potters had no taste for mechanical precision, anyhow before the Hellenistic period, and their products are by modern standards often decidedly asymmetrical. So far there is nothing unusual about Greek technique.

Before describing the next processes, those of decoration and firing, some explanation is wanted of two curious features of fine Attic pottery (and in lesser degrees of most other Greek pottery with painted ornament). One is the conjunction of red and black (or reddish and blackish) colour. The other is the sheen, stronger on the black paint and weaker on those reddish surfaces that were meant to be seen. These effects were obtained not by using basically different materials, but by the nature of the clay, its preparation and the firing. Since modern practice is here quite different, at least in Europe, students for a long time could not understand the ancient methods and there are still some points not altogether elucidated by chemists.

Both the red and the black colour of Attic pottery are due, as analyses have proved, to the presence in the natural clay of a fair quantity of ferric oxide, which can be fired red or black according to conditions in the kiln. If the atmosphere is oxidizing, the ferric oxide is unaffected and the fired clay will keep its red colour. But if the atmosphere is reducing – that is, short of oxygen – then oxygen is absorbed from the ferric oxide (Fe_2O_3) which thereby becomes one or other of the iron oxides that show black (FeO or the blacker Fe_3O_4). Conversely, if a black oxide is exposed to an oxidizing fire, it will absorb oxygen and become the red Fe_2O_3. So Attic clay – and the painting medium was clay too – can be fired red or black. What is at first puzzling is that it was fired both red and black on the same pot. This can be managed in two ways. First, since both oxidation and reduction are retarded if the particles of the clay are finer and so more compact, the paint which is more refined than the clay of the rest of the pot changes colour more slowly. If then a pot so painted is exposed in the firing first to a reducing atmosphere – till the paint as well as the rest of the pot is black – and then to an oxidizing atmosphere, a time comes when the rest of the pot is red but the paint still remains black. There was besides an initial oxidizing stage, necessary for good firing. This sequence of oxidation, reduction and partial reoxidation was the normal method of producing the contrast of black and red till the early sixth century and, as can be imagined, the last stage was tricky; indeed a very large proportion of the pots so produced show some reoxidation of the paint, whether through unequal exposure of different parts during the firing or because the thickness of the paint varied.

Secondly, in the same sequence of firing, reoxidation of the black oxides can be prevented by sintering, a partial vitrifaction which in the clays used by the Greeks results at temperatures between 825 and 950 °C. Here the particles of iron oxide become enclosed within crystals of quartz, present in Attic clay, and so – if already reduced – they are insulated against reoxidation until the temperature is raised to 1,050 °C and the quartz softens. Sintering, to be effective for protecting the black colour, requires a considerable refinement of the clay and, though the paint remains black, the rest of the pot can be reoxidized; presumably in its coarser constitution the particles of iron oxide and quartz are too scattered for much enclosure. This fixing of the black paint by sintering occurred from time to time in earlier wares, but perhaps as much by accident as intentionally; the controlled use of the sintering method was a discovery of Attic potters soon after the beginning of the sixth century.

The explanation of the sheen is rather less certain. This used to be called 'varnish' and is still often called 'glaze', but it is not any kind of varnish nor yet one of the familiar silicate or lead glazes. On pots made of some natural illite clays of fine quality it is said that the plate-like particles tend simply through evaporation to align themselves with the plane of the surface, smoothly enough to reflect light; but this effect is improved by careful preparation. First, the clay can be refined by levigation till the particles are of colloidal dimensions. Secondly, an electrolyte (or peptizing agent) can be added to break down excessive coagulations of particles: potash, which was usually at hand in potters' yards, is a good electrolyte and has the further advantage that when added to a solution of clay it makes it thinner and more fluid. Thirdly, burnishing of the surface helps to compact and align the outermost particles. Fourthly, the partial vitrifaction produced by sintering increases the reflective quality of the surface. At present it is not clear how much each of these improvements contributed to the Greek sheen. The higher sheen that becomes regular in Attic work of the early sixth century evidently makes more use than before of controlled sintering and burnishing.

The constitution of the clays used in Greek pottery and of those available in Greek lands is now being studies, and it is clear that what was used for fine Attic ware was a secondary iron-bearing clay of the illite variety, perhaps – because of the quartz – containing celadonite. This clay was used both for the pot itself and in a more refined colloidal solution for the paint and the thin shiny film over other exposed surfaces. Since refinement of the clay eliminates the coarser particles and the particles of iron are finer, this solution has a higher proportion of iron than the less refined clay and therefore a deeper tone, both before and after firing. Before starting his work the painter needed supplies of the finer solution in two or more concentrations.

A first, though not obligatory, stage in decorating the leather-hard pot (if it was to be painted in the red-figure style) was to make a rough preliminary sketch. This sketch was made with some hard instrument, since in many red-figure paintings, if they are turned to catch the light, the preliminary lines are visible as slight depressions in the surface. If, as may be expected, the sketch was reinforced by some pigment, it was a pigment (such as charcoal) that disappeared in firing; not only does no trace of it survive, but also the final drawing does not exactly follow the preliminary sketch, as with the collar-bone of Plate 37A. In black-figure painting, whatever the reason, these depressions are much rarer, though they are known as far back as the middle of the seventh century.

Next the visible surface of the pot was coated with a thin film which dried quickly and often with a slight sheen. Opinions differ on whether this film was a weak solution of the more refined clay or a wash of ochre or a mixture of the two. Ochre (probably the ancient 'miltos') is anyhow the constituent of the deep plummy red of which there are traces here and there on many pots of the red-figure period and especially on the underside of the feet of kotylai. This ochre has not worn well and the period and extent of its popularity are uncertain, but it is not likely that it was used before the sixth century.

For the best results the surface was burnished before and after coating. The painting followed. Its medium was the clay solution in the strong concentration, stiff enough not to run, and the instruments were for the broader surfaces a brush – the marks of its strokes can very often be seen – and for the line-work a fine brush or quill or a syringe, or even a loose hair, all these methods work, and the fine groove that runs down the middle of some relief-lines does not depend on the instrument used. The painter first marked out carefully with a broad thick outline the areas that were to be painted black (see Plate 37B), following more or less closely his preliminary sketch. Then he filled those areas in with an even coat of his solution and added details according to the style in which he was painting. Incised lines were engraved with a sharp point, relief-lines were drawn with a thick concentration and lines intended to fire brown with a thinner, and purple and white enhancements were put on. The painting of bands round the pot was preferably done on the wheel.

At this stage the colour of the pot, or at least of the surfaces coated with the finer solution of the clay, varied only in tone, according to the density and nature of the solution. As has been said, the final contrast of reddish surface and black paint resulted from firing, not from the addition of any special pigment. Of the subsidiary colours, which showed more or less their final tone, the purple seems to come from red ochre, powdered and mixed in a fine solution of the ordinary clay; and the white is probably a primary clay with very often slight traces of iron – enough to produce in an oxidizing fire an ivory-yellow tone. The purple regularly, and the white frequently, has no sheen. Neither of these colours adheres very firmly to the pot. As for yellow, used occasionally in some Greek schools, a satisfactory recipe is to dilute the white with a solution of the ordinary 'paint'.

The Greek kiln was a small and simple structure of clay, but its details are uncertain. The reconstruction shown in Figure 41 is based on the plaques from Penteskouphia (see p. 336), some excavated remains and modern analogy. The kiln proper was domed and may have been sunk partly in the ground; the size varied. It contained a lower fire-chamber and an upper larger chamber in which the pots were stacked; the floor separating the two was perforated to allow the circulation of air and gases, which could escape through a vent in the top of the kiln. In the wall of the upper chamber there was a door, plastered up with clay during firing, and in it a

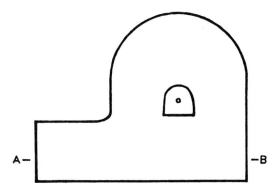

SIDE ELEVATION

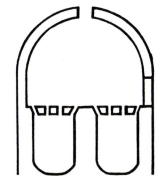

SECTION AT C D

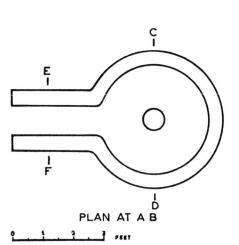

PLAN AT A B

SECTION AT E F

Figure 41 Conjectural restoration of a Greek kiln.

spy-hole through which the potter could watch the progress of his pots. A low tunnel for stoking about 70 cm long ran into the fire-chamber: the opinion that it was divided into two channels is unfounded and improbable. The draught could be regulated by closing the mouth of the tunnel and the vent at the top. In a kiln of this type, if wood or charcoal is used as fuel, a temperature of 900–1,000 °C is practicable. This reconstruction is not beyond criticism. First, all Greek potters' kilns were not of circular plan; the earliest kilns yet found at Corinth, which are said to be (like the plaques) of the sixth century, were probably apsidal, and at Athens Classical kilns are becoming rectangular at their far end. Secondly, though some sort of door with spy-hole is regular on the plaques, its size seems too small for inserting very large pots or even for stacking small ones, though it would have been useful for withdrawing test pieces; perhaps the roof of the kiln was not always permanent, but a temporary crust of straw and clay, put on after the unfired pots had been arranged in the kiln and demolished when the firing was over. Thirdly, by analogy with Romano-British practice, there may not always have been a raised (perforated) floor – for instance, large (unfired) pots could have bridged the gap between central pier and wall. Fourthly, the floor of tunnel and fire-chamber may have sloped upwards from the mouth at an angle of 5–10 degrees.

After they had been decorated and left to dry out the pots were put in the kiln. Since neither the paint nor the rest of the surface became fluid at the temperature reached, there was no regular need of spurs or stilts and the pots could be stacked one on another without danger that they would stick together, though such stacking might sometimes prevent even firing. A fire was now lit of dry wood and a strong draught admitted, and the temperature was gradually raised to about 800 °C. In this oxidizing atmosphere the pots fired red, deeper and more shiny on the painted parts. The second stage required a reducing atmosphere. This can be produced simply by damping the fire and closing the stokehole and the vent; it seems to have been unnecessary to use green wood for fuel. The temperature was now raised to about 950 °C. So the pots turned towards black, the intensity of the colour depending again on the density of the concentration of iron oxide, and some sintering occurred, especially in the paint. Finally, when the heat had dropped to about 900 °C, oxidizing conditions were restored by admitting some draught, and the pots started turning back from black through brown to red; but well-prepared paint, because of its compacter structure or sintering, did not reoxidize during this stage of slow cooling and stayed black. When the cooling was complete, the pots were taken out of the kiln, ready after wiping to be sold. Ancient potters could probably judge the critical temperatures fairly well by eye, though some test pieces have been found.

All these processes required delicate and accurate craftsmanship. The writer of the Homeric epigram to the potters named five devils who plagued them, and there were mistakes. The commonest fault is that areas intended to be black have fired brown or deep red; this may be the result of misfiring, but often the paint had been laid too thinly on the affected parts (as probably on Plate 37B) and so was more susceptible to reoxidation. Sometimes indeed the contrast of red and black paint was deliberate, as on many Corinthian Late Geometric pots and in the Wild Goat style of Aeolis. Sagging of the shape is also common, though generally slight. But the average technical standard was high. Greyness of the unpainted surface is more often the result of a subsequent reduction, especially when pots or sherds were burnt in a funeral pyre.

These technical processes of preparing the clay and of firing are subtle, but simple. They could easily have been discovered empirically and independently. Pottery with a sheen and the contrast of reddish ground and darker brown-black paint, which seem to have been similarly produced has a wide distribution in time and space. The earliest known is the Tell Halaf ware of northern Mesopotamia, which goes back to the fourth millennium BC. In Greece the first appearance of these techniques – whether independently invented or derived from Asia is not known – is in Neolithic in the later fourth millennium: in Crete it was adopted a little later. During the Bronze Age it was the normal Greek practice, except for the matt-painted wares of the Middle Helladic period, and the Iron Age inherited it. But the refinement of the sheen and the regular achievement of a black colour were the work of Attic potters in the sixth century, and their successors and imitators carried on the tradition into Hellenistic times. Arretine and some other Sigillata wares made full use of the shiny property of their clays, though the sifting of the particles was less fine; but, perhaps to simplify factory production, only a single oxidizing firing was employed. Later the sheen in its turn was gradually neglected.

OTHER PROCESSES

Bucchero, unlike the black-painted wares, is dark all through. It too used a very fine illite solution, though in its dilute form, so that the surface has only a faint sheen. But the firing ended with the reducing stage. The dirty yellowish tinge of some bucchero pots comes from incomplete reduction. It has been asserted that added carbon was needed.

The *red wares*, of which Sigillata is the most notable, have undergone only a single stage of oxidation.

The varying technique of *relief wares* has already been mentioned (pp. 204–5), and the methods used for *impressed decoration* (pp. 203–4) are obvious enough.

The white-ground wares with friable *polychrome decoration* have not all been investigated satisfactorily. The Attic lekythoi and their relations were evidently fired in the normal three stages, but some at least of the colours were put on afterwards – this is why the bodies of figures were sketched in the ordinary paint before the firing. In the early Orientalizing of Crete and the Hellenistic Hadra ware there are instances of polychrome painting over the ordinary decoration; here too the second painting presumably followed firing. In general polychrome wares were made as grave furniture and not for ordinary use, and in some instances the pots were so lightly fired that they would disintegrate if soaked in water.

A few Attic pots of the later sixth and earlier fifth centuries make play with a deliberate contrast of black and 'coral' or 'intentional' red. One explanation is that this red comes through mixing ochre with the standard paint; another that kaolinitic clay was added as an ingredient; a third that a less-refined solution of the paint was used, the purpose being to lower the reoxidation point of this 'coral red'. It does not adhere very firmly.

LOCAL CLAYS

The Mansell Colour Charts provide accurate recording of the colour of clays and paints, more accurate in fact than is usually needed. But these charts are relatively new, nor are they always available to students, to that very often one has to rely on verbal descriptions, which differ from one student to another and anyhow are usually imprecise. So, for example, 'red' is variously used of the subsidiary colour which this book loosely calls 'purple', of the brownish unpainted clay of Attic pots (hence the term 'red-figure'), of the ruddier miltos, and – more justly – of the surface of Sigillata wares. In the paragraphs that follow the brief descriptions aim more at consistency than precision.

Mycenaean pottery is remarkably uniform in its technique. Specimens from the Argolid, Attica and Rhodes have a similar light-brown surface, dark-brown paint and good sheen. The use of clays with a fair content of iron oxide and illite and the process of firing in three stages are regular, though through uneven application of the paint or bad arrangement in the kiln the colour of the decoration on one pot often ranges from dark-brown to dark-red. In Submycenaean there is a decline in technical accomplishment, most obvious in the weaker sheen, and neither the Protogeometric nor the Geometric craftsmen recover the Mycenaean standard.

In the Geometric period there is rather more divergence between local schools. But the differences in style are not much more than parochial and the technical ideal is generally to produce a lightish brown surface painted with a brownish black. The unpainted surface is rather darker than is regular in Protogeometric. The paint varies in depth of colour according to its concentration – in the hatching of meanders the paint is often intentionally dilute – and the browns often shade into reds. Before the end of the

Geometric style wares with a whitish slip appear to be regular in Laconia, some Cycladic and Euboean workshops, and Chios. By 'slip' Greek archaeologists mean a coat of clay of a different constitution from that of the pot to which (after the turning) it was applied. Greek slips are generally primary clays with a very low iron content, and so fire to tones ranging from white to yellow. Some local clays were perhaps such that they could not practicably or profitably be refined; or there may have been an aesthetic preference for a lighter ground, as presumably later induced East Greek potters to change their technique when they adopted the Wild Goat style.

The break-up of Geometric increases the local variety of technique as well as style. Athens, the metropolis of the old style, continues the old technique, occasionally (perhaps in emulation of Corinthian effects) reviving the yellowish slip that had been known in its Protogeometric and early Geometric; about 580 BC the colour of the surface deepens from buff to orange, and this with the rich black of the paint sets a new standard for Greek potteries. Corinth on the other hand had in the late eighth century produced a very smooth pale clay, fired at first a yellowish to pinkish tinge, but in the Ripe period more often faintly green: about 575 BC the new Attic tone provokes the painting of an orange background to the principal field of elaborate works. Few other cities used such fine clay for making pots. The Boeotians had access to a clay scarcely inferior to Attic, but also made slipped pottery. Laconia preferred a pink clay with a cream slip. In Crete the clay is generally brownish with or without a pale slip. The Orientalizing schools of the Cyclades have usually a yellowish slip over rather coarse, brownish clay. Most East Greek fine wares after Geometric are slipped. The clay is coarse and varies from buff to pink, the slip ranges from the white of Chiot through cream to yellow, and the paint is generally brownish and streaky. But the Subgeometric Bird bowls continue the Geometric technique; and during the sixth century there is imitation of Attic, often palish, by the Ionian Little Master cups and by Clazomenian and other black-figure ventures. In Italy the abler makers of painted pottery copied with varying success first Corinthian and then Attic clay and finish. The red-figure style of Athens carries on the black-figure technique of clay and paint. At the end of the sixth century a thin white slip sometimes occurs, especially on small black-figure lekythoi. From this develops the very white but friable slip of the white-ground lekythoi. During the fourth century Attic clay tends to be yellower than before. The red-figure of South Italy uses various clays, mostly pale, and often, as at Corinth, the potter felt obliged to cover the surface with a reddish wash.

The technical decline of the fourth century continued in the Hellenistic period. Attic potters for some while remained superior to their rivals, but even Attic clay is less regularly fine and deep in colour, and the paint takes a bluish tinge or becomes streaky. A little more has been said on p. 202.

Students of Greek vase-painting are very ready to assign pots and sherds to local schools on the appearance of the clay or paint to the unaided eye. In this they are within limits successful. Corinthian clay, for example, is pale and clear, Etruscocorinthian pale but slightly muddy; and Attic clay is unusually free of what is called mica. This crude practice is bound to continue because of its simplicity and speed, but now there are scientific ways of determining the peculiarities of particular clays.

Natural clays may vary widely in constituents from one district to another and even sometimes in the same district, nor is this always obvious to the naked eye. Most of these constituents survive refining and firing. At present examination is done by either chemical or petrological analysis. Petrological analysis looks for inclusions of distinctive rocks and, since many or them may be eliminated when a potter refines his clay, it is more suited to coarse wares. Chemical analysis, of which there are several methods, estimates the proportions of various elements in the sample. In these ways groups of pots can be distinguished by the composition of their clays. So it should be possible to determine which pots can have been made of clay from the same beds and which cannot and further, if local beds of clay have been examined, whether a particular pot can or cannot have been made of a particular local clay. Some cautions are necessary. First, there is some arbitrariness in deciding the limits of variation acceptable within a group of pots. Secondly, clays of similar constitution may appear over a large area or recur in distant areas. Thirdly, through exhaustion or erosion or even because they have been overlooked, relevant beds of clay may not be taken into account. Fourthly, in the course of time a pot may have been contaminated by contact with other minerals, so falsifying the analysis. Lastly, clay may have been transported from one district to another, though so far there is no evidence that this was at all regular in ancient times. Even so, results are impressive and have given answers to several questions that perplexed archaeologists and also to some they had not thought of. So far, for the period dealt with in this book, the most important concern the Archaic wares of the East Greek region, where the local clay resources have been investigated in most detail.

MENDING

Many Greek pots were mended. Mending was usually done with lead or bronze rivets for which holes about the diameter of a matchstick were drilled along the edges of breaks. Usually only the holes are left. Often even inferior small pots were repaired, and an early Protoattic krater of moderate size has over forty pairs of rivet holes. Occasionally a piece of another pot was inserted as a patch, or a tall foot cut down.

CHAPTER X

INSCRIPTIONS

— ·◆· —

GENERAL COMMENTS

Inscriptions first appear on Greek pots in the later eighth century, but do not become at all numerous till the sixth and even then are relatively few. They may be painted or incised, or even written in ink or stamped. A more significant distinction is whether they were executed before or after firing, by the painter or by the merchant or purchaser. As it happens, nearly all painted inscriptions other than merchants' marks were put on before firing and nearly all incised inscriptions after firing. The exceptions can easily be detected, since incision before firing (when the pot is leather-hard) leaves a clean and not a ragged edge to the cut, and painting after firing is usually under the foot and – if the test is permitted – can be removed by methylated spirit or some other solvent.

The main classes of inscriptions painted before firing are captions, signatures, mottoes (for all of which nonsensical groups of letters sometimes serve), and fourthly dedications. Inscriptions incised after firing mostly record dedication or ownership. Many of the inscriptions painted after firing and some of those incised are the marks of merchants; normally they are under the foot. Writing in ink is an alternative to incision for the bare epitaphs added to some Hadra urns. Stamping, of course before firing, appears on some Megarian bowls and many Calene phialai, and also on many Classical and Hellenistic coarse amphorae and on Sigillata wares of the Roman period. All these inscriptions were put on whole pots. There are also 'ostraka', sherds already broken and casually picked up to make jottings on or inscribe with a vote. But though ostraka have their importance, it is not for the study of Greek pottery.

Till the fifth century inscriptions on pots, though brief, are both more numerous and more securely dated than most other inscriptions that survive. So they offer much of the evidence for the date when the Greeks adopted their alphabet, for some of its local varieties and their development, and for early orthography. They offer something too to the knowledge of Greek dialects, especially if the origin of the writer is known. Conversely, the forms of a painter's alphabet and dialect may help to decide where he worked. But some of the results are perplexing; for example, around the middle of the seventh century the Polyphemus painter, a notable Attic vase-painter, wrote like an Aeginetan, and the painter of the Chigi vase, a leader of the Corinthian school, was not a Corinthian, if judged by his writing. There is also much for prosopographers and for those who can reconstruct social history from personal names.

INSCRIPTIONS BEFORE FIRING

Inscriptions put on a pot while it was being decorated are usually painted. Where the ground was light, they were done in the ordinary dark paint. Where the ground was dark, as normally in red-figure, first purple and later white was the obvious medium, though occasionally a signature might be incised in some remote place like a handle or the edge of the foot. But most of these inscriptions belong to the principal field.

In the placing and lettering of an inscription painters took more or less pains to conform to the decorative scheme of the vase, but there is one class of Attic pottery in which it has become a regular and integral part of the decoration. The lip cup, created in the 560s, is remarkable for its rejuvenation of old artistic forms and it uses inscriptions with equal virtuosity. A fairly typical specimen is illustrated on Plate 25A (though inscriptions on the lip are rare). Here, as also on some band cups, the handle frieze contains between the terminal palmettes a neat row of fine letters, which spell out sometimes a signature, sometimes an invitation to drink and sometimes – for the sense does not really matter – what is partly or wholly nonsense. Since the proportions of the field are fixed and the inscription should have an appropriate length, signatures are often padded out, and so we know (less from piety than because his name was a short one) that the prolific maker Tleson was the son of Nearchos. There are also some curious instances of the misspelling or muddling of words, such as Χσενοκλες εποκλεσεν and ενεοινοιοιεν, which are best explained if the painter could not himself spell but was drawing from a text set before him or his memory of such a text.

Captions

Names written against figures first appear during the second quarter of the seventh century. In the second quarter of the sixth they suddenly become excessive; on the François vase in the scene of Troilus the well-house, Polyxena's water pot and Priam's seat are labelled superfluously κρενε, hυδρια, θακος – a fashion vaguely known to Aelian (*VH* x. 10) – and on Tyrrhenian amphorae there are often meaningless blobs to simulate lettering. In the fifth century these names grow much fewer. It is usually individual figures that are named, rarely objects or groups of figures, and very rarely whole scenes. The captions are written against the figures to which they belong, forward or backward, and at whatever angle space and convenience recommend. Occasionally the words of a speaker issue from his mouth as on an amphora of Exekias in the Vatican where Achilles calls 'four' and Ajax 'three'. A few red-figure pots of the end of the sixth century express the ebullient feelings of the vase-painter; so in the remarkable anatomical study of Plate 39 Euthymides appends the comment hoς ουδεποτε Ευφρονιος – as never Euphronios', and he in turn is toasted by Phintias with σοι τενδι Ευθυμιδει in a scene that makes the compliment ambiguous.

Since captions are an addition to scenes of human and especially mythological figures, they are not to be expected in all groups of Greek pottery. They are comparatively frequent in the more ambitious products of Corinthian, Attic and 'Chalcidian'; in Laconian around the middle of the sixth century there were two or perhaps three painters who could write; in Boeotia the naming of figures is least rare in the Cabiran style; and some red-figure Etruscan and South Italian workshops follow the Attic example. In other schools of vase-painting examples are few and isolated. The naming of figures appears also on plaques, free paintings and sculptures in relief, lingering on into fully illusionist pictures such as the Odyssey landscapes from the Esquiline and on mosaics continuing till the end of antiquity. But there is no rule for captions. At first, when mythological scenes were a novelty, names may have been thought necessary to explain who the characters were, but often the scene is self-explanatory or in its action or spirit anonymous, and more often still – at least in vase-painting – the artist does without names. Nor does the placing of the letters usually improve the decorative composition. In general captions were a convention of Archaic and Early Classical art, which Greek taste did not feel unpleasant or obligatory. They add some new names to the catalogue of mythical persons, usually supplied by the painter's invention or faulty memory.

The legends of official Panathenaic amphorae form a special class of captions. On these conservative monuments the formula τῶν 'Αθήνηθεν ἄθλων ('a prize from Athens') continues till the end, though the names of magistrates that begin in the fourth century are painted in the modern style. Some of these magistrates can be dated, and so their inscriptions have a little value for the chronology of vase-painting.

Signatures

In number much fewer, signatures rank first in interest for the student of Greek pottery, since they give an insubstantial existence to its personalities. These signatures – the term is loose, since not all can be autographs – are of two kinds, one naming the painter, the other the maker; Σοφιλος εγραφσεν and Αμασις μ εποιεσεν are typical. The oldest certain signatures are of the first half of the seventh century and come from unexpected places. The earliest – a name ending in . . inos – is on a krater found on

Ischia (Pithecusae) and apparently local work in a Euboean style of about 700 BC; and a generation or more later there follow a banded aryballos imitating Protocorinthian and signed by Pyrrhus in a Euboean alphabet, a krater probably made in Italy by Aristonothos (or Aristonophos), and a 'candlestick' of the Ithacan school by Kalikleas. All these were makers. The first Corinthian to leave us his name is the painter Timonidas, who was working in the 580s, and in the next generation Chares painted a miserable pot and Milonidas a plaque. Sophilos, a contemporary of Timonidas, begins the long line of Attic painters and makers whose names we know. Attic signatures reach their peak about 500 BC and are rare again by the end of the fifth century. A few Boeotians thought themselves worth recording, two Paestans, Praxias in Etruria and some late manufacturers of relief ware.

Ἔγραψε and ἐποίησε are the two normal verbs of signature – 'so and so painted (me)' and 'so and so made (me)'. It is plain that the painter and the maker were not always the same person, since for example the pots that Andocides signed as maker are painted by more than one hand and on the François vase the joint signatures distinguish between the painter Clitias and the maker Ergotimos. 'Painted' is clear enough, but 'made' is ambiguous in Greek as in English and whether on Greek vases it means maker in the narrow sense of the man who shapes the pot on the wheel or in the wider sense of the master of the workshop can be debated for ever. Little is known of the organization of Greek potteries except that they were often small, and so one man might combine two or all three of the roles of master, shaper and painter. Those who hold that 'made' refers to the shaper claim first that the Greeks valued shape as much as decoration, and secondly that vases signed by the same maker were in fact shaped by the same shaper. The opposite school asserts that the owner of a workshop would sometimes at least have insisted that he should be advertised rather than his employees, that two men cannot have combined to shape a band cup though in a couple of instances two combined to 'make' one, and that it is lexically irrational to limit 'making' to shaping. None of these arguments is beyond question. We do not know how the ancient Greeks rated the shape of a pot and the painting on it, though it does not seem likely that shape was closely valued before the refinements of the second quarter of the sixth century. The claim that all pots signed by one maker are by one shaper has been tested extensively only for Attic cups of the later sixth and earlier fifth centuries, and not many of these are signed. Two relevant results are that cups signed by one maker are or may be by the same shaper and that cups painted by one man are very often shaped by one man: if then painter and shaper were separate persons, they worked together faithfully, and it is no harder to believe that painter and master of the workshop stayed together. That the master should neglect to advertise his products by putting his name on them is by modern notions absurd, but so few Greek pots are signed that such advertisement cannot have been valued – an exception should be made perhaps for Nikosthenes. Even so, it is worth noting that the signatures of makers are more than twice as common as those of painters – an unnatural instance of unselfishness if the painter (who wrote the signature) was advertising a colleague and not a master. There are two minor arguments that point opposite ways. A few Attic pots have the signature of one man as both painter and maker; of these men Duris also painted pots made by Python both before and after those he made himself. Euphronios is the name of an Attic painter of the end of the sixth century, of a maker of the early fifth and of a man, from his attributes a potter who, before 480 BC made an expensive dedication as a tithe on the Acropolis at Athens; unless we accept coincidence, it appears that Euphronios began as a painter and then became a maker and, since he was or grew wealthy, that he was owner of a workshop. So three conclusions are possible. First, 'made' means 'shaped'; this is now the orthodox opinion, with the two optional provisos that 'making' was occasionally extended to other manual processes and that the shaper was usually the master of the workshop. Secondly, the 'maker' as such was the master. Thirdly, the term 'made' did not necessarily have the same meaning at different times, or even at the same time. The second and third solutions seem to me the more likely.

This account assumes that the signatures on pots are those of the makers and painters of those pots, but a recent theory would transfer them to metalworkers: potters acquired drawings prepared for engravers and copied even the signatures. The evidence is flimsy.

Mottoes

Convivial phrases like χαῖρε καὶ πίει εὖ though appropriate to drinking cups, are not common. They occur principally on Attic lip cups where an inscription of any kind was useful, and round the lip of some Hellenistic kantharoi. There are also a few oddities like καλόν εἰμι ποτήριον – 'I am a good cup'.

More curious are the καλός inscriptions (or love-names) of the pattern of Λεαγρος καλος or more cannily ho παις καλος and simply καλος. These inscriptions which record more than two hundred names, are fairly frequent on Attic pots from the third quarter of the sixth to the third quarter of the fifth century, after which the fashion quickly disappears. The range of the Greek καλός includes the English 'beautiful', and the accepted interpretation of these phrases is that they celebrate the homosexual charms of the popular aristocratic youths of the day. This fits with the short currency – normally five to ten years – of individual names, some of which after a proper interval recur among leaders of the Athenian state. Thus Leagros, the most celebrated of the καλοί, should have been in his teens within the years 510–500 BC and could well have grown up to be the Leagros who was a general in Thrace in 465. These inscriptions are an interesting commentary on fashion, since they were not bespoken solely (if at all) by the intimates of the beautiful youth, but were put on pots for public sale, many of which were exported to Etruria where young Leagros and the rest can have had no admirers. Occasionally a woman's beauty too is celebrated, and there are instances where the epithet is applied to a god or a hero. The normal καλός inscriptions are useful for chronology; pots with, for example, the legend Παναιτιος καλος should have been made about the same time.

Dedications and owners' names

Inscriptions recording dedication or very much less often private ownership are usually added after the firing. But a few bespoke pieces received such inscriptions in the workshop.

Dedications painted before firing are preserved on Chiot chalices, kantharoi, and phialai around the 570s. The formula is of the type of Ζωιλος μ ανεθηκε τηι Αφροδιτηι – 'Zoilos dedicated me to Aphrodite'. Many examples have been found at Naucratis in Egypt, some in Aegina and a few in Chios. The most obvious explanation was that outside Chios these pots were dedicated by merchants, since the same dedicators recur too often to be casual visitors, and that some merchants had regular connections with certain potters, since the inscriptions for each dedicator are usually written by one painter; and though at least one dedicator turns out to be female, this may be right in general. Outside this class of Chiot pottery fired dedications are very rare.

Fired inscriptions of private ownership are rare still. The earliest is perhaps an Attic cup not much after the middle of the seventh century with . . . υλο ειμι – 'I am . . yl(l)os's' – on the rim. Only one known painter, a Corinthian of the second quarter of the sixth century, made anything like a regular practice of adding customers' names; he has left four specimens on simple quatrefoil aryballoi.

INSCRIPTIONS AFTER FIRING

Inscriptions put on pots already fired are mostly incised. These vary greatly in carefulness of planning and execution, but even the best are a little ragged along the edges of the cut or scratch. Inscriptions painted after firing are usually in purple or white. Of these unfired inscriptions most were added by or for the ultimate purchaser, and their obvious place is on the lip or shoulder. A few are merchants' or dealers' notes, scribbled usually under the foot. Generally, it may be presumed, these inscriptions were incised or painted while the pot was still fairly new, but some may be considerably later, and a few are modern, to be detected only by the forger's negligence or faulty knowledge.

Dedications

Formulas of dedication vary, but regularly give the name of the recipient deity and not so regularly the name of the giver, occasionally supplemented at international sanctuaries by his ethnic. The commonest formulas are of the types of Εϱμησιφανης μ ανεθηκεν τηφϱοδιτηι and Απολλωνος εμι and, especially in Hellenistic times, Αφϱοδιτης and Υγιειας, though this is often a toast or invocation rather than a gift. These dedications are useful principally for identifying the deities of sanctuaries and shrines and sometimes their cult titles.

Owners' names

A number of pots, mostly from graves, are inscribed with the name of a private owner, for instance Χαϱιλεο εμι or Ευθυμο. Sometimes the assertion is expanded, as in Θαϱιο ειμι ποτεϱιον, and a very few longer inscriptions add the occasion when the pot was acquired or a curse on anyone who should steal it. At Athens pots which were public property might be marked δημοσια or in abbreviated ligature δη, but these are coarse ware.

Mottoes and captions

Unfired convivial inscriptions would perhaps be less uncommon if excavators had picked through more dumps from private houses and taverns. There are also some obscene comments on friends or enemies. Titles designating a pot as a prize are very rare apart from the fired inscriptions of Panathenaic amphorae, but they provide what may be the earliest incised text; this is on the so-called Dipylon jug, an Attic oinochoe of Late Geometric style offered as a prize for dancing – hος νυν οϱχεστον παντον αταλοτατα παιζει it reads in a good hexameter, and then tails off into incomprehensibility.

Epitaphs

Some of the Hadra hydriai from the early Hellenistic cemeteries of Alexandria give in ink or incision the name of the dead person and the date of death or burial.

Merchants' marks

Merchants' and dealers' marks, incised or painted after firing, are as nowadays mostly cryptic. A few longer texts give prices, but not usually of the pot on which they are inscribed.

CHAPTER XI

CHRONOLOGY

—— .◆. ——

INTRODUCTION

Chronology may be absolute or relative. Absolute chronology is tied accurately to calendar years. Relative chronology states more or less loosely the relation in time between one event and another, which may or may not itself be absolutely dated. But for convenience, if nothing worse, it is usual to express relative dates in absolute terms. For example, the pots illustrated on Plates 2B, 3A and 3B are in the captions dated to the tenth, the second quarter of the ninth, and the middle or later ninth centuries BC but it would be truer to say that the first was of the beginning of the Greek Iron Age, the second appreciably later than the first and the third rather later than the second. In studies concerned with Greek pottery it is often important to remember which dates are absolute and which relative, and also how secure those dates are.

RELATIVE CHRONOLOGY

In many schools of fine Greek pottery, anyhow before the Hellenistic period, style and to a smaller degree technique developed more or less consistently, and the study of these developments (which requires a good eye and the judgement and knowledge to pick out the significant characteristics) has enabled specialists to determine sequences of pots in various schools and is in fact the basis of what we know or think we know of their courses and ties. It allows also more subtle inferences if the pieces compared are connected closely. But where there is no close connection, as for instance between the Boeotian Bird cups and other Orientalizing schools, the internal evidence provided by style is inadequate or even misleading.

The external evidence comes mostly from graves and stratified deposits. In a stratified deposit – that is a deposit which accumulated gradually or in successive layers – the depth at which an object is found should show how early it was deposited. But stratification usually deals in periods of not less than fifty years, and the excavators of Greek sites have not reported many strata of any sort. Graves are more frequent and informative, if they were used only once. The ancient Greeks and their neighbours regularly put pottery in graves, so that we have many groups of pots that were buried at the same time. Though it does not follow that they were made at the same time, comparison suggests that the range of the pots in any one interment is usually not more than twenty or perhaps thirty years. So grave groups are excellent for synchronisms between different schools or trends within a single school. But it is dangerous to argue from a single instance; to allow for heirlooms and the negligence of excavators several similar contexts are wanted before a synchronism or its absence can be accepted.

By combining these two methods, the stylistic and the external, a system of parallel sequences may be obtained. Such a system is essentially relative. Occasionally there may be hints of the absolute intervals between various points in a sequence. If style allows the recognition of individual painters, the period of their works is limited by the span of human life. A close series of grave groups might perhaps excuse a rough reckoning in steps of some twenty years, and the ingenuous student can try to divine the annual rate of deposit in a stratified site. For Attic vase-painting in its prime the Καλός names seem normally to have been current for not more than ten years, though they are most useful for synchronisms and sequences. But such checks hardly become available till they are no longer needed.

The results so far reached by these methods are set out perfunctorily in Figures 42 and 43. The two principal sequences are the Attic, which runs from the beginning of Protogeometric to the end of red-figure, and the Corinthian, which is clear from Late Geometric till the end of the Animal style. These sequences are fairly well tied to each other by connections in style and by grave groups, and other schools are linked to them. Some of the links are weak. For Protogeometric and Geometric the synchronisms, depending mainly on stylistic resemblances to Attic, are not much more than tentative till near the end, when first Attic and then Corinthian influence became strong. Of the Orientalizing and black-figure schools Laconian III is tied mainly to Corinthian by style and grave groups. For Bocotia grave groups have dated the Bird cups and style its Archaic black-figure. The connections for Cycladic are stylistic, loose for the early schools and close for 'Melian'. Of East Greek wares the Bird bowls are tolerably fixed by grave groups and other contexts; the Wild Goat style appears in useful grave groups about the Early phase of Ripe Corinthian; Chiot depends mostly on stylistic parallels, Fikellura on grave groups, Clazomenian black-figure on style and one context, and the Clazomenian sarcophagi on style with little help from grave groups. For Crete there is an increasing supply of internal and external evidence. In Italy grave groups and lax stylistic links are at hand for Geometric, Italocorinthian and Bucchero; and for Etruscan black-figure, 'Chalcidian' and the Caeretan hydriai stylistic comparison with Attic is good enough. In red-figure Attic till its late stage influences and dates the other schools. For Hellenistic, where style is no longer coherent, contexts are necessary. But even in the well-explored periods of mature black-figure and red-figure new discoveries may be surprising.

ABSOLUTE CHRONOLOGY

Greek and Oriental literature and records offer a large number of dated events. The Greek sources are accurate enough from the fifth century onwards, when historical study had begun and public archives became extensive. The period before 500 BC is more obscure. Greek events are few and dates less certain, since it does not seem that there was much official recording, anyhow before writing was introduced, nor did the ancients themselves agree on the very bare chronologies that they constructed in Classical and later times; and though in the older civilizations of the East there are many accurately dated events, only rarely have they been linked to Greece. Besides, not all events are relevant to pottery, and all that are relevant are not equally valuable. In general the most valuable fixed dates are those given by the sealing of a rich deposit, in a communal grave or a destroyed settlement. The foundation of a settlement is not so definite, since the earliest deposit may be poor, escape notice or have been cleared away. Parallels with sculpture and free painting are mostly delusive in the Archaic period, since the dating of those arts is almost always dependent on pottery, and afterwards the arts no longer proceeded in step. Nor is there much help from small independently dated objects, such as coins, which often prove much older than the context in which they are found; so an isolated object of this sort is usually suspect, though if the association is repeated it becomes more trustworthy.

The useful dates for Archaic and earlier pottery, few and regressively more unreliable, must be considered critically. For later times a statement of the more important dates is enough.

Late Bronze Age

At Amarna in Egypt, in contexts of the second quarter of the fourteenth century – the date is safe to ten or fifteen years – there has been found Mycenaean pottery of the Late Helladic IIIa stage; and two centuries later there is a less secure and less direct synchronism for the Late Helladic IIICI style in the new settlements of the Philistines. From this comes the generally accepted date of 1050 BC for the beginning of Attic Protogeometric, though 1000 BC may be likelier.

Protogeometric and Geometric periods

The next five or six hundred years after Amarna have so far no good fixed points. The Dorian invasion (whatever that was) is disappointing; its date is uncertain and its traces have not been recognized in pottery. From Tell Abu Hawam in Palestine there are three pieces of imported Greek ware, which look contemporary with Attic Early and Middle Geometric and were found in a stratum thought to be no later than the end of the ninth century. From Megiddo we have two Attic sherds of the beginning of Middle Geometric and two other sherds that appear to imitate Greek work of much the same time; these were at first assigned to a stratum thought to end no later than 850 BC and the beginning of Attic Middle Geometric was based on this context, but later they were reassigned to the following stratum, so that here again, current Greek chronology may be too high. From Samaria come seven Attic or Atticizing sherds of Middle (or very early Late) Geometric style and sealed in a stratum thought to end no later than 750 BC. At these three sites the dates given above depend on the contents of the strata and their relative chronology according to the system constructed by Palestinian archaeologists, but unfortunately there is no agreement yet on their absolute values. It is different with Hama, which was destroyed by the Assyrians – as their records tell us – in 720 BC: so the one example of Attic Middle Geometric II and the three Late Geometric fragments should be earlier. Al Mina is delusive, since its beginning is dated only relatively by comparing the earliest Oriental finds with those from other Syrian and Palestinian sites, and there is no certainty that its earliest Greek finds are as old.

Archaic period

With the Western colonization of the Greeks we are approaching their historical times. For the Sicilian foundations Thucydides gives some relative dates in two distinct series and Eusebius absolute dates which tally very roughly with Thucydides and a chance remark of Pindar's. Modern students generally combine Thucydides and Eusebius, though the ancients were less agreed. At four of the colonies so dated – Syracuse in 733, Megara Hyblaea in 728, Gela in 688 and Selinus in 628 BC – there has been enough excavation to raise the hope that the plentiful Corinthian pottery goes back to within a few years of their founding, though where the earliest pieces are from graves a few perfectionists profess to allow a longer lag for the first settlers to grow old and die. The relative order of these foundations is confirmed by the sequence of the pottery, Syracuse and Megara Hyblaea of course appearing contemporary. For the earlier absolute dates two contacts with the East give some support. In a grave at Pithecusae (Ischia) which contained three Corinthian pots little later than the earliest from

Syracuse and earlier than any from Gela there was a scarab with the cartouche of the Egyptian Bocchoris whose reign can be fixed with a margin of a few years to 718–712 BC. If the scarab is Egyptian (as has been asserted) it was probably made during and not after the reign of that inglorious king, but the context can be used to suggest a more precise result. It is obviously improbable that all three pots should be much older than the time of the burial and therefore than the scarab; but, to judge by the generations of Attic Geometric painters, the interval between these pots and those from Samaria cannot be more than some sixty years; if then the latest date of the Samaria pots is 750 BC and the earliest date of the Pithecusae pots is 718 BC (since the scarab of king Bocchoris cannot be earlier than the beginning of his reign), then the range of error in the absolute dating here should not be more than twenty-five years and the chronology followed in this book cannot be raised or lowered by more than ten or fifteen years. The importance of this Bocchoris scarab is exceptional; other scarabs found in Greece have not been helpful.

Selinus is troublesome. Till 1958 it was believed that its earliest finds were Early Ripe Corinthian, and the beginning of that stage was related to the fixed date of 628 BC which Thucydides gives for the foundation of the colony. Then it was noticed that Transitional or even Late Protocorinthian had been found in a cemetery there. However it now appears that the graves in that cemetery also contained indigenous pottery, while at the Greek colonial settlement there was nothing earlier than Early Ripe Corinthian. So the cemetery may have been a native pre-colonial one – natives elsewhere imported Greek pots – and the accepted chronology can be justified without the shifty device of preferring Eusebius here to Thucydides. Still, it is as well to be cautious about foundation dates.

For another colony, Aziris in Cyrenaica, dates can be obtained by a combination of statements of Herodotus and Eusebius. This puts its beginning in 637 and its end in 631 BC. If the site has been identified correctly, the Archaic objects found there should be of, or not much before, that time. The very few finds recorded include fragments of Protocorinthian pots and examples of East Greek Bird bowls and banded cups.

In the East the sources of our tradition may be different. At three colonial sites there has been much excavation – Naucratis, Istria and Olbia; Eusebius puts their foundations in 749, 657 and 647 BC, but to judge by the finds they should all be rather later than the settlement at Selinus. Perhaps the earliest pottery of these eastern sites has not been revealed, or more likely they were founded later than Eusebius thought. Certainly the earliest finds so far made at those colonies are little, if any, earlier than the latest from destruction deposits at Old Smyrna, which Herodotus says was destroyed by king Alyattes of Lydia, that is on his reckoning (which may well be a little inflated) not before 613 BC, since Alyattes was occupied elsewhere in his first five years. It is easiest to conclude that though

Eusebius's dates cannot be trusted consistently, the western series is more or less right. But Greek history in the early Archaic period is so shadowy that an absolute error even of thirty or forty years should not be disturbing.

A little absolute evidence comes from Oriental sites. Tarsus was destroyed by Sennacherib in 696 BC and Protocorinthian and East Greek Bird bowls were found there; unfortunately it is not yet agreed whether they belong before or after that destruction. There is also Meṣad Ḥashavyahu near Askalon, where a small fort which was in use only a short time contained pottery of the Middle II Wild Goat style – not, I think, the earliest – and also several Hebrew inscriptions. Since the inscriptions are Hebrew and this area was occupied by the Egyptians in 609 BC, it is reasonable to suppose that the pottery too is earlier and consequently that the Middle I Wild Goat style and, since it seems contemporary, Early Ripe Corinthian did not begin later than 620 BC. Yet Early Ripe Corinthian, so the finds at Old Smyrna show, was not yet at its end when that city was sacked and so can hardly have ended earlier than 605 BC. If then, as is likely, early Ripe Corinthian lasted for no more than twenty-five or thirty years, its absolute dating can be fixed within ten or fifteen years and the system generally accepted by archaeologists should not, so it happens, be over five or ten years out. Suspicious though this result is, the main framework for the chronology of Archaic pottery seems reasonably sound, though when applied to lesser schools the error may be considerably more.

The next fixed date is 566 BC when, according to Pherecydes and Eusebius, the Panathenaic festival or its games were instituted, and with them – it is assumed – the officially inscribed Panathenaic amphorae: so the earliest surviving amphorae, one near Lydos in Halle, Burgon's in the British Museum (Plate 21B) and a fragment in Athens, are dated in the later 560s. There is also the famous Laconian cup that shows a man labelled Arcesilas presiding over the weighing of wool: if this is a contemporary record of a king Arcesilas of Cyrene, then to conform with our other fixed dates he must be the second of that name and the cup was made in the 560s or not much later. Some students also hold that since, as Herodotus and inscribed fragments say, king Croesus of Lydia gave columns to the new Artemisium at Ephesus, the surviving sculpture from columns of that temple can be dated about 550 BC; but the Artemisium was a very big building, and work, even on the pedestals, may have been spread over many years.

Herodotus also records that, after the building of the Siphnian treasury at Delphi, Siphnos was attacked by Samian exiles who had taken part in the Spartan expedition against Polycrates, and that that expedition took place while Cambyses was invading Egypt in (as we know) 525 BC: though the story is probably in part false and the interval between the building and the attack is not stated, archaeologists assume that it was only a year or two and so roundly date the sculptures of the Siphnian treasury about 525 BC. Another fixed point at 525 BC may come from the same invasion of Egypt by Cambyses. According to Herodotus Daphnae was the frontier fortress to the east of Egypt and there were Greek mercenary troops in the Egyptian army that was defeated by the Persians: if, as seems likely, Daphnae is the modern Tell Defenneh, then the latest Greek pottery from that site may be not later than 525 BC.

Three later Archaic dates are owing again to the Persians. Miletus was sacked in 494 BC, but the finds are not yet very helpful. At Marathon in 490 BC the Athenians raised a mound over their dead and duly furnished them with pottery. At Athens, sacked in 480 BC, rich pockets of debris have been recovered on the Acropolis and in the Agora; admittedly there is contamination from later periods, but it is very small. Further, in Sicily, Megara Hyblaea was destroyed in 483 BC and the finds are well published.

Classical period

With the fifth century, dates in Greek history became exactly reliable. After the sack of Athens in 480 BC the next useful peg is the refounding of Camarina in 461 BC. In 426–425 BC the Athenians purified Delos, digging up the graves and removing their contents to Rheneia; there the Purification deposit has been found and only slightly (so it seems) contaminated by later objects. After the battle of Delion in 424 BC the Boeotians buried their dead and local pottery in the Polyandrion at Thespiae. A little later is a grave of Lacedaemonians in Athens of 403 BC. Motya was sacked in 397 BC. Olynthus came to an end, or nearly so, in 348 BC. Gela, destroyed in 405, was refounded about 340 BC and destroyed again some sixty years later: the second settlement is now being useful for South Italian wares. At Chaeronea the Thebans killed in the battle of 338 BC were buried in a communal grave, which is not yet published properly. Alexandria was founded in 331 BC, and an earlyish cemetery has been unearthed at Chatby (or Sciatbi). The effect of Alexander may be seen also on some Apulian red-figure pots, which show a Greek attacking a Persian king; if rightly interpreted, these must have been painted after 334 BC, but probably not long after, since the vase-painters had not yet learnt that Alexander had no beard. There are also from 379 till 312 BC Panathenaic amphorae painted before firing with the name of an annual archon.

Hellenistic period

Alexandria offers not only its foundation, but also a number of funerary dates inscribed on Hadra hydriai; these dates give the year of the reigning Ptolemy and if the identifications are right (as seems likely) they extend

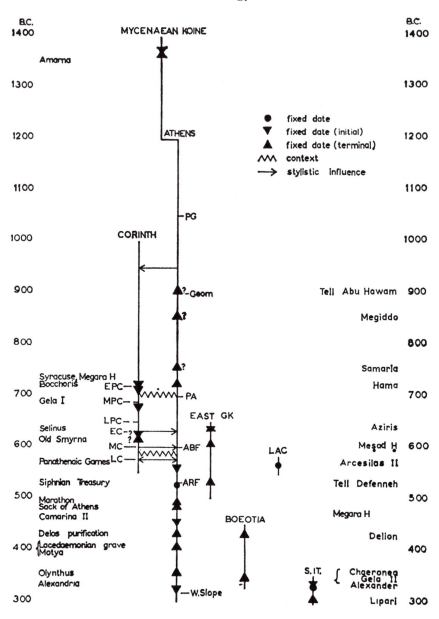

Figure 42 Main structure of system of dating.

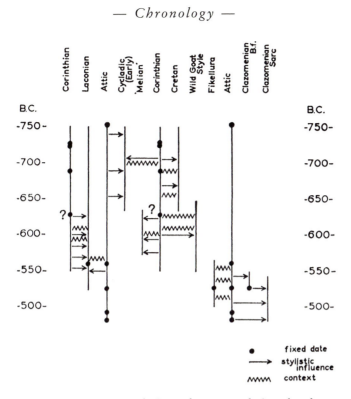

Figure 43 Cross-dating of some archaic schools.

from 271 to 209 BC. The Panathenaic amphorac continue to show names of officials, but after about 310 BC archons are replaced by treasurers and agonothetes, and very few of these can now be identified. Lipari was wasted in 304, to the benefit of South Italian specialists. An excavated fort at Koroni in Attica, occupied only from 265 to 261 BC, is useful especially for black-painted ware. In Crete Lyttos was destroyed in 220 BC and Apollonia in 171. The destruction of Carthage in 147 BC has little value, while that of Corinth in 146 BC has much value. The keen student of Hellenistic pottery can probably find other good dates that are fixed more or less precisely.

Other absolute chronologies

Besides dates based on historical records there are physical methods of computing time. Calculation of the decay of radiocarbon, by now indispensable to prehistorians, is not precise enough to help students of Greek vase-painting. Measuring thermoluminescence also has the convenience that the material is provided by the pottery itself, but for the first millennium

BC a hundred years is an optimistic limit to its accuracy. As for thermo-remanent magnetization of fired clays, there is the advantage that the point of reference is not the present but the nearest ascertained magnetic date; but it is uncertain how far it will be practicable to fix such dates, and even then the margin of error is not likely to be less than fifty years. For the time being it looks as if Classical archaeologists, with resignation or relief, had better stick to their old methods.

THE RECONCILIATION OF RELATIVE AND ABSOLUTE CHRONOLOGIES

Once a relative chronology has been established, it is easy to peg it to the relevant absolute dates. But in spacing the sequences between pegs some assumption must be made, either that the output (or rather the surviving output) of pottery or that the development in style continued at a uniform rate. Usually development in style seems more scholarly and is preferred, though students tend to consider it as proceeding not continuously but by stages. So, till small shifts were made to accommodate Samaria and Gela, Attic Geometric was often presented in four parts, to each of which fifty years was allotted, and the Orientalizing style of Corinth was marked out in phases of twenty-five years. On the other hand the early phase of Attic Protogeometric has been made short to fit the rarity of its products.

The absolute dating of early Greek pottery is precarious. Towards the middle of the fourteenth century there are good contacts with the secure chronology of Egypt, and in the late eighth the Sicilian colonies provide dates that may be correct to about fifteen years. Between these two pegs lie over six hundred years and rather more than the Submycenaean, Protogeometric and Geometric styles. To assign dates to those styles is convenient, to rely on them foolhardy. During the seventh century the normal range of error should not be more than ten or twenty years. By the end of the sixth century the fixed dates should be strictly accurate.

Figures 42 and 43 summarize very roughly the structure of the relative chronology and its attachment to the absolute dates. The relative chronology is moderately secure, though it may need minor adjustments; for instance, grave groups at Sindos and Tarentum suggest that Middle Ripe Corinthian corresponds to a rather earlier stage of Attic black-figure than has been supposed. The absolute dating is more arbitrary: the system followed here is that most commonly used, but there are others which prefer lower chronologies for the seventh and earlier sixth centuries. Still, for the present, since these dates have little value for other purposes, uniformity is more convenient than attempted accuracy.

CHAPTER XII

THE POTTERY
INDUSTRY

———— ·◆· ————

Greek writers show little interest in economics, perhaps because their economy was simple and obvious. Anyhow, the few literary references to pottery say nothing useful about the industry. What we know or guess comes from the pots themselves and a few inscriptions set up in public by potters.

Excavation of a potters' quarter at Corinth and the name Ceramicus at Athens show that in those cities potters had their workshops close together. Fine pottery was not their only product. Others were coarse pottery, tiles, architectural revetments, plaques, figurines and larger statuary; and till the fifth century vase-painters may well have painted in other media too. How far workshops specialized in one or more of these lines we do not know, but it is natural to suppose that tiles and revetments were more suited to larger establishments.

For the size of workshops or parts of workshops that made fine pottery there are a few scraps of evidence. Several Corinthian plaques and Attic pots of the sixth and fifth centuries illustrate potters at work. Most of these have room for only one or two figures, but a black-figure hydria of near 500 BC shows the manager, one painter, one man shaping a pot and five assistants, and on a red-figure hydria of about 460 BC four painters (unless they are metalworkers) are being honoured by celestial visitants. Round the middle of the fifth century a group of Attic painters associated with the Penthesilea painter occasionally collaborated two together on the same cup, so that plainly they worked in the same shop; there are more than a dozen of these collaborators, spread over a period of perhaps thirty years. Yet in the early fourth century the Jena painter, one of the leaders of his generation, was the only regular painter in his workshop, to judge by the debris found in its ruins. Stylistic analysis gives similar results. The hackneyed sameness of the Penthesilean group is fair proof that its members worked together; so this workshop during its forty years had over twenty painters. But in several decent red-figure establishments there were, it seems, not more than two or three qualified painters at one time. The study of shapes also points in the same direction. There is not much sign of factory methods, at least till the Hellenistic period. In the great period of Attic fine pottery, the later sixth and earlier fifth centuries, it appears more or less often (according to the interpretation taken of the 'maker's' signature ἐποίησε) that cups and presumably other pots were shaped by one man and painted by another, but division of the painter's labour remained very rare.

The status of potters need not have been uniform. At Athens during the last quarter of the sixth and the first of the fifth centuries several potters including Andocides and Euphronios, who are reasonably identified with the makers and painter of fine pottery, were able to erect impressive dedications on the Acropolis. In the later fourth century the brothers Kittos and Bacchius, potters and Athenian citizens, were honoured with the citizenship of Ephesus and an inscription to record it; and another potter, Bacchius, probably their father, has left a respectable gravestone in Attica. The family of Bacchius may have been owners who did not work with their hands, since though by the fourth century literary Athenians looked down on manual work, they admitted the propriety of owning a workshop. But in an earlier age Euphronios as a painter used his hands, and yet was prosperous and presumably reputable. These men were masters. Of their workmen we know less. A Boeotian kotyle perhaps of the earlier fourth century shows a potter's workshop in which one of the men is suffering servile punishment. But the mobility of such a painter as Oltos, who painted for at least six makers, argues that he was a free agent. There is little in inferences from names, that for example Skythes and Brygos were Scythian and Phrygian slaves; foreign ethnics and personal names were naturalized in Archaic Greece.

It has been alleged that vase-painters and other potters migrated freely within the Greek world, and in particular from Ionia to Athens. But though in most schools of pottery foreign influences are visible at one time or another, there are not so many signs of painters trained and matured in a foreign tradition. In Etruria the Swallow painter should have been an immigrant, and so too rather later the painters of the Campana group. The Eretrian black-figure of the mid-sixth century, the South Italian red-figure of the later fifth and perhaps some Faliscan red-figure of the early fourth all start in a style too Attic to have been learnt outside an Attic workshop, and some Boeotian painters may have trained at Athens. But normally the vase-painters of any city appear to have been brought up in the local tradition of that city, and the odds are that they were born there. Signatures very rarely help. In the third quarter of the sixth century Lydos signs two Attic pots ho Λυδος, of which the simple meaning is 'the Lydian'. The contemporary painter of a wooden plaque from Pitsa is Corinthian in style and calls himself a Corinthian. In the fourth century there are two pots of Attic style inscribed as made by the Athenian Xenophantos. As for the generality of inscriptions painted before firing, the painters of any school usually follow the local alphabet and dialect, and though sometimes these may not have been their own, the cumulative effect is telling. It might perhaps be expected that, as a local school of fine pottery declined, unemployment would drive its craftsmen to emigrate; but fine pottery was only a part of the production of potters, and its decline was usually gradual.

The general character of Greek industry makes it very unlikely that potters themselves engaged in merchanting. Presumably they sold in the workshop to ordinary purchasers and to dealers or merchants, who in turn sold to other merchants and dealers overseas. Even a regular connection between a potter and a merchant or market was unusual, if we may judge by the dispersal of the works of individual painters. There are a few probable or possible exceptions. Some Chiot workshops around the 570s appear to have had close ties with particular merchants; at least Chiot cups found at Naucratis and on Aegina have dedications painted before firing, the dedications of the same man are too numerous for a casual traveller, and each dedicator has usually his own painter. The Attic Tyrrhenian amphorae run a little later, a showy class of pots almost all found in Etruria; perhaps, then, they were made specially for the Etruscan trade. Towards the end of the century the Attic maker Nikosthenes seems also to have studied the Etruscan market, since his peculiar variety of amphora not only occurs principally (if not exclusively) in Etruria, but also looks suspiciously like a native Etruscan shape. It has been argued that the griffins and Arimaspians of many Attic pelikai of the mid-fourth century were chosen to appeal to the Greeks and Scythians of Ukraine, but they are as common at Spina in Italy.

For the Chiot pottery just mentioned it may be inferred from the painted dedications that export from Chios to Naucratis and Aegina was direct; it may also be inferred that the exporters were Chiots, since in four or five instances the dedicator adds his ethnic and that ethnic is o Χιος. For exports from the Aegean to Italy and Sicily the route was more difficult, requiring transhipment at the Isthmus or the hazardous rounding of the Peloponnese. Who handled the western trade we do not know, but the merchants' marks on Attic pots imported into Italy during the later sixth and early fifth centuries suggest that at some stage the trade was not in Attic hands.

For the prices of pottery we have a few scribbles on the bottoms of pots mostly found in Italy. They are not all certainly intelligible, and those that are do not show in what currency or at what point in the journey the price was given, nor always what was included in the lot. We read, for example, on several Attic bell-kraters of the later fifth century that six kraters were offered or sold for four drachmas, and on two Attic hydriai of much the same date the letters υδιδραχποι and υδτριδραχποι presumably signify that ὑδρίαι ποικίλαι (or decorated hydriai) cost three drachmas and two drachmas. A practical potter might perhaps estimate the cost of production. But evidently in most of the Greek world it was over long periods cheaper to import fine and moderately fine pottery than to produce it at home, and even in distant Italy the advantages of local manufacture were not overwhelming.

The industry making painted pottery was small, even when it was flourishing. This can be demonstrated from J. D. Beazley's *Attic Red-figure Vase-painters* – I use the first edition since I have not made detailed counts for the second, though generally this gives similar results. In *ARV¹* close exploration of Attic vase-painting of the fifth century assigned two-fifths of the known pots to some five hundred painters and workshops. Balancing new painters still to be detected against old painters to be combined, one may reasonably conclude that the true total (casuals excluded) is not likely to be far from five hundred. Since the average working life of a painter was evidently not more than twenty-five years, the average number of vase-painters working at any time should not be more than a hundred and twenty-five. Another and perhaps sounder method gives a comparable result. Some red-figure painters have been more closely studied and are more widely known, so that it is likely that most of their extant works have been identified. Lekythoi and cups had, of course, better chances of survival than large pots; but on average it seems that the number of extant works of these painters, as listed in *ARV¹*, is equivalent to not less than three for every year of their working lives. The number of red-figure pots that had been examined competently when *ARV¹* was written may be estimated at not more than forty thousand or, on this calculation, the equivalent of thirteen thousand painting years. Since the period over which these pots extend is something like one hundred and thirty years, the average number of painters at work throughout this period should, be about a hundred. To the number of painters must be added a complement of shapers, which can hardly have been larger even if the painters rarely shaped the pots they painted, and also various assistants and labourers. So the total of workmen, skilled and unskilled, required to produce the decorated and the fine black-painted Attic pottery of the fifth century is likely to have been in the order only of hundreds. Yet the Attic potters of the fifth century supplied the greatest part of the fine pottery used throughout the Greek world. It is because pottery survives that its industrial importance has appeared great.

CHAPTER XIII

USES FOR
OTHER STUDIES

——— •◆• ———

Greek historians have usually learnt little about archaeology and Greek archaeologists have thought little about history, so that the historical conclusions they draw from archaeological evidence are often discreditably naïve. But pottery has a limited usefulness for historians.

DATING

Greek pottery is plentiful and can be dated with some precision, according to the system explained in Chapter XI. Briefly, that system is reliable from the end of the sixth century, but before then depends on stylistic sequences that are at a few points pegged to dates taken from the literary tradition. But the intervening stretches are not necessarily measured out correctly nor are all the literary dates necessarily of comparable validity. So it is one thing to say of the oinochoe of Plate 4B that it was made about twenty-five years before the earliest finds from Syracuse, but something of a different kind to say that it was made about twenty-five years after the institution of the Olympic Games.

The theory of stratification is well known. Objects found in the same stratum are of the same date as the stratum and – within its limits – as each other, and a lower stratum is earlier than a higher stratum. These bald statements are true only in general, and a single association or dissociation is not very important. But at some Greek sites enough has been found to date various stages of their development, usually by deposits connected with levels of destruction or rebuilding. Other sites have been only partially explored or casually inspected, and there is a special difficulty in determining when a settlement was founded, since small beginnings (especially on a new site) may easily have been destroyed or missed. Before using pottery to date a site it is necessary to consider how complete and efficient was the excavation, how reliable the report, and how frequent the pottery on which conclusions are to be based. It is helpful to remember that it was more than fifty years before the excavators of Corinth struck a Mycenaean deposit.

TRADE

The more relevant facts until the Hellenistic era are roughly these. All Greek cities used Greek pottery, and so did some other peoples of the West and of Anatolia, but not the older communities of the Orient. Greek cities used only Greek pottery. Most Greek cities, anyhow from the seventh to the fourth century BC, imported rather than made fine pottery. The favourite imports in that period were till the early sixth century Corinthian and afterwards Attic, but a few other wares have a considerable distribution in limited areas. The importation and the quality of fine pottery were both declining from the later fifth century onwards.

The reasonable inferences from these and more general facts are disappointing. First, the presence or absence of Greek pottery has different meanings in different places. In Europe an urban settlement using an appreciable quantity of pottery that was not Greek was itself not Greek; if it also used Greek pottery it traded with Greeks, and if it did not use Greek pottery it did not trade with Greeks. But in the East an appreciable quantity of Greek pottery is evidence of Greek residents, commercial or military, and the absence of Greek pottery does not preclude trade with Greeks. Secondly, though pottery made up a part of Greek trade, it was presumably a minor and inconstant part, so that the total value of trade cannot be estimated from pottery. Thirdly, the comparative value of the exports of different cities cannot be related to the pottery they made, since most Greek cities made no pottery to export. Fourthly, Greek trade was not organized strictly or elaborately. If pottery of one of the less important wares was exported in some quantity from the place where it was made to some other place, the likeliest explanation of its export is direct trade between the two places. But the universally admired wares may often have been traded indirectly. These last two assertions have a little support in merchants' marks on a few Attic pots and perhaps in the painted dedications on Chiot chalices; on the other hand the Attic Nikosthenic amphora looks to have been designed particularly for the Etruscans.

It should always be remembered that the total quantity of pottery that happens to have been found varies greatly from one site to another, and so it is not the absolute as much as the relative quantity of a ware that is important. Few archaeological aids have been more delusive than those distribution maps which mark where specimens of a particular class of objects have been found, but not in what frequency. An isolated find is of very little importance.

POLITICAL RELATIONS

There is no evidence that private purchasers of Greek pots regularly let political reasons impair their tastes. If politics had effects on the distribution of pottery, it was through the promotion or restriction of trade and especially direct trade. Such effects should be visible, if at all, in the exports of those minor wares which depended on direct trade. Two possible examples will serve. East Greek pottery is less rare at Gela than at most western sites; Gela had an East Greek mother-city. Laconian pottery of the mid-sixth century appears to be less rare on Samos than at other East Greek sites; according to Herodotus Laconia interfered in Samos a little later. But whether the proportions of those wares is significant may be doubted.

PROSPERITY

It is likely enough that at any one time the Greeks were uniform in their uses, domestic and dedicatory, of painted pottery. So it should be possible to compare the prosperity of contemporary settlements and sanctuaries by the amount and quality of the pottery found in them, if the finds are representative. That condition is not often satisfied. It is true that some sanctuaries, like that on Mount Hymettus, appear from the character of the pottery to have been poor, but such conclusions can usually be proved more clearly by the architectural remains. For comparing sites of different periods there is the extra difficulty that from the fifth century onwards fine pottery was losing in importance.

In most Greek graves pottery was the principal part of the furniture, and very often this pottery is complete. But local fashions and individual piety make comparisons less reliable. In general early graves vary more in lavishness than later graves.

ICONOGRAPHY

From the eighth to the fourth century BC scenes with human figures are regular on Greek pottery. Some are based on ordinary life, and even in those that are mythological many details are contemporary. A few artistic conventions must be discounted, notably the representation of youthful males as naked in almost every context: this convention, which is sometimes explained as 'Heroic nudity', was a dominant characteristic of Greek art. Another convention, demanded as much by pictorial composition as by epic tradition, was the resolving of a battle into separate duels. But paintings on pots offer valuable illustrations of much of Greek life – at home, parties, exercise, ceremonies, work and war.

The interpretation of these subjects is called iconography. In a simple form it is concerned with identification of the incidents, persons and objects depicted; the results are often convincing, though for instance the recognition of scenes from lost tragedies is usually dubious. A more sophisticated inquiry, which has become popular again in recent years, aims at recovering the inner message or meaning of the subjects. So some students look for political propaganda, disguised as mythology. Others, often called iconologists, use the findings of social anthropology to elucidate the mentality of fifth-century Athenians (which was different from ours). Too often, though, the premises cannot be demonstrated, so that the conclusions remain speculative. A complication, perhaps not sufficiently considered, is that the painters were artisans and so may not have been fully acquainted with the life, especially at home, of the leisured class they so often depicted.

CHAPTER XIV

PRACTICAL COMMENTS

—— ·◆· ——

So much Greek pottery survives that most students have occasion to handle or acquire examples. Experience is learnt by trial and reflection, But some unsystematic hints may be helpful to the beginner.

HANDLING

Pottery is fragile, especially if like many old pieces it has been cracked or broken and repaired. So continuous care is expected in handling Greek pots, and no strain should be added to the weaker parts. An amphora such as that of Plate 32A ought not to be picked up by the handles or lip but by putting both hands under the belly, and in the same way the cups of Plate 25 should be supported below the bowl. When set down again, a pot should be lowered gently to avoid jarring. It is prudent too, when lifting a pot off a shelf or putting it back, to watch the bottom of the shelf above, since often there is little clearance and if the shelves are of glass they are easily overlooked.

EXAMINATION

Many pots have been restored, some misleadingly. Sherds may be inserted in the wrong places, parts of different pots combined, a fragmentary shape wrongly completed in plaster, lost or damaged decoration repainted, and occasionally there are more creative forgeries. The character and extent of restoration varies from one collection to another and even within the same collection. At present the approved practice is to distinguish original and restored parts of a pot by leaving the plaster white or (more considerately) tinting it to a colour not too near that of the clay, and the painting in of missing decoration is done, if at all, with unobtrusive faintness. But earlier ethics, still observed by some dealers, preferred complete restoration or improvement. Plaster repairs and damaged surfaces were coloured to match the original parts. Missing pieces of the decoration were supplied faithfully or imaginatively, and occasionally indecent parts were painted out. Damaged or vanished paint and colours were renewed. Often too the whole surface, ancient or modern, was treated to a coat of varnish that has since become opaque. A variant method, especially inside cups, was to apply a skin of plaster over a damaged surface and on that to paint in the original or some novel design. In some arrant forgeries the decoration, painted or incised, is wholly modern. Though elaborate restoration or forgery is relatively uncommon, any pot should first be examined for signs of modern work.

Where parts of a pot (especially the base, handles or neck) have been wholly or largely reconstructed in plaster, the profiles and proportions of those parts may be wildly wrong and are rarely quite right. This is a truism, though sometimes forgotten. But it is much less easy to determine whether genuine fragments come from the same pot – feet are the commonest intruders – or whether they have been put in the right place. For the thickness of the wall may vary greatly at different levels and slightly at the same level, and colour of clay and paint may range widely because of some fault in the making or a later accident. But the quality of the clay should be uniform, and the agreement of the decoration and of wheel-marks should help. Here practice and a knowledge of style are the quickest guides.

Wheel-marks are worth attention. When a pot is being thrown on the wheel, the pressure of the fingers on the moist clay produces a series of grooves and ridges of varying sizes but all approximately horizontal, and though the later process of turning may remove these wheel-marks the removal is not always complete and such parts of a pot as are not meant to be seen are usually not turned. If a sherd with wheel-marks is held up at the level of the eye and twisted about till the chosen wheel-mark appears as a straight horizontal line, the sherd must then be at its correct angle to the horizontal plane of the pot. It may, of course, be upside down, but that can usually be decided by experience or common sense. Bands of paint also often run horizontally, but are less reliable than wheel-marks. Once the angle of the sherd is fixed its curvature, unless the sherd is very small, allows a calculation of the diameter at its level and a surmise about the profile. Further, the finish of the inside generally shows whether the pot was open or closed, and the decoration too may be suggestive of the shape. Wheel-marks may also have a pattern sufficiently distinctive to decide whether sherds come from the same level of the same pot, or even to allow an estimate of their distance from each other: Figure 44 should make this clear.

Where restoration is thorough and tries to conceal itself, the commonest clues are some fault in style or a messy appearance. Plaster tends to have a rough or flattened surface without wheel-marks, the dark paint may be dull or thick, the white rather coarse. Such differences in texture show best in a glancing light, though if the whole pot has been varnished the underlying texture is usually invisible. Sometimes the inside of the pot reveals what is plaster, but often the plaster has been smeared too widely for any precision. A few museums have ultra-violet equipment, which distinguishes

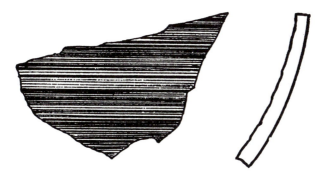

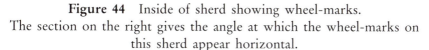

Figure 44   Inside of sherd showing wheel-marks.
The section on the right gives the angle at which the wheel-marks on this sherd appear horizontal.

clearly between clay and plaster. But it is best if the restorations can be cleared away.

Older forgeries do not give much trouble. Occasionally genuine ancient pots have been provided with new painting in their blank fields or with black-figure decoration cut out of a dark band; but the new and unfired paint usually dissolves in spirit, incision on a pot already fired is ragged and scratchy, and a surface from which paint has been scraped is implausibly rough. As for wholehogging imitations of Greek pots, ignorance of ancient techniques made them rare and mainly unconvincing till the 1960s, when recent research had been assimilated; but some later productions are admirable. Here the claim that a fake is always betrayed by some contemporary mannerism seems optimistic, and the safest test of antiquity is by thermoluminescence, though a method has been devised of adjusting the radiation, if not completely.

If, as is more usual, a pot has not been restored, its decoration may be badly worn. The standard dark paint is very durable, the purple colour moderately so, but the white disappears easily and other colours are worse. Yet even the dark paint may be destroyed by prolonged damp or exposure. In general surfaces once covered by paint lack sheen, and if the only damage is the loss of the paint they show distinctly, especially in a glancing light. Similarly, dull patches and lines in the shiny dark paint often betray the loss of purple or white additions. In Attic and some other black-figure work, where detail on white was done by incising through it, faint incisions on the dark paint are another indication of lost white. Occasionally the whole surface has been equally worn away, so that the parts once reserved have become rough while the paint survived long enough to protect the smooth ground beneath it.

TAKING NOTES

In taking notes it is convenient to follow some system. Models may be found in most of the recent catalogues of active museums. For objects in a museum the inventory number ought always to be quoted, whether or not there is a catalogue number too; for the inventory is a permanent record, but catalogues may be replaced or forgotten. Measurements, usually of the height though idealists demand the diameter too, should be on the metric system.

The shape and decoration of a pot or sherd may be learnt by inspection but its provenance often cannot be checked. If an object in a reputable collection is said to have been found in an authorized excavation, the statement can generally be trusted. So too with objects attributed to some of the less official enterprises. Even so, if sherds are left uninventoried for a long time, they are liable to become mixed with aliens. Dealers' provenances have always been suspect, perhaps more so since the Greeks and Italians enacted laws to control the exhumation and export of antiquities; sellers wish to protect the source of their supply or oblige a customer with information to his taste. But in general purchases made in Athens have been found in what at the time was Greek territory. The market in Rome has been supplied principally from Etruria and Latium, that in Naples from South Italy. Smyrna till 1912 attracted clandestine finds from western Anatolia but not the islands off its coast. Cairo and Alexandria drew and perhaps still draw much of their stock from across the Mediterranean. Elsewhere in Greek lands there has been no established trade in antiques, and objects bought for example in Rhodes or Cyprus or Boeotia have almost always been found in those parts.

DRAWING AND PHOTOGRAPHING

In tracing or sketching the decoration of a pot there are recognized conventions. Solid areas of dark paint are simply outlined, incision is distinguished by a darker or heavier line, purple is shaded or hatched: Plate 9B is exemplary. White too is outlined, if its position is obvious; but if there might be confusion, some sort of hatching or shading is permitted. For direct tracing from pottery the more transparent the material the better, and so plastics are preferable to paper.

In photographing for study the aim is a clear, sharp and clean negative, suitable for publication without any retouching. The illumination should be evenly distributed over the object, avoiding heavy shadows or highlights, and the background should be neutral, of uniform tone, and plainly distinguished from the pot. Highlights, which are dazzling if the paint is shiny, can be evaded by lighting a pot only from the sides, so that there is no strong reflection from its surface to the lens of the camera. Oblique lighting is useful also for bringing out faded or damaged details. These and other reasons recommend artificial lighting in a darkened room or a portable tent. Some experts have a dirty habit of dulling highlights by smearing the spot with plasticine. There is no particular difficulty about complete pots which can be photographed upright, though some thought should be taken to find the best eye-level. Sherds are usually laid out flat and photographed from above. To avoid shadows it is best to arrange them on a sheet of ground glass not less than 45 × 30 cm in size and supported at the corners some 15 cm or more above a sheet of white paper: to reflect the light evenly onto the glass above it the paper may have to be tilted or curved, and if artificial light is being used an extra lamp may be needed to shine on the paper. If several sherds are being photographed together, they should be arranged in a sort of grid so that each sherd is in a separate rectangle: then, if the prints are chopped up, each sherd is properly framed, and there is no temptation to the discreditable makeshift of cutting round the edges of a sherd or masking out its background. When photographing sherds it is useful to include a scale, but the scale should be placed in the right alignment and towards the edge of the field so that it can at will be trimmed off the print. In spite of what some authorities declare, scales are valueless for complete pots which have depth of perspective. Photography needs practice, but the amateur who knows what he wants is more likely to succeed than the professional who does not.

Copying the shape of a pot (which the eyes see only in perspective) can be done in several ways. The quickest should be photographing with a long-focus lens from a distance of thirty or more times the longer dimension of the pot; at that range distortion is negligible. Polarized light and sand boxes have not yet proved successful. Templates are unwieldy and expensive for large pots, though useful for sherds. A copying frame, with one arm touching the profile of the pot and another tracing an outline on a vertical board, is practicable and exact. Lead wire is handy and useful: a suitable length of it is rolled flat on a board, moulded against the profile of the pot till it takes its shape, then carefully removed and laid flat on a sheet of paper, where it must be held in position while the inner outline is traced with a sharp pencil; since the wire springs back a little the ends of each section should be fixed by measurement with dividers, and sharp angles must be corrected by eye. But most students, who only rarely need a precise shape, rely on measured drawings: the height of the pot is noted and its diameter at lip and foot, other points are transferred by the combined use of a vertical ruler and of a horizontal ruler or calipers, and intermediate contours are sketched by eye. Figure 27 is a measured drawing, showing on the left a profile and on the right a section (though current fashion prefers to black in the wall of the section). But for complete pots it is often impracticable to calculate a complete section. Profiles and sections are demanded much more now than in the past, especially for undecorated pottery where shape is a principal criterion of date.

CLEANING

When a piece of pottery is dug up from the ground, it is usually incrusted with mud or some other deposit. This incrustation should not be picked off nor immediately scrubbed, since it is liable to take the paint with it. The proper preliminary is to soak the specimen in water for some hours or days; this may dissolve the deposit or loosen it so much that it comes off with light brushing. If water is not enough – and it rarely is – a more efficient solvent is dilute hydrochloric acid. Though neat hydrochloric acid does not damage well-made and well-preserved Greek pottery, one part of acid to twenty parts of water is normally ample. The specimen should be saturated with water before it is put into the solution of acid. If it fizzes or bubbles there is no cause for alarm. After twenty-four hours or so it may be taken out and brushed lightly. If a deposit still remains, it can be steeped longer or in a stronger solution of the acid. When finally removed the specimen should again be soaked and rinsed in water, and then put aside to dry. Incrustations that survive this treatment are best left to experts. But there are many pieces in collections which have not even been washed.

Pottery that has been cleaned sometimes develops whitish crystals on its surface, caused by salts that have penetrated the clay. The cure is soaking in plain water.

The removal of restorations may be troublesome. Varnish and unfired paints can be more or less slowly dissolved by wiping them with methylated spirits. Plaster usually loosens in water and breaks up in a weak solution of hydrochloric acid. The treatment of the adhesives used to join sherds is mentioned in the next section.

MENDING

Before joining sherds the order in which the joins are to be made needs to be thought out. If the join between any two sherds is not immediately obvious, it helps to hold them together in their correct position and to draw a pencil stroke on the inside across the join; then, when the adhesive is applied, no time is lost in fumbling for the fit. Of adhesives there is a choice. In the past the favourite has been shellac dissolved in hot or cold methylated spirit and brushed onto the edges to be joined. But some menders now prefer the proprietary adhesives made specially for repairing domestic china. Whatever adhesive is used, it should not be put on too thickly and the join should be made when it is tacky. Then the two fragments should be pressed tightly together for a little while and when they are holding left to set without any strain, as for instance by standing them with the join upright in a box filled with sand. Any surplus adhesive that may ooze out of the join should be removed before it dries hard. Shellac can be loosened again by heat and may give through prolonged dampness, but it is very difficult to break down the china adhesives, though methylated spirit may weaken them slowly. Durability is not always an advantage.

To fill a gap with plaster a strip of plasticine should be put at the back of the gap and the plaster pressed in from in front. When it is set, any roughness can be cut or sandpapered away and smears or splashes wiped off with water, though it may be difficult to remove plaster from incisions. Plaster is easily tinted with watercolour.

More complex mending may need some sort of form to ensure that circuit of the pot is made regularly and that the final sherd joins on both sides. For weak joins a plaster backing may be advisable. But anything elaborate is best left to an expert.

COLLECTING

In Geneva, London, Paris, New York and elsewhere there are dealers who specialize in Greek pottery, and since the market is free – that is, since purchasers are not thwarted by laws restricting export – the prices are high. Ordinary antique shops in northern Europe and America rarely have Greek pots. In Greece and Italy, the principal sources of supply, the unlicensed export of antiquities is forbidden by law and at present only poor or mediocre pieces receive a licence. So in Athens prices are relatively moderate, and in the rest of Greece low. In Rome and Italy generally prices are higher, perhaps because evasion of the law is more regular. Even so, to judge by the pottery on sale in free markets, there must be some smuggling of good pieces from Italy (especially Etruria), Turkey and Greece.

Sherds can be picked up by any visitor to Greek lands (if the police do not object), and unless they are exceptional the authorities usually permit their export, though official permission may be slow. It is worth emphasizing that much of the interest of sherds is in where they were found, and so any sherd intended for a collection should be promptly marked with its provenance, preferably in Indian ink on a clean patch of the clay.

CHAPTER XV

THE HISTORY
OF THE STUDY OF
VASE-PAINTING

——— •◆• ———

Though ancient sherds are always turning up and the rarer complete pots
are likely to be preserved, if only for re-use, they were for long ignored.
The Middle Ages have left few records, but Arretine relief ware is
mentioned from the late thirteenth century on. Ristoro d'Arezzo in his
della Composizione del Mondo of 1282 wrote that artists supposed its
maker divine or the fragments fallen from heaven. Giovanni Villani
who died in 1348 also thought it superhuman in his *Cronaca Fiorentina*,
and in the mid-fifteenth century Giorgio Vasari (according to his grandson,
the biographer of painters) succeeded in imitating it. Giulio Romano in
1524 possessed an ancient cup of terracotta and M. Negri in 1557 in his
Commentarium Geographicum mentioned pottery from Adria, but neither
said anything of decoration. A few pieces, no doubt, could be found in
the cabinets of the time, as for instance the painted vases of Cardinal Carpi,
praised for their garlands by U. Aldroandi in L. Mauro's *Antichità della
Città di Roma* of 1558, and there were the black-figure pots found about
1565 in a chamber tomb at Orbetello by a Spanish engineer who was
building fortifications there for Philip II. But such specimens were hardly
noticed, and Thomas Dempster, a Scots papist who read and remembered
everything, did not include vase-painting in the ceramic accomplishments
of the paragons of his encyclopaedic and uncritical panegyric *de Etruria
Regali*, compiled while he was professor of Law at Padua from 1616 to
1619. Avid though they were for other kinds of antiques, it is clear that
writers and collectors, at least till the middle of the seventeenth century,
had generally no interest in ancient painted pottery and, since it was available and its material not despised, this must have been from some stylistic
repugnance. What that repugnance was may by elimination be inferred.
After the end of antiquity, though technical standards had sunk, formulas
survived for oblique views of faces and modelling by shading, so that to
inquisitive painters of the late Middle Ages and still more so of the
Renaissance the drawing of figures on the Greek pots commonly found in
central Italy would have appeared primitive. For the same reason the earliest
known facsimiles of Greek red-figure vase-painting mostly correct their
originals by supplying heavy shading. These facsimiles – now at Windsor
Castle or lent to the British Museum – are part of a large collection of

drawings procured in the mid-seventeenth century by Cassiano dal Pozzo (or perhaps his brother) and reproduce a dozen Attic and South Italian figured pots accurately enough to allow the identification of their schools and in some instances of their painters. About the same time the French sculptor F. Girardon who studied in Rome around 1650, possessed two examples of South Italian red-figure; and it was perhaps through him that C. A. du Fresnoy, in his versified *de Arte Graphica* of 1668, listed vases among the examples of ancient art to be noticed. The next honour, that of first publishing an ancient vase (to be distinguished from an urn, which at that time meant a cinerary casket) belongs, it seems, to M. A. de la Chausse (or Causeus), a French resident in Rome and the author of the *Romanum Museum*. In this enlightened folio, which first came out in 1690, there are tolerable drawings with commentaries of a Calene phiale and of an Attic black-figure pelike (on sale again in Rome in the 1930s). A few years later, probably in 1701, L. Beger produced the third volume of the *Thesaurus Regius et Electoralis Brandenburgensis*: among the items, most of which had recently been bought from the estate of G. P. Bellori in Rome and were soon after traded from Berlin to Dresden for a regiment of dragoons, there are illustrated one piece of Attic and one of South Italian red-figure as well as an Italocorinthian alabastron. In another context and so un-noticed for more than a hundred years was the publication of a Panathenaic amphora from Benghazi, which Lemaître, French consul at Tripoli, contributed to P. Lucas's second *Voyage* of 1712. In 1719 and 1724 B. de Montfauçon, in his *l'Antiquité Expliquée*, added several red-figure pots, mostly bought in Naples, but was as much interested in shape and use as in decoration. Then from 1723 to 1726 F. Buonarroti inserted in Dempster's work, at last being published, drawings of over thirty vases and appended a long disquisition about them.

Buonarroti had an advantage over his predecessors; there were more pots for him to see. In Rome and Tuscany, where the vocal antiquaries lived or sojourned, it appears that in spite of the statements of la Chausse and Montfauçon painted pots were still rare in the early years of the eigh-teenth century. In Naples they were commoner, since the graves of Campania were already being exploited, but Naples was in another realm. We know very little of the early Neapolitan cabinets apart from that of the lawyer Joseph Valletta, whose heirs about 1720 sold to Cardinal Gualtieri what became the first Roman collection of Greek vases. By 1725, as Buonarroti's captions show, there were several connoisseurs in central Italy who owned a few specimens, mostly of South Italian red-figure. Gualtieri's collection, which also contained an assortment of bucchero and other local finds made by Bargigli, the bishop of Chiusi, passed to the Vatican, where in 1744 Cardinal Quirini furnished a separate vase room, though according to a precept still honoured in certain museums visitors were not permitted – so Uhden and Millin say – to make close examination or drawings of the exhibits. Thus the taste for painted vases was becoming acceptable; they were convenient in size and not too scarce or expensive.

The antiquaries also indulged their fancy. Of these the most eminent were A. F. Gori, G. B. Passeri and the Count de Caylus. Gori, whose Tuscan patriotism (so he boasts) impelled him to publish his *Museum Etruscum* from 1737 to 1743, illustrated and expounded several ancient painted pots and one modern forgery. Passeri, best remembered for his *Picturae Etruscorum in Vasculis* (1767–75), devoted three hundred plates to specimens from forty collections throughout Italy and even beyond the Alps. Caylus was more critical and observant, though there is not much pottery in his *Recueil d'Antiquités égyptiennes, étrusques, grecques et romaines*, which began to appear in 1752.

All these writers believed that the painted vases were Etruscan. The reason is probably not, as is usually asserted, that the earliest examples had been unearthed in Etruria; in fact most of them were made and so probably found in South Italy. But the Etruscomania that still visits the credulous was virulent in the seventeenth and early eighteenth centuries. It goes back to the forged Etruscan histories which began in the late fifteenth century and, though recognized as impostures by critical scholars, fed the prejudice, convenient to contemporary Tuscan pride and politics, that in the past the Etruscans had been a great and creative people. In effect all ancient monuments that were not obviously Roman or Greek (then barely known) nor yet Egyptian were likely to be classed as Etruscan. Antiquaries, as Paciaudi remarked of Gori, found something Etruscan everywhere, and the frequency of painted vases in South Italy was a proof only of Etruscan suzerainty. This attitude was strong enough in Rome and Tuscany to dub Greek vase-painting Etruscan, and Rome and Florence were then the homes of antiquarian curiosity and speculation. But the collectors of Naples and Sicily were less disposed to accept the incidental notes of Servius and supposedly Philargyrius that the Etruscans were once masters of almost all Italy, and besides the painted vases were found chiefly in their own territories. However that may be, the Etruscan addicts soon felt obliged to defend their attribution. La Chausse had used the term 'Hetruscan' casually and loosely, since he dated his Attic pelike to the epoch of the Roman emperors. Beger simply followed la Chausse, and Montfauçon identified the pot as Martial's Arretine. But Buonarroti gave ampler reasons, that painted vases were found throughout Etruria and that their Bacchic scenes – his repertory was largely South Italian – had details alien to both Greeks and Romans. Gori, a more fanatical Tuscan who concluded that Homer was taught in Etruria, deplored the error of those who claimed vase-painting for the Greeks, and where Pliny says that most of mankind uses earthenware pots he would have liked to emend *terrenis* to *Tyrrhenis*. But by 1749 even Gori had to concede to the Sicilian

Benedictine Blasi that some of the painted vases then being found in Sicily had been made by the Greeks of Sicily, a claim repeated two years later by the Theatine G. M. Pancrazi in his *Antichità Siciliane*. Still Caylus next year resisted, and even proposed that owl-kotylai were made in Etruria to suit Athenian customers. Gradually logic prevailed. In 1745 S. Paoli noted that some painted inscriptions on red-figure pots were in Greek, and nine years later A. S. Mazocchi argued that their painters must have been Greeks. A. R. Mengs, the most respected artist of his day and a judicious critic, was converted by 1759; and in 1764 in the first edition of the *Geschichte der Kunst des Alterthums* J. J. Winckelmann gave his sanction to the Greek origin of painted vases, though three years later he conceded to the Etruscans those found in Etruria, not that he had seen any. Passeri in 1767 still tried to compromise – vase-painters may mostly have worked in Campania, but despite Winckelmann Campania was then Etruscan – and in 1769 the learned potter Josiah Wedgwood christened his new factory Etruria. But serious students were soon agreed that most painted pottery was Greek – Greek, that is, of South Italy and Sicily – though the old name persisted on the fringes of scholarship and is not yet quite extinct.

About this time a new and much more influential personage was busying himself with painted vases. William, later Sir William, Hamilton had been appointed at the age of thirty-three as British envoy to the king of the Two Sicilies, a post he occupied from 1764 till 1800. Hamilton was a man of parts – diplomatist, amateur and collector of objects of virtu, natural philosopher, promoter of manufactures and scholar of some acumen. Within two years of his establishment in Naples he had amassed his first remarkable collection of vases, part bought and part excavated by his own enterprise. Till then the principal interest in painted pottery had been the scholarly interpretation of its subjects, and the drawings published (with few exceptions) had been of an improbable crudity or carelessness; and though Winckelmann preached the study and appreciation of style, his own illustrations were bad enough. Hamilton was impelled by the new idea, apparently more practical, of providing correct models for the designers of his own time and in particular of his own country. He resolved to publish his collection worthily, and when Winckelmann refused enlisted the quick-witted adventurer P. F. Hugues or, as he chose to call himself, the Chevalier P. V. d'Hancarville. D'Hancarville's *Collection of Etruscan, Greek and Roman Antiquities from the Cabinet of the Honble Wm Hamilton* issued in four volumes dated 1766 and 1767, is the first great work on Greek pottery. The drawings of the decoration, large and coloured, are recognizably close rather than pedantically accurate, and the novel diagrams of the shapes have a precision that is not always equalled today. The text too, a mixture of shrewdness and negligence, had its value. Soon after the British Parliament bought Hamilton's collection for £8,400, convinced of its utility to contemporary potters and artists, and so in 1772 the British Museum became the first public gallery to exhibit Greek pots. But though Wedgwood, with whom Hamilton corresponded, painfully copied the ornate Apulian red-figure and John Flaxman formed his gentle style from Classical models, the trade which most benefited was that of the dealers in antiques. Ancient vases became a requisite of the connoisseur's outfit and prices rose infinitely higher, as Hamilton lamented when he built up his second collection. This too was published handsomely, though incompletely, by Wilhelm Tischbein in the *Collection of Engravings from Ancient Vases mostly of Pure Greek workmanship*, four volumes of which were printed from 1791 to 1795. Hamilton himself wrote the introduction, Italinsky interpreted the subjects, and Tischbein and his pupils prepared the illustrations. These illustrations, which established the current practice of outline drawing that ignores the contrast between dark and light areas, set a standard worthy of an art master, officiously correcting such inelegancies as the archaic eye to conform with perspective and good taste. Twenty years later J. B. Millingen published the first honest reproductions; and later generations have accepted that ideal, even if they have not always bothered to achieve it.

The students of the eighteenth century did two services to vase-painting; they discovered it and they recognized it as Greek. In their other inquiries they were handicapped by want of material, of general evidence and of sound method. The pottery they knew was mostly red-figure, South Italian of the fourth century but also Attic of the fifth. There was next some Attic black-figure and a little Corinthian. Black-painted ware and Etruscan bucchero were fairly plentiful, Italogeometric cannot have been rare, and native Apulian appears occasionally. This at least is the effect of the publications, though it must be remembered that the interests of the time were in subject and politeness of style and so naturally concentrated on red-figure. The material was very soon divided into three main classes – red-figure, black-figure and what was called Egyptian – and their order was deduced rightly from the sophistication of their style. The Egyptian class corresponded roughly to what we know as Orientalizing, though it might include Geometric too. The reasons for its name were the belief, clearly formulated by Caylus, that art had originated in Egypt and the observation that this class of painted pottery was the most primitive; it was then easy to discover a resemblance between Orientalizing animals and Egyptian hieroglyphics, though the closest parallels were supplied by the forgers. It is hard to say how seriously students took the name Egyptian: Caylus for instance, in 1752 was sure that the Egyptians did not paint their pottery, Passeri in 1767 was sure that (unlike the Phoenicians) they did, and F. Münter in 1790 in his *Nachrichten von Neapel und Sicilien* contended that the style, though crude, was not at all Egyptian. But even in the middle of the nineteenth century some reputable scholars believed that Geometric pottery was imported into Greece from the East. The distinction between vases with black figures and vases with red (or yellow) figures is obvious.

The earlier writers supposed that both black-figure and red-figure vases were Etruscan. When about the middle of the eighteenth century it was admitted that most of them were Greek, antiquaries turned to the reasonable assumption that pottery was made in the neighbourhood where it was most commonly found. The chances of discovery seemed to confirm this assumption. Attic red-figure was best known from Nola, Apulian from Apulia, black-figure from Sicily, bucchero from Etruria and the experts soon learnt to see subtler local differences. But generically red-figure was regarded as Italian Greek and black-figure as Sicilian Greek, and such terms as Sicilian, Campanian and Italo-Greek became current.

The accurate dating of pottery proved impracticable. It was natural to rely on the Greek and Roman authors, and they said little about pottery and almost nothing about painted pottery. A few events from historical records appeared to be relevant and there were rare clues in inscriptions or comparisons with coins, but the choosing of evidence was chancy and its use incidental. La Chausse's dates are so strange that they can hardly have been based on any system. Montfauçon, relying on Athenaeus, fixed the end of pottery made from clay in the time of Alexander. Gori, to suit his theory of Etruscan priority, could put painted vases before Homer. But generally it came to be accepted that there was a connection between the Dionysiac scenes of South Italian red-figure and the Senatus Consultum de Bacchanalibus of 186 BC and that Demaratus about 660 BC introduced vase-painting into Etruria. From these and other faulty data it could be concluded that the period of painted pottery was from the eighth to the second century BC. Only d'Hancarville, taking advantage of the general neglect, examined dating in much detail and his results were not orthodox: characteristically he appreciated and neglected the evidence of the coins of Sybaris, destroyed about 510 BC, to provide a fixed date for archaeologists.

The erudite found a readier and more congenial exercise in the subjects of vase-painting. La Chausse patently did not yet know the rules. But Buonarroti had observed how popular Dionysus was in the red-figure he studied, and discerned in its pictures the rites and mythology of the Bacchic mysteries. This mode of interpretation, or rather intuition, was popular for more than a hundred years. A second and lesser school, founded by Passeri, held that the paintings on vases symbolized the major events of their owners' lives: so draped youths denoted success in the gymnasium and Heracles (to the Etruscomaniacs) the assumption of the toga virilis. It is at first startling and then depressing to read the descriptions that accompany the illustrations in the works of this period and of the early nineteenth century. But the connoisseurs were not blind to artistic quality and admired

Attic red-figure (or Nolan) more than South Italian, even if their eyes were not yet opened to the modern merits of the primitive.

With the nineteenth century the German scholars arrived, to impose a new discipline on archaeology. The French for a time still held second place. The British contributions, few and amateurish, had the virtue of considering the pottery found in Greece and so admitted to have been made there. Hamilton, it seems, had been the pioneer. In the introductions to his volumes of 1791 and 1795 he pointed out that though a particular variety might be commoner on one site than another, in general vases found in Greece and the Two Sicilies were in all respects so alike that they might be supposed of the same manufacture; either then there was one centre of manufacture or, as he thought more likely, an established method was brought to the Western colonies by emigrants from Greece and presumably from Athens, since he recognized that many of the subjects were Attic. E. Dodwell added that duplicate vases, evidently copied from the same original, were found on both sides of the Adriatic. Dodwell was one of the travellers and had visited Corinth: there in 1805 he bought his pyxis, a work in the Egyptian style with Greek – in fact Corinthian – inscriptions, and this he published admirably in 1819. Thomas Burgon is famous for the Panathenaic amphora (Plate 21B) which he excavated at Athens in 1813 and Millien illustrated in 1822, dating it correctly enough a little before 562 BC. Some Geometric pots also turned up in Athens and Melos, but though examples were displayed in the British Museum and Leyden they were ignored elsewhere for at least forty years. During the first quarter of the century publications of collections became frequent, though the text was often restricted to describing and interpreting the subjects. The sanest of the broader students of vase-painting was J. V. Millingen, who suggested that the misnamed Egyptian class originated in Corinth (citing Athenaeus's etymological derivation of Thericlean from θηρίου), denied that black-figure was specifically Sicilian, and though he still preferred to classify painted vases by subjects rejected their symbolical interpretation.

The second quarter of the century was dominated by Eduard Gerhard. This indefatigable scholar settled in Rome in 1822 and six years later succeeded in organizing the Instituto di Corrispondenza Archeologica, which regularly published reports of new discoveries and other papers in its *Bullettino, Annali* and *Monumenti*. The timing was happy. In the past Etruria had yielded little painted pottery, but during the spring of 1828 the necropolis of Vulci was found and by the end of 1829 over 3,000 painted vases had been unearthed. The lucky proprietors (of whom the luckiest was Napoleon's slippery brother Lucien, the Prince of Canino) were soon selling off their booty to European collectors, but not before Gerhard had seen most of it. In the years that followed other sites in Etruria were tapped and there was renewed discovery in South Italy, although the Nolan landlords at first left their fields fallow till the markets should recover. But Vulci was the richest of all the sites, providing especially Attic black-figure from the second quarter of the sixth century onwards and red-figure of the earlier phases, as well as some 'Chalcidian', Pontic and Corinthian. It is surprising how many of the famous examples of those classes come from this one obscure Etruscan city.

Gerhard perceived at once the importance of the new finds and prepared himself for their study by a tour of South Italy and a paper on the local red-figure manufactures, especially those of Nola, Avella, Sant' Agata de' Goti, Capua, Basilicata, Apulia and Lucania. Accustomed to such neat taxonomy he was able in his *Rapporto Volcente* (in *Annali* 1831) to detect three contemporary schools at Vulci – the Nolan, the Tyrrhenian and the Etruscan. The Nolans were Greeks or Italo-Greeks and their work was the finest; the Tyrrhenians, Greeks permanently settled in Etruria, were coarser and more old-fashioned and fonder of inscriptions; the native Etruscans betrayed themselves by negligent style and Etruscan details and dipinti. Gerhard also kept the three familiar classes or (as he preferred) manners, naming them the Egyptian, the Archaic and the Perfect; the Egyptian began before the Archaic and the Archaic before the Perfect, but all three continued together. Though vase-painting was invented a little before 660 BC, when Demaratus landed in Etruria, the finds from Vulci were more advanced in development and for historical reasons should be dated between 480 and 280 BC: Apulian and Lucanian lasted another century until the Romans suppressed Bacchanalia. On the black-figure and red-figure pottery from Vulci the subjects and inscriptions were undeniably Attic; they must then have been painted in Etruria by Greeks of Attic stock, and perhaps Vulci was an Athenian colony. Gerhard's classification shows keen observation and some of his distinctions are valid, but he was misled by his choice of evidence and his love of system.

Most of Gerhard's colleagues were impressed by his enthusiasm and authority. They accepted the coexistence of the three manners, not realizing that many of the tombs at Vulci were family vaults in use for a long while; besides, Heinrich Meyer, C. A. Böttiger and Millingen had already declared that the periods of black-figure and red-figure overlapped. To support this theory it had to be assumed that much vase-painting was 'affected' – that is, consciously archaizing – as, for example, the Affecter's group in Attic black-figure. But though the Duc de Luynes laid down the rules by which later imitations could be detected, they proved too subtle for general application. The dating also was acceptable and evidence was chosen to support it, especially from ancient notices about the development of the alphabet, parallels in sculpture, and historical records and silences. So C. O. Müller in 1831 identified the Leagros of the Archaic καλός names as the butt of the comic poet Plato, and de Luynes in 1833 recognized the fourth Arcesilas on the famous Laconian cup, which otherwise he interpreted admirably. The comparison between black-figure and the coins of Sybaris, which Böttiger had stressed in 1811, was dismissed by Bunsen as valid only for Sybaris. In general the early pottery, in so far as it was not considered affected, was dated with fair accuracy; so Müller put the Dodwell pyxis about 580 BC, though others went a century further back. But black-figure was usually dated too late, so that some students assigned even the Burgon amphora to the fifth century, and the beginning of red-figure was commonly fixed about 450 BC.

What most puzzled the archaeologists of the 1830s was the great quantity of the painted pottery found at Vulci. Canino with his claque at once insisted that it was Etruscan and with the virtuous indignation of the monopolist threatened by competition clamoured that the vases being found in Greece were planted by agents who had stolen them from his Tuscan estate, or else were ancient exports from Etruria. But the majority of students were resolute in believing that black-figure and red-figure were Greek. Either then Greek vase-painters worked at Vulci or the Vulcentines imported Greek painted vases. Gerhard's first explanation was an Attic colony at Vulci, his second an isopolity of Athenians and Etruscans. F. G. Welcker postulated a hereditary guild of emigrant Attic potters. L. Hirt thought of Athenian refugees from Thurii. Millingen more simply made the Etruscans Greek. Those who preferred import were troubled by distances. D. Raoul-Rochette chose South Italy or Sicily for his factories. C. O. Müller risked Athens, but quickly switched to Cumae. The scholarly diplomat C. K. J. Bunsen, later Baron von Bunsen, after neatly dissecting his predecessors, allotted most black-figure to Athens and most red-figure to South Italy, since the import of pottery was not necessarily more expensive than local manufacture, particularly when trade was not yet restricted by governments. These Greek theories and their historical consequences may now seem extravagant, but their authors were honest and reputable students and, granted their premises, they argued with tolerable logic. Their statements are mostly printed, in full or in summary, in the early volumes of *Annali* and *Bullettino*.

A more radical solution was published in 1837. Gustav Kramer was a textual critic, still respected for his edition of Strabo, but in 1835 he visited Italy and on his travels examined the collections of painted pottery. His conclusions, lucidly and courteously expressed in the pamphlet *Über den Styl und die Herkunft der bemalten griechischen Thongefässe*, were founded on stylistic observation and epigraphic forms, since chemical analysis of clay and paint had proved useless or impracticable. He began by denying the multiplicity of local fabrics. The Egyptianizing style (which Bunsen had recently dubbed Doric) was at least in part Corinthian. The Old style – his name for black-figure – was Attic, as he had seen. But Bunsen's argument could be extended to red-figure, which also must be Attic, even – and here he deserted his epigraphic principle – the late group commonly called Apulian. What is now named Gnathian was connected with Apulian, but perhaps later in date and Italian. In his chronology Kramer was conventional, comparing for instance his Severe (our Archaic) red-figure to the Aegina pediments and his Free (our Classical) red-figure to Praxiteles' female nudes and so dating them respectively from 460 to 420 and from 420 to 380 BC. But he could not see archaistic imitations, except in some Panathenaic amphorae. Kramer's argument was too fundamental to be accepted at once; seven years later C. Lenormant and J. de Witte wrote that the problems of vase-painting had seemed nearer to solution before Vulci was exhumed, and in the 1850s Gerhard would concede only wandering guilds of Attic potters.

The publication of painted vases was continued busily, notably by Gerhard after he had moved on to Berlin. But almost all that was published came from Italy. In Greece discovery was slow and not well known. L. Ross, who was in charge of the antiquities of the kingdom, observed in 1835 that there were red-figure sherds in the debris from the Persian sack of the Acropolis of Athens; but Ross was difficult and often wild, and his observation was at the time ignored, if indeed it became known before his paper in *Allgemeine Monatschrift* in 1852. The most promising work was on the Orientalizing and Geometric styles. Even before 1830 the Sicilians had preferred to speak of Phoenician rather than Egyptian, and as knowledge of Oriental art grew de Witte and Müller and Raoul-Rochette pointed to parallels in Phoenicia and Babylonia. Geometric was slowly being suspected. In 1837 Gerhard commented on the big Late Geometric amphorae from Thera and Baron O. M. von Stackelberg published a couple of Attic Geometric pots; since the beginning of the century travellers had been noting Geometric and Mycenaean sherds at Mycenae; and there was, of course, Geometric and Subgeometric from Italy. The tendency now was to distinguish Geometric as genuine Phoenician, and Orientalizing as Greek imitation. While the experts were groping towards a solution, the veteran Burgon published in 1847 the results of observations he had made in Greece nearly forty years before. He saw that Geometric (with which he mixed a few Mycenaean sherds) was a separate, earlier and probably universal stage of Greek pottery, dated it from the twelfth to the tenth century, and included it with the subsequent Orientalizing in his Pelasgian or Heroic class, which preceded true Hellenic. Burgon's paper was printed in the *Transactions of the Royal Society of Literature* and escaped the notice of continental students.

The study of subjects was waning, in spite or because of T. Panofka's brilliant follies. Panofka also supplied ancient names for the shapes of Greek pottery in his *Recherches sur les véritables noms des vases grecs* of 1829, and Gerhard in *Annali* 1831 proposed a rival system that was no more veritable. More than a century before Montfaucon had seen that such researches were futile, and A. Letronne rightly attacked both Panofka and Gerhard. But their new nomenclature was thought more reputable than the current Italian names, which were attributed to the Neapolitan dealers. Later students have proposed various modifications and additions, and the more fanciful names have gradually lost favour, though 'stamnos' and 'olpe' for example still survive. A convenient key to the three early systems is given in note 619 of the introduction to O. Jahn's *Beschreibung der Vasensammlung*.

Jahn's book, published in 1854, makes a good epilogue to the early epoch of the study of Greek painted pottery. He accepted the three classes and analysed them neatly, in general recognizing Kramer's attributions, except for South Italian, and retaining and refining some of Gerhard's juster distinctions. So he derived black-figure from Orientalizing (a term that he used incidentally) and marked the transition just after the Attic François vase, and he had a notion (though misplaced) of 'Chalcidian' and was sound enough on later Etruscan black-figure. He denounced the symbolic interpretation of subjects, and recommended that the place where a pot was found should be recorded at the time and not invented to suit its supposed style. In dating he was more judicious and accurate than his predecessors. The Oldest style began at a time not yet ascertained and lasted at least till 460 BC; black-figure was established well before the Oldest style ended and, except for some Panathenaic amphorae, ended in the 430s; in Attic red-figure the Severe phase was current from before 480 till 436, the Fine phase from 436 till the end of the fourth century; Etruscan red-figure, such as it was, belonged mainly to the third century; South Italian flourished from the third to the first century BC. The most important chronological pegs were Ross's report of red-figure in the Persian stratum at Athens, the Pronomos krater, a grave at Panticapaeum (or Kerch) containing a coin of the early fourth century, and the Panathenaic amphorae from Benghazi inscribed with the names of Athenian archons of the late fourth century. Jahn had a cool and shrewd intelligence and his survey was thorough and systematic, so that it deservedly became the primer of the next generation. It also lays bare how little had been achieved by the first four generations of students. They had, of course, the excuse (so often trotted out by their successors) that published illustrations were few and bad, and there was the further hazard that till 1859 all plates were engraved by hand. Yet the successful specialists of the 1920s, when photography was still cumbrous and expensive, made do for the most part with the old – and irreplaceable – aids of careful notes and tracings.

Soon after the middle of the nineteenth century a new spirit was transforming the study of vase-painting. It can be glimpsed even in S. Birch's *History of Ancient Pottery*, published in 1858, only four years after Jahn's *Beschreibung*. Birch was an Orientalist, who approached Classical antiquity with an open, if not empty, mind; and in his Greek chapters, ignorant and grossly careless as they are, the emphasis is towards stylistic evolution. It was the specialized study of style that marked the new epoch, encouraged and supported by excavation in Greek lands east of the Adriatic. Greece itself was becoming more attractive than Italy to foreign students and welcomed them more generously. So new schools and periods of Greek pottery were soon discovered.

Within the modern epoch the First World War, or rather the publication of E. Pfuhl's *Malerei und Zeichnung* in 1923, is a convenient point near which to halt. The excavations undertaken in this period varied greatly in standard, but on most there was some interest in sherds and even in contexts. Of those significant for Hellenic pottery the first occurred in what was then Turkish territory. In 1859 A. Biliotti and A. Salzmann, the British and French consuls at Rhodes, were encouraged by C. T. Newton to exploit the cemeteries of Camirus and Ialysus, where their most novel finds were Mycenaean, Rhodian Geometric, Wild Goat style and Fikellura; this new material became available very quickly, since like good patriots they sold the greater part to the British Museum and the Louvre. In Greece, where the export of antiquities was restricted by law, it was more necessary for excavators to publish what they found, and some of them did. New Prehellenic wares were revealed in Therasia and Thera in the years 1866–7, when among others the geologist F. Fouqué struck Middle Cycladic remains below the deposits of an unrecorded eruption; in Cyprus especially in 1868 and the next few years, while General L. P. di Cesnola was ransacking sites of all periods; and at Troy and Mycenae in H. Schliemann's campaigns of 1871–3 and 1874–6. More directly important was the Geometric cemetery near the Dipylon gate of Athens, where J. Palaiologos and G. Hirschfeld delved from 1871–2. New East Greek of the sixth century came in the period 1884–6 from the operations of W. M. Flinders Petrie and E. A. Gardner at the Egyptian sites of Naucratis and Tell Defenneh. The turn of Cycladic was later; H. Dragendorff in 1896 and E. Pfuhl in 1902 excavated much Theran Late Geometric and Linear Island wares on Thera, and D. Stavropoullos in 1898–9 exhumed other groups from the Purification enclosure on Rheneia, though the release of the bulk of his finds did not begin till 1934. For Protocorinthian and Ripe Corinthian the key sites were the western colonies, for which ancient author offered fairly consistent dates. Here L. Mauceri in *Annali* 1877 published a small and P. Orsi in *NSc* 1893 and 1895 a large sample of recent finds at Syracuse; for Megara Hyblaea Orsi in *MA* in 1892 could offer little, but his account of work just done at Gela, published in *MA* in 1906, was full; E. Gábrici in 1913, also in *MA*, surveyed the results of the last thirty-five years at Cumae; and from the 1880s onwards some information slipped out about Selinus. Laconian was augmented by R. M. Dawkins at Sparta from 1906–10. In Attica and Boeotia the local wares turned up constantly; of sites regularly excavated the most relevant were for later Boeotian the Theban sanctuary of the Cabiri in the years 1887–8; and for Submycenaean Salamis in 1893. An important find of Middle Protoattic was made soon after on Aegina, but mostly concealed. For Attic of the fourth century southern Ukraine had been providing material since about 1840, some of it admirably published by L. Stephani, and for early Hellenistic Alexandria from about 1885. In Turkey excavation was politically difficult and in its outcome unlucky, though after 1882 the dealers of Smyrna could lay their hands on Clazomenian sarcophagi. The chronological order of these excavations and finds gives a clue to the course of study.

In surveying the work of the specialists it is simpler to follow one style at a time. Geometric is conveniently taken first. In 1870 in the *Sitzungherichte* of the Vienna Academy A. Conze produced *zur Geschichte der Anfänge der griechischen Kunst*, where he catalogued some sixty Geometric pots. Generally he elaborated and improved Burgon's notions, giving a clear, though incomplete, analysis of the style. Two years later in *Annali* G. Hirschfeld published many of the new finds from the Dipylon graves and added human figures to Conze's repertory. The students of this time necessarily concentrated on Attic Geometric, though they recognized more or less close relatives in Thera and Italy and tended to include what Mycenaean they knew as well as some early Orientalizing. Mycenaean was abruptly detached in 1879 by A. Furtwängler and G. Loeschcke in their *Mykenische Thongefässe*, and gradually local Geometric schools were distinguished. Furtwängler, in particular, from 1879 to 1886 could refer understandingly to Rhodian, belated Apulian, Italogeometric and Cypriot, and in 1888 he discovered the Geometric which preceded Protocorinthian. J. Boehlau in *JdI* 1887 recognised Protoattic and its position, so finally establishing against Furtwängler and Loeschcke that the dominant Geometric school had its home in Athens: in *JdI* 1888 he studied Boeotian; in 1895 in *zur Ornamentik der Villanovaperiode* he gave reasons for deriving the earliest Italian Geometric from Greek. Then in *JdI* 1899 and 1900 the diligent Sam Wide roughly summarized the present state of knowledge: he collected examples of the Theran, Melian, Cretan, Boeotian, Laconian, Argive and Attic schools, noted the Mycenaean connections of some Protogeometric pots, and saw, but refused to believe, the stages of Attic development. H. Dragendorff in *Thera* II, which appeared in 1903, was less timid: he outlined the course of Attic and Theran, transferred Linear Island from Boeotia to Euboea, commented on the Protocorinthian school which inspired Italogeometric, and made a division between the vigorous Geometric style of mainland Greece (with Melos and Thera) and the weak and arrested Geometric of Cyprus, Crete and the East Greek region, though Rhodes slowly submitted to western influence. F. Poulsen, two years later, in his *die Dipylongräber und die Dipylonvasen* gave an admirable conspectus of earlier work, supplemented Wide's lists, and made a close and sensible examination of Attic development. There was still a gap between Mycenaean and Geometric; this was partly filled by the Submycenaean finds from Salamis, cited by Dragendorff and published in

AM 1910 by Wide, though he named them Protogeometric. A fuller study of Argive Geometric followed in 1912, contributed by W. Müller and F. Oelmann in *Tiryns* I. Finally, in 1918, K. F. Johansen in *Sikyoniske Vaser* gave a clear account of Protocorinthian (that is, Late Corinthian) Geometric, and B. Schweitzer in his *Untersuchungen zur Chronologie [und Geschichite] der geometrischen Stile in Griechenland* (of which the first part was printed separately and the second in *AM*) at last defined Proto-geometric, though more broadly than is accepted now, noticed the existence (which by now could not be denied) of other East Greek schools besides Rhodian, and with the aid of some new metaphysical terms made a brave and generally successful analysis both of Protogeometric and Attic Geometric. Schweitzer's was almost the last major work to speak of the Dipylon style. 'Dipylon' had superseded 'Pelasgian' about 1880 as a general name for what we now call Geometric, but within twenty years was normally restricted to the Attic school. 'Geometric' itself had been mentioned by Semper and was afterwards always current, if only as a term of description.

The dating of Geometric (including Protogeometric) could hardly be far wrong. From the first it was seen that Geometric came immediately before Orientalizing, and the Dipylon graves showed that it still belonged to the Iron Age. So it was easy to reject Conze's choice of the second millennium BC based on a mistake over Theran geology, and when Mycenaean had been recognized and dated most students put the beginning of Geometric in the tenth or else the eleventh century. But in fixing the end of Geometric they found two extra difficulties. First, they did not agree on what was Geometric and what early Orientalizing. Secondly, they presumed that some Greek regions were little affected by Geometric and so Orientalizing could be its contemporary rather than its successor. So Furtwängler, who included the SOS amphorae, maintained that Geometric was widespread in the seventh century and in Athens was current in the mid-sixth. Boehlau reclassified some of Furtwängler's Attic Geometric as early Protoattic, and the second half of the seventh century became the limit of his own Geometric Attic. Wide tried in vain to compress the period of Geometric generally. Dragendorff made progress, he took account of the finds from Italy and Sicily and inferred that the Protocorinthian and Attic schools of Geometric must end with the eighth century. Müller and Oelmann for the same reason went back to the middle of that century. It was left to Schweitzer to examine the evidence thoroughly and to conclude that his Protogeometric belonged mainly to the eleventh and tenth centuries, Geometric to the ninth and eighth. There still was, and is, some doubt on how long the lesser Geometric and Sub-geometric schools persisted or lingered.

The earlier students found more interest in the origin of Geometric and its relation to Orientalizing than in the development of its style. In 1860 and 1863 G. Semper in his influential treatise, *der Stil in den technischen Künsten*, had observed that geometrical ornaments were widespread among primitive peoples and by the principle of the spontaneous evolution of art derived them from textiles and wickerwork (as indeed Burgon had suggested for his Greek pots, though with less ado). This derivation, which some still maintain, had the convenience of allowing a geometric pottery to appear suddenly and unheralded. Semper also observed a close similarity in the Geometric style of the Greeks (of which he had a vague notion from Birch) and that of other early Europeans. In 1870 Conze developed this theory: the Geometric of Greece (and Italy too) originated in the primitive style of northern Europe, brought by the Indo-German invaders and then adapted to pottery. This explanation accorded with notions becoming prevalent among philologists and in one form or another has had a long life. An older theory was refurbished by W. Helbig in *Annali* 1875: in Greece and Italy the Indo-Germanic Geometric (which he conceded) was a rough, incised ware, but the painted Geometric had a highly developed system and came through the Phoenicians from the East. The problem shifted with the isolation of Mycenaean pottery. Little notice had been taken of the finds from Rhodes in the Louvre and the British Museum and none of a collection from Cephallenia exhibited since 1836 in Neuchâtel; a few sherds from Mycenae had been noticed, but classed with Geometric. Then in 1876 A. Milchhöfer, reporting in *AM* on Schliemann's excavation of that site, hinted at a local ware with vegetable ornament that was not Orientalizing. Three years later this new Mycenaean style was clearly displayed in the *Mykenische Thongefässe* of Furtwängler and Loeschcke. It was now apparent that though Geometric resembled Mycenaean in technique and perhaps in some ornaments, it differed greatly in style, the more so since the intervening stages had not yet been discovered. It was also apparent that the change from one style to the other coincided more or less with the traditional invasion of the Dorians. Yet the Geometric pottery found at Athens, where traditionally the Dorians did not penetrate, was the most richly and thoroughly Geometric. Furtwängler and Loeschcke, adapting Conze, saw in Geometric the combination of Mycenaean technique with the European style of the Dorian invaders; this began perhaps at Argos, but spread elsewhere; Athens imported her Geometric. But in 1887 Boehlau demonstrated that Protoattic, undeniably Attic itself, developed out of the Geometric of Athens. In his solution, offered eight years later in *zur Ornamentik der Villanovaperiode* and elaborated by Wide in *AM* 1896, the Geometric style had its origin in the peasant style of Middle Helladic, which was suppressed by Mycenaean, but re-emerged with a modern technique after the collapse of Mycenaean rule and art. Thus the contribution of the Dorians was negative, and in his *Dipylongräber* of 1905 Poulsen (inspired perhaps by E. Curtius and K. J. Beloch) denied even this, arguing that the Mycenaean kingdoms were overthrown by aristocratic revolution. But the theory that the Dorians brought the Geometric style, though the hardest to support, remained the most popular and was given a new prop by A. J. B. Wace and M. S. Thompson in their *Prehistoric Thessaly* of 1912. Continuity from Mycenaean to Geometric was asserted by Dragendorff in 1903, demonstrated by Schweitzer in 1918 and afterwards slowly accepted. This new view can be, or rather is, reconciled by die-hards with the Dorian theory and perhaps something may be salved even from Helbig's, if (as some of his opponents admitted) such Geometric types as the recumbent goat have Oriental ancestors.

Orientalizing, black-figure and red-figure were still the regular divisions of Greek vase-painting at the middle of the nineteenth century. For Orientalizing there was then no upper limit, except to Burgon and his intimates. But when after 1870 the separate character of Geometric was recognized generally, a natural zeal at first gave it much of what we call early Orientalizing and a little more. To the students of the mid-century, familiar mainly with Italian finds, the core of Orientalizing was Ripe Corinthian, to which were appended the Tyrrhenian class of Attic, Pontic, 'Chalcidian' and a few strays of other groups in which rows of animals were frequent. Black-figure as a stylistic term was reserved more or less to the mature and late phases of the Attic school and to late Etruscan. As earlier Attic became known, the boundary of black-figure was slowly and unevenly pushed back and by the First World War was near its present vague position. But since at the same time interest had been shifting from styles to schools, the definition between Orientalizing and black-figure, always rather arbitrary, became unimportant as well.

The term 'Orientalizing' did not establish itself till the 1870s. 'Egyptian' was already condemned as misleading before 1850 and the other veteran, 'Phoenician', had not become reputable when the Assyrian discoveries of the 1840s suggested that it too was inaccurate. An improved name, 'Asiatic' or 'Asianizing', had some currency in the third quarter of the century, but was perhaps thought too narrow. 'Oldest' or 'Ancient' became absurd when a still earlier style was admitted, though in Germany the derivatives 'altkorinthisch' and 'altrhodisch' survived till the end of the century to denote Ripe Corinthian and the Wild Goat style. 'Dorian' and 'Corinthian' had seemed reasonable to the adherents of Kramer, but as new schools of Orientalizing were discovered could no longer be accepted as generic descriptions. There was no difficulty over 'black-figure', which had always been used as a sort of sub-title and soon after 1850 began to replace 'Archaic' and its variants as the proper name of a style.

Most of the Orientalizing studied in the 1850s was rightly considered to be Corinthian or in its later stage Attic adaptation of Corinthian. The first new school detected was 'Melian', represented by three large amphorae in Athens and a sherd in Berlin. Conze, who published them in his *Melische Thongefässe* of 1862, the earliest and most lavish of special studies, concluded from their place of finding that they were made in Melos by Greeks still influenced by their Phoenician predecessors, and he compared their style to the so-called Corinthian. The excellence of Conze's illustrations made 'Melian' familiar and the size of his amphorae enlarged its reputation, since archaeologists are too often impressed by size. It was commonly supposed that 'Melian' was the earliest of the Orientalizing schools and the transmitter of the new style to Corinth and Athens. J. Boehlau in *JdI* 1887 argued that 'Melian' (as then known) was short-lived and slavishly imitative of the Wild Goat style; and H. Dragendorff in *Thera* II, which was published in 1903, dated it from after the middle of the seventh century till some time in the sixth. But such radical criticisms could hardly be accepted completely, and even now 'Melian' is sometimes over-valued. In part that is because the main find of that ware, from the Purification enclosure on Rheneia, has only lately been published. Only one other study needs mentioning, J. H. Hopkinson's in *JHS* 1902, which gave a summary but useful analysis of the style of the Rheneian finds: Hopkinson believed that 'Melian' influenced European Greece, but found it difficult to fit into the evolution of Greek vase-painting. His suggestion that it was made at Delos had some effect.

Among the finds from Vulci were several 'Chalcidian' pots, notable for their subjects, quality and painted inscriptions. Gerhard had put them in his Tyrrheno-Egyptian school, Kramer in the appendage to his Corinthian and Jahn among Attic imitations of Corinthian. But the inscriptions were puzzling. Kramer noted that their dialect was not Doric, Jahn that they were neither Corinthian nor completely Attic. The answer came from the epigraphist, A. Kirchhoff, who in 1863 in the first edition of *Studien zur Geschichte des griechischen Alphabets* (in the *Abhandlungen* of the Berlin Academy) showed that their alphabet was that of the Chalcidian colonies of South Italy and in his third edition fourteen years later that of Chalcis too. The group was at once called Chalcidian, though for a time it was defined more by its inscriptions than its style. The style was first examined, not very satisfactorily, by W. Klein in his *Euphronios* of 1879, and then more accurately by F. Studniczka in *JdI* for 1886. In the same year G. Loeschcke announced a comprehensive study of 'Chalcidian', but though he lived another thirty years did little more than deter other students from attempting it. The task was at last executed in 1927 in A. Rumpf's *Chalkidische Vasen*. A close relation between 'Chalcidian' and later Corinthian had always been perceived, and at first 'Chalcidian' was seen to be the borrower. But Chalcis was 'ethnically' Ionian, and so believers in Ionian pre-eminence tended for historical reasons to make Corinth dependent. This was Klein's opinion, endorsed by Loeschcke in *AM* 1894. But Studniczka resisted in *JdI* 1887 and by the First World War the priority of Corinthian was usually admitted, although 'Chalcidian' was still dated about a generation too early. 'Chalcidian' influence on Attic was accepted by Pfuhl as late as 1923. It was, of course, generally assumed that 'Chalcidian' was made in Chalcis, though the ambiguity of the evidence was shown in 1883 by A. Milchhöfer in *die Anfänge der Kunst in Griechenland* and by A. Dumont (who proposed Cumae) in *les Céramiques de la Grèce propre*: it was not till the 1930s that serious doubt reappeared.

By an unlucky chance the Phineus cup, the chief representative of the later stage of 'Chalcidian', had suffered restoration and its painted inscriptions, originally Chalcidian, had become misleadingly Ionic. So from the first the Phineus group was separated from 'Chalcidian'. Furtwängler in 1880, in *der Satyr aus Pergamon*, naturally diagnosed the style of the Phineus cup as Ionian; J. Endt in 1899 in *Beiträge zur ionischen Vasenmalerei* more moderately proposed Naxos. The style was now recognized as dependent on 'Chalcidian', with of course a more easterly flavour. The collection of a Phineus group began in the 1890s. The first considerable list of cups was that of J. Boehlau in *AM* 1900, though it included much that was alien. Two years later Furtwängler in FR made some sensible corrections, and R. Zahn in *BPW* added several amphorae. Finally in 1921 the Phineus cup was cleaned down to the genuine inscriptions and Rumpf in *AM* proved them and it 'Chalcidian'.

Laconian too emerged from Vulci, and one hydria and half a dozen cups (including the Arcesilas cup) were published before 1850, but their similarity had not been noted. J. de Witte in the *Gazette des Beaux Arts* for 1863 connected five of the cups and in 1871 H. Brunn made a list of seven in his *Probleme in der Geschichte der Vasenmalerei* (from the *Abhandlungen* of the Bavarian Academy). Brunn, an otherwise able student, was the last notable adherent of the theory of 'archaism' and the most extreme, and till he died in 1894 maintained with a perverse logic that most of the best pots found in Etruria were painted in the third or second centuries in imitation of much earlier styles. So some of his Laconian cups were early and some archaistic. An eye trained to imaginary distinctions did not miss true ones, and Brunn observed that on style the Arcesilas cup should be contemporary with the second Cyrenaean king of the name. So far the group had not been located: the dialect of the inscriptions of the Arcesilas cup was evidently Dorian, but the alphabet was unknown. In 1879 in the first edition of his *Euphronios* W. Klein showed that this was Laconian and drew the unpalatable but correct conclusion. Next year G. Loeschcke appended to his *de Basi quadam prope Spartam reperta* a list of two dozen Laconian pots; he noted that the group was provincial enough for Sparta, but would not commit himself till the alphabets of Cyrene and other places were known. This evasion was accepted by O. Puchstein, who claimed in *AZ* 1880 that the Arcesilas cup must be Cyrenaean: after all its subject was set in Cyrene and adapted from the neighbouring art of Egypt. Puchstein also, in *AZ* 1881, enlarged Loeschcke's list to twenty-nine, dated the school from the mid-sixth century to the beginning of the fifth, found it more closely connected to the Wild Goat style and 'Melian' than to Corinthian, and traced its development no more accurately than Loeschcke. Most students accepted Cyrene, especially after Studniczka in his *Kyrene* of 1890 had revealed Cyrenaean interpretations of other cups, and they regarded the style as dominantly Ionic. This was still Dugas's position in 1907, when he listed in *RA* over eighty examples, dating them between 600 and 525 BC. But the excavations at Sparta were now finding that Cyrenaean was the normal pottery there and could be followed back to Geometric. So after a short hesitation J. P. Droop in *BSA* XIV, published in 1909, demonstrated that Cyrenaean was Laconian, and in *JHS* 1910 he proceeded to classify the style in six stages, some of which are still valid. Though a few recalcitrants insisted on a branch factory at Cyrene, the Laconian origin was soon established and Corinthian influences were once again admissible.

Corinthian of the Ripe style was the base of the first of the old three divisions of Greek vase-painting, and by the middle of the nineteenth century most students had accepted at least in part Kramer's argument that it was made in Corinth and fathered the black-figured style of Athens. It fell easily into two parts, the Animal style and the Red-ground style (to which were attached other pots with human scenes): the Red-ground style was considered late Corinthian, even though some laggards attributed it to Corinthian emigrants in Etruria. When in the 1860s 'Melian' and the Wild Goat style and soon after Geometric came to light, the technical sequence – silhouette, reservation, incision – and the degree of sophistication suggested that Ripe Corinthian was not the earliest version of the Orientalizing style. During the 1870s its relations to Attic were probed more exactly, and in *Annali* 1878 Loeschcke asserted that the Red-ground style, which appeared when the Animal style was dying, showed a reverse influence from Attic. About the same time Protocorinthian was discovered. But this early promise was blighted by the new orthodoxy which saw Ionian models everywhere, and so replaced Corinthian influences by 'Chalcidian'. The only bold study of the next generation was that of E. Pottier in 1899 in the second part of the *Catalogue des Vases antiques du Louvre*: Pottier had some imperfect notions of the development of Ripe Corinthian, included an abnormal quantity of Etruscocorinthian, recognized Ionian traits, and dated it from the early seventh to the middle of the sixth century. Such early datings were general and not clearly explained, since the refusal to consider Ripe Corinthian as the continuation of Protocorinthian was as much an effect as a cause. It was rather that 'Melian' and East Greek were also dated too early, and they were linked to Ripe Corinthian by style and the contexts of graves in Rhodes; perhaps also the finds at Syracuse were misunderstood. In the twentieth century these early dates were gradually reduced and the present chronology was established in 1931 in H. G. G. Payne's *Necrocorinthia*, a thorough and impressive analysis of the Ripe Corinthian style. Though its main stages were more or less perceived, as catalogues show, it is surprising that a special study of the school had been undertaken only once before, in 1892, and that had been immediately and justly condemned. In spite of the Panionist perversion, Ripe Corinthian had remained important as the parent or foster-parent of the black-figure technique, so that even in the 1890s the incising Late Wild Goat style was without much opposition accepted as an imitation of Corinthian, and before the First World War Corinthian was again seen to have a strong influence on Attic and 'Chalcidian'. Possibly the great number of Corinthian pots overfaced earlier students.

Protocorinthian excited much more speculation, once it was discovered. First W. Helbig in *Annali* 1877 noted the uniformity of some simple aryballoi found in Italy and Sicily, and by historical reasoning suggested that the group was made by Chalcidians. Two years later in *die Italiker in der Poebene* he published Loeschcke's information that similar aryballoi occurred in Athens, Corinth and Aegina, favoured distribution in the West by Chalcidian colonists, and claimed that this was the first group of Greek pottery imported into Italy: as evidence he could cite finds beneath the Servian wall at Rome and Mauceri's useful contexts at Syracuse, which also had been published in *Annali* 1877. Then Furtwängler took over. In 1879 in *die Bronzefunde aus Olympia* he observed that Helbig's group was intermediate between Geometric and Ripe Corinthian, and dated it (according to the low chronology then regular for Geometric) to the seventh and sixth centuries. About the same time he privately invented the name 'Protocorinthian', for want of a better as he explained when others had established its use. In *AZ* 1883 he added two aryballoi with polychrome figures, commented acutely on the Protocorinthian style, and while maintaining that it was older than Ripe Corinthian and closely connected to it could not yet decide on its home: in spite of Ionian traits it was presumptuous to give judgement for Chalcis. He further recognized Italian imitations, which Helbig had not distinguished. In his Berlin catalogue, published in 1885, Furtwängler made a partly successful division between early and late stages; in *die Sammlung Sabouroff* in 1886 he asserted manufacture in Corinth; and finally in *JdI* 1888 he identified correctly the local Geometric from which Protocorinthian developed. Other students did little more than dispute about origins. Although all agreed that Ripe Corinthian was in the main derived from Protocorinthian, many thought that the two schools were largely contemporary and, if transitional pieces were discounted as imitations, there were obvious differences in style and shapes: since, then, Ripe Corinthian was made at Corinth, Protocorinthian must have been made in some other place or places, preferably not far away. Even so, Corinth always had some supporters, of whom P. Orsi and L. Pallat must be mentioned. Orsi in *NSc* 1895 used his finds at Syracuse to show the development of Protocorinthian, and especially of its aryballoi, and he regarded Ripe Corinthian as a subsequent stage. Pallat had worked on Corinthian sherds at Aegina and his demonstration in *AM* 1897 of the unity of Protocorinthian and Ripe Corinthian is hardly less complete than Payne's more than thirty years later. Chalcis, which seemed to have as good a historical claim as Corinth to trade with the West, had fewer backers: if Ripe Corinthian was hard to reconcile to Protocorinthian, 'Chalcidian' was harder. In the 1890s some students rashly proposed Ionia and Boeotia, and others Aegina, Argos and Sicyon, which Johansen supported in his *Sikyoniske Vaser* of 1918. But opinions were still divided between Sicyon and Corinth till in 1931 Payne's *Necrocorinthia* crushed the dispute. On the development of Protocorinthian and its importance for the black-figure style knowledge came slowly. Pallat's was the most notable contribution before Johansen's thorough and exemplary study. As for chronology, the colonies in the West fixed the beginning of Protocorinthian in the mid-eighth century, but before Johansen its end was still often prolonged into the sixth.

Very little East Greek was known by the middle of the nineteenth century. Jahn in 1854 could describe a good dish of the canonical Wild Goat style only as an unusual example of Orientalizing, and eighteen years later L. Urlichs ingenuously published two Chiot chalices of the corresponding phase under the title *Zwei vasen ältesten Stils*. The first considerable finds were made by A. Biliotti and Salzmann in Rhodes in 1859 and the following years, to the immediate benefit of the British Museum and afterwards of the Louvre. But except for the Euphorbos plate, unique for its painted inscriptions, heroic subject and polychromy, they were not much noticed by active students, who like Conze in *AA* 1864 classed the Wild Goat style vaguely with 'Melian'. The first important step was A. de Longpérier's *Musée Napoléon III*, published in 1868 and the earliest album of vase-paintings to exploit photography. His plates included examples of the Wild Goat style, Fikellura and Chiot, and his text shows intelligence. Other pieces were illustrated with haphazard captions in Salzmann's *Nécropole de Camiros* in 1875. From now on various classes of East Greek began to be considered separately.

At this stage the new theory of Panionism perverted the study of Orientalizing and particularly of East Greek. As far back as 1833 Millingen had casually suggested the priority of Ionian pottery and in 1864 C. Bursian in Ersch and Grulow's *Allgemeine Encyclopädie* asserted that Greek art originated in Ionia, in much the same way as literature. These untimely claims were ignored. But in 1879 Furtwängler and Loeschcke made clear the existence and character of Mycenaean pottery. Furtwängler at once observed an affinity between Mycenaean and Orientalizing, and the same year in *die Bronzefunde aus Olympia* declared that Rhodian (by which he meant the Wild Goat style), 'Melian' and Boeotian, though borrowing something from Oriental sources, yet evolved directly out of Mycenaean without ny Geometric interval. Boeotian was anyhow negligible, and Furtwängler's theory was interpreted as setting the origin of the Orientalizing style in Ionia, an Ionia usually expanded to take in not only the whole East Greek region from Rhodes to Lesbos, but also the Cyclades and Euboea. By another sleight of logic the dominance of this Ionia was extended to black-figure too. The Panionian theory when first propounded was not demonstrably wrong, and it was quickly and universally accepted: after all, the Ionians were historically Mycenaean refugees, Homer and other poets and thinkers testified to the early primacy of Asiatic Greece, and Ionia was in Asia and that much closer to the sources of Orientalizing art. So the students of vase-painting were disposed, even against the evidence, to date East Greek too early, to hail as East Greek any unidentified group of pots, and to see East Greek influence wherever it could not certainly be disproved. At first new discoveries seemed to confirm Panionism. In 1882 Clazomenae began to disgorge its enormous sarcophagi with their curious mixture of Wild Goat, black-figure and even red-figure styles: Clazomenae, some believed, was destroyed by the Persians about 540 BC. Elsewhere too in Ionia the Persian conquest must have driven creative artists to emigrate. In the later 1880s there came the excavations, roughly but quickly published, of Naucratis and Tell Defenneh in Egypt, the first introducing to students Bird bowls and their derivatives, the Late Wild Goat style and the more striking phases of Chiot, and the second its Situlae and Clazomenian black-figure: by an arbitrary interpretation of ancient writers, the period of Tell Defenneh was fixed as the first third of the sixth century and the foundation of Naucratis about the middle of the seventh, though a few dissenters preferred a date about 570 BC without closely considering the consequences. Some students, notably F. Dümmler, turned to Etruria and claimed much of the local manufacture as Ionian, whether imported or made by emigrants: again a terminal date was found about 540 BC, when the battle of Alalia ousted the Greeks from Etruscan lands. So by a series of prejudiced errors the chronology of East Greek was set some thirty or forty years too high, and perhaps for that reason Biliotti's records of his graves appeared unreliable and though consulted several times in the 1880s were never published. But even when dated so early Ionian art did not provide the models that Panionism required, and in the 1890s some students began to restore to Corinth the credit that had been transferred to Chalcis and more easterly Ionia, while others searched desperately for the elusive proof. Of these the most distinguished was Boehlau, who in 1898 in his *aus ionischen und italischen Nekropolen* contended that the black-figure style began in Aeolis and culled from Etruscocorinthian a sample for his original Aeolian school. In 1902 he bravely tested his theory on the site of 'Larisa' in Aeolis, and then from disillusion or some other cause retired into silence for the last forty years of his life. Boehlau's Aeolian claim had few supporters and by 1900

Panionism, though generally professed, was on the wane. Studniczka in *AA* 1899 attacked it radically, but Hopkinson in *JHS* 1902 expressed the moderate attitude most logically: Ionia provided the models for the vase-painting of European Greece, but those models were not painted vases. Even so, the old reverence for East Greek pottery and especially for the Clazomenian sarcophagi was sometimes noticeable till the 1930s, and traces can still be found in studies of Italian material. The chronology, of course, survived independently and was not comprehensively set right till Rumpf's paper in *JdI* 1933.

The students of the 1860s and 1870s hardly noticed the Wild Goat style except to assign it to Rhodes, where almost all their examples had been found, and to date it rather later than 'Melian'. Puchstein in *AZ* 1881 listed fifteen pieces and Dumont in 1883 in *les Céramiques de la Grèce propre* made the first analysis. In 1885 in his Berlin catalogue and the next year in *JdI* Furtwängler showed that he understood the general development. So far only the reserving 'Rhodian' was known, but now Naucratis provided a mass of incised sherds. At first some students claimed the incised Wild Goat style as Naucratite, and a few thought it a Corinthian copy of 'Rhodian'. Another heresy was propagated by Dümmler in *AM* 1888 and *JdI* 1891. The Euphorbos plate had the only text by a 'Rhodian' painter and its alphabet was Argive. This had been noted in 1867 by Kirchoff, who inferred that the Argive alphabet was current in Rhodes before the epichoric Rhodian. Dümmler, with his flair for the wrong conclusion, claimed the Euphorbos plate for Argos and with it all 'Rhodian' except a few poor plates. More serious was Loeschcke's assertion in *AM* 1897 that the Wild Goat style belonged to Miletus. The experts veered first to 'Milesian', then back again to 'Rhodian'; and Pfuhl compromised with 'Rhodian-Milesian'. A wiser solution, that the Wild Goat style was made in several East Greek cities, had perhaps been glimpsed by Dumont in 1883 and was clearly proposed by R. Zahn in *AM* 1898: its acceptance was slow. So too was stylistic study. Pottier in his *Catalogue* of 1896 and Boehlau in his *aus ionischen und italischen Nekropolen* of 1898 made some useful comments. Prinz in 1908 appended to his *Funde aus Naukratis* a long list of 'Milesian' pottery, but gave a muddled development of the style, which in 1912 in *der Orient und die frühgriechische Kunst* F. Poulsen supported by an ingenious misuse of Oriental parallels. The same faulty system was elaborated by K. F. Kinch two years later in *Fouilles de Vroulia*, which contained the first well-illustrated and detailed, though unsatisfactory, account of the Wild Goat style. Most of these students agreed on their dates: the style ran from the beginning of the seventh century till the early sixth, the younger contemporary of 'Melian' and the older of Ripe Corinthian. The problems of the Wild Goat style are still far from solved.

A poor Fikellura amphoriskos had been illustrated by Gerhard in 1831 as Orientalizing made by Greeks, but the school to which it belonged could not be recognized before the excavations in Rhodes that began in 1859. The best examples went to the British Museum, where the keepers saw that they represented a distinct and late class of Rhodian Orientalizing and named them Fikellura. Though this was stated by A. S. Murray in *RA* 1882, the Germans, less amateurish but here worse informed, still lumped Fikellura in the Wild Goat style; and Murray's notes of stylistic and stratigraphical connections with mature Attic black-figure and even red-figure were soon forgotten. In the late 1880s new groups of Fikellura were found at Naucratis and Tell Defenneh by Petrie, who dated them in the first half of the sixth century. Still more turned up in 1894 in Boehlau's cemetery on Samos, admirably published four years later in his *aus ionischen und italischen Nekropolen*. Here Boehlau gave a catalogue and a careful study of the school, which (following Loeschcke) he assigned provisionally to Samos; observed a direct influence of Mycenaean that was absent in 'Milesian' (as he called the Wild Goat style); and concluded that 'Samian', datable in the first half of the sixth century at Tell Defenneh and in the second at Samos, was a school parallel and not subsidiary to 'Milesian'. His successors discarded the Mycenaean survivals and tended to raise the dating, so that it could overlap more plausibly with the Wild Goat style. But no important advance was made till the Italian campaigns in Rhodes in the mid and late 1920s confirmed the observations that Biliotti had recorded nearly seventy years before.

The Chiot school was revealed suddenly in 1886 in Petrie's *Naukratis* I. Although three chalices had been published by the 1870s, their peculiarities were not evident till compared with the new and rich haul of sherds from Naucratis, which still provide so much of our evidence. Petrie naturally argued that this new school must be Naucratite and dated it according to his stratigraphy from 620 to 530 BC. Though Boehlau in 1898 did not distinguish 'Naucratite' from 'Milesian', Prinz ten years later in his *Funde aus Naukratis* found a neat compromise: 'Naucratite A', the reserving style, was made at Naucratis but derived from 'Milesian' (and from Boehlau's 'Aeolian' too), and the black-figure 'Naucratite B' remained a late derivative of 'A'. A new uncertainty was introduced in *A Delt* 1916 by K. Kuruniotis, who had found 'Naucratite' on Chios and suggested that it was made there, at least in part. Pfuhl of course hankered after 'Chiot-Naucratite' and summed up competently from his predecessors. E. R. Price in *JHS* 1924 denied manufacture in two places and preferred Naucratis to Chios: she also made a detailed study of the school, dividing Prinz's 'Naucratite A' into the earlier Wild Goat style influenced by 'Rhodian' and the later Chalice style influenced by Clazomeman. Price it seems was the only student since Petrie and his collaborators who had looked closely at the finds.

Bird bowls, Eye bowls and Rosette bowls were other groups which first caught students' attention at Naucratis in 1885. On Bird bowls *Naukratis*

I, published the next year, candidly offered two opinions. Petrie thought they were made at Naucratis, approximately between 620 and 530 BC. C. H. Smith more shrewdly saw that the group was partly Orientalizing and was already finishing when Naucratis was founded, as he thought, about 650 BC. But if Smith was right – and this was generally agreed – Bird bowls must have been made in some other place than Naucratis. The Geometric motifs suggested Rhodes, though Pottier in his *Catalogue* of 1896 denied the attribution. Pallat in *AM* 1897, following Dümmler's bad example in *JdI* 1887, claimed that the Bird bowls belonged or were closely related to Protocorinthian; and Dragendorff in 1903 in *Thera* II thought them probably Cycladic, yet correctly recognized their ancestry. But these heresies, surprising in students who were expert in the wares to which they as signed the Bird bowls, made few converts. The solution of widespread manufacture in the East Greek region was left to Price in her paper in *JHS* 1924. The Eye bowls too had been assigned by Petrie to Naucratis, and neither style nor distribution was against him. Pfuhl in 1923, connecting them again with the Bird bowls, assumed a Rhodian factory in Naucratis, and Price agreed. The Eye bowls were regularly dated in the sixth century and had some repute as the ancestors of black-figure eye cups. The Rosette bowls, numerous but uninteresting, were probably considered, when considered at all, as poor relations of the Eye bowl.

Since the 1880s at the latest Vroulian has usually been credited to Rhodes, and till after the First World War was dated in the seventh century as an immediate successor of the local Geometric. The only study of the group was that of Kinch in 1914 in *Fouilles de Vroulia*, where the name 'Vroulian' was first given. G. Karo in 1896 in his *de Arte Vascularia Antiquissima Quaestiones* had related it to Etruscocorinthian, and Boehlau two years later in *aus ionischen und italischen Nekropolen* labelled Karo's mixture 'Aeolian' and recommended it as the first Greek black-figure style. But these aberrations had no wide effect, though Kinch still fancied that Vroulian might have taught Protocorinthian potters to incise.

The Clazomenian sarcophagi brought out the worst in most of their many students. A poor late example from Rhodes had entered the British Museum in 1863 and received several harmless mentions, but the rot began with the discoveries in Clazomenae in 1882 and the thirty years that followed. These offered, separately or in conjunction, a reserving Wild Goat style and an imitation of a developed black-figure style, a few specimens even attempted red-figure, and there were others with wholly linear decoration. The size of the sarcophagi, their variety of style, the prevailing mood of Panionism and the lack of datable contexts combined to inflate the credit of these deplorable monuments. A favourite principle of study seems to have been to date each sarcophagus by the most primitive element in its decoration: those supposed the earliest were put back to the middle of the seventh century or before, and the end of the school was connected by the more credulous with a Persian destruction of Clazomenae about 540 BC. This chronology granted, it was logical to make the Clazomenian painters the first great masters of black-figure and the inventors of red-figure, and the judicious Zahn even turned Pliny's Cimon of Cleonae into a Clazomenian. Equally ingenious were the interpretations of subjects and the recognition that the shape and the ritual of the sarcophagi were derived from Egypt. Sober students, though not denying the premises, ignored the consequences, but there were also a few radicals. In particular F. Studniczka in *JdI* 1890 dated some, of the elaborate scenes in the later sixth century, F. Winter in *AA* 1898 insisted that the black-figure style was inanely decorative and that the example from Rhodes could not be much earlier than the middle of the fifth century; and Hopkinson in *JHS* 1902 observed that the Wild Goat style too was a degenerate relic. Zahn also in *AM* 1898, though greatly overrating the sarcophagi, saw that their period was short and not before the middle of the sixth century. But it was not till the 1930s that the old fantasies were abandoned, whether through Rumpf's insistence or the death of his adversaries.

For Clazomenian black-figure the only important find was at Tell Defenneh, and Petrie though not a Greek specialist saw quickly that this was a new school. In his report of 1888, which was bound up in *Tanis* II, he gave some useful drawings, claimed local manufacture and fixed the date (according to his notions of the history of the site) in the first third of the sixth century. Though A. S. Murray, also in *Tanis* II observed that the style of this pottery could be later, Petrie's dating was accepted by most students till the 1930s. Zahn in *AM* 1898 added some sherds from Clazomenae and showed a connection with the sarcophagi, and his conclusion that Petrie's group too must be Clazomenian was disputed only by Endt. Prinz in 1908 in *Funde aus Naukratis* listed the pots and sherds he knew. As the only certain school of East Greek black-figure Clazomenian soon attracted a number of strays and small groups, East Greek and Etruscan. The most notable of these, the Campana dinoi and the Northampton group, were still loosely attached to Clazomenian as late as the 1930s, if not later.

The East Greek Situlae too were first recognized at Tell Defenneh, and again Petrie in 1888 in the supplement to *Tanis* II published them sketchily and argued that they were made locally in the early sixth century. This dating was thought if anything too low, till Rumpf's paper in *JdI* 1933. Zahn in *AM* 1898 noted Rhodian connections and Kinch in 1914 in *Fouilles de Vroulia* argued for manufacture in Rhodes, it seems rightly.

At the middle of the nineteenth century the Attic school of vase-painting had been traced back to the François vase, and the next generation went little if any further. The Attic black-figure style was still thought to develop out of Ripe Corinthian and the known pieces from the seventh century were treated as sports. Of these there were a fair number, notably from earlyish Protoattic, the Burgon dinos and the small jugs from Phaleron, of which Dumont had illustrated a sample in *RA* 1869, and at the other end the Nessos painter's late bowl in Berlin. But they were not considered as a series, so that even Furtwängler in *AM* 1881 maintained that the 'Dipylon' style (which was not yet linked to Attic black-figure) could not be an Attic school of Geometric. Only C. H. Smith in JHS 1884 showed some glimmering of the truth. Then in *JdI* 1887 Boehlau published a remarkable paper that was not superseded for fifty years. Boehlau took some thirty pots and fragments, arranged them in early and late groups, explained their position in the Attic sequence, and called his new style 'Early Attic' – a name soon translated into 'Protoattic'. His dating – around 600 BC – was sound according to the low chronology still current when he wrote, and his recognition of an originally Ionian impulse was only to be expected. In 1898 in *aus ionischen und italischen Nekropolen* Boehlau returned to Protoattic, listing late pieces in which he saw the effects of Protocorinthian: but his sequence was faulty, since he took the extent of incision as his index, and his dating, tied now to an unduly high dating of Protocorinthian was not generally accepted. Other students detected a 'Melian' influence. But the Ionian theory also persisted; it was openly affirmed by G. M. A. Richter in *JHS* 1912, where Protoattic was more subtly deployed in three stages, and had Pfuhl's guarded blessing as late as 1923.

Of early Attic black-figure Jahn in 1854 was aware only of what are now called the Tyrrhenian amphorae and the François vase (which had been found in 1844). Following Kramer he regarded them as the Attic transition from Corinthian. There was little or no progress till the 1870s when Brunn and Loeschcke published observations based on style rather than epigraphy. Brunn, whose peculiar belief in archaistic imitations obliged him to examine style more closely than was then usual, put the François vase at the head of Attic black-figure and about the middle of the sixth century. This was in 1871 in his *Probleme in der Geschichte der Vasenmalerei*, and in 1877 in T. Lau's *die griechischen Vasen* (intended like d'Hancarville's album a century earlier to provide models to working potters) he noted that the François vase was both more advanced and more old-fashioned than the Tyrrhenian group. Loeschcke in *AZ* 1876 emphasized the dependence of Attic on Corinthian for its early types, but in *Annali* 1878 recognized that the one-piece amphora with decoration in a reserved panel was invented at Athens and that here Corinth was the imitator. The new Panionist theory of course persuaded many students that it was not Corinthian, but Ionian and especially 'Chalcidian' influence that they saw in early Attic black-figure. Others were more resolute and in 1890 even invented the term 'Attic-Corinthian' to describe the Tyrrhenian group and the new Animal style of the first quarter of the sixth century; this Animal style, made known by V. Stais in *AM* 1890 in his publication of graves at Vurva, soon itself acquired the name 'Vurva'. In the late 1890s two important studies show how stylistic perception was improving. P. Wolters in *JdI* 1898 divided early Attic into a coarse series that proceeded from the Vurva group through Sophilos to the Tyrrhenian amphorae and a fine series leading from Clitias to Exekias and the Amasis painter: Clitias, he insisted, was a younger contemporary of Sophilos and his François vase was therefore not so old as was commonly believed. H. Thiersch's *'Tyrrhenische' Amphoren*, published in 1899, was the first thorough analysis of any group of Greek pots and much of it is still valid. Thiersch, who fixed the name 'Tyrrhenian' in its present meaning, refined Wolters' scheme by inserting the Polos group as the immediate precursor of Tyrrhenian and Nikosthenes' workshop as its successor. It is perhaps a tribute to Thiersch's lucid presentation of the material that his successors rejected his extravagant claims of Ionian influences. Of other Attic pottery of this period the Burgon Panathenaic amphora was from the 1880s regularly dated about 560 BC (as it still is), but its stylistic connections were not obvious. The Siana cups were first noted by C. H. Smith in *JHS* 1884: he hinted that they were Attic and this opinion became dominant after 1900; but others made them Rhodian or 'Chalcidian' or Corinthian, and Pfuhl in 1923 could describe them as 'Attic-Chalcidian' and perhaps of Cycladic manufacture. That the Comast cups were Attic had been suggested by P. Orsi in *MA* 1909; but till A. Grefenhagen's demonstration twenty years after they were usually reckoned Corinthian or Boeotian. In their dating some of these students tended to go too high, putting the Vurva style in the last quarter of the seventh century and stretching Tyrrhenian over the first half of the sixth. The present chronology was first clearly stated by Payne in 1931 in his *Necrocorinthia*.

Mature and later Attic black-figure had always interested students because of the subjects and the occasional signatures, but the detailed consideration of its style hardly began before the last quarter of the nineteenth century. An important landmark was Loeschcke's assertion in *AZ* 1881 that Exekias was the painter of the Memnon amphora in the British Museum, although one of its inscriptions gave the name 'Amasis'. The three great, because known, masters were Exekias, Amasis and Nikosthenes, and in the late 1880s their dating was fixed more or less as it is now. Here too Panionism intruded, the more strongly as it was expelled from earlier Attic: plainly the Persian conquest of the 540s must have driven many Ionians overseas. Since the red-figure style was admitted to be essentially Attic, Exekias as its predecessor could be ranked a true Athenian. But Amasis was betrayed by his name as well as the details and decorative character of his style: Studniczka in *EA* 1886, revived C. O. Müller's innocent suggestion of 1831 that Amasis came from Egypt, Loeschcke in 1894 in his article for Pauly-Wissowa preferred Samos, and the conservative Pfuhl in 1923 still thought he might be an Ionian immigrant. The Affecter smacked even more of Ionia, if indeed he did not live there. Nikosthenes was notable for his special shape of amphora and the white-ground technique that he was supposed to have introduced into Athens. His origin and quality were disputed. Loeschcke in *AZ* 1881 before his conversion to Panionism believed that the Nikosthenic amphora was adapted from Etruscan, but afterwards Ionian metalwork seemed more plausible; Pottier in his *Catalogue* of 1893 made Nikosthenes the chief apostle of the Ionian influx; Thiersch in 1899 degraded him to the unprogressive side of Attic black-figure. The Little Master cups, which were at first dated too late, and the Attic eye cups also showed East Greek or 'Chalcidian' tutelage, and after Droop's paper in *JHS* 1910 the cups since called after him were often said to imitate Laconian. Pfuhl's synopsis in 1923 collected the general opinions held in the twenty years before the First World War, but he did not comprehend the fine distinctions and attributions which were a more important achievement of that time.

Boeotian became known in the late 1880s. Besides true Geometric, four later classes were especially distinguished. The big Subgeometric and Orientalizing amphorae received some attention in the 1890s, and were at first confused with the Linear Island group; but after 1903, when Dragendorff in *Thera* II separated the two schools, it became usual to see here a Cycladic influence on Boeotian. Boeotian Bird cups had been shown to Furtwängler in 1878, and in *JdI* 1888 they were studied by Boehlau with exemplary thoroughness: to him and his successors they were transitional between Geometric and Orientalizing, that is of the late eighth and early seventh centuries. The next advance was made in 1909 in *BSA* XIV by R. M. Burrows and P. N. Ure, two representatives of the new, more scholarly generation of British students: from their excavation at Rhitsona they concluded that the Bird cups, now divided into an earlier and a later group, were mostly of the sixth century. This dating, unexpectedly low, was accepted with reluctance. Examples of Boeotian black-figure of the sixth century were published occasionally: their general dependence on Attic was obvious. For the Cabiran style H. Winnefeld's paper in *AM* 1888 was an able introduction: he dated its human scenes to the early and middle fourth century, and so tempted others to find a connection with the Hadra hydriai.

Cycladic other than 'Melian' is still a puzzle. Conze in 1870 in *zur Geschichte der Anfänge der griechischen Kunst* listed in his Geometric a few examples of Theran Late Geometric and added the late stage of the Linear Island group for the transition to Orientalizing. In 1903, Dragendorff published much new material in *Thera* II: he divided Theran into a Geometric phase of the ninth and eighth centuries and an Orientalizing of the seventh and very early sixth, suggested the Heraldic group might be the style of Melos before about 650 BC, and distinguishing Linear Island from Boeotian assigned it to Euboea and the seventh century. Pfuhl added many pots and few comments in *AM* 1903. F. Poulsen and

C. Dugas in *BCH* 1911 gave a foretaste of the more varied finds from Rheneia, but their classification was not satisfactory.

A few Cretan Orientalizing pots were illustrated by Orsi in *AJA* 1897 and some more by Pfuhl in *AM* 1903. Pfuhl in his thoughtful commentary noted influences from Cypriot and parallels in Protocorinthian. Hopkinson, publishing the Praisos plate in *JHS* 1902, denied that there was any Orientalizing style in Crete, and Poulsen in *AM* 1906 considered that Cretan art of the seventh and sixth centuries was sterile. But as Panionism declined some students, notably E. Löwy in *ÖJh* 1909 and 1911, attempted to substitute Crete as the creator and first teacher of the new Greek art that replaced Geometric. So E. Buschor in 1912 in his perceptive handbook, *Griechische Vasenmalerei*, gave Crete and Rhodes the original schools of Orientalizing and asserted Cretan influence on Protocorinthian. Though as finds increased it became still clearer that Cretan vase-painting was generally dull and the few good pieces were eccentric, its primacy was accepted by Johansen and Payne and was not challenged before the Second World War.

Etruscan pottery was continually produced in the spoliation of Etruria; and although for the maintenance of prices the Princess of Canino ordered her workmen to smash all the plainer ware they found, most collections were soon well stocked. But its study was left to a few conscientious excavators and curators and to some devoted Panionists. Bucchero, as it came to be called in the 1870s was generally admitted to evolve from the native impasto though influenced by Greek shapes and ornaments, and in the later part of the century the stamped red ware was often cited for its subjects. A few students maintained that Etruscan bucchero was inspired from Aeolis and red ware from Rhodes, or that they were produced in Greek colonies in the West; and till the 1950s it was still sometimes claimed that the finer bucchero kantharoi were made in Sicily, where several had been found. The most important publications were S. Gsell's *Fouilles dans la Nécropole de Vulci* of 1891, which is still valuable, and Pottier's half-informed discussion in his *Catalogue* of 1899. Etruscocorinthian (then known as Italocorinthian) though mentioned earlier, was not clearly distinguished from Corinthian before Furtwängler's *Beschreibung der Vasensammlung* in 1885. Karo in 1896 in his *de Arte Vascularia* transferred much to Greek workshops in Sicily, and two years later Boehlau in *aus ionischen und italischen Nekropolen* almost made the black polychrome and Animal groups Aeolian. These vagaries were rejected, and so too though less immediately was the corollary that the Animal style of Etruscocorinthian owed more to Ionia than Corinth. The best collection of material was by J. Sieveking and R. Hackl in 1912 in *die königliche Vasen-Sammlung zu München*: this helped greatly to define the school, but detailed study came much later. Of Etruscan black-figure the best and most colourful pieces were in the 1870s still included in the Tyrrhenian group of Attic;

the rest, as Jahn had seen, were unequivocally Etruscan. Dümmler's Panionism gave them a new aspect. In *RM* 1887 he collected two dozen of the earlier pieces and by detailed but shaky argument satisfied himself that they were made around 600 BC by Ionians, probably working in the Pontic colonies. In *RM* 1888 he applied the same methods to the later black-figure, detected the influence of the Caeretan hydriai, and unable to ignore the provincial sterility of his 'Italo-Ionic' school assigned it (or most of it) to Greeks in South Italy. Dümmler's notions were readily believed, but with some modifications. For the first group Pontic manufacture was too absurd to be misleading and so the name was adopted. But gradually the Ionian originators of Pontic were shifted to Etruria, barbarization of the style was admitted and the date brought down to the first half of the sixth century. In the later group of 'Italo-Ionic' the Etruscan character was undeniable and Dümmler's successors made less of its Ionic origins and even recognized that in the end its models were Attic. Endt's *Beiteräge zur ionischen Vasenmalerei* of 1899 had added many new pieces, but Sieveking and Hackl in their Munich catalogue of 1912 not only illustrated a large collection but classified it with intelligence. The next clear advance was not made till the later 1930s.

It is easy to guess the course of opinions about the Caeretan hydriai. The first illustration was published in 1842, but interest was confined to subjects, and it was not till 1863 that Helbig in *Annali* put together three Caeretan and two Corinthian pots and pronounced them Etruscan archaistic versions of Corinthian. Jahn in 1870 in *die Entführung der Europa* (from the Vienna *Denkschriften*) listed six hydriai and recognized the group's independence. Furtwängler in *AZ* 1882 still thought them Etruscan, but saw a kinship with 'Chalcidian'; and till the 1950s the Ionian character of the hydriai was accepted without question, though its home was less obvious. After the discoveries at Naucratis the Busiris hydria suggested to some students that the Caeretan group was made in Egypt, but the usual choice was and still is between northern Ionia and Etruria as the situation of this ultimately East Greek workshop. That the group was short-lived has never been disputed. In the 1880s progressive students dated it around the middle of the sixth century, in the 1920s to the third quarter, and in the 1930s to the last third. The Campana dinoi, first studied by Pottier in *BCH* 1893, and the Northampton group, which Studniczka collected in *JdI* 1890, were loosely annexed to Clazomenian by Zahn in *AM* 1898: but though dated too early and often cited, the claim that they were important soon proved incredible.

Red-figure pottery was very frequent in the early finds and invited study by its curious range of subjects as well as its accomplished draughtsmanship. It is not surprising that in the hundred years that followed the opening of Vulci more than twice as much was written on this style as on all others. The main development was plain, since there were no big gaps in the sequence, and Jahn's account (which was adapted from Kramer's) is still broadly instructive. But detailed investigation of schools and painters began only in the last quarter of the nineteenth century: till then, as might be inferred from the illustrations of the time, students put subjects and inscriptions before style. For Attic red-figure the signatures seemed an easy key. It was reasonable to claim that all works signed with the same painter's name were painted by the same hand; and it was further claimed, without much reason, that if a pot was signed only by a maker, then making included painting. So stylistic interest was usually confined to lists of signatures and the forms of letters, though occasionally some students looked further. For instance in 1837 Kramer had thought that it would be instructive to compare the signed works of Epictetus and de Witte that his unsigned works could be recognized; but as late as 1873 R. Kekule in *AZ* was reserved in claiming that Euthymides had a character of his own. Brunn's archaistic heresy, though generally denied, provided another distraction.

A new stage began with W. Klein, whose *Euphronios* and *die griechischen Vasen mit Meistersignaturen* were first published in 1879 and 1883 in the *Denkschriften* of the Vienna Academy and afterwards were revised and issued separately. Klein's service was rather in collating and refining current opinions than in correcting them. He argued that the founder of the red-figure style was Epictetus, since black-figure and red-figure were often used together on his cups; he insisted that normally the maker was the painter too, even boasting that without this aid Euphronios's development could not have been comprehended; and he felt safer dating by the lettering of inscriptions than by the drawing of figures. But he had some grasp of the relations between his Archaic vase-painters, gave a good account of their new shapes and noted that the incising of the outline of the hair was a mark of early date. In attributing unsigned pieces to their painters Klein was no more successful than others of his contemporaries, though C. H. Smith in 1883 in *JHS* IV pointed to the Charmides painter. Even Furtwängler, whose *Beschreibung der Vasensammlung* of 1885 intimated a clearer understanding of the red-figure style, was right in only a third of some fifty attributions. Much more ambitious was P. Hartwig's *die griechischen Meisterschalen*, published in 1893, which tried to identify the major and some minor painters of Archaic cups. Hartwig's analysis was detailed and subtle, and many of his conclusions were just, especially when he trusted to style: unhappily he also thought makers painters and assumed too readily that each καλός name was peculiar to one painter. His many illustrations, or the best of them, were notably accurate. Furtwängler's review next year in *BPW* made some corrections: the pioneer of red-figure was not Epictetus but the Andocides painter (as Jahn had hinted and de Witte proposed), 'made' did not mean 'painted' nor even 'shaped', and Euthymides must be ranked a great master. Classical and later red-figure were now being neglected. The first important study was F. Winter's *die jüngeren attischen Vasen* of 1885, which Milchhöfer with less perception supplemented and tried to correct in *JdI* 1894.

It was now Furtwängler's turn and in 1900 in partnership with K. Reichhold he began the serial *Griechische Vasenmalerei*, which flourished before the First World War and lingered on till 1932. The object was to publish the most important vase-paintings, especially of the red-figure style, in accurate, full-size drawings and an authoritative text. The exemplary drawings were Reichhold's, as were the technical observations. Furtwängler's commentary illumined the whole range of Attic red-figure; among much else he detached the Panaitios painter from Euphronios, added substance to the Niobid and Eretria painters, and fixed the period of the progressive school of the fourth century. Lesser students too were busy.

Furtwängler died in 1907. The next year J. D. Beazley, the other great exponent of Classical Archaeology, published the first of his many papers. Beazley rejected the hardy prejudice that the isolation of red-figure vase-painters must start from their signatures, and he very soon showed an unrivalled eye and memory. So in *JHS* 1910 he trebled the dozen known works of the Cleophrades painter, and in *JHS* 1911 revealed an unsuspected master, the Berlin painter, to whom he at once assigned nearly forty pieces. In 1918 *Attic Red-figured Vases in American Museums* besides more such lists gave what is still a subtly illuminating survey of red-figure, and in 1925 *Attische Vasenmaler des rotfigurigen Stils* was a general catalogue of the painters and their works. This comprehensive progress shocked some older students, who felt it improper to attribute unpublished pieces so freely; even in 1923 Pfuhl's *Malerei und Zeichnung*, though useful for its detailed analyses and references, betrays a puzzled reluctance in accepting the new orthodoxy. But others, notably Buschor in his *Griechische Vasenmalerei* of 1912 and his later continuation of Furtwängler and Reichhold's great album, were converted to Beazley's method, and to the next generation it seemed fundamental. In his *Attic Red-figure Vase-painters* Beazley scrupulously noted the good attributions of other students, but only made it plainer how many more are his own. It is pleasant to reflect that his unique achievement was honoured by a knighthood and the Order of Merit.

Attic white-ground lekythoi with black-figured and with outline decoration were familiar from Sicily and South Italy, and acquired the name of Locrian vases. But the later, more polychrome lekythoi are very rarely found outside Greece and so were neglected till 1870 when O. Benndorf published fair drawings of thirty examples in the second part of his *Griechische und Sicilische Vasenbilder*. In the next generation much was written about the lekythoi, but only R. C. Bosanquet in *JHS* 1896 and 1899 showed stylistic insight. A. Fairbanks in his *Athenian White Lekythoi* of 1907 and 1914 compiled a credulous and too methodical catalogue; W. Riezler's *Weissgrundige attische Lekythen*, sensible and well illustrated, though timid in its attributions, also appeared in 1914, as did J. D. Beazley's account in *JHS* of the Achilles painter. When Pfuhl wrote his summary in 1923 the personalities of the white-ground painters were still obscure: afterwards they were explored by Buschor and Beazley.

The Panionist theory did no harm to the study of Attic red-figure which was beyond doubt Attic and Attic alone. Zahn in *AM* 1898 had logically but unconvincingly derived the red-figure technique from Clazomenian sarcophagi. Some stalwarts, Pfuhl included, thought the Andocides painter an Ionian immigrant, though more followed Loeschcke's assertion made in 1879 that he was a dependant or pupil of Exekias. Duris had a Samian namesake and must be a Samian too, for Dümmler and even Furtwängler and Langlotz. B. Schröder in *JdI* 1914 suspected Ionian influences in the early Classical period. But no one concocted a red-figure school that worked in Ionia. Boeotia had more luck, being often credited with poor Attic works of the fourth century: the distinction is perhaps not yet entirely sure.

In the later 1850s there were three systems of dates for Attic red-figure besides the fantasies of 'archaism'. Ross, who had found red-figured sherds on the Acropolis of Athens in the debris of the Persian sack of 480 BC fixed its span from the early sixth century to the early fourth, but Birch was his only notable adherent. Jahn admitted Ross's evidence so far as to start red-figure a little before 480 BC, and he let it continue in Athens till the late fourth century. But some students, incredulous of Ross's observation, still put the invention of the new technique about 470 or 460 BC. These lower chronologies were based principally on the forms of letters painted on red-figure pots: it was not guessed that private inscriptions might be a generation or more ahead of the official script. Although U. Koehler corrected this error incidentally in *AM* 1885, it was the new excavation of the Acropolis, cited by Studniczka in *JdI* 1887, that stirred students. Not only had red-figure begun before 480 BC, but its severe (or Archaic) stage was by then almost over. In a few years 530 BC was agreed to be the date when the style began, and Furtwängler's chronology of the Archaic phase stood the test of E. Langlotz's thesis of 1920, *zur Zeitbestimmung der strengrotfigurigen Vasenmalerei*. Once the beginning of red-figure had been pushed back, there followed inevitably the attempt, led by Milchhöfer in *JdI* 1894, to push back its end and cram all Classical and later Attic into the fifth century. But Furtwängler's authority established the general dating that remains current. A few painters were still misplaced and some of the white-ground lekythoi dated too late, but gradually assurance has become more precise. For all these various chronologies connections in sculpture, painting and history were found and accepted: the educated eye and mind are very accommodating.

South Italian red-figure has never been scarce, and since the 1760s the experts have generally been right about its origin. This was at first because they presumed that pots were made where they were found, and most red-figure pots were found in South Italy. Later, when (thanks to Kramer) Attic red-figure was recognized, the residue (in spite of Kramer) remained South Italian, except for a few obvious Etruscan products. Gradually the many supposedly local fabrics were condensed into three schools, though still very impure and hazy round the edges, and by Jahn's time the terms Apulian, Lucanian and Campanian meant more than the place of finding. Because of the subjects much South Italian was published, notably in Gerhard's *Apulische Vasenbilder* of 1845, but its style (as de Luynes had once observed) was not attractive. The Paestan painter Asteas had signed several of his works and so was particularly noticed: in 1890 in *Bonner Studien* H. Winnefeld carefully analysed his style, six years later in the *Catalogue of Vases* in the British Museum H. B. Walters made a special class for the style of Asteas of Paestum, and in 1897 G. Patroni extended his school and named it simply Paestan. Meanwhile in 1893 Furtwängler in his *Meisterwerke* had detected the early stage of South Italian, noting its relation to Attic, with which till then it had been confused, and arguing for manufacture in the Greek coastal cities of Thurii, Heraclea and Tarentum. This was too much for Patroni, who saw in these schools of vase-painting an Italian genius which could have flowered only in the native towns of the interior. But his *la Ceramica antica nell'Italia meridionale* (which appeared in 1897 in *Atti dell' Accademia di Archeologia, Lettre e Belle Arti di Napoli*) was the first broad study of these red-figure schools, and important. Furtwängler, Hauser, Buschor and Zahn made good additions and corrections in the text to FR; B. Macchioro in *RM* 1912 and elsewhere perhaps included no useful observations among his fantasies; and in 1923 in *The Hope Vases* E. W. M. Tillyard offered a sane and intelligent summary. Tillyard also discovered the early stage of Paestan and abolished the so-called Saticulan fabric, seeing that it was not Campanian but Attic. More recently the detailed search for painters has gone far, through the lifelong devotion of A. D. Trendall. Dating was difficult. After the 1830s it was regarded as the successor of Attic, taking over more or less where the other left off. For its end the evidence seemed conflicting. Many students held the old opinion that figured vase-painting was suppressed in 186 BC through the Senatus Consultum de Bacchanalibus. Others had it continue till the next century, deluded by the report of red-figure at Canosa in a grave of 67 BC. There were also those who thought the third century late enough, finding a cause – if one were wanted – in the Second Punic War. A fairly sound chronology began at last to emerge from the observations of Furtwängler, Patroni and Furtwängler's successors.

Etruscan red-figure has had still fewer investigators than South Italian. That it existed was allowed even by those who first claimed painted pottery for the Greeks, and Jahn in 1854 had a rough grasp of its character and development. But the earliest close study, of the late school of Clusium and Volterra, was C. Albizzati's in *RM* 1915. Since then progress has been considerable.

Of Hellenistic pottery knowledge is still vague. Though its Italian schools were soon observed, the first special studies came mostly in the early twentieth century. Gnathian, which by its showy elegance appealed to some collectors, was evidently related to Apulian red-figure and often considered its successor: the name, given by Neapolitan dealers, was accepted reluctantly by archaeologists around 1880. The Pocolom group with its early Latin inscriptions exercised epigraphists; stylistically it was attached to Gnathian, and its place of origin was often put in Campania. The polychrome ware of Canosa, becoming known towards the end of the century, was studied with moderate competence by M. Jatta in *RM* 1914. The still more polychrome products of Centuripae had turned up as early as 1830, but obtained only passing mentions. It was of course seen that both these groups were late. A Calene phiale had been one of the first two Greek pots published; here too students were preoccupied with Latin inscriptions, but Benndorf in 1883 in *Griechische und Sicilische Vasenbilder* illustrated several pieces and R. Pagenstecher in *die Calenische Relief-keramik* of 1909 was thorough, though not always right.

West Slope ware was cited casually as Gnathian till and even after 1901, when C. Watzinger defined and analysed it excellently in *AM*; since then it has been found regularly in excavations and museums. The Hadra hydriai, noted already in the 1850s, offered inscribed dates to be determined; their style was first considered, with too much reference to Cabiran, by R. Pagenstecher in *AJA* 1909 and four years later in *Expedition E. von Sieglin* and also by E. Breccia in *la Necropoli di Sciatbi* in 1912. Zahn in 1904 in *Priene* made a few sound observations on the light-ground lagynoi, and G. Leroux in 1913 in *Lagynos* assembled the group and examined it with care and judgement. The 'Megarian' bowls, as they came to be called in the 1880s, were soon attributed in part to Athens, though many supposed that at least the technique of moulding came from Alexandria; their dating, within the Hellenistic period, was and is not altogether certain.

The Black-painted wares had always been exhibited in collections, but they remained too plain and difficult for students. The credit for the first thorough inquiry should go to P. N. Ure for his *Black Glaze Pottery from Rhitsona* of 1913, a work noteworthy as much for its devotion as its precision.

Since the First World War progress has been remarkable. New excavations, when published or made available, have contributed something. But the main reason is that students, taught by the example of Beazley and Johansen, have seen that the examination of style can be pushed much further than it was before and they expect that in any figured school of painted pottery they will probably find some painter. Much more can be done by this method, as is evident in current work on Hellenistic. For most of the Protogeometric and Geometric schools other than Attic and Euboean – at least till their latest phases – for the earlier Orientalizing wares of the Cyclades, and for much East Greek Orientalizing and black-figure, new evidence is the first need. But whether all these subjects are worth probing is a question that may well be asked.

The history of the study of vase-painting, like the history of all studies, offers entertainment to the curious or cynical mind and is sometimes useful for understanding older books and papers. But it is also instructive. Although there are rare students of genius, most are clever only in detail, normally uncritical of their methods or presumptions and blind to the further consequences of their arguments. So such fashionable theories as the Etruscan origin of painted vases, the representation of the ancient Mysteries and the artistic dominance of Ionia have in their time been accepted as fundamental truths. We may laugh at these past follies, but they are also a warning to look for equal follies of our own.

ABBREVIATIONS

—— •◦• ——

A (in description of a pot) = the front.

AA *Archäologischer Anzeiger* (supplement since 1889 to *JdI*, previously to *AZ*).

ABSA = *BSA*.

ABV J. D. Beazley, *Attic Black-figure Vase-painters*.

AC *Archeologia Classica*.

Acta A *Acta Archaeologica*.

AD *Antike Denkmäler*.

A Delt Ἀρχαιολογικὸν Δελτίον.

AdI = *Ann*. (1).

AE = *EA*.

AJA *American Journal of Archaeology*.

AK = *Antike Kunst*.

AM *Mitteilungen des Deutschen Archäologischen Instituts, Athenische Abteilung* (shortly *Athenische Mitteilungen*).

Ann (1) *Annali dell'Instituto di Corrispondenza Archeologica*. (2) = *ASA*.

Anz = *AA*.

ARV¹ J. D. Beazley, *Attic Red-figure Vase painters*.

ARV² J. D. Beazley, *Attic Red-figure Vase-painters* (2nd edn).

ASA *Annuario della Scuola Archeologica di Atene*.

Ath Mitt = *AM*.

AZ *Archäologische Zeitung*.

B (in description of a pot) = the back.

BCH *Bulletin de la Correspondance Hellénique*.

BdI *Bullettino dell'Instituto di Corrispondenza Archeologica*.

Bf black-figure.

Bg black-glazed (or black-painted).

BICS *Bulletin of the Institute of Classical Studies*.

BM British Museum.

BPW *Berliner Philologische Wochenschrift*.

BSA *Annual of the British School at Athens*.

BSR *Papers of the British School at Rome*.

Bull (1) = *BdI*. (2) = *RM*.

BWP *Programm zum Winckelmannsfeste der Archäologischen Gesellschaft zu Berlin* (shortly *Berliner Winckelmannsprogramm*).

Cl Rh *Clara Rhodos*.

CRAI *Comptes Rendus de l'Académie des Inscriptions et Belles-Lettres.*

CVA *Corpus Vascrum Antiquorum.*

Delt = A Delt.

EA = Ἐφημερὶς Ἀρχαιολογική, since 1910 Ἀρχαιολογικὴ Ἐφημερίς.

Eph = EA.

EVP J. D. Beazley, *Etruscan Vase-Painting.*

FR A. Furtwängler and K. Reichhold (and others) *Griechische Vasen-malerei.*

GGP J. N. Coldstream, *Greek Geometric Pottery.*

Hesp *Hesperia.*

I (in description of a cup) = the inside.

Jahreshefte = ÖJh.

Jb = JdI.

JdI *Jahrbuch des Deutschen Archäologischen Instituts.*

Jh = ÖJh.

JHS *Journal of Hellenic Studies.*

MA *Monumenti Antichi per cura della R. Accademia dei Lincei.*

MdI (1) *Mitteilungen des Deutschen Archäologischen Instituts.* (2) = *Mon Ined.*

MEFR = MEFRA.

MEFRA *Mélanges d'Archéologie et d'Histoire publiés per l'école française de Rome,* since 1971 in two parts, the relevant one subtitle *Antiquité.*

Mél = MEFR(A).

ML = MA.

MMS *Metropolitan Museum Studies.*

Mon Ant = MA.

Mon Ined *Monumenti Inediti pubblicati dall'Instituto di Corrispondenza Archeologica.*

Mon Inst = Mon Ined.

Mon Piot *Fondation Eugéne Piot, Monuments et Mémoires.*

MuZ E. Pfuhl, *Malerei und Zeichnung.*

NC H. G. G. Payne, *Necrocorinthia.*

NM National Museum.

NSc *Notizie deglie Scavi.*

OJA *Oxford Journal of Archaeology.*

ÖJh *Jahreshefte des Oesterreichischen Archäologischen Instituts.*

PAE Πρακτικὰ τῆς ἐν Ἀθήναις ἀρχαιολογικῆς ἑταιρείας.

PBSR = BSR.

PGP V. R. d'A. Desborough *Protogeometric Pottery.*

Praktika = PAE.

RA *Revue Archéologique.*

Rf red-figure.

RM *Mitteilungen des Deutschen Archäologischen Instituts, Römische Ab-teilung* (shortly *Römische Mitteilungen*).

SA   Sovetskaya Archeologiya.
SE   Studi Etruschi.
Vroulia   K. F. Kinch, *Fouilles de Vroulia.*
VS   K. F. Johansen, *les Vases sicyoniens.*
Wg   white-ground.

NOTE ON MUSEUMS

———— •◆• ————

Most museums outside Greek lands, that is museums which have no local sites to fill them with Greek pottery, are much the same in their composition. That is because they have been formed in much the same way. Since the first and by far the largest supplies came from Italy, there is a core of Corinthian, later Attic black-figure, Attic red-figure till the end of the fifth century, South Italian red-figure and Etruscan (especially bucchero). Part of this went originally to private collectors, but private collections generally end in public museums, large or small. A much scantier and less evenly spread contribution from Rhodes provides Rhodian Mycenaean and Geometric, Wild Goat style and Fikellura, as well as more Corinthian and Attic black-figure. Attic Geometric, which can still be obtained, is dispersed widely. There is also more than enough Cypriot pottery of the Early Iron Age. Besides these constituents, which since they come from graves consist mainly of whole pots, East Greek and Attic sherds from Naucratis, mostly of the sixth century, were widely distributed. Examples of other wares are comparatively rare; their possession depends on the luck or management of each museum. Of the largest collections the most varied are those in the British Museum and the Louvre, which were active in acquiring pottery at the time when opportunities were good, though if money can do it Malibu may rival them.

In the regions where Greek pottery is unearthed the museums are no more complete in their range, since they contain local finds and little else. It is easy to guess the character of Italian museums, though not their quality. In Greece the standard of finds has been poorer, but since the free export of ancient pottery was prohibited before much had been discovered there are several schools and groups that are rarely or never to be seen elsewhere.

Generally the museums of Greece and Italy will continue to grow as long as excavation flourishes. Some of them are already badly overcrowded, but national and professional pride are not likely to allow the reasonable solution of selling off the surplus. In most other countries the supply of pots is short. There is some reshuffling of ownership, when the dwindling private collections come onto the market, but in recent years only the Russians have honoured the ancient custom of taking works of art as reparations of war, though they too soon weakened so far as to send back the Pergamum frieze. Selections of second-rate sherds are sometimes given to

317

honest excavators and may fill some gaps in foreign collections. But fine or rare pieces are likely to be got only through the antique trade, and their nature depends on where at the time clandestine digging is being successful. The casuists might well consider the proper conduct of the director of a museum.

Most museums of any importance have published some sort of catalogue. In the nineteenth century these catalogues were usually fairly complete in their listing, but neither detailed nor illustrated; and even when their numbering is still retained they have little value except for the history of scholarship or of the collection. Later catalogues are often illustrated and sometimes learned, but more rarely comprehensive. In general the bigger and established museums are dilatory; Copenhagen is a notable exception. But some of the museums of middling size, especially when connected with a university, have produced good catalogues, of which Würzburg's are exemplary.

The list that follows is only a rough guide to the major collections. The principle of choosing varies from one country to another, or the Italian entry would be still longer. The citing of catalogues too is unjust, particularly for those museums which are stocked from excavations; for some excavators publish their pottery satisfactorily and it would be extravagant to do the job again.

I. GREECE, TURKEY AND ITALY

Museum	Principal source	Illustrated catalogue
Greece		
Athens, NM	Greek mainland (and some Aegean islands)	*CVA*. M. Collignon and L. Couve. *Catalogue des vases peints* (1902–4). B. Graef, *Die antiken Vasen von der Akropolis zu Athen* (1909–33)
Athens, Agora Mus.	Athens, Agora	*Hesp* (casually) and *The Athenian Agora* 8, 12, 21, 22, 23 (1962–)
Athens, Ceramicus Mus.	Athens, Ceramicus	*Kerameikos* 1, 4, 5, 6, 12 (1939–)
Corinth	Corinth	*Corinth* 7, 1–4, 13, 15.3 (1943–)
Aegina	Aegina	*Alt-Ägina* 2.1 (1982)
Heraklion	Crete	
Mykonos	Rhencia (Purification deposit)	*Délos* 15, 17, 21 (1934–). Ph. Zapheiropoulou, Προβλήματα τῆς Μηλιακῆς Ἀγγειογραφίας (1985)
Thera	Thera	H. Dragendorff, *Thera* 2 (1903). E. Pfuhl, *AM* 1903, 1–290
Rhodes	Rhodes, Nisyros	*Cl Rh* 3, 4, 6/7, 8 (1929–36)
Turkey		
Istanbul	Asia Minor and Rhodes	
Smyrna	Western Asia Minor (recent finds)	
Italy		
Rome, Vatican	Etruria and S. Italy	*Vasi antichi dipinti del Vaticano* (1925– : C. Albizzati; A. D. Trendall). J. D. Beazley, *La Raccolta Benedetto Guglielmi* 1 (1939)
Rome, Villa Giulia	S. Etruria	*CVA*. P. Mingazzini, *Vasi della Collezione* Castellani (1930)
Florence, Mus. Arch. Etr.	N. Etruria: Rhodes	*CVA*
Bologna, Mus. Civ.	Emilia	*CVA*. G. Pellegrini, *Catalogo dei Vasi greci dipinti delle necropoli Felsinee* (1912)
Ferrara, Mus. di Spina	Spina	N. Alfieri, P. E. Arias and M. Hirmer, *Spina* (1958)
Naples, NM	S. Italy	*CVA*
Taranto, NM	S. Apulia	*CVA*
Lecce, Mus. Prov. Castromediano	S.E. Apulia	*CVA*
Palermo, NM	Sicily	*CVA*
Syracuse, NM	E. Sicily	*CVA*

II. OTHER LANDS

Museum	Unusual sources	Illustrated catalogue
Australia Sydney, Nicholson Mus.		
Austria Vienna, Kunsthistorisches Mus. (incorporating former Oesterreichisches Mus.)		*CVA*. K. Masner, *Die Sammlung antiker Vasen und Terracotten im k. k. Oesterreichischen Museum* (1892)
Belgium Brussels, Mus. du Cinquantenaire		*CVA*
Canada Toronto, Royal Ontario Mus.		*CVA*. J. W. Hayes, *Greek and Greek-style Painted and Plain Pottery* (1992); *Etruscan and Italic Pottery* (1985); *Greek and Italian Black-Gloss Wares* (1984). D. M. Robinson, C. G. Harcum and J. H. Iliffe, *A Catalogue of the Greek Vases* (1930)
Denmark Copenhagen, NM		*CVA*
France Paris, Louvre	Rhodes; Athens (Geometric)	*CVA*. E. Pottier, *Vases antiques du Louvre* (1897–1922)
Paris, Bibliothéque Nationale		*CVA*. A. De Ridder. *Catalogue des vases peints* (1901–2)
Germany Munich, Mus. Antiker Kleinkunst		*CVA*. J. Sieveking and R. Hackl, *Die k. Vasen-Sammlung* (1912)
Berlin Antikenmuseum	Rhodes; Aegina (Protoattic)	*CVA*. K. A. Neugebauer, *Führer durch das Antiquarium* 2 (1932). U. Gehrig, A. Greifenhagen and N. Kunisch, *Führer durch die Antikenabteilung* (1968)
Würzburg, Martin von Wagner Mus.		E. Langlotz, *Griechische Vasen* (1932). *CVA*
Great Britain London, British Mus.	Rhodes; Naucratis; Tell Defenneh	*CVA*
Oxford, Ashmolean Mus.		*CVA*
Cambridge, Fitzwilliam Mus.		*CVA*

Museum	Unusual sources	Illustrated catalogue
Holland		
Leyden, Rijksmus. van Oudheden	Aegean	*CVA*
Amsterdam, Allard Pierson Mus.		*CVA* and *CVA Hague* (mostly now in Amsterdam)
Poland		
Warsaw, NM		*CVA* (including fascicules on [formerly] Goluchow and Wilanow)
Russia		
St Petersburg, Hermitage	South Ukraine	A. A. Peredolskaya, *Krasnofigurniye Atticheskiye Vaz y v Ermitazhe* (1967): for Attic Rf
Spain		
Madrid, Mus. Arqueológico		*CVA*. G. Leroux, *Vases grecs et italo-grecs* (1912)
United States		
New York, Metropolitan Mus.		*CVA*. G. M. A. Richter and L. F. Hall, *Rf Athenian Vases in the Metr. Mus. of Art* (1936)
Boston, Mus. of Fine Arts		*CVA*. A. Fairbanks, *Catalogue of Greek & Etruscan Vases* (1928). L. D. Caskey and J. D. Beazley, *Attic Vase Paintings in the M.F.A., Boston* (1931–63). J. M. Padgett *et al.*, *Vase-painting in Italy: red-figure and related works in the MFA, Boston* (1993)
Philadelphia, University Mus.	Near East	*CVA* E. H. Dohan, *Italic Tomb-Groups* (1942)
Malibu, J. Paul Getty Mus.		*CVA*

NOTE ON SITES

——— •◆• ———

It would be useful if someone would compile a list of sites, noting in each instance what pottery has been found, where it is published, and which museum or museums now exhibit or conceal it. Lists which include many relevant publications up to 1925 are given in the second edition of the *Katalog der Bibliothek des deutschen archäologischen Instituts in Rom* 1, 83–600; 1 Supplt, 76–414; 2, 579–84); studies on sites are tabulated in the *Bibliographie* appended to *JdI*; and from 1946 to 1970 more information can be extracted from *Fasti Archaeologici*. But most excavations remain unpublished, in whole or in part. The fact is that too many excavators still prefer the thrill and glory of discovery to the drudgery of publishing their finds, and even those who are conscientious too often refuse to make their evidence available till they have at last elaborated a learned commentary on it. There are, of course, distinguished exceptions. But what is wanted is a strict code of excavation with heavy penalties for failure or delay in reporting what has been found. It is less easy to understand why so many reports forget to say where the finds have been deposited. A rough rule is that the greater part remains in the local museum, if there is one, and the finer pieces are taken to one of the more important and better-guarded museums; but as new museums are founded or old ones raised in status, even this rule may be misleading.

A GLOSSARY OF TERMS
NOT ALREADY EXPLAINED

———— •◆• ————

AEGIS. A sort of breast-plate worn by Athena, fringed with snakes and bearing the Gorgoneion on its front. (Plates 21B and 38 show only back and side views.)

ANIMAL STYLE. A style in which animals are the principal subject of the decoration.

APOTROPAIC. A term used of objects that avert evil. Archaeologists are too fond of invoking this sort of magic.

ARCHAIC. The style and period between Geometric and Classical, conventionally 720–480 BC.

ARGIVO-CYCLADIC. *Obsolete.* Used of an incompatible assortment of Cycladic Geometric and Orientalizing.

ATTIC-IONIC. *Obsolete.* A Panionist term for Attic pottery supposed to be influenced by East Greek of 'Chalcidian': it was used first as a replacement for Attic-Corinthian (see p. 301), and later as a complement to it.

BALLOON AMPHORA. *Rare.* A large amphora with very swelling body, especially of the SOS group.

BALSAMARIUM. Another fancy name for Fusiform Unguentarium.

BAROQUE. A term misapplied by some archaeologists to the late, full-blown phase of a style.

BARREL AMPHORA. In South Italian Rf an amphora with concave profile to the body.

BELLY AMPHORA. A one-piece amphora.

BILINGUAL. An unpleasant designation of those Attic pots on which one field is Bf and another Rf.

BLACK DIPYLON. *Obsolete.* Attic Geometric pottery largely covered with dark paint (e.g. Plate 3A).

BOEOTIAN CYLIX GROUP. The Boeotian group of Bird cups.

BOMBYLIOS. *Obsolete.* Alabastron of Corinthian type (Plate 10C). The name is possibly justified.

BUCCHERO ITALICO. *Obsolete.* Impasto.

BUCCHERO PESANTE. Heavy, generally late, Etruscan bucchero, especially with relief decoration.

BUCCHERO SOTTILE. *Obsolete.* Fine, generally early, Etruscan bucchero.

BUTTERFLY ORNAMENT. A variant for Opposed Triangles, when the decorative emphasis is lateral.

CADUCEUS. The herald's twining staff, often carried by Hermes. Examples appear on Plates 34 and 53.

CAMIRAN. *Obsolete.* An alternative name for the Wild Goat style.

CARCHESION. *Rare.* A kind of footless kantharos. The name is possible.

CHITON. A fine sleeved dress (see Plate 43, women).

CHLAMYS. A short cloak, worn especially by riders (see Figure 31).

CHTHONIC. Connected with the underworld and its gods (as opposed to the gods above).

CLASSICAL. The style and period between Archaic and Hellenistic, conventionally 480–323 BC. But in Attic Rf 'Classical' does not extend beyond 400 BC.

COMAST. A participant in a comos or drunken dance.

CONNOISSEURSHIP. A pretentious new name for the study of style.

CORINTHIAN-ATTIC. *Obsolete.* A short-lived variant for Attic-Corinthian.

COTHON. A conventional name for a large saucer with rim turned over inwards: this may have been a bowl for unguent or a lamp. The name belongs properly to some kind of drinking vessel, once certainly a mug.

DAUNIAN. The native school of northern Apulia.

DELIAN. A name sometimes ventured for this or that group of Cycladic.

DIPINTO. A painted inscription, especially one added after the firing of the pot.

DIPYLON. An overworked term used once for all Geometric, then for Attic Geometric, lastly for Attic Geometric with funerary scenes (see p. 288). In a still more restricted sense Dipylon is sometimes applied in the big Attic Geometric kraters with high stems and scenes of human figures. More reasonably it is confined to the Dipylon painter (see pp. 21–2) and his school.

DOUBLE AXE ORNAMENT. A variant for Opposed Triangle, objectionable because it suggests a connection with Minoan.

DÜMMLER'S GROUP. A german variant for Pontic.

EPICHYSIS. A small oinochoe, especially frequent in Apulian Rf, with narrow neck and a body shaped like a reel. The name was used of some sort of jug.

EPINETRON. A kind of thigh-guard, used in spinning.

ETRUSCO-CAMPANIAN. *Obsolete.* A class of Bg ware, mostly Campanian.

EUBOEAN. *Obsolete.* An early name for Linear Island. But there is also true Euboean.

EUBOEO-CYCLADIC. *Obsolete.* Another name for Linear Island.

EXERGUE. The segment of a circular field below the base-line of the main decoration. The term is borrowed from numismatics.

FENESTRATED. Used of pedestals with rectangular holes cut through the wall.

FIGURE STYLE.   Often used of decoration with human figures, in contrast to Animal style.

FINE STYLE.   In Attic Rf an alternative to 'Classical'.

FUSIFORM UNGUENTARIUM.   A coarse little tubular pot, bulging in the middle; on Greek sites Hellenistic, but elsewhere once (and perhaps misleadingly) reported in a context as early as the seventh century.

GLOSS. A term recently floated to describe the shiny black or later red of fine Greek pottery.

GRAFFITO.   An incised or scratched inscription.

GREEK KEY.   An unarchaeological name for the key meander.

GUILLOCHE.   Cable-pattern.

GUTTUS.   Strictly a pot like a flat askos but with a single ring-handle to one side. But sometimes used for Askos.

HANDLE PLATE.   A rectangular projection from the rim (especially of a column krater), meeting and covering the handle.

HEAD-VASE.   A pot in the shape of a human head, with the lip or spout at the top.

HELLADIC.   A term conveniently used to distinguish the Bronze Age from the Iron Age in Greece.

HELLENIC.   The counterpart of Helladic.

HELLENISTIC.   The style and period following Classical, conventionally dated 323–27 BC.

HELMET ARYBALLOS.   A small pot in the form of a helmeted head with a narrow mouth at the top. Most examples are East Greek of the early sixth century.

HERAEUM.   A sanctuary of Hera.

HEROÖN.   A sanctuary of a hero.

HIMATION.   A heavy cloak or mantle (see Plate 38, Heracles; and Figure 34).

HOLKION.   A name misused by some bucchero specialists for the handle-less chalice.

HOMERIC BOWL.   *Obsolete.* A Megarian bowl of the class, perhaps Macedonian, that is decorated with scenes from Homer.

HORROR VACUI.   A psychological explanation, once fashionable, of the thick filling ornament of many Geometric and Orientalizing scenes.

HOURGLASS ORNAMENT.   A variant of Opposed Triangles, when the decorative emphasis is vertical.

HYDRISKE.   *Rare.* An unpleasant name for a miniature hydria.

IAPYGIAN.   Native Apulian.

IMPASTO.   A native Italian ware, characterized by its coarse, poorly fired clay.

IONIAN BOWL.   *Obsolete.* A generic name for East Greek Bird, Eye and Rosette bowls.

KALATHOS. A pot shaped like a basket or inverted bell. The name was certainly used of wicker baskets.

KELEBE. *Obsolete.* A conventional name for a column-krater.

KERCH. The usual name for the progressive school of Attic Rf around the middle of the fourth century: the first important finds were made at Kerch (Panticapaeum).

KEY MEANDER. The ordinary continuous meanders, as on Plate 3B.

KRATERISKOS. (1) A small krater. (2) A rare alternative for Lydion.

KYATHOS. (1) a kind of ladle, frequent in Mature and Late Bf: it resembles a tea-cup with very high handle: the name seems credible and is in fact inscribed on two metal specimens. (2) A confusing and unnecessary name for the small, footless kantharos (especially that of earlier Protocorinthian).

KYLICHNIS. *Rare.* An Attic name that was used of some pyxides.

LACRYMATERIUM. Another modern name for Fusiform Unguentarium.

LEKYTHOS-OINOCHOE. An aberrant name for the conical oinochoe.

LEPASTE. *Obsolete.* A conventional name for what is now called Lekanis.

LYDION. A conventional name for a small pot shaped like a krater with high foot, but without handles. It may have been used to hold ointment. Most lydia are of the sixth century: some are supposed to be Lydian, some are East Greek, some are Etruscan.

MASTOS. A cup in the shape of a woman's breast. The name is likely.

MERRYTHOUGHT HANDLE. A handle shaped like a wishbone.

MESSAPIAN. The native school of southern Apulia.

METOPE DECORATION. A misleading name for the system of decoration of Plate 6A.

MINOAN. The conventional name for the Bronze Age of Crete.

MYCENAEAN. A generic name for the Late Bronze Age in Greek lands. Mycenaean specialists prefer Late Helladic.

NECKING RING. A projecting ridge or moulding on a pot where the neck fits into the shoulder.

ONE-HANDLER. A low cup with one handle common in Attic Bg in the fifth and fourth centuries. One example is inscribed with a variant of the name 'kanastron'.

ONOS. Used, perhaps wrongly, as an alternative to Epinetron.

OPEN CABLE. A simple cable pattern in which the links do not join (as on Plate 14B, behind the horses and before the lions' jaws).

OVERLAP CUP. A name for those Siana cups on which the row of figures extends across lip and handle frieze (as on Plate 24B).

OXYBAPHON. An ancient name for some kind of small dish. Some students, on the ambiguous evidence of a graffito, have identified it with the fish-plate.

PEPLOS. A heavy sleeveless garment (see Plates 22 and 45, female figures).

PETASOS. A hat with a broad brim, especially for travelling (see Figure 31, middle boy).

PEUCETIAN. The native school of central Apulia.

PHALERON. *Obsolete.* A name for small Protoattic pots, especially jugs and mugs, of the Early and Middle periods. So called from finds in graves at Phaleron, published in 1869.

PHOCAEAN. A name sometimes given to Grey ware found in Provence on the unlikely plea that it was imported to Marseilles from Phocaea.

PHORMISKOS. A conventional name for a bulbous object of terracotta, pierced for hanging, that was common in Attic graves of the sixth century.

PINAX. (1) Plaque. (2) *Obsolete.* Plate.

PLASTIC VASE. A pot made in the shape of a human figure, animal or other natural object.

PLEMOCHOE. A low lidded bowl with wide shoulder and high foot.

POLOS. A pill-box hat.

POT-PAINTER. A painter of large pots in contrast to a cup-painter (*ARV*).

PREHELLENIC. A useful and proper definition of the cultures of Greece before the Hellenic (and Iron) Age.

PROCHOUS. A kind of jug. The name is ancient.

PROTHESIS. The lying in state of a corpse.

PROTO-. A prefix denoting the forerunner of a style that had previously been recognized and called by a simple name. So Protogeometric, Protocorinthian and Protoattic. Mercifully other formations of this sort have been stillborn.

PROTOME. The upper part of a human figure or the of the forepart of an animal.

PSYKTER. A rare pot, in Attic usually of mushroom shape. Presumably a cooler, and so reasonably named.

RESERVED. When a figure or detail is deliberately left unpainted within an area of dark paint, that figure or detail is said to be reserved. Examples of reservation are the light stripes of the lower part of the pot of Plate 1C, the inner markings of the animals of Plate 31, and figures in the red-figure technique.

RHYTON. A cup in the shape of a horn (as on Figure 22) or an animal's head. There is ancient authority for the name.

RUNNING DOG. Another name for Open Cable.

SACRED TREE. A vertical combination of volutes. The motive is derived from Oriental art, where it had some religious meaning.

SAKKOS. A kind of snood.

SAMIAN. (1) *Obsolete.* A name for Fikellura, since supposedly made in Samos. (2) A general term for Geometric and Orientalizing found and probably made in Samos. (3) An obsolescent name for Sigillata. (4) A name for a class of Sigillata, perhaps made in Samos.

SECOND WHITE. The whiter paint used for female flesh over the less white slip of many of the earlier white-ground lekythoi.

SEVERE STYLE. (1) In Geometric this term is often used of the early part of the Middle phase and conventionally dated 850–800 BC. (2) In Attic Rf it is equivalent to Archaic.

SITULA. A name given conventionally and loosely to deep pots of rather cylindrical shape.

SIX'S TECHNIQUE. The application of colour over the dark paint to give the effect of the reservation of the true Rf technique; inner details are incised through the colour to the dark paint.

SLIP. In potter's parlance a slip is a roughly equal mixture of clay and water, but archaeologists usually mean by 'slip' a coating of clay different in colour and character from the clay of the pot it covers.

STEP MEANDER. A continuous form of the meander, popular especially in Late Argive Geometric. The name explains itself.

STIRRUP VASE. A pot with more or less globular body, and on the shoulder a narrow false spout in the middle, two thin handles joining the false spout, and a genuine spout forward of it. The shape is typically Mycenaean.

STRONG STYLE. A mistranslation of the German 'streng' = severe.

SUB-. A prefix denoting a degenerate extension or survival of a recognized style.

SYMPLEGMA. An interlocked group, usually erotic.

TERMINUS ANTE QUEM. A date *before* which something occurred or was made. So pottery which the Athenians put in their grave-mound at Marathon must have been made before the mount was constructed in 490 BC.

TERMINUS POST QUEM. A date *after* which something occurred or was made. For example a scarab naming King Bocchoris must have been made after his accession about 718 BC.

THERICLEAN. A class of vases celebrated in antiquity, perhaps including some Corinthian terracotta relief ware of around 400 BC.

THYMIATERION. An incense-burner. The name is given, probably with justice, to some smallish bowls attached to high, elaborate pedestals.

TROZZELLA. A more modish name for Nestoris.

TRIPOD-PYXIS. A pyxis supported by three feet.

UNGUENTARIUM. See 'Fusiform Unguentarium'..

VOTIVE. Used loosely of all offerings at a sanctuary. A votive deposit is usually a heap of such offerings thrown out at some clearance of the sanctuary.

WASH. A term sometimes used by archaeologists for a thin slip.

WAVE PATTERN. A row of spiral hooks used as a border.

BIBLIOGRAPHY

——— ·◆· ———

These lists are not complete. Where a good comprehensive study is available, references to earlier and more particular studies can be found there. I have added the ostensible date of publication, as a guide to what the writer could not have known. For abbreviations see pp. 313–15.

CHAPTER I:
INTRODUCTION

General studies

B. A. Sparkes, *Greek Pottery: An Introduction.* A helpful and unbiased survey of topics other than style. 1991.

E. Simon, M. Hirmer and A. Hirmer, *die griechischen Vasen.* Admirable photos and a useful text. 1976.

Museum Catalogues

Most museums of any importance have published catalogues of their more noteworthy exhibits. These catalogues vary greatly in the quality and number of their illustrations and in the accuracy and fullness of the commentaries.

Corpus Vasorum Antiquorum [CVA]. An international series, which has published nearly 300 fascicules each of about 50 large plates. The quality of text and illustrations is uneven, but generally the more recent fascicules are better. Methods of numbering and citing the plates vary: old-fashioned citation is by the code symbols at the top of each plate, but it is more usual now (and convenient) to use the serial number of the fascicule also at the top of the plate or, if the plates are not so numbered, there is the national serial number at the bottom. For a survey of the contents of the first 233 fascicules see T. H. Carpenter, *Summary Guide to the CVA.* (1984). 1922–.

E. Langlotz, *Griechische Vasen in Würzburg.* An exemplary catalogue of a well-balanced collection. 1932.

Current work

JdI, Archäologische Bibliographie (section 'Gefässe'). Annual list of studies.

Révue des Études Grecques, Bulletin Archéologique-Céramique, Biennial list, selective but critical.

Archive

The Beazley Archive, Ashmolean Museum, Oxford (OX1 2PH) maintains a computerized index of Attic black-figure and red-figure pottery, with data for shapes, attributions, subjects, etc.

CHAPTER II:
THE PROTOGEOMETRIC STYLE

General

V. R. d'A. Desborough, *Protogeometric Pottery [PGP]*. A comprehensive and detailed study. (His final Transitional stage is now classed as Geometric.) 1952.
V. R. d'A. Desborough, *The Greek Dark Ages*. Supplements and modifies *PGP*. 1972.

Athens

W. Kraiker and K. Kübler, *Kerameikos* 1, and K. Kübler, *Kerameikos* 4. Publication and analysis, perhaps too precise, of Attic Protogeometric. 1939 and 1943.

Outside Attica

B. Wells, *Asine* 2.4, 149–297. For Protogeometric at Asine (Argolid). 1983.
M. E. Voyatzis, *The Sanctuary of Athena Alea, 800–600 BC*. Includes Protogeometric from Arcadia. 1990.
V. R. d'A. Desborough, in M. R. Popham and L. H. Sackett, *Lefkandi* 1, 281–354. Detailed analysis of Euboean Protogeometric. 1980.
R. W. V. Catling and I. S. Lemos, in M. R. Popham *et al.*, *Lefkandi* 2.1. A full and revised study of Euboean Middle Protogeometric. 1990.
R. Kearsley, *BICS* Suppl. 44. On PSC cups. 1989.
N. M. Verdelis, ὁ Πρωτογεωμετρικὸς 'Ρυθμὸς τῆς Θεσσαλίας. A useful collection of Protogeometric in Thessaly. 1958.
M. Sipsie-Eschbach. *Protogeometrische Keramik aus Iolkos in Thessalien*. For finds at Iolcus in Thessaly. 1991.
W. D. E. Coulson, *BSA* 80, 29–84. A meticulous provisional account of Laconian Protogeometric. 1985.
W. D. E. Coulson, *The Dark Age Pottery of Messenia*. Ditto for Messenian Protogeometric. 1986.
W. D. E. Coulson, *BSA* 87, 43–64. Ditto for Ithacan. 1991.
C. A. Morgan, *Athletes and Oracles*, App. 1. For Protogeometric and Geometric in Elis. (App. 2. is on Phocis). 1990.
I. P. Votokopolou, *ADelt* 24A, 74–94. Finds credibly from Agrinion (Aetolia). 1971.
L. Morricone, *ASA* 56. For Protogeometric and Geometric at Cos. 1982.
J. K. Brock, *Fortetsa*. For Cretan Protogeometric at Cnossus. 1957.
J. N. Coldstream, *Knossos, the North Cemetery: Early Greek Tombs*. Important additions to Brock (Announced).

Note on Mycenaean

A. Furumark, *the Mycenaean Pottery: Analysis and Classification,* and *the Chronology of Mycenaean Pottery*. Fundamental and detailed, but too precise. 1941.

P. A. Mountjoy, *Mycenaean Decorated Pottery: a guide to identification.* Well-informed and useful. 1986.
F. H. Stubbings, *BSA* 42, 1–75. Mycenaean in Attica. 1947.
V. R. d' A. Desborough, *The last Mycenaeans and their Successors,* 1–28. Reconsiders the latest Mycenaean pottery. 1964.

CHAPTER III: THE GEOMETRIC STYLE
General

J. N. Coldstream, *Greek Geometric Pottery* [*GCP*]. A fundamental, though not final, conspectus, which should be consulted when use is made of most of the special studies listed below. 1968.
J. N. Coldstream, *Geometric Greece.* Includes some additions and modifications to *CGP*. 1977.

Athens

K. Kübler, *Kerameikos* 5.1. Publication of an Attic Geometric cemetery and a detailed analysis of the style; the last phase is dated about twenty-five years earlier than seems likely to me. 1954.
R. S. Young, *Hesp* Supplement 2. Contains much useful information about later Attic Geometric, but the chronology is improbably compressed. 1939.
E. T. H. Brann, *Hesp* 1961, 93–146. A useful collection of Late Geometric from the Agora of Athens.
E. T. H. Brann, *The Athenian Agora* 8. Complementary to the last item. 1962.
J. M. Davison, *Attic Geometric Workshops* (Yale Classical Studies 16). Useful for illustrations of the figure style. 1961.
J. M. Cook, *BSA* 42, 139–55. A neat review of progressive Late workshops. 1947.
CVA Louvre 11 (F. Villard), pls 777–92. For illustrations of human figures. 1954.

The Argolid

P. Courbin, *La Céramique Géométrique de l'Argolide.* A detailed analysis. (See also pp. 29–34 for 'Argive Monochrome'.) 1966.
C. Morgan and T. Whitelaw, *AJA* 1991, 79–108. An interesting attempt to distinguish local variations.
N. Kourou, *BCH* 111, 31–55. For 'Argive Monochrome' other than Argive. 1987.

Corinth

S. S. Weinberg, *Corinth* 7.1, 9–32. For illustrations. 1943.
C. W. Neeft, *MEFRA* (93.1, 7–88. Detailed study of Thapsos group. 1981.
R. S. Young, in *Corinth* 13, 13–49. Adds useful material and contexts. 1964.

Note: Weinberg's and Young's names for Middle and Late Geometric are Late and Protocorinthian Geometric.

Laconia

E. A. Lane, *BSA* 34, 101–89. A survey of the Late phase. 1936.
W. von Massow, *AM* 1927, 46–53. Useful for finds from Amyklai.
J. P. Droop, in R. M. Dawkins, *Artemis Orthia,* 54–68. Useful for finds from Sparta. 1929.

Western Greece

[C.] M. Robertson, *BSA* 43, 60–113. A solid account of Ithacan, but including much Corinthian and too high in its dates. 1948.

S. Benton, *BSA* 48, 255–358. Supplements and in part corrects Robertson. 1953.

Boeotia

A. Ruckert, *Frühe Keramik Böotiens*. (*AK* Beiheft 10). A close study of some Late Geometric. 1976.

Euboea

J. Boardman, *BSA* 47, 1–13. Some useful notes on Late Geometric from Eretria. 1952.

A. Andreiomenou, *EA* 1977, 128–63. Geometric from Eretria.

J. Boardman and M. J. Price, in M. R. Popham and L. H. Sackett, *Lefkandi* 1, 57–79. Geometric from Lefkandi (and Cesnola painter). 1980.

J. N. Coldstream, *BICS* 18, 1–15. On the Cesnola painter. 1971.

The Cyclades

C. Dugas and C. Rhomaios, *Délos* 15. For the Geometric from Delos and Rheneia; the classification is unreliable. 1934.

H. Dragendorff, *Thera* 2, 133–76. For Theran Geometric. 1903.

E. Pfuhl, *AM* 1903, 98–121. For Theran Geometric.

E. Buschor, *AM* 1929, 142–63. Illustrates some sherds from Paros and Naxos, and attempts to define local schools.

E. Walter-Karydi, *AA* 1972, 386–421. On finds from Naxos.

J. K. Breck, *BSA*, 44, 33–45. On the finds from Siphnos; see also pp. 74–9 on general classification. 1949.

N. M. Kondoleon, *EA* 1945–7, 1–21. Illustrates some elaborate pieces, but claims too much for Cycladic.

(On the classifications of these writers see the table on pp. 340–1).

The East Greek Region

Rhodian

K. F. Johansen, *Acta Archaeologica* 1957, 1–192. An admirable conspectus of later Geometric. (Usually cited as *Exochi*.)

Clara Rhodos 6/7 (G. Jacopi), 119–32, 189–203, 360–3. For illustrations and grave groups. 1933.

Clara Rhodos 3 (G. Jacopi), graves lvi-lxiv. Ditto. 1929.

Coan

L. Morricone, *ASA* 56. For Protogeometric and Geometric at Cos. 1982.

Samian

Samos 5 (H. Walter), nos. 15–300. Useful for illustrations (see J. N. Coldstream, *JHS* 1971, 202–4). 1968.

Chiot

J. Boardman, [*Excavations in Chios, 1952–1955*]: *Greek Emporio*, 101–47. A good presentation and classification of the finds. 1967.

Lesbian Grey ware (Bucchero)

W. Lamb, *BSA* 32, 51–6. For finds at Antissa. 1934.

North-east Aegean

C. W. Blegen *et al.*, *Troy* 4, 253–5, 281–3. A brief description of G2–3 ware. 1958.

Carian

C. Özgünel, *Carian Geometric Pottery*. Useful preliminary study. 1979.

Crete

J. K. Brock, *Fortetsa*. Instructive on Protogeometric B and Geometric at Cnossus. 1957.

J. N. Coldstream, *BSA* 67, 62–98. Further information for Cnossus. 1972.

J. N. Coldstream, in *Knossos, the North Cemetery: Early Greek Tombs*. Supplements and corrects the last two items. (Announced).

J. Boardman, *BSA* 62, 57–75. On the Oriental connections of Protogeometric B. 1967.

H. G. G. Payne, *BSA* 29, 224–98. Tombs at Cnossus and a general account; but Protogeometric B is not recognized. 1928.

M. Hartley, *BSA* 31, 56–114. Illustrates material from various sites in Crete. 1933.

D. Levi, *ASA* 10/12. Finds from Arkades (Afrati). 1931.

J. D. S. Pendelbury, *Archaeology of Crete*, 316–26. Useful for list of sites. 1939.

Italy

Å. Åkerström, *Der Geometrische Stil in Italien*. An important attempt at a general survey; but the chronology is too low and the Greek parallels are hazardous. 1943.

G. Vallet and F. Villard, *Mégara Hyblaea* 2, 139–57. A well illustrated account of the local Geometric of that site. 1964.

F. Villard and G. Vallet, *MEFR* 1956, 7–27. An important introduction to the classification of Geometric in Sicily.

T. J. Dunbabin, *The Western Greeks*, 487–96. A still valuable bibliography which includes Geometric finds; see also the index, *s.v.* 'Siculan pottery' and 'Lucanian pottery'. 1948.

F. Canciani, in M. Martelli, *La Ceramica degli Etruschi*, 9–15, 242–54. A useful illustrated introduction to Etruscan Geometric. 1987.

D. Yntema, *the Matt-painted Pottery of Southern Italy*. A comprehensive, but necessarily provisional account of native Apulian and Lucanian. 1985.

CHAPTER IV:
THE ORIENTALIZING AND
BLACK-FIGURE STYLES

There is no comprehensive term which describes all the schools of Greek vase-painting of this chapter. '*Archaic*' would be convenient, if it did not also include the early phase of the red-figure style. '*Orientalizing*', which implies dependence on Oriental models, may with caution be applied to the Animal style, but is improper for the human figures which are purely Greek, '*Black-figure*' conventionally defines the incising technique and the style based on that technique; it therefore excludes much Protoattic that is not Orientalizing either, while on the other hand such pieces as those of Plate 11 can be described both as Orientalizing and black-figure.

General

J. Boardman, *The Greeks Overseas* (2nd edn). A knowledgeable assessment of the relations between the Greeks and the East. 1973.

E. Akurgal, *The Birth of Greek Art*. A helpful illustrated survey of much relevant Oriental art. 1968.

C. Decamps de Mertzenfeld, *Inventaire commenté des ivoires phèniciens et apparentés découverts dans le Proche-Orient*. Convenient for illustrations. 1954.

R. D. Barnett, *A Catalogue of the Nimrud Ivories*. A well-illustrated and informed account of a large collection of Oriental ivories. 1957.

Corinth

K. F. Johansen, *Les Vases sicyoniens*. The fundamental study of Protocorinthian, though the dates are too early and the attribution to Sicyon has proved wrong. 1923.

H. G. G. Payne, *Protokorinthische Vasenmalerei*. A good short sketch of Protocorinthian, though the dating is rather too early. 1933.

H. G. G. Payne, *Necrocorinthia*. The fundamental study of Ripe Corinthian. 1931.

D. A. Amyx, *Corinthian Vase-painting of the Archaic Period*. A comprehensive study of the figured style with a catalogue by painters. 1988.

C. W. Neeft, *Addenda et Corrigenda to D. A. Amyx, CorVP*. Self-explanatory. 1991.

C. W. Neeft, *Protocorinthian Subgeometric Aryballoi*. An exhaustive study. 1987.

R. J. Hopper, *BSA* 44, 162–257. A useful commentary and supplement to Payne's *Necrocorinthia*. 1949.

Antike Denkmäler 1, pls. 7–8; 2, pls. 23–4, 29–30, 39–40. For illustrations of the plaques from Penteskouphia. 1886–1901.

M. T. Campbell, *Hesp* 1938, 560–4. For illustrations of Corinthian imitation of Attic Bf.

H. Palmer, in *Corinth* 13, 97–149. Instructive on late wares, including imitations of very late Attic Bf lekythoi. 1964.

E. G. Pemberton, *Hesp* 1970, 265–307. Useful comments on local styles of the later fifth century.

Ithaca

C. M. Robertson, *BSA* 43, 60–113. A careful publication of the material, but the dates are too high and some Corinthian is included. 1948.

S. Benton, *BSA* 48, 255–358. Supplements and occasionally corrects Robertson. 1953.

A concordance of terms and dates for Protocorinthian may be helpful. I accept Coldstream.

Coldstream	Weinberg	Payne	Johansen
720 Early Proto-corinthian	725 Early Proto-corinthian	750 Early Proto-corinthian	800 époque des aryballes pansus: style de transition
690 Middle Proto-corinthian I	700 Middle Proto-corinthian I	700 Middle Proto-corinthian I: 1st Bf and Orientalizing styles	725 époque des aryballes ovoides: style archaïque A
670 Middle Proto-corinthian II	675 Middle Proto-corinthian II	675 Middle Proto-corinthian II: 2nd Bf and Orientalizing styles	690 époque des aryballes ovoides: style archaïque B
(650 Late Proto-corinthian)	650 Late Proto-corinthian	650 Late Proto-corinthian	650 époque des aryballes piriformes: style archaïque C

The periods of Protocorinthian are often abbreviated to EPC, MPC (I and II) and LPC. Similarly the periods of Ripe Corinthian, which is usually called simply 'Corinthian', are abbreviated to EC, MC, LC I (to 550 BC), and LC II (for the Ripe and other styles after 550 BC).

Some students now put the end of Early Ripe Corinthian at 590 or 585 BC with corresponding adjustments of the dates of other periods of Corinthian: they may be right.

Athens

Protoattic

J. M. Cook, *BSA* 35, 165–219. A lucid analysis of the Early and the Black and White phases, but sketchier for the later phase. 1938.

K. Kübler, *Altattische Malerei*. A good survey with representative illustrations, but stretches the chronology at both ends. 1950.

R. Hampe, *Ein frühattischer Grabfund*. Adds to understanding of the Early phase (see J. M. Cook, *JHS* 1961, 220–2). 1960.

CVA Berlin 1 (R. Eilmann and K. Gebauer). A valuable publication of Early and of Black and White pottery from Aegina (see J. M. Cook, *JHS* 1939, 151–2). 1938.

S. P. Morris, *The Black and White Style*. Reclassifies painters and attributes much to Aegina. 1984.

S. Papaspyridi-Karouzou (S. Karouzou), Ἀγγεῖα τοῦ Ἀναγυροῦντος 1. A detailed and well-illustrated study of some Late Protoattic works. 1963.

J. D. Beazley, *Attic Black-figure Vase-painters*, 1–7. Lists works of some painters whom J. M. Cook and I call late Protoattic. 1956.

R. S. Young, *Hesp* Supplement 2. Contains useful information about Protoattic, but dates its beginning twenty years later than Cook. 1939.

E. T. H. Brann, *The Athenian Agora* 8. An illuminating survey of finds in the Agora. 1962.

E. T. H. Brann, *Hesp* 1961, 305–79. Supplements the last item.

K. Kübler, *Kerameikos* 6.2. A detailed publication of finds from the Ceramicus cemetery. 1970.

Cook (as adjusted by J. N. Coldstream) divides Protoattic into Early (700–675 BC), Middle (675–630 BC) and Late (630 to a little before 600 BC). Beazley classes Cook's Late Protoattic (or most of it) as early Black-figure. My division is nearer Cook's.

Attic black-figure

J. D. Beazley, *Attic Black-figure Vase-painters (ABV)*. A monumental catalogue by painters of 10,000 pieces. 1956.

J. D. Beazley, *Paralipomena (Para)*. Supplements *ABV* 1971.

T. H. Carpenter, *Beazley Addenda²*. Supplementary bibliography for *ABV* and *Para*. 1989.

J. Boardman, *Athenian Black Figure Vases*. A good illustrated survey. 1974.

J. D. Beazley, *The Development of Attic Black-figure*. A good selective survey. 1951, and with minor revision 1986.

I. Scheibler, *JdI* 1961, 1–47. A good study of the Gorgon painter.

G. Bakir, *Sophilos*. A good study. 1981.

A. Birchall, *JHS* 1972, 46–63. Classifies Horsehead amphorae.

A. Furtwängler and K. Reichhold, *Grieshische Vasenmalerei*, pls. 1–3 and 11–13. Complete drawings of the François vase. 1900–1.

H. Thiersch, *'Tyrrhenische' Amphoren*. Still useful for Tyrrhenian amphorae. 1899.

D. von Bothmer, *AJA* 1944, 161–70. Groups Tyrrhenian amphorae by painters.

H. A. G. Brijder, *Siana Cups I and Komast Cups* and *Siana Cups II: the Heidelberg Painter*. A detailed study. 1983 and 1991.

J. D. Beazley, *MMS* 5, 93–115. An account of the C painter (mainly Siana cups). 1934.

J. D. Beazley, *JHS* 1932, 167–204. A lucid account and list of signed Lip cups and Band cups.

P. N. Ure, *JHS* 1932, 55–71. A good account and list of Droop cups. (Supplemented in *Studies Presented to D. M. Robinson* 2, 45–54. 1953.)

A. Rumpf, *Sakonides*. A good and well-illustrated study of Lydos, Sakonides and their connections, whom Rumpf combines into one painter. 1937.

M. A. Tiberios, ὁ Λυδὸς καὶ τὸ ἔργο του. A detailed and well-illustrated study of Lydos. 1976.

J. D. Beazley, *JHS* 1931, 256–85. On the Amasis painter and the earlier Heidelberg group of Siana cups.

D. von Bothmer, *The Amasis Painter and his World*. A detailed and well-illustrated study. 1984.

H. Mommsen, *Der Affecter*. A detailed and well-illustrated study. 1975.

D. von Bothmer, *RA* 1969, 3–15. A short study of 'Elbows Out' and comments on the Affecter.

E. Böhr, *Der Schaukelmaler*. A detailed and well-illustrated study of the Swinger. 1982.

W. Technau, *Exekias*. A well-illustrated account of Exekias and his group. 1936.

J. Burow, *Der Antimenesmaler*. A detailed and well-illustrated study of the Animenes painter. 1989.

C. H. E. Haspels, *Attic Black-figure Lekythoi*. A detailed analysis of late black-figure painters. 1936.

J. D. Beazley, *AJA* 1943, 441–65. Notes on Panathenaic amphorae by known painters.

K. Peters, *Studien zu den panathenäischen Preisamphoren*. Notable for attributions to red-figure painters. 1942.

G. R. Edwards, *Hesp* 1957, 320–49. On Hellenistic and Roman Panathenaic amphorae. (See also H. A. Thompson, *Hesp* 1960, 366–7.)

D. A. Jackson, *East Greek Influence on Attic Vases*. Salutary, though speculative. 1976.

A. W. Johnston and R. E. Jones, *BSA* 73, 103–41. A helpful account of SOS amphorae. 1978.

The Argolid

J. M. Cook, *BSA* 48, 42–50 and 57. An intelligent summary of finds from Mycenae. 1953.

P. Courbin, *BCH* 1955, 1–32. For illustrations of the Polyphemus krater from Argos.

Laconia

E. A. Lane, *BSA* 34, 99–189. Still valuable for the earlier stages. 1936.

C. M. Stibbe, *Lakonische Vasenmaler des sechsten Jahrhunderts*. A thorough and fully illustrated study of the developed black-figure style. 1972.

J. P. Droop, in R. M. Dawkins, *Artemis Orthia*, 66–109. Useful for illustrations of finds from Sparta. 1929.

J. (W.) Hayes, in J. Boardman and J. Hayes, *Excavations at Tocra* 1, 87–95. A preliminary survey of the Plain ware. 1966.

C. M. Stibbe, *Laconian Black-glazed Pottery* 1 and 2. A thorough study of the Plain ware. 1989 and 1994.

Boeotia

A. Ruckert, *Frühe Keramik Böotiens*. For earlier Orientalizing. 1976.

A. Andreiomenou, τὸ κεραμεικὸν Ἐργαετήριον τῆς Ἀκραιφίας. A good discussion of Bird cups, based on grave groups. 1980.

B. Schmalz, *Marburger Winckelmann-Programm* 1977/8, 21–60. For lists and illustrations of Bird cups, but his chronology is insecure.

K. Kilinski II, *Boeotian Black Figure Vase Painting of the Archaic Period*. A convenient survey. 1990.

A. D. Ure, *JHS* 1929, 160–71. Early silhouette black-figure.

G. Bruns, in P. Wolters, *des Kabirenheiligtum bei Theben* 1, 95–128. A general study of Cabiran. 1940.

K. Braun, *das Kabirenheiligtum bei Theben* 4. Supplements and corrects Bruns. 1981.

A. D. Ure, *BSA* 41, 22–8. Some late black-figure groups. 1946.

Concordance of Classifications of Cycladic

(Note: the equations are approximate)

Délos xv, xvii & x	Brock	Boardman	Buschor (AM 1929, 142–63)	Payne	Dugas (Céramique des Cyclades)	Pfuhl	Strøm	Coldstream Greek Geometric Pottery
(Geom. & Subgeom.) Aa	Parian Geom.	Parian (Geom.) n. 79	Parian I(–II)	–	–	–	Parian Geom.	'Parian' Geom.
(Geom.) Bb	Naxian (Geom.)	Naxian Geom. n. 8	Naxian	–	–	–	Naxian Geom.	Naxian Geom.
Wheel grp Ab <1–7>	Parian Trans.	Parian n. 49 & Theran n. 79	Parian (Trans. I – II)	–	Island Geom.	Euboean 'Besondere Gruppe' J. 14–18	Parian	'Parian' Geom.
Theran Geom. –	Theran	Theran Geom.	Theran Geom.	–	Theran Geom.	Theran	Theran Geom.	Theran Geom.
Linear Island –	Parian Or. I	Theran n. 79	Parian II	Linear Island Geom. & Or. I	Island Geom.	Euboean	Southern Cycladic	–

Leyden grp	–	Parian Or. II	–	–	Linear – Island Or. II	–	–	Southern Cycladic (late) –	–
Ad grp	Ad	Ad	–	? Siphnian II	–	–	–	Parian (preceding 'Melian')	'Parian'
Heraldic grp	Ba	Naxian Or. I (Heraldic grp)	Naxian (Or.) p. 21	Löwen-wappen grp	Proto-Melian	Argivo-Cycladic Or. I	–	Naxian	Naxian
Protome grp	C <1–7, 9>	Naxian Or. II (Protome grp)	Naxian Or. n. 94	Parian III	Linear Island Or. III	Argivo-Cycladic Or. IV	–	?	–
Grp D	D	D	–	? Siphnian III	–	Argivo-Cycladic Or. V	–	–	–
'Melian'	Island (Or.)	Melian	'Melian'	Melian	Melian	Island Or.	Melian	'Melian' (Parian)	–

(Geom. = Geometric; Trans. = Transitional; Or. = Orientalizing).

A. D. Ure, *JHS* 1926, 54–62. Late black-figure cups of southern group.
A. D. Ure, *Hesp* 1946, 27–37. Late black-figure cups of northern group.
CVA Louvre 17 (A. Waiblinger). For illustrations of Boeotian of all sorts. 1974.

Euboea

J. Boardman, *BSA* 47, 1–48. A comprehensive study of pottery from Eretria, supplemented in *BSA* 52, 15–22, 1952 and 1957.
J.-P. Descoeudres, *BCH* 1972, 269–82. On an Early Orientalizing painter.
D. von Bothmer, *Metropolitan Museum Journal* 2, 27–44. Attempts to isolate imitations of Attic Black-figure. 1969. (See A. D. Ure, *BSA* 68, 25–31. 1973.)
A. D. Ure, *BSA* 55, 211–17; 58, 14–19; 65, 265–70. For black-figure mainly of the fourth century. 1960, 1963, 1970.
I. R. Metzger, in *Eretria* 6, 63–79. Late Black-figure from Eretria. 1978.

The Cyclades (see Concordance on p. pp. 340–1)

I. Strøm, *Acta* 1962, 221–78. Useful but partly speculative examination of Orientalizing groups before 'Melian'.
H. Dragendorff, *Thera* 2, 198–210. Linear Island. 1903.
E. Pfuhl, *AM* 1903, 183–93. Linear Island.
C. Dugas and C. Rhomatos, *Délos* 15 (Ab and Ad). 1934.
C. Mustakas, *AM* 1954/5, 153–8. Publishes finds of Ad group from Kimolos.
K. A. Sheedy, *BSA* 80, 153–90. A detailed study of the Ad group and group D. 1985.
C. Dugas, *Délos* 17 (all pots classed as Cycladic and some classed as Rhodo-Ionian). The classification is unreliable. 1935.
Ph. Zapheiropoulou, Προβλήματα τῆς Μηλιακῆς Ἀγγειογραφίας. A welcome and thorough study of 'Melian' from Rhenesia. 1985.
A. Conze, *Melische Thongefässe*. Coloured plates of large 'Melian' amphorae. 1862.
J. Boardman, *BSA* 47, 24–6. Useful comments on 'Melian'; other comments on Cycladic elsewhere in this paper. 1952.
J. K. Brock, *BSA* 44, 33–49. Finds from Siphnos; see also pp. 74–80 on general classification. 1949.
H. G. G. Payne, *JHS* 1926, 203–12. On Leyden group and general classification.
C. Karusos, *JdI* 1937, 166–97. Publishes an amphora from Naxos and comments on classification; he dates too early.

The East Greek region

General

Clara Rhodos 3, 4, 6/7 (G. Jacopi), 8 (L. Laurenzi). For grave groups from Camirus and Ialysus in Rhodes. 1929, 1931, 1933, 1936.
K. F. Kinch, *Fouilles de Vroulia*. For grave groups from Vroulia in Rhodes and illustrations of other Rhodian finds. 1914.
Samos 5 (H. Walter), nos. 301–631. Illustrates finds from Samos till late seventh century. 1968.
Samos 6.1 (E. Walter-Karydi). Useful illustrations of East Greek from late seventh century on, but local attributions idiosyncratic. 1973.
P. Dupont, *Dacia* 17, 19–43. Fundamental for clay analyses. 1983.
P. Dupont, *Istanbuler Mitteilungen* Beiheft 31, 57–71. Clay analysis of Milesian products. 1986.

— Bibliography —

Bird bowls

J. N. Coldstream, *Greek Geometric Pottery*, 298–301. A concise analysis of the development. 1968.

Wild Goat style

C. Kardara, Ροδιακὴ Ἀγγειογραφία. A valuable and detailed study, but unequal (see R. M. Cook, *Gnomon* 1965, 502–7). 1963.
W. Schiering, *Werkstätten Orientalisierender Keramik auf Rhodes*. A valuable detailed study, but the classification into Camirus, Euphorbos and Vlastos groups does not convince me. 1957.
Samos 5 (H. Walter), nos. 502–631. Publishes the material from Samos (with some from elsewhere). 1968.
Samos 6.1 (E. Walter-Karydi). Admirably comprehensive illustrations of East Greek from the end of the seventh century on, but arbitrary in attributions. 1973.
Clara Rhodos 6/7 (G. Jacopi), 475–543. Publishes the material from Nisyros. 1933.
J. Boehlau and K. Schefold, *Larisa am Hermos* 3. For Aeolian, but the classification is too precise and the chronology hazardous. 1942.
E. Walter-Karydi, *AK* Beiheft 7. Valuable on Aeolian, but overbold. 1970.

Chiot

A. A. Lemos, *Archaic Pottery of Chios*. A detailed and fully illustrated study. 1991.
J. Boardman, [*Excavations in Chios, 1952–1955*] *Greek Emporio,* 102–53 and 156–75. A valuable survey. 1967.
D. [J. R.] Williams, *AA* 1983, 155–86. Chiot finds in Aegina.
J. Boardman, *BSA 51, 55*–62. A partisan claim for manufacture in Naucratis with some useful general comments. 1956.

Ionian Little Master Cups

E. Kunze, *AM* 1934, 81–122. A detailed study.

Fikellura

R. M. Cook, *BSA* 34, 1–98. Attempts a detailed analysis. 1936.
G. R. Schaus, *BSA* 81, 251–95. A closer study of painters and chronology. 1986.
CVA British Museum 8 (R. M. Cook), pls. 568–81. For illustrations 1954.

Clazomenian and other East Greek Black-figure

J. M. Cook, *BSA* 60, 114–42. A good account of various groups from Smyrna. 1965.
R. M. Cook, *BSA* 47, 123–52. A short provisional analysis of Clazomenian 1952.
CVA British Museum 8, pls. 582–95. for illustrations of Clazomenian. 1954.

Clazomenian Sarcophagi

R. M. Cook, *Clazomenian Sarcophagi*. Detailed; the early chronology needs revising. 1981.

Situlae

CVA British Museum 8 (R. M. Cook), 29–37 and pls. 596–605. For illustrations and a speculative account. 1954.

Vroulian

K. F. Kinch, *Frouilles de Vroulia*, 168–90. For illustrations. 1914.

East Greek Cups

F. Villard and G. Vallet, *MEFR* 1955, 14–34. A useful general study, though too precise and claiming too much as East Greek.
J. [W.] Hayes in J. Boardman and J. Hayes, *Excavations at Tocra 1963–65: the Archaic Deposits* I, 111–34. Venturesome correction and refinement of the classification of V*illard* and V*allet.* 1966.

Grey Ware (bucchero)

W. Lamb, *JHS* 1932, 1–12. For finds from Lesbos. (*Cf.* also *BSA* 32, 51–6. 1934.)
J. Boehlau and K. Schefold, *Larisa am Hermos* 3, 99–128. For finds from Larisa in Aeolis. 1942.

Thasos

Études Thasiennes 7 (L. Ghali-Kahil). A selection of finds from Thasos. 1960.
A. A. Lemos, *Archaic Pottery of Chios*, 209–22. For pottery of Chiot style. 1991.

Crete

J. K. Brock, *Fortetsa.* Contains much information on Orientalizing at Cnossus. 1957.
J. Boardman, *BSA* 56, 78–80. Isolates the Fortetsa painter. 1961.
D. Levi, *Hesp* 1945, 1–32. Useful for illustrations.
H. G. G. Payne, *BSA* 29, 277–98. Exaggerates the earliness and importance of Cretan. 1928.
D. Levi, *ASA* 10/12. Material from Arkades (Afrati). 1931.

Italy

Greek colonial

G. Buchner and D. Ridgway, *Pithekoussai* I. For Pithecusan versions of Protocorinthian (and of Corinthian and Euboean Geometric). 1993.
G. Vallet and F. Villard, *Mégara Hyblaea* 2, 137–99. An intelligent account of local pottery at Megara Hyblaea. 1964.
P. E. Arias, *BCH* 1936, 144–51. Publishes the Fusco kraters from Syracuse, but supposes them imported.

Apulian and Lucanian

D. Yntema, *The Matt-Painted Pottery of Southern Italy.* A comprehensive, if exploratory, survey of the native schools. 1985.

Etruscan earlier Orientalizing

M. Martelli, *La Ceramica degli Etruschi*, 16–22, 255–68. A helpful illustrated survey. 1987.

CVA Tarquinia 3 (F. Canciani). For Tarquinian versions of Protocorinthian. 1974.

S. S. Leach, *Subgeometric Pottery from Southern Etruria*. A general study of the Heron style. 1987.

Etruscocorinthian

J. G. Szilágyi, *Ceramica Etrusco-Corinzia Figurata: Parte 1,650–580 a.C.* The standard study though not yet completed. 1992.

J. G. Szilágyi, *Etruszko-Korinthose Vázafestészet*. In part superseded by the preceding item: the lists are useful to readers without Hungarian. 1975.

J. G. Szilágyi, in A. Alföldi. *Römische Frühgeschichte*, 183–93. A clear general account. 1976.

J. Sieveking and R. Hackl, *Die k. Vasensammlung zu München*, nos. 610–795. A comprehensive set of illustrations. 1912.

Etruscan Bucchero

T. B. Rasmussen, *Bucchero Pottery from Southern Etruria*. A comprehensive study. 1979.

T. [B.] Rasmussen, in J. Swaddling, *Italian Iron Age Artefacts in the B.M.*, 273–81. On Campanian bucchero. 1988.

J. W. Hayes, *Etruscan and Italic Pottery in the Royal Ontario Museum*, 62–130. For illustrations and notes on North Etruscan bucchero. 1985.

Etruscan Black-figure

M. A. Rizzo, in M. Martelli, *La Ceramica degli Etruschi*, 31–42, 297–312. A helpful illustrated survey and up to date. 1987.

T. Dohrn, *Die schwarzfigurigen Etruskischen Vasen*. A detailed study till the early fifth century. 1937.

J. D. Beazley, *La Raccolta B. Guglielmi* 1, nos. 87–106, and *Etruscan Vase-painting*, 11–24. Enlarges and rearranges Dohrn's groups. 1939 and 1947.

J. Sieveking and R. Hackl, *Die k. Vasensammlung zu München*, nos. 796–1014. A good series of illustrations. 1912.

L. Hannestad, *The Paris Painter* and *The Followers of the Paris Painter*. A lucid study of Pontic. 1974 and 1976.

A. Drukker, in H. A. G. Brijder *et al.*, *Enthousiasmos* 39–48. The latest list for the Ivy (-Leaf) painter. 1986.

M. Zilverberg, in H. A. G. Brijder *et al.*, *Enthousiasmos* 49–60. The latest list for the La Tolfa group. 1986.

N. J. Spivey, *The Micali Painter and His Followers*. A close study. 1987.

'Chalcidian'

A. Rumpf, *Chalkidische Vasen*. A thorough and fully illustrated study. 1927.

H. R. W. Smith, *The Origin of Chalcidian Ware* (Univ. of California Publications in Classical Archaeology 1, 85–149). Asserts against Rumpf its Etruscan manufacture. 1932.

G. Vallet, *Rhégion et Zancle*, 211–28. Puts the case for Rhegion. 1958. M. Iozzo, *Ceramicá 'Calcidese'*. For additions to Rumpf's lists. 1994.

Northampton group

CVA München 6 (E. Walter-Karydi), 42–3. For illustrations and references. 1968.
CVA Castle Ashby (J. Boardman), 1–2. For more illustrations and references. 1979.

Campana group

F. Villard, *Mon Piot* 43, 33–57. A good study, but assigns group to Rhodes. 1949.
R. M. Cook and J. M. Hemelrijk, *Jarhbuch der Berliner Museen* 1963, 107–20. Modify Villard's account.

Caeretan hydriai

J. M. Hemelrijk, *Caeretan Hydriae*. Comprehensive. 1984.

Campanian Black-figure

CVA Capua 3 (P. Mingazzini), pls 1293–1303. Illustrations of earlier and later classes, with useful comments and references. 1958.
F. P. Badoni, *Ceramica Campana a Figure Nere*. A general study of the earlier class. 1968.
E. Rohde, *Wissenschaftliche Zeitschrift der Universität Rostock*, Ges. und Spr. Reihe 7/8, 499–505. Useful comments on the earlier class. 1967.
R. Hurschmann, *JdI* 1988, 39–66. A general study of the later class.

The Eastern fringes

P. Gercke, *Funde aus der Antike*, 28–89. A good batch of Carian. 1981.
R. M. Cook, *OJA* 1993, 109–15. On a Carian Wild Goat (and Fikellura) painter.
C. H. Greenewalt Jr, *California Studies in Classical Antiquity* 1, 139–54; 2, 55–89. Some Lydian versions of the Wild Goat style. 1968, 1970.
A. Della Seta, *EA* 1937, 629–54. For illustrations of some of the finer pieces from Lemnos.
D. Mustilli, *ASA* 15/16. Useful for grave groups from Lemnos and for illustrations. 1942.
E. Akurgal, *Phrygische Kunst*, 1–59. A pioneering study of Phrygian pottery; well illustrated. 1953.
G. K. Sams, *Early Phrygian Pottery (Gordion Excavations 1950–73: Final Reports 4)*. A detailed account. 1994.

CHAPTER V:
THE RED-FIGURE STYLE

Attica

General works

J. D. Beazley, *Attic Red-figure Vase-painters* (2nd edn) [*ARV* ²]. The indispensable catalogue by painters of 21,000 red-figure and white-ground pieces. 1963.

J. D. Beazley, *Paralipomena (Para.)*, Supplements *ARV* ². 1971.

T. H. Carpenter, *Beazley Addenda* (2nd edn), Supplementary Bibliography for *ARV* ² and *Para*. 1984. .

[C]. M. Robertson, *The Art of Vase-painting in Classical Athens*. A leisurely and expert commentary on Beazley's lists. 1992.

J. Boardman, *Athenian Red Figure Vases: The Archaic Period*. A good general account 1975.

J. Boardman, *Athenian Red Figure Vases: The Classical Period*. Ditto. 1989.

I. Wehgartner, *Attisch weissgrundige Keramik*. A good account of the white-ground style, not only on lekythoi. 1983.

J. D. Beazley, *Attic White Lekythoi [AWL]*. A short general account. 1938.

D. C. Kurtz, *Athenian White Lekythoi*. A detailed study of ornaments and shapes. 1975.

W. Riezler, *Weissgrundige attische Lekythen*. Most useful for illustrations of white-ground lekythoi. 1914.

K. Schefold, *Kertscher Vasen*. A well-illustrated short account of the progressive late painters. 1930.

K. Schefold, *Untersuchungen zu den Kertscher Vasen*. A detailed, but not wholly reliable study of the progressive late painters. 1934.

L. Talcott and B. Philippaki, *Hesp* Supplement 10, 1–77. Valuable for the poorer red-figure of the fourth century. 1956.

L. D. Caskey and J. D. Beazley, *Attic Vase Painting in the Museum of Fine Arts, Boston* 1–3. A catalogue with excellent illustrations and commentary. 1931, 1954 and 1963.

A. Furtwängler and K. Reichhold (and others), *Griechische Vasenmalerei* 1–3 [FR]. Contains accurate drawings and descriptions of many important pieces. 1900–32.

R. Lullies, *Griechische Vasen der reifarchaischen Zeit*. Admirable photographs of some Archaic pieces. 1953.

E. Simon, M. Hirmer and A. Hirmer, *Die griechischen Vasen*. Admirable photographs and informative notes. 1976.

E. Pfuhl, *Malerei und Zeichnung der Griechen [MuZ]*. Useful for the number of illustrations. 1923.

P. Jacobsthal, *Ornamente griechischer Vasen*. A detailed and well-illustrated study, mainly of red-figure ornaments. 1927.

E. Bloesch, *Formen attischer Schalen*. A pioneer study of the shapes of red-figure cups till *c*. 450 BC. 1940.

Special studies

H. Marwitz, *ÖJh* 46, 73–104. An interesting examination of the Andocides painter. 1961–3.

A. Bruhn, *Oltos and Early Red-figure Vase Painting*. A well-illustrated survy. 1943.

H. R. W. Smith, *New Aspects of the Menon Painter* (University of California Publications in Classical Archeology 1, 1–64). A good account of the painter now identified as Psiax. 1929.

W. Kraiker, *JdI* 1929, 141–97. A useful paper on Epictetus.

Euphronios der Maler (Antikenmuseum Berlin). A well-illustrated catalogue. 1991.

J. D. Beazley, *The Kleophrades Painter*. A lucid and well-illustrated estimate of the Cleophrades painter. 1974 [1933].

J. D. Beazley, *The Berlin Painter*. A comparable study of the Berlin painter. 1974 [1930].

D. C. Kurtz, *The Berlin Painter.* Instructive for a microscopic examination of the painter's style. 1983.

D. Buitron-Oliver, *Douris.* A detailed and well-illustrated account of Duris. 1995.

J. D. Beazley, *The Pan Painter.* A well-illustrated study of the Pan painter. 1974 [1931].

F. P. Johnson, *AJA* 1945, 491–502. A useful study of Hermonax.

J. D. Beazley, *RM* 1912, 286–97. A close analysis of the Villa Giulia painter.

M. Prange, *Der Niobidenmaler.* A useful, if contentious, study of the Niobid painter and his school. 1989.

H. Diepolder, *BWP* 110. A well-illustrated account of the Pistoxenos painter. 1954.

H. Diepolder, *Der Penthesilea-Maler.* A well-illustrated account of the Penthesilea painter, but conflating the Pistoxenos painter (pls 1–8) with him. 1936.

H. R. W. Smith, *Der Lewis-Maler.* A well-illustrated analysis of the Lewis painter and his group. 1939.

J. D. Beazley, *JHS* 1914, 179–226. A close analysis of the Achilles painter.

A. Lezzi-Hafter, *Der Schuwalov-Maler.* A detailed and well-llustrated study of the Shuvalov painter. 1976.

A. Lezzi-Hafter, *Der Eretria-Maler.* A similar study of the Eretria painter and his connections. 1988.

J. H. Oakley, *The Phiale painter.* Another similar study. 1990.

S. Papaspyridi [S. Karouzou], *A Delt* 1923, 117–46. A good account of the Reed painter.

W. Hahland, *Vasen um Meidias.* A well-illustrated survey of painters of around the end of the fifth century. 1930.

V. Paul-Zinserlina, *Der Jena-Maler und sein Kreis.* A detailed and well-illustrated study of the Jena painter. 1994.

F. P. Johnson, in *Studies Presented to D. M. Robinson* 2, 96–105. A useful study of owl-kotylai. 1953. (Supplemented in *AJA* 1955, 119–24.)

S. Howard and F. P. Johnson, *AJA* 1954, 191–208. A classification of the St Valentin group, consisting of small pots with simple ornaments and mostly of the second half of the fifth century.

M. Crosby, *Hesp* 1955, 76–84. Publishes an early fourth-century group with polychrome comic figures.

Corinth

S. Herbert, *Corinth* 7.4. A detailed study of the red-figure. 1977.

A. N. Stillwell and J. L. Benson, *Corinth* 15.3, 368–71. Gives list of Sam Wide group. 1984.

Boeotia

R. Lullies, *AM* 1940, 1–27. A good account of fifth-century painters.

A. D. Ure, *AJA* 1958, 389–95. On two painters of the later fifth century.

A. D. Ure, *AJA* 1953, 245–9. On the group with women's heads.

Etruria

J. D. Beazley, *Etruscan Vase-painting* [*EVP*]. A fundamental study and catalogue, though now in part superseded. 1947.

M. Christofani, in M. Martelli, *La Ceramica degli Etruschi*, 43–53 and 313–31. An informative recent survey with useful references. 1987.

G. Pianu, *MEFRA* 1978, 161–95. On the Sokra and Phantom groups.

M. M. Pasquinucci, *Le Kelebai Volterrane*. A well-illustrated catalogue of the (later) school of Volterra. 1968.

M. A. del Chiaro, *Etruscan Red-figured Vase-painting at Caere*. On the fourth-century products. 1975.

M. A. del Chiaro, *The Genucilia Group* (Univ. of California Publications in Classical Archaeology 3, 243–372). On the Genucilia plates. 1957.

South Italy

Red-figure

A. D. Trendall, *The Red-figure Vases of Southern Italy and Sicily*. A painstaking survey. 1989.

A. D. Trendall, and A. Cambitoglou, *The Red-figured Vases of Apulia* 1, 2 and Index [*RVAp*]. Lists by painters, with commentary and illustrations, over 9,000 pieces. 1978, 1982, 1982. (Additions in *BICS* Supplement 42 and 60, 1983 and 1991.)

A. D. Trendall, *The Red-figured Vases of Lucania, Campania and Sicily* [*LCS*]. A similar classification of some 5,000 pieces. 1967. (Additions in *BICS* Supplement 26, 31 and 41. 1970, 1973 and 1983.)

A. D. Trendall, *The Red-figured Vases of Paestum*. Does the same for Paestum (nearly 2,000 pieces). 1987.

L. Bernabo Brea and M. Cavalier, *La Ceramica policroma liparese di età ellenistica*. On late Sicilian, but the chronology too low. 1986.

A. D. Trendall, *BICS* Supplement 19. Lists Phlyax vases and gives a short account 1967.

I. McPhee and A. D. Trendall *Greek Red-figured Fish-plates*. Lists and discussion (not only of South Italian pieces). 1987. (Additions in *AK* 1990, 41–51.)

H. Hoffmann, *Tarentine Rhyta*. A catalogue and study of South Italian rhyta. 1966.

J. M. Moret, *l'Ilioupersis dans la céramique Italiote*. A salutary examination of mythical subjects and more widely instructive. 1975.

H. Lohmann, *Grabmäler auf unteritalischen Vasen*. On grave monuments, but more generally useful and well illustrated. 1979.

H. Sichtermann, *Griechische Vasen in Unteritalion*. Excellent illustrations of Apulian. 1966.

Gnathian

L. Forti, *La Ceramica di Gnathia*. A useful preliminary survey. 1965.

J. R. Green, *Gnathia Pottery in the Akademisches Kunstmuseum, Bonn*. A handy short account. 1976.

M. Bernardini, *Vasi dello Stile di Gnathia; Vasi a Vernice Nera*. A good set of illustrations of finds in North Apulia. 1961.

CVA Naples 3 (A. Rocco). Another good set of illustrations (of finds from Campania?). 1954.

Miscellaneous

I. McPhee, *BSA* 81, 153–65. On Laconian red-figure (with references for some other local schools in n. 6). 1986.

I. McPhee, *BSA* 76, 297–308. Local red-figure of Chalcidice. 1981.

L. Stephani, *Compte-Rendu de la Commission Impériale Archéologique* 1874, 42–51. An account of some Ukrainian attempts at red-figure.

CHAPTER VI:
HELLENISTIC POTTERY WITH
PAINTED DECORATION

West Slope ware

S. I. Rotroff, *Hesp* 1991, 59–102. The most recent study of the Attic school.

G. R. Edwards, *Corinth* 7.3, 20–6 etc. Meticulous publication of Corinthian fragments. 1975.

D. Behr, *Istanbuler Mitteilungen* 1988, 97–188. A good study of the Pergamene school.

P. J. Callaghan, *BSA* 76, 35–58. Indicates local style of Crete. 1981.

The Lagynos group

G. Leroux, *Lagynos*. Still the only comprehensive study. 1913.

J. Schäfer, *Hellenistische Keramik aus Pergamon*, 101–15. Helpful comments based on finds at Pergamum. 1968.

Hadra ware

R. Pagenstecher, *Expedition E. von Sieglin* 2.3, 32–52. Illustrates both light-ground and polychrome hydriai. 1913.

P. J. Callaghan and R. E. Jones, *BSA* 80, 1–17. Clay analysis. 1985.

P. J. Callaghan, *BSA* 75, 33–47. Basic for origins and dating of light-ground ware. 1980.

L. Guerrini, *Vasi di Hadra*. Classifies and illustrates the light-ground group; dating and connections are dubious. 1964.

B. F. Cook, *Inscribed Hadra Vases in the Metropolitan Museum of Art*. Makes some good general points. 1966.

B. F. Cook, in N. Bonacasa and A. Di Vita, *Alessandria e il Mondo Ellenistico-Romano* 3, 804–18. Some light-ground groups. 1984.

H. Braunert, *JdI* 1950/1, 231–63. A generally sound equation of regnal with calendar years.

B. F. Cook, *Brooklyn Museum Annual* 10, 115–38. Some additions and corrections to Braunert. 1968/9.

A. Yiannikoyri, in Γ'Επιστημουική Συναντήση γιά τήν Ελληνιστική Κεραμική, 302–10. A preliminary study of the polychrome hydriai of Rhodes. 1994.

Canosa ware

H. Lohmann, *AA* 1979, 187–213. A useful survey.

Centuripae ware

U. Wintermeyer, *JdI* 1975, 136–241. A comprehensive account.
G. M. A. Richter, *MMS* 2, 187–205 and 4, 45–54. Good coloured illustrations. 1930 and 1932.

Miscellaneous

T. N. Knipovitch, *Sovetskaya Archeologiya* 7, 140–51. A short account of the light-ground group from Ukraine. 1941.
F. Maier, *JdI* 1963, 218–55. A provisional study of 'Galatian' light-ground ware.
E. Pottier, *Mon Piot* 20, 163–79. A short description of Carthaginian oinochoai. 1913.

CHAPTER VII:
BLACK-PAINTED AND RELIEF WARES

B. A. Sparkes and L. Talcott, *The Athenian Agora* 12. An excellent detailed account of Attic black-painted ware from the sixth to the third century, but the later chronology is too high. (See Rotroff, below, 107–12). 1970.
A. D. Ure, *JHS* 1936, 205–15 and 1944, 67–77. Lists Attic red-figure cups with impressed decoration.
G. Kopcke, *AM* 1964, 22–84. A good study of fourth-century Attic black-painted ware with gilded decoration.
H. A. Thompson, *Hesp.* 1934, 429–38. A useful survey of Attic black-painted ware of the third and second centuries, but the dating is too high (see Rotroff below, 107–12).
P. N. Ure, *Black Glaze Pottery from Rhitsona*. A careful study of some Boeotian black-painted ware. 1913
G. R. Edwards, *Corinth* 7.3, 18–102. A close study of the Hellenistic black-painted of Corinth. 1975.
P. J. Callaghan, *BSA* 73, 6–21 and 76, 35–58. Informative on the black-painted of Cnossus. 1978, 1981.
J. Schäfer. *Hellenistische Keramik aus Pergamon*, 32–44. For black-painted at Pergamum. 1968.
J.-P. Morel, *Céramique Campanienne: les Formes*. An exhaustive study, not only of products of Campania. 1981.
H. Comfort in Pauly-Wissowa-Kroll, *Real-Encyclopádie* Supplementband 7, 1295–1352. Still a useful survey of Sigillata. 1940.
C. Meyer-Schlichtmann, *Die pergamenische Sigillata aus der Stadtgrabung von Pergamon.* For Pergamene Sigillata. 1988.
R. J. Charleston, *Roman Pottery* (2nd edn). A brief illustrated survey of the pottery of the Roman Empire. 1972.
J. W. Hayes, *Late Roman Pottery* and *Supplement to Late Roman Pottery*. The standard work on the Late Roman red wares. 1972, 1980.
F. Courby, *Les Vases grecs à Reliefs*. A comprehensive account of Greek relief wares, but needing much revision, 1922.
J. Schäfer, *Studien zu den griechischen Reliefpithoi des 8.-6. Jahrbunderts v. Chr. aus Kreta, Rhodos, Tenos and Boiotien*. A useful arrangement of the material. 1957.
N. M. Kondoleon, *EA* 1969, 215–36. For early Cycladic relief ware.
M. E. Caskey, *AJA* 1976, 19–41. Some additions to the previous two entries.

C. A. Christou, *A Delt* 1964, 164–265. For early Laconian relief ware.

D. Feytmans, *BCH* 1950, 135–80 and 1952, 197–200. For Rhodian coarse amphorae with stamped decoration.

S. S. Weinberg, *Hesp* 1954, 109–37. Collects earlier stamped and relief wares from Corinth.

E. A. Zervoudaki, *AM* 1968, 1–88. A detailed study of polychrome Attic relief ware of the late fifth and fourth centuries.

S. I. Rotroff, *The Athenian Agora* 22. A good study of the Attic 'Megarian bowls'. 1982.

G. R. Edwards, *Corinth* 7.3, 151–87. Defines the Corinthian variety of 'Megarian bowl'. 1975.

C. M. Edwards, *Hesp* 1986, 389–419. Modifies some of the conclusions of the last entry.

G. Siebert, *Recherches sur les ateliers de bols à relief du Péloponnèse a l'époque hellénistique*. Defines some characteristics of the 'Megarian bowls' from various workshops in the Peloponnese (and elsewhere). 1978.

A. Laumonier, *Délos* 31. A careful study of East Greek (probably Ephesian) 'Megarian bowls' at Delos. 1977.

U. Sinn, *Die Homerischen Becher*. Another careful study. 1974.

J. Schäfer, *Hellenistische Keramik aus Pergamon*, 64–100. For local relief ware. 1968.

R. Pagenstecher, *JdI* Erganzungsheft 8. A detailed study of Calene, though in part wrong on its dates and relations. 1909.

M.-O. Jentel, *Les Gutti et les Askoi à reliefs étrusques et apuliens*. An incomplete replacement of Pagenstecher. 1976.

L. Hannestad, *Ikaros: the Hellenistic Settlement* 2. A tentative assessment of the influence of Hellenistic Greek pottery in the Near East. 1983.

V. R. Grace, *Hesp* Supplement 10, 113–89. A good entry into the study of unpainted amphorae with stamped handles. 1956.

Much useful material and criticism is included in the more conscientious reports of excavations, such as those of Labraunda, Olympia, Olynthus, Pergamum, Priene, Samaria, Sparta and Tarsus.

CHAPTER VIII:
SHAPES

M. G. Kanowski, *Containers of Classical Greece: A Handbook of Shapes*. A useful general survey. 1984.

M. B. Moore and M. Z. Pease Philippides, *The Athenian Agora* 23, 4–72. An account of Attic black-figure shapes. 1986.

B. A. Sparkes and L. Talcott, *The Athenian Agora* 12, 47–235. A fuller account of Attic black-painted (and other) shapes; the dating of the later groups is too high. (A discussion of their names on pp. 3–9). 1970.

I. Scheibler, *JdI* 1961, 1–47. On the Attic olpe.

B. Philippaki, *The Attic Stamnos*. A detailed study. 1967.

R. M. Becker, *Forman attischer Peliken*. A detailed study as far as the Early Classical Period. 1977.

E. Diehl, *Die Hydria*, 49–64, 223–36. An account of the development of the hydria till Hellenstic. 1964.

J. R. Green, *BICS* 1972, 1–16. Classifies Attic red-figure oinochoai.

J. R. Green, *AA* 1978, 262–72. A close study of some Attic red-figure oinochoai.

J. R. Green, *BSA* 66, 189–228. A detailed account of the chous. 1971.

G. Leroux, *Lagynos*. A fair account of the lagynos. 1913.

T. Bakir, *Der Kolonettenkrater in Korinth und Attika zwischen 625 und 500 v. Chr.* A careful account of the early column krater. 1974.

K. Hitzl, *Die Entstehung und Entwicklung des Volutenkraters.* An account of the early development of the volute krater. 1982.

S. Drougou, *Der attische Psykter.* A careful study. 1975.

H. Bloesch, *Formen attischer Schalen.* A meticulous and well-illustrated analysis of the shapes of Attic cups from *c.* 540 to *c.* 450 BC. 1940.

S. R. Roberts, *The Attic Pyxis.* A careful account. 1978.

L. D. Caskey, *Geometry of Greek Vases.* Excellent measured drawings of Attic shapes of the later sixth and fifth centuries, and some fanciful theory. 1922.

M. L. Lazzarini, *AC* 1973/74, 341–75. A useful collection of the evidence for the ancient names of shapes.

F. Brommer, *Hermes* 1942, 356–73. A cautionary examination of the names of pots in Homer.

M. Vickers and D. [W. J.] Gill, *Artful Crafts*, 154–66. Asserts that fine pottery was dependent on metalware for shapes, decoration and even colouring (black for silver, red for gold). On shapes some good points are made; on decoration the evidence is weaker; and on colouring the initial argument is ingenuous, that in Greek society (but not after the second century BC some (but not all) silver was kept sedulously tarnished. 1994.

D. K. Hill, *AJA* 1947, 248–56. A salutary, but exaggerated denial of the influence of metal on earthenware shapes.

Many special studies on particular schools or groups of vase-painting include a discussion of the relevant shapes.

CHAPTER IX:
TECHNIQUE

J. V. Noble, *The Techniques of Painted Attic Pottery* (2nd edn). A comprehensive and generally reliable compendium, 1988.

A. Winter, *Die antike Glanztonkeramik.* An instructive study, especially for clays and firing, based on long practical experiment. 1978.

R. E. Jones, *Greek and Cypriot Pottery.* An invaluable and judicious account of methods of scientific analysis with a survey of work on Greek wares. 1986.

P. Dupont, *Dacia* 17, 19–43. An exemplary, though provisional, examination of East Greek clays. 1983.

CHAPTER X:
INSCRIPTIONS

Inscriptions before firing

P. Kretschmer, *Die griechischen Vaseninschriften.* The only comprehensive study, and still useful. 1894.

D. A. Amyx, *Corinthian Vase-painting of the Archaic Period*, 547–615. Lists and discusses inscriptions on Corinthian pots. 1988.

J. D. Beazley, *Attic Black-figure Vase-painters*, 664–78 and 847–51. Lists signatures and καλός names in Attic black-figure. 1956.

J. D. Beazley, *JHS* 1932, 167–204. Lists and discusses inscriptions on Attic Little Master cups.

J. C. Hoppin, *A Handbook of Greek Black-figured Vases*. For signatures on black-figure other than Attic. 1924.

R. M. Cook and A. G. Woodhead, *BSA* 47, 159–70. List and discuss inscriptions on Chiot pots. 1952.

A. Rumpf, *Chalkidische Vasen*, 40–53. Lists and discusses inscriptions on 'Chalcidian' pots. 1927.

J. D. Beazley, *Attic Red-figure Vase-painters* (2nd edn), 1553–1616. Lists signatures and καλός names in Attic red-figure. 1963.

M. Vickers and D. [W.J.] Gill, *Artful Crafts*, 154–66. For the theory that signatures are silversmiths'. 1994.

Inscriptions after firing

H. Braunert, *JdI* 1950/1, 231–63. Discusses the dated inscriptions on Hadra hydriai.

A. W. Johnston, *Trademarks on Greek Vases*. A thorough and scrupulous study of merchants' marks. 1979.

D. A. Amyx, *Hesp* 1958, 275–307. Good on prices.

Many excavation reports include some inscriptions on pots. Generally the fewer that were found the more fully are they published. Captions are the first to be omitted, then dedications.

Epigraphically important inscriptions are examined in L. H. Jeffery, *The Local Scripts of Archaic Greece* (2nd edn, revised by A. W. Johnston). 1990.

CHAPTER XI: CHRONOLOGY

Most special studies of particular schools discuss the relevant evidence for their dating. The references listed below are for the material associated with the fixed absolute dates rather than for the interpretation of that material, which is usually done better in the special studies: of these J. N. Coldstream's *Greek Geometric Pottery* may be singled out for its discussion of Tell Abu Hawam, Megiddo, Samaria and Hama (pp. 302–11), of Syracuse, Megara Hyblaea and Gela (pp. 324–6) and of the Bocchoris grave at Pithecusae (Ischia) (pp. 316–17). For a lower chronology of Protogeometric, see V. Hankey, *JdI* 1988, 33–87). For the bracketing of Samaria with the Boccdhoris grave and of Old Smyrna with Meṣad Ḥashavyahu see *BSA* 64, 13–15.

Amarna. W. M. F. Petrie, *Tell el Amarna*, 16–17. 1894.
Philistines. A. M. Snodgrass, *The Dark Age of Greece*, 107–9. 1971.
Tell Abu Hawam. R. W. Hamilton, *Quarterly of the Department of Antiquities in Palestine* 1935, 23–4 and 67–8; W. A. Heyrtley, *ibid.* 181.
Megiddo. C. Clairmont, *Bérytus* 1955, pl. 20, 1–2; P. J. Riis, *Sukas* 1, 144–6. 1970.
Samaria. J. W. Crowfoot, *Samaria-Sebaste* 3, 210–13. 1957.
Hama. K. F. Johansen, *Acta Archaeologica* 1957, 107.
Syracuse. G. Vallet and F. Villard, *BCH* 1952, 329–35.
Megara Hyblaea (foundation and destruction). G. Vallet and F. Villard, *Mégara Hyblaea* 2, 1964.
Ischia (Pithecusae), Bocchoris grave. M. W. Stoop, *Antiquity and Survival* 1955, 265 (fig. 17).

Tarsus. G. M. A. Hanfmann, in H. Goldman, *Excavations at Gözlü Kule, Tarsus* 3, 19–20, etc. 1963. But see J. Boardman, *JHS* 1965, 5–15.

Gela I. P. Orsi, *MA* 17. 1906.

Aziris. J. Boardman, *BSA* 61, 150–2. 1966.

Selinus. G. Vallet and F. Villard, *BCH* 1958, 16–26 (for the earliest finds). E. Gabrici, *MA* 32, 1927, R. Martin, *Comptes Rendus de l'Academie des Inscriptions et Bolles Lettres* 1977, 46–63.

Old Smyrna J. K. Anderson, *BSA* 53/54, 143–8. 1958/9.

Meṣad Ḥashavyabu J. Naveh, *Israel Exporation Journal* 1960, 129–39; 1962, 27–32 and 89–113.

Scarabs. T. G. H. James, in T. J. Dunbabin, *Perachora* 2, 461–4. 1962.

Siphnian Treasury. E. Langlotz, *Zur Zeitbestimmung der strengrotfigurigen Vasenmalerei,* 17–23. 1920.

Tell Defenneh. CVA *British Museum* 8 (R. M. Cook), 57–60. 1954.

Marathon. V Stais, *AM* 1893, 46–63.

Athens, Persian sack. B. Graef, *Die antiken Vasen von der Akropolis zu Athen.* 1909–33. T. L. Shear Jr, *Hesp* 1993, 383–482.

Camarina II. P. Orst, *MA* 14, 783–892. 1904.

Delos, purification. C. Dugas, *Délos* 21, 1952.

Thespiae, Polyandrion. R. Lullies, *AM* 1940, 8–10. D. U. Schilardi, *The Thespian Polyandrion.* 1978.

Athens, grave of Lacedaemonians. J. D. Beazley, *ARV*[2], 1344. 1963.

Motya. (Material mostly unpublished.)

Olynthus. D. M. Robinson, *Excavations at Olynthus* 5 and 13. 1933 and 1950.

Gela II. P. Orlandini, *AC* 1957, 44–75.

Chaeronea. (Material in Chaeronea Museum and National Museum, Athens.)

Alexandria. E. Breccia, *La Necropoli di Sciathi.* 1912.

Alexander, representations. A. Furtwängler in FR 2, 150–5. 1906.

Lipari. A. D. Trendall, in *Meligunìs-Lipára* (L. Bernabò-Brea and M. Cavalier) 2, 269–89. 1965.

Karoni. E. Vanderpool, J. R. McCredie and A. Steinberg, *Hesp* 1962, 26–61 and 1964, 69–75.

8th and 7th centuries generally. T. J. Dunbabin, *EA* 1953/4, 2, 247–62. A valuable examination, though in parts questionable.

Early 6th century. M. A. Tiverios, Μακεδονικα 25, 70–87. Questions synchronisms of Attic and Corinthian (Sindos). 1985–6.

Scientific Aids. M. J. Aitken, *Science-based Dating in Archaeology.* An expert general account. 1990.

(Perhaps it is worth mentioning that in the 1980s M. Vickers and E. D. Francis campaigned for the lowering by some sixty years of all dates for Archaic art; but they made few converts and by now interest seems to have disappeared. For references to their many publications see *JHS* 1989, 164 – in a paper that examines their arguments and finds them wanting.)

CHAPTER XII:
THE POTTERY INDUSTRY

J. D. Beazley, *Potter and Painter in Ancient Athens.* Offers some shrewd comments on Attic workshops. 1946.

D. P. S. Peacock, *Pottery in the Roman World* (especially chs 6–7). An intelligent and stimulating approach, but not to be followed uncritically for Greek fine wares. 1982.

See also the Bibliography to Chapter X.

CHAPTER XIII:
USES FOR OTHER STUDIES

Most special studies of the schools of Greek pottery include sections on distribution and subjects.

R. M. Cook, *JdI* 1959, 114–23. A rather fuller statement on trade.

F. Villard, *La Céramique grecque de Marseille*, 72–161. The most rational, though not entirely convincing, attempt to make economic sense of Greek pottery. 1960.

F. Brommer, *Vasenlisten zur griechischen Heldensage* (3rd edn). An invaluable catalogue of heroic subjects in Greek vase-painting. 1973.

H. Metzger, *Les Représentations dans la Céramique attique du IV siècle* and *Recherches sur l'Imagerie athénienne*. A good study of the subjects of later Attic Rf. 1951 and 1965.

Lexicon Iconographicum Mythologiae Classicae (LIMC). An ambitious illustrated compendium. 1981–   .

C. Bérard. *La Cité des Images* (translated as *A City of Images*). A convenient batch of iconographical studies of varying complexity. 1984 [1989].

CHAPTER XV:
THE HISTORY OF THE STUDY
OF VASE-PAINTING

This subject has been neglected. Even the writers of special studies usually do not go far back. The notable exceptions are for Geometric.

F. Poulsen, *Die Dipylongräber und die Dipylonvasen* (1905), 50–71, and for 'Chalcidian' A. Rumpf, *Chalkidische Vasen* (1927), 1–6.

O. Jahn, *Beschreibung der Vasensammlung*, ix-lxxxv. Gives a brief account of the history of the study and early collections, and a fuller account of places of finding. (The introduction to the *Beschreibung* is sometimes cited as Jahn, *Einleitung*.) 1854.

C. B. Stark, *Handbuch der Archäologie der Kunst*. Useful for its short biographies. 1880.

Katalog der Bibliothek des deutschen archäologischen Instituts in Rom 2, 1, 560–732 and 809–23. Classifies by title most books and papers published from 1825 till 1925 and some earlier works. 1932.

INDEX

abbreviations 313–15, 336
absolute chronology 251–8
Abu Hawam 252, 354
acanthus leaf 174
Acarnania: Geometric 28;
  Protogeometric 7, 12
Achaea: Geometric 28; Protogeometric
  7, 12
Achilles painter 171, 172–3, 188, 308,
  346
Acropolis see Athens, Acropolis
Acropolis 606, painter of 80, 81
Ad group 102–3, 210, 342
added colour see applied colour
Adria 275
Aegina 23, 26, 35, 68, 122, 123, 127,
  286, 295, 321, 337; Museum 319
aegis 325
Aeolian: Bucchero 34, 45, 110, 116,
  144, 334, 342; misattributed 296,
  299, 304; Protogeometric 10; Wild
  Goat style 110, 112, 116–17, 129,
  237, 342
Aetolia 51; Geometric 28;
  Protogeometric 7, 12
Affected style 282; see also
  Archaism
Affecter 81–2, 148, 282, 302, 338
Afrati see Arkades
Agora see Athens, Agora
Aitken, M.J. 354
Åkerstrom, A. 335
Akraiphia 97
Akurgal, E. 336, 346
alabastron 138, 143, 221, 222, 276
Alalia, battle of 296
Albizzati, C. 310
Aldroandi, U. 275
Alexander, C. 355

Alexander the Great 255
Alexandria 195, 197, 198–9, 205, 247,
  255, 270, 355
Al Mina 26, 29–30, 32, 35, 41, 103,
  118, 119, 252
alphabet see epigraphy
altars, terracotta 152
alt-korinthisch 290
alt-rhodisch 290
Alyattes 253
Amarna 251, 252, 353
Amasis painter 80, 81–2, 211, 302, 38
Amisos 117
amphora 209–13; panel decorations 70,
  71, 77, 86–7
amphoriskos 210
Amsterdam, Allard Pierson Museum
  321
Amyklae 26
Amyx, D.A. 336, 352
Analatos painter 63–5, 67, 68
analysis of clay 17, 110, 117, 233,
  238–40, 268–9, 342, 350, 353
Anatolian influence 34, 36, 117, 118,
  264
Ancient style 290
Anderson, J.K. 353
Andocides 158, 244, 260
Andocides painter 82, 85, 162, 306,
  308, 346
Andreiomenou, A. 333, 339
Andros 30
Animal style 3, 42, 43, 52–7, 76, 79,
  119, 142, 150, 301, 325, 335
Antimenes painter 85, 339
antiquities laws 273, 317–18
Antissa 36, 115, 334
Apollonia Pontica 118, 123
apotropaic 325

applied colour 163, 184, 187, 189, 191, 202–3, 269; *see also* white on dark decoration
Apulian: native style 40, 139, 195, 199, 343; Red-figure 182–3, 185–91, 193, 200, 226, 255, 279, 282, 310, 349
Arcadian: Geometric 16, 24, 27; Protogeometric 10
Arcesilas: cup 93, 254, 292; king 254, 292; painter 93
Archaic 163–5, 193, 251, 252–5, 325
Archaism 292, 306, 308
archons 255, 257, 285
Argive 297; Geometric 16, 17, 23–4, 27, 332; misattributed 88, 139, 287, 289; Monochrome 24, 333; Oriental-izing and Black-figure 45, 88, 338; Protogeometric 6, 10, 12, 332–3
Argivo-Cycladic 325
Arias, P.E. 343
Arimaspians 261
Aristonothos krater 88, 142, 244
Arkades 137, 334, 343
Armento 188
Arretine 201, 202, 205, 237, 275, 277
aryballos 46–7, 49–50, 222, 337
Asianizing style 290
Asiatic style 290
Asine 23, 35
askos 221, 222–3; *see also* duck vases
Assyrian: influence 41, 54, 252; lion 55–6
Asteas 190, 309
Athenaeus 280, 281
Athens: Acropolis 255, 284, 308, 353; Agora 7, 18, 63, 255, 332, 337–8, 350, 351; Agora Museum 319; Ceramicus 7, 9, 18, 259, 319, 338; Ceramicus Museum 319; Dipylon 286–7, 288; Geometric 18–23; Lacedaemonian grave 255, 353; National Museum 319, 353
Attic: Black and White style 67–71; Black-figure 3, 44, 46, 63, 71–86, 129, 131, 135, 210, 258, 317, 337–8; Black-painted 201, 202–3, 351; Geometric 7, 16–23, 24, 26, 210,

216, 258, 281, 284, 317, 332; Mycenaean 317; Protoattic 63–71, 287, 288, 301, 337; Protogeometric 2, 6, 7, 9–13, 332; Red-figure 3, 158–78, 250–1, 262, 306, 307–9, 317, 339, 346–7, 349; relief ware 204–5, 350; West Slope *see* West Slope; White-ground 165, 168–9, 207, 307, 345
Attic-Chalcidian 302
Attic-Corinthian 301
Attic-Ionic 325
Avella 282
Aziris 101, 253, 355

Bacchanalia 280, 282, 309
Bacchic mysteries 280
Bacchius 260
Badoni, F. 344
bail-amphora 185, 189
Bakir, G. 337
Bakir, T. 351
balloon amphora 325
balsamarium 325
band cups 78, 79, 80, 224, 242, 338
Banded ware 134
Bargigli, bishop of Chiusi 276
Barnett, R.D. 335
baroque 325
barrel amphora 325
Basilicata 182, 282
battlement meander 18
Beazley, J.D. 215, 262, 307, 308, 310, 338, 344, 345, 346, 347, 348, 352, 353–4
Beazley Archive 332
Becker, R.M. 352
Beger, L. 276, 277
Behr, D. 348
bell-krater 172, 175, 177, 189, 190, 219, 261
Bellori, G.P. 276
belly amphora 325
Beloch, K.J. 289
Benghazi 276, 285
Benndorf, O. 307, 310
Benson, J.L. 347
Benton, S. 334, 337

Bérard, C. 356
Berezan 110, 118, 122, 127, 129
Berlin museums 320
Berlin painter 87, 307, 346
Bernabo Brea, L. 347, 353
Bernardini, M. 349
bibliography 331–56
Big Bird group 106
bilingual 325
Biliotti, A. 286, 295, 296, 298
Birch, S. 285, 289, 308
Birchall, A. 337
Bird bowls 91, 110–11, 133, 224, 225, 239, 250, 254, 298–9, 342
Bird-cup group 96–7, 226, 249, 250, 302–3, 309, 339
Bisenzio 39
Black and White style 66–8, 69, 87–8, 337
Black Dipylon 325
Black Droop cups 79
Black-figure: name 279–80, 336; style 2–3, 44, 45, 46–153, 155, 168–9, 193, 210–11, 228, 229, 250, 280, 336–46; technique 87–8, 233, 239
Black-glazed *see* Black painted ware
black 'paint' 226, 227, 234, 236–7
Black-painted ware 177–8, 201–5, 279, 310–11, 351–2
Black Pattern style 61, 337
black polychrome technique 52, 118, 140, 142
Blasi 278
Blegen, C.W. 334
Bloesch, H. 347, 353
Boardman, J. 333, 334, 335, 338, 342, 343, 347, 355
Bocchoris 253, 353
Boehlau, J. 287–9, 291–2, 296–9, 301, 303, 304, 342
Boeotian: Bird-cup group 96–7, 226, 249, 302, 303, 339; Black-figure 97–8, 228, 303, 339; Black-painted 349; Cylix group 325; Geometric 16, 23, 28–9, 333; misattributed 308; Orientalizing 44–5, 96, 303, 339; Protogeometric 6–7, 10; Red-figure 179–80, 308, 347; relief

ware 203, 350; Subgeometric 96, 303, 339
Bohr, E. 338
Bologna, Museo Civico 319
bolsal 225
bombylios 325
Bonaparte, L. *see* Canino, Prince of
Boread 55, 71
Boread painter 93, 94
Bosanquet, R.C. 307
Boston Museum of Fine Arts 321
Bothmer, D. von 337, 338, 342
Böttiger, C.A. 282, 283
bowls 217–20
Brann, E.T.H. 332, 337
Braun, K. 339
Braunert, H. 350, 354
Breccia, E. 310, 355
Brijder, H.A.G. 338
British Museum 82, 85, 275, 279, 317, 320
Brock, J.K. 334, 339, 342, 344
Brommer, F. 351, 355
Bruhn, A. 346
Brunn, H. 292, 301, 306
Bruns, G. 342
Brussels, Musées du Cinquantenaire 320
Brygos 260
Brygos painter 165
Bucchero: Aeolian 34, 45, 110, 116, 144, 335, 343; Cretan 137, 345; Etruscan 45, 86, 141, 144–7, 203, 204, 212, 215, 217, 222, 226, 304, 317, 344; italico 325; Lesbian 34, 116, 34, 342; pesante 325; sottile 325; technique 237
Buchner, G. 344
Buitron-Oliver, D. 348
Bunsen, C.K.J. 283
Buonarroti, F. 276, 277, 280
Burgon, T. 281, 284, 287, 289, 290
Burgon amphora 80, 86, 254, 283, 301, 302
burial ware *see* funerary ware
burnishing 234
Burow, J. 339
Burrows, R.M. 303

Bursian, C. 295
Buschor, E. 304, 307, 308, 309, 333, 340–1
Busiris hydria 151–2, 305
butterfly ornament 325

C painter 75, 337
Cabiran 97–8, 227, 243, 303, 310
caduceus 326
Caere 39, 70, 141, 181, 182, 345, 347
Caeretan hydriai 46, 140, 148, 151–2, 250, 305, 344
Calene ware 205, 241, 310, 350
Callaghan, P.J. 350, 351
Calydon, metopes 51, 57, 167
calyx-krater 177, 189, 219
Camarina 255
Cambitoglou, A. 347
Cambridge, Fitzwilliam Museum 320
Cambyses 254–5
Camel group 129
Camiran 326
Camirus 286, 343
Camirus group 118, 343
Campana group 130, 151, 260, 305, 346
Campanian: Black-figure 152–3, 344; Black-painted 201, 205, 350; Impressed ware 203, 350; Red-figure 181–5, 187–9, 190, 191, 276, 309, 349
Campbell, M.T. 336
Canciani, F. 335
Canino, Prince of 283
Canino, Princess of 304
Canosa, Roman grave 309
Canosa ware 199–200, 222, 310, 350
captions 242–3, 247, 353
Capua 189, 282
carchesion 326
Caria 10, 36, 115, 118, 127, 153, 335, 345
Carpenter, T.H. 331, 338, 347
Carpi, Cardinal 275
Carthage: destruction 257; local ware 194, 349
Caskey, L.D. 347, 353
Caskey, M.E. 351
Cassel cups 79

'catagrapha' 160
catalogues 318–21, 331
Catling, R.W.V. 332
Causeus *see* Chausse, M.A. de la
Cavalier, M. 347, 353
Caylus, Count de 277, 278, 279
celadonite 233
centaur 50, 67, 83
Centuripae ware 189, 200, 219, 310, 349
Cephallenia 289
Ceramicus *see* Athens, Ceramicus
Cerveteri *see* Caere
Cesnola, General L.P. di 286
Cesnola painter 29, 333
Chaeronea, battle of 255, 353
'Chalcidian' 46, 98–9, 140, 149–51, 211, 243, 250, 290–4, 303, 344, 348, 355
Chalcis 29, 98–9, 291–2, 295, 296
chalice 119–22, 197, 209, 219, 223, 224, 246, 264, 342
Chares 244
Charleston, R.J. 351
Charmides painter 306
Chatby 255
chattering 204
Chausse, M.A. de la 276, 277, 280
Chiaro, M.A. del 347
Chigi vase 51, 241–2
Chimera group 56
Chios 33, 35–6, 110, 116, 298, 342
Chiot: Black-figure 110, 116, 120–2, 134, 296, 298, 342; Chalice style 119–22, 197, 209, 219, 223, 224, 246, 264, 342; Geometric 35–6, 334; painted inscriptions 246, 261, 352; Wild Goat style 45, 12, 116, 119–22, 127, 296, 298, 343
Chiot-Naucratite 296
chiton 83, 85, 326
Chiusi: Black-figure 146; Bucchero 146; Red-figure 181, 310
chlamys 326
chous 174, 215, 216, 351
Christou, C.A. 352
chronology 17, 186, 249–58, 354–5
chthonic 326

Cilicia 118
Cimon of Cleonae 160, 300
Clairmont, C. 354
Classical 326
clay 17, 110, 117, 233, 238–40, 268–9, 343, 350, 354
Clazomenae 33, 115, 122, 299, 300
Clazomenian: Black-figure 110, 115–16, 127–30, 300; sarcophagi 45, 109, 110, 122, 129–30, 157, 250, 287, 296–7, 299–300, 308; Wild Goat style 109, 128, 130, 299
cleaning 272
Cleophrades painter 85, 87, 165, 168, 307, 346
Clitias 73, 74, 76, 80–1, 244, 302
Close style 6
closed pots 209, 268
Clusium, school of 181, 310
Cnossus 13, 26, 37, 135, 334, 343, 350
Coldstream, J.N. 334, 335, 337, 338, 340–1, 343, 354
collecting 273
colonial wares (Western) 38–9, 343
colonies 252–4, 289
column-krater 218, 353
comast 326
Comast cups 58, 74–5, 302, 337
Comast group 87, 97
Comfort, H. 350
conical oinochoe 216–17
connoisseurship 326
Conventionalizing style 61
Conze, A. 287, 288, 289, 290–1, 295, 303
Cook, B.F. 349
Cook, J.M. 333, 337, 339
Cook, R.M. 343, 346, 354, 355, 356
cooler *see* psykter
Copenhagen National Museum 318, 320
coral-red 238
Corcyra 62
Corinth 239, 259; destruction 257; Museum 319
Corinthian: Black-figure 45, 115; Black Pattern style 61, 338; Conventionalizing 61; Geometric 16,

17, 22, 23–7, 279, 281–3, 333; imitations 2, 3, 62, 106, 108, 179, 291, 294; krater 218; Linear 57, 60–1; misattributed 290, Orientalizing style 43–5, 46–63, 113, 138–9, 290, 336–7; Protocorinthian *see* Protocorinthian; Protogeometric 2, 6, 10, 11, 333; Red-figure 178–9, 347; Red-ground 57, 59–60, 62, 68, 77; relief ware 349–50; Ripe 54–60, 113, 214, 222, 250, 254, 258, 286, 290, 294–5, 300, 335, 336; Subgeometric 60–1, 336; terracotta altars 152; West Slope 196; White style 61
Corinthian-Attic 326
Corpus Vasorum Antiquorum 331, 332, 338, 342, 344, 345, 349, 355
Cos: Geometric 33, 34–5, 335; Protogeometric 10, 335
cothon 326
Coulson, W.D.E 332
Courbin, P. 332, 338
Courby, F. 350
Cretan: Bucchero 137, 344; Geometric 16, 17, 23, 36–8, 135, 287, 335; Orientalizing 45, 62, 135–8, 304, 343; Protogeometric 6, 7, 12, 335; Protogeometric B 36–7, 41, 335; relief ware 351
Cristofani, M. 349
Croesus 254
Crosby, M. 348
Crowfoot, J.W. 353
Cumae 30, 32, 39, 45, 141, 189, 200
Cumaean 39, 62, 138, 141
cup 132–4, 223–7, 352
cup-kotyle 75, 79, 81, 177, 225
cup-painters 86, 159, 162
Curtius, E. 289
Cycladic 17, 22, 29, 250; classification 340–41; Geometric 11, 16, 30–3, 286, 303, 333, 340–1; misattributed 299; Cycladic (continued) Orientalizing 43, 45, 62, 96, 100–9, 286, 296, 303, 340–1, 342; Prehellenic 286; Protogeometric 6, 10–11; relief ware 352

cylix 223, 224
Cynosarges amphora 69
Cypriot 9, 11, 23, 30, 33–5, 37–8, 125, 127, 136–7, 198, 286–7, 304, 317, 353
Cyrenaean 92, 93, 292–3
Cyrene 27, 122

D group 99, 106, 342
daily life 265, 266
dancers, padded 57
Daphnae *see* Tell Defenneh
Darius painter 184
dates *see* chronology
dating by pottery 257, 263
Daunian 222, 326
Davison, J.M. 332
Dawkins, R.M. 286
dealers (modern) 273, 279
dealers' marks 248, 261–2, 264
Decamps de Mertzenfeld, C. 335
dedications 246, 247, 352
Defenneh *see* Tell Defenneh
Delian 291, 326
Delion, battle of 255
Delos 30, 255, 340; purification deposit *see* Rheneia purification deposit
Delphi 26; Siphnian treasury 254–5, 353
Demaratus 280, 282
Dempster, Thomas 275, 276
Desborough, V.R.d'A 332
Descoeudres, J-P. 342
Diehl, E. 353
Diepolder, H. 348
dinos 117, 217, 220
Dinos painter 174, 175, 176
dipinto 326
Dipylon: amphora 21–2, 64; cemetery 286, 287; jug 247; painter 21–2, 41, 326; style 288, 301, 326
Dirce painter 189
dish 227–9
distribution maps 264
Dodecanese *see* Cos; Rhodes
Dodwell, E. 281
Dodwell pyxis 283
Dohrn, T. 345

Dorian/Doric style 15, 34, 51, 283, 290, 292
Dorian invasion 2, 6, 252, 289–90
double axe ornament 326
Dragendorff, H. 286–91 passim, 299, 303, 333, 339
drama, influence of 98, 185, 187, 190, 348
drapery *see* dress
drawings 270–2
dress 86, 152, 169–70, 174, 175–6, 190
Droop, J.P. 293, 303, 333, 339
Droop cups 78–80, 83, 92, 93, 95, 97, 224, 303, 339
Drougou, S. 353
Drukker, A. 345
duck vases 12, 181, 185, 222
Dugas, C. 293, 304, 333, 339–41, 353
Dümmler, F. 296, 297, 299, 305, 308
Dümmler's group 326
Dumont, A. 292, 297, 301
Dunbabin, T.J. 335, 354
Dupont, P. 343, 353
Duris 164, 245, 308, 348

Early Roman 201
Early South Italian 181–2, 183–5, 308–9, 347–8
East Greek 95, 239, 250, 254; banded cups 83, 92, 132–3, 224–5; definition 33; Geometric 17, 23, 33–6, 109, 133, 224–5, 286–8, 296, 299, 334; misattributed 134, 295–7, 300; Orientalizing and Black-figure 45, 77, 100, 109–34, 295–6, 317, 343; political relations 265; Protogeometric 10, 288; relation to Etruscan 109, 146, 151, 304; Subgeometric 111
Eastern fringes 153, 346
Edwards, C.M. 350
Edwards, G.R. 244, 339, 350, 352
Εγραψε 244
Egypt, Persian conquest 254–5
Egyptian: influence 41, 42, 110, 277, 290, 292, 300; name for Orientalizing 277, 279, 284, 290
Egyptian Greek 131, 305

Egyptianizing 283
Eilmann, R. 337
El Amarna 251, 252, 354
Elbows Out (painter) 81–2, 339
Eleusis 18
Elis: Geometric 28; Orientalizing 45;
    Protogeometric 7, 12
embattled border 190
Endt, J. 292, 305
Enmann class 129
Ephesus 33, 117, 130, 260
epichysis 326
Epictetus 159–60, 162, 165, 306, 347
Epigram to the Potters 236–7
epigraphy 241–2, 276–9, 283–4, 298, 352
epinetron 326
epitaphs 247 244, 259
ἐποίηε 244, 259
Eretria painter 172, 174, 307, 346
Eretrian: Geometric 29, 333, 339;
    Orientalizing and Black-figure 45,
    98–100, 339; *see also* Euboean
Ergotimos 73, 79, 244
Eteocretan 36
Etruscan: Black-figure 140, 147–9, 250,
    344; Bucchero 45, 86, 141, 144–7,
    203, 204, 212, 215, 217, 222, 226,
    304, 317, 343; Earlier Orientalising
    62, 119, 141–2, 345;
    Etruscocorinthian 62–3, 142–4, 222,
    228, 240, 343; generic name for
    Red-figure 277–8, 280; Geometric
    39, 140, 336; Gerhard's
definition 282; Red-figure 140–1,
    180–2, 309, 347; relation to East
    Greek 109, 146, 151, 304
Etruscans 38, 139–40, 277–8
Etrusco-Campanian 326
Etruscocorinthian *see* Etruscan
Etruscomania 277–8, 80
Euboean: Geometric 16, 17, 27, 29–30,
    35, 38–40, 333, 339; influence 38, 39,
    40; misattributed 303, 326;
    Orientalizing and Black-figure 41,
    96, 98–100, 339; Protogeometric 6,
    7, 10–11
Euboeo-Cycladic 96, 326
Euphorbos: group 118; plate 295, 297

Euphronios 159, 162, 163, 243, 245,
    260, 306, 307
Eurytos krater 58, 72
Eusebius 252, 253–4
Euthymides 159, 162–3, 165, 243, 306
examination of pottery 267–9
Exekias 44, 72, 74, 80–3, 85, 123, 155,
    158, 161–2, 243, 302, 308
exergue 326
exports 62–3, 261
eye bowls 111, 298–9
eye cups 83, 86, 149, 299, 303

Fairbanks, A. 307
Faliscan Red-figure 181–2, 260
false spiral 32
fenestrated 326
Ferrara, Museum de Spina 319
ferric oxide 231, 232
Feytmans, D. 350
figure style 327
Fikellura 61, 95, 110, 115, 123–30, 133,
    210, 250, 317, 345
Filottrano painter 178
Fine style 327
fish plate 185, 228, 348
fixed dates 251–8
Flaxman, J. 279
floral band cups 79
Florence, Museo Archeologico Etrusco
    319
foreshortening 86, 156, 159–60, 164,
    168
forgery 247, 269
Fortetsa painter 344
Forti, L. 348
Fouqué, F. 286
Francis, E.D. 354
François vase 72–4, 76, 77–78, 80, 84,
    242, 244, 285, 300, 301–2, 338
free painting *see* painting
Fresnoy, C.A. du 276
funerary ware 21, 69, 187, 194, 237
Furtwängler, A. 287–9, 292, 294,
    296–7, 301, 303–4, 306–9, 338, 347,
    355
Fusco krater 88, 139, 343
fusiform unguentarium 327

G2–3 ware 36, 335
Gabrici, E. 286, 355
Galatian ware 194, 351
Gardner, E.A. 286
Gebauer, K. 337
Gela 109; foundations 252–3, 255, 258, 265, 353; local pottery 35, 138
Genucilia group 182, 347
Geometric: origin 1, 2, 5, 11, 15, 223, 252; style 5–6, 10, 15–40, 210, 218, 250, 258, 317; technique 238–9
'Geometricizing' 97
Gerhard, E. 281–5 *passim*, 297, 309
Ghali-Kahil, L. 343
gilding 155, 174
Gill, D.W.J. 351, 352
Girardon, F. 276
glaux *see* owl-kotyle
glaze 233
gloss 327
Gnathian 186, 191–3, 201, 213, 216, 310, 348
Gordion 345; cups 79, 80
Gorgon 42, 55, 69, 71, 73
Gorgon painter 71–2, 76, 77, 337
Gorgoneion 56, 58, 83, 93, 126; group (Corinthian) 55; group (East Greek) 91
Gori, A.F. 277, 280
Grace, V.R. 352
Graef, B. 355
graffito 327
graves 110, 173, 209, 249–50, 265
Greece (museums) 319
Greek key 327
Green, J.R. 349, 352
Greenewalt, C.H. 345
Greifenhagen, A. 302
Grey ware *see* Bucchero
Group E 82
Group R 175
Gsell, S. 304
Gualtieri, Cardinal 276
Guerrini, L. 349
guilloche 327
guttus 327
Gytheion 95

Hackl, R. 304, 305, 343
Hadra ware 194, 195, 197–9, 214, 241, 247, 255, 303, 310, 350, 354
Hague (former collection) 321
Hahland, W. 346
Haloa group *see* Sam Wide group
Hama 252, 354
Hamilton, R.W. 354
Hamilton, Sir William 278–9, 281
Hampe, R. 337
Hancarville, P.V.d' 278, 280, 301
handle ornament 190
handle plate 327
handles, development of 207–8
handling pottery 267
Hanfmann, G.M.A. 355
Hannestad, L. 345, 352
Hankey, V. 354
Hartley, M. 335
Hartwig, P. 306
Haspels, C.H.E. 338
Hauser, F. 309
Hayes, J.W. 338, 343, 350
head vase 327
Heidelberg group 338
Heidelberg painter 338
Helbig, W. 289, 290, 294, 305
Helladic: definition 327; Late *see* Mycenaean; Middle 5, 237
Hellenic (definition) 327
Hellenistic: definition 327; pottery with painted decoration 193–200, 211, 310–11, 348–9; wares 233, 238
helmet aryballos 91, 327
Hemelrijk, J.M. 346
hemispherical bowl 227
hemitomos 227
Hephaestus painter 73, 93
Heraclea 188, 309
Heraeum 23, 68, 327
Heraklion Museum 36, 319
Heraldic group 103–4, 211, 303
Herbert, S. 348
Hermitage 321
Hermogenes 80
Hermonax 348
Herodotus 253, 254–5, 265
Heroic Age 43

heroic nudity 265
Heroic style 284
Heron style 141–2, 343
heröon 327
Hesychius 221
Heurtley, W.A. 355
high lighting 185
Hill, D.K. 353
himation 84, 327
Hirmer, A. 331, 347
Hirmer, M. 331, 347
Hirschfeld, G. 286, 287
Hirt, L. 283
historical value of pottery 263–6
history of the study of vase-painting 275–311, 355–6
Histria *see* Istria
Hittite: influence 41; lion 55
Hitzl, K. 353
Hoffmann, H. 349
holkion 327
Homer 80, 205, 277, 280, 296, 353
Homeric bowls 327, 353
Hopkinson, J.H. 291, 297, 300, 304
Hopper, R.J. 336
Hoppin, J.C. 354
horror vacui 327
horsehead amphorae 77, 338
hourglass ornament 327
Howard, S. 348
Hugues, P.F. *see* Hancarville, P.V. d'
human figures 3, 57–60
Hunt painter 93
Hurschmann, R. 344
hydria 63–6, 84, 94–5, 173, 175, 190, 197–9, 213–14, 352
hydriske 327

Ialysus 131, 286, 343
iapygian 327
Iberian 192, 194
iconography 265–6
iconology 266
illite 233, 238
impasto 39, 327
impressed decoration 34, 146, 203–4, 237
incision: in Black-figure 48–9; in Geometric 16; in Hellenistic 196, 198; in Red-figure 153, 163, 167; technique 45, 48
Indo-Germans 289
industrial organization 259–62, 355–6
Inscription painter 149
inscriptions 241–8, 353; *see also* epigraphy
Instituto de Corrispondenza Archeologica 281
intentional red 238
Ionia 45, 128; bowls 327; Geometric 34, 35–6, 38; Little Masters 110, 122–5, 127, 133, 239, 303; misattributed 134, 295–6, 297, 300; Persian conquest 110, 296, 300, 302; Protogeometric 10; Wild Goat style 109–10, 112–16; *see also* Panionism
iron oxides 231, 232
Ischia *see* Pithecusae
Island style *see* Cycladic
Istanbul Museum 319
Istria 110, 118, 122, 127
Italian 342; Geometric 17, 33, 38–40, 138, 279, 287–8, 289, 335; Greek 138–53, 277–8, 280, 289; native wares *see* Apulian; impasto; Lucanian; Siculan; Villanovan; *see also* South Italian
Italinsky 279
Italiot *see* South Italian
Italocorinthian *see* Etruscan
Italogeometric *see* Italian, Geometric
Italo-Greek 280, 284
Italo-Ionic 305
Italy (museums) 319
Ithaca 45, 244; Geometric 26, 27–8, 333; imitation of Protocorinthian 62, 336; Protogeometric 7, 12
ivory 2, 41
Ivy-leaf group 123, 148, 346

Jackson, D.A. 339
Jacobsthal, P. 347
Jacopi, G. 335, 343
Jahn, O. 285, 291, 295, 301, 305–6, 308–9, 355
James, T.G.H. 355

Jatta, M. 310
Jeffery, L.H. 354
Jena painter 176, 177, 259, 348
Jentel, M.O. 352
Johansen, K.F. 288, 295, 304, 310, 335, 337, 354
Johnson, F.P. 348
Johnston, A.W. 338, 352
Jones, R.E. 339, 353

K at beginning of Greek words and names *see also* under C
kadiskos 210
kados 210
Kahil L. Ghali 343
kalathos 9, 12, 208, 328
Kalikleas 244
καλός inscriptions 245, 246
kalpis 213–14
Kanowski, M.G. 351
kantharos 209, 223, 226–7
Kardara, C. 343
Karo, G. 299, 304
Karoni 355
Karouzou, S. 338
Karusos, C. 342
Kearsley, R. 332
Kekule, R. 306
kelebe 328
Kerch/Kerch style 285, 328
key meander 328
Kilinski, K. 339
kilns 234–6, 256, 354
Kimolos 30, 31, 100, 103, 339
Kinch, K.F. 297, 299, 300, 344
Kirchhoff, A. 291, 297
Kittos 260
Klein, W. 291, 292, 306
Knipovitch, T.N. 351
Knipovitch class 129
Koehler, U. 308
Kondoleon, N.M. 334, 351
Konnakis painter 191
Kopcke, G. 351
Koroni 257
kotyle 25, 223, 224, 225–6
kotyle-krater 218, 229
Kourou, N. 333

Kraiker, W. 332, 347
Kramer, G. 283–4, 285, 290, 291, 293, 301, 306, 309
krater 217–20
krateriskos 328
Kretschmer, P. 353
Kübler, K. 332, 338
Kurtz, D.C. 347, 348
Kuruniotis, K. 298
kyathos 226, 328
kylichnis 328

Labraunda 352
Lacedaemonian grave at Athens 255, 353
Laconian: Geometric 16, 17, 26–7, 287, 333; krater 219; Orientalizing and Black-figure 45, 88–96, 121, 287, 292, 338; plain ware 95–6; Protogeometric 7, 10, 12, 332; relief ware 351
lacrymaterium 328
lagynos 194, 196–7, 217, 353
Lagynos group 196–7, 350
lakaina 89, 224
Lamb, W. 335, 343
Lane, E.A. 333, 339
Langlotz, E. 308, 331, 355
'Larisa' in Aeolis 33, 110, 116, 296
Late Roman 201, 202, 351
La Tolfa group 148, 345
Lau, T. 301
Laumonier, A. 352
Laurenzi, L. 343
laws about antiquities 273, 317–18
Lazzarini, M.L. 353
Leach, S.S. 345
Leagros 245–6, 282
Leagros group 85
lebes 217
lebes gamikos 220, 239
Lecce, Museo Castromediano 319
Lefkandi 10, 29, 332, 334
lekane 135, 227, 228
lekanis 227, 229
lekythos 221–2, 237, 239, 339, 347
lekythos-oinochoe 328
Lemaitre 276

Lemnos 36, 153, 346
Lemos, A.A. 343
Lemos, I.S. 332
Leningrad, Hermitage Museum 321
Lenormant, C. 284
lepaste 328
Leroux, G. 310, 348, 351
Lesbian Grey ware 34, 116, 335, 343
Lesbos 33, 34, 36, 334
Letronne, A. 284
Levi, D. 335, 344
Lewis painter 348
Leyden group 101–2, 281, 342
Leyden, Rijksmuseum 281, 321
Lezzi-Hafter, A. 348
lids 229
life, daily 265, 266
Linear: Geometric 25, 28–9; Island
    group 96, 100–1, 106, 211, 287, 303,
    339; style 49, 57, 60–1
lions 52, 53–5, 112
Lipari 257, 353; group 188; painter 200
lip cups 75, 78–80, 83, 123, 208–9, 224,
    338
Little Master cups 75, 78, 80–1, 83,
    110, 123–5, 127, 133, 239, 303, 354
Locrian vases 307
Loeschcke, G. 287, 289, 291–4, 297,
    301, 302–3, 308
Lohmann, H. 348, 350
Longpérier, A. de 295
Lotus bowls 36, 111, 113, 116–17
loutrophoros 175, 211, 213
loutrophoros-hydria 213
Louvre 76, 77, 317, 320, 332
love-names *see* καλός inscriptions
Löwy, E. 295
Lucanian native ware 40, 139, 335,
    344; Red-figure 182, 183, 187–8, 282
Lucas, P. 276
Lullies, R. 347, 348, 355
Luynes, Duc de 282, 309
Lycia: Geometric 36; wall paintings
    166
Lycurgus 95
Lydian: Geometric 34, 36;
    Protogeometric 10; Wild Goat style
    118, 119, 153

lydion 328
Lydos 80, 83, 260, 338
Lysippides painter 158
Lyttos 198, 257

Macchioro, V. 309
McCredie, J.R. 355
Macedonian 23; Megarian bowls 215;
    Protogeometric 11
Macmillan aryballos 50
McPhee, I. 350
Madrid Archaeological Museum 321
magnetization 258
makers 158, 244–5, 306
Maier, F. 351
Makron 165
Malibu, J.Paul Getty Museum 321
Mansell Colour Charts 238
mantle figures 84
Marathon, battle of 85, 255, 355
market (modern) 273
Marseilles 355
Martelli, M. 345
Martial 277
Martin, R. 355
Marwitz, H. 346
Massow, W.von 333
mastos 328
Mauceri, L. 286, 294
Mauro, L. 275
Mazocchi, A.S. 278
Megara Hyblaea 24, 35; destruction
    255, 354; foundation 252, 286, 335;
    local ware 106, 138–9, 151, 343
Megarian bowls 202, 204–5, 208, 226,
    227, 241, 310, 350
Megiddo 252, 354
'Melian' 45, 71, 99, 100, 106–9, 134–6,
    210–11, 214, 250, 290–1, 293, 295,
    297, 301, 303, 339
Melian Geometric 31, 281, 287
Melos 30, 31, 100, 106, 109, 291
Memnon group 151
mending: ancient 240; modern 272–3
Mengs, A.R. 278
Menon painter 347
merchants 248, 261, 354
merchants' marks 248, 354, 261

merrythought cup 83; handle 328
Mesad Hashavyahu 255, 354
Messapian 188, 328
Messenia: Geometric 28; Orientalizing
  45; Protogeometric 7, 12, 332
metalwork 2, 17, 37, 41, 48, 95, 227,
  228, 353
metope decoration 51, 328
Metope style 39, 141, 142, 168
Metzger, H. 356
Metzger, I.R. 342
Meyer, H. 282
Meyer-Schlichtmann, C. 350
Micali painter 148–9, 180, 345
Middle Helladic 5–6, 237
Midias painter 174–5
Mikon 168
Milchhöfer, A. 289, 292, 307, 308
Milesian (name for Wild Goat style)
  297, 298
Miletus 127; destruction 255; finds 33,
  123; Geometric 33, 35;
  Protogeometric 10; Wild Goat style
  112, 115, 116, 124, 297
Millin, A.L. 276
Millingen, J.V. 279, 281, 282, 283
Milonidas 244
miltos 234, 238
Mingazzini, P. 346
Minoan 7, 12, 328
Mistress of the Beasts 55, 73
modelling 165, 169, 172, 191
Mommsen, H. 38
Montfauçon, B.de 276, 277, 280, 284
Moore, M.B. 352
Morel, J-P. 351
Moret, J.M. 349
Morgan, C.A. 333
Morricone, L. 334
Morris, S.P. 337
mottoes 245–6, 247
Motya 255, 353
mug 216, 227
Müller, C.O. 282–3, 284, 302
Müller, W. 288
Munich, Museum Antiker Kleinkunst
  320
Münter, F. 279

murals *see* painting, free
Murray, A.S. 298, 300
Musée Rodin 181
museums 276–7, 317–21, 331
Mustakas, C. 339
Mustilli, D. 346
Mycenaean: style 1–2, 5–9, 11, 12,
  23–4, 38, 43, 88, 210, 221, 238, 252,
  286, 287–90, 317, 328, 339; tablets
  208
Mykonos Museum 319
Myrina 117, 199
Myson 165
Mystae painter 98

names of shapes 207–8
Naples Museum 319
narrative style 74
Naucratis painter 93
Naucratis 305; attributed 117–19, 123,
  296; finds 110, 115, 122, 127, 129,
  261, 298; foundation 253, 296
'Naucratite' 119, 122
Naveh, J. 353
Naxian: attributed 104, 292, 339–41;
  Geometric 29–31, 33, 333;
  Orientalizing 104, 105, 106
Nearchos 80–1, 242
neck-amphora 190, 210–11
necking ring 328
Neeft, C.W. 333, 336
Negri, M. 275
negro alabastra 165
Nessos amphora: in Athens 69–72; in
  New York 67–8, 69, 72
Nessos painter 69–72, 76, 301
nestoris 185, 188
Newton, C.T. 286
New York, Metropolitan Museum 321
Nikosthenes 212, 245, 261, 302–3
Nikosthenic amphora 86, 145, 210,
  212, 264, 303
Niobid painter 167, 171, 307, 348
Nisyros 33, 110, 118, 228, 348
Noble, J.V. 353
Nolan: amphora 164, 170, 173, 210,
  211; style 281, 282
nonsense inscriptions 243

Northampton group 130, 151, 305, 344
note-taking 270

Oakley, J.H. 348
oblique views *see* foreshortening
Oelmann, F. 288
oinochoe 102, 170, 173, 175, 214–17, 349
Olbia (Ukraine) 100, 110, 118, 122, 127, 253
Old Smyrna *see* Smyrna
'Old' style 283
'Oldest' style 283, 285, 290
olpe 217, 285, 381
Oltos 159, 162, 260, 347
Olympia 91, 352
Olynthus 255, 352, 354
one-handler 328
one-piece amphora 210, 212, 301
one-piece oinochoe 215–16
Onesimos (Panaitios painter) 165, 307
onos 328
open cable 328
open pots 209, 268
Orbetello 275
Oriental: imports 41, 140; influences and models 2, 22, 37, 41–5, 49, 60, 110–11, 114, 140, 146, 169, 227, 285, 287
Orientalizing 26–8, 32, 35–6, 39, 239, 249, 285, 335–45; definition 41–6, 194, 210–11; inception 17, 23, 41–6, 141–2, 288; schools 46–153, 290–1; Subgeometric 110–11; survivals 169
Orlandini, P. 355
ornaments 170, 347, 348
Ornate style: Apulian 186–8, 190, 191; Attic 176
Orsi, P. 286, 294, 302, 304, 353
Orvieto group 146, 149
ostraka 241
outline technique 23, 37, 58, 65, 67–8, 88, 89, 99, 168
overlap cup 328
owl-kotyle 226, 278, 348
Owl-Pillar group 182, 183, 189
owners' names 246, 247

Oxford, Ashmolean Museum 320, 332
oxidation 232, 236, 237
oxybaphon 328
Özgünel, C. 335

Paciaudi, P.M. 277
padded dancers 57
Paestan Black-figure 154
Paestan Red-figure 182–3, 185, 187–8, 190–1, 309, 349
Pagenstecher, R. 310, 350, 352
Pagenstecher group 153
paint 232, 236
painted decoration 193–200, 202–3
painters 243–4, 306–7; *see also individual painters*
painting, free 1, 3, 57, 157, 166–8, 195, 251
painting, vase 275–311, 355–6
Palaiologos, J. 286
Palermo National Museum 319
Pallat, L. 294–5, 299
Palmer, H. 336
Pan painter 171, 346
Panaitios painter (Onesimos) 165, 307
Panathenaic amphorae 80, 85–7, 164–5, 193–4, 198, 210–11, 243, 247, 254, 255, 257, 281, 285, 302, 339
Panathenaic festival 86, 254
Pancrazi, G.M. 278
panel decoration on amphorae 70, 71, 77, 86–7
Panionism: applications 299, 301–5, 308; general theory 295–7
Panofka, T. 284
pansu, aryballos 47
panther 42
Panticapaeum 129, 285
Paoli, S. 278
Papaspyridi-Karusu, S. 338, 348
Parian (attributed) 30–1, 33, 101, 103, 109, 134, 333
Paris: Bibliothäque Nationale 93, 320; Louvre 76, 77, 317, 320, 332; painter 345
Parthenon 171
Pasquinucci, M.M. 349
Passeri, G.B. 277, 278, 279, 280

Patroni, G. 309
Paul-Zinserling, V. 348
Payne, H.G.G. 293–5, 302, 304, 334, 336, 339, 340–1, 343
Peacock, D.P.S. 354
Pease Philippides, M.Z. 351
'Pelasgian' style 284, 288
pelike 178, 213
Peloponnesian War 179
Pemberton, E.G. 336
pendent semicircles 10–11, 33
Pendlebury, J.D.S. 335
Penteskouphia plaques 57–8, 60, 231, 234, 336
Penthesilia painter 166, 171, 259, 346
peplos 170, 328
peptization 233
'Perfect' style 282
'Pergamene' 196, 201, 202, 204, 205, 348
Pergamum 196, 348, 350
Persian: conquest of Egypt 254–5; conquest of Ionia 110, 296, 300, 302; sack of Miletus 255
petasos 329
Peters, K. 339
Petrie, W.M.F. 131, 286, 298–9, 300, 355
Petrie group 128
Petrie painter 129
petrological analysis 240
Peucetian 329
Pfuhl, E. 286, 292, 297–9, 301–4, 307, 308, 333, 339, 340–1, 347
Phaleron style 329
phallus cup 12
Pherecydes 255
phiale 227, 347
Philadelphia University Museum 321
Philargyrius 277
Philippaki, B. 347, 352
Philistines 253, 355
Phineus: cup 292, painter 149
Phintias 243
Phlyax vases 185, 347
Phocaea 34
Phocaean attributed 329
Phoenician: palmette 140, 142–3; style

290, 291
phormiskos 209, 329
photography 270–2
Phrygian 79, 153, 346
Phrynos 80
Pianu, G. 349
pinax 228, 329
Pindar 252
piriform aryballos 47
Pistoxenos painter 171, 346
Pitane 34, 110, 117, 122, 130
pitcher 209, 216
Pithecusae 41; Bocchoris grave 253, 353; finds 30, 35, 38, 138, 343; local ware 39, 45, 62, 138
pithos 32, 37, 38, 135, 137
Pitsa plaques 60, 166, 260
Plain manner, Apulian 186–7, 188
plain ware 95–6, 338
plaques 57–8, 60, 166, 231, 234, 260, 336
plastic accessories 22, 65, 125, 129, 137, 186, 194, 199, 231, 236
plastic vases 329
plates 227–8
Plato 282
plemochoe 329
Pliny 160, 277, 300
Pocolom group 310
pointed amphora 210
political influences 265
polos 329
Polos: group 214, 302; painter 76, 211
polychrome plates (Cycladic) 109
polychromy 51, 57, 69, 109, 118, 140, 188, 194, 197, 199–200, 237–8, 347–50; *see also* black polychrome technique
Polygnotus: free painter 168; vasepainter 172–4, 186, 188
Polyphemus: group 142, 151, 339; painter 241
Pontic 147–8, 196, 210, 305
Pothos painter 188
'Potnia theron' 55, 73
pot-painters 86, 161, 162, 329
Potters, Epigram to 236–7

pottery: historical value of 263–6; industry 259–62
Pottier, E. 293, 297, 299, 303, 304, 305, 351
Poulsen, F. 287, 289, 297, 303–4, 355
Pozzo, Cassiano dal 276
Praisos plate 304
Prange, M. 348
Praxias group 180, 244
Prehellenic 329
preliminary sketch 233
Price, E.R. 298, 299
Price, M.J. 333
prices 261, 273
Priene 350
Primato painter 188
Prinz, H. 297, 300
prochous 329
Pronomos krater 285
prosperity 265
prothesis 329
Proto- 329
Protoattic *see* Attic
Protocorinthian: Geometric 25–7, 35, 44, 45–54, 62, 68, 286–8, 293–5, 299, 301, 336; name 293–4; *see also* Corinthian
Protogeometric 1–2, 5–13, 24, 210, 238–9, 250–1, 258, 332–5
Protogeometric B 36–7, 41, 334
protome 329
Protome group 101, 104–6
PSC cups 10–11, 29, 332
Psiax 85, 162
psykter 209, 329
Ptolemies 198, 255
Puchstein, O. 292, 297
purification deposits *see* Rheneia
Pyrrhus 244
Python 198, 245
pyxis 223

quatrefoil aryballoi 56
Quirini, Cardinal 276

R group 175
radiocarbon 257
Ram Jug painter 67

Raoul-Rochette, D. 283, 284
Rapporto Volcente 282
Rasmussen, T.B. 343
Red-figure: style 3, 85, 140–1, 149, 155–92, 200, 211, 226–9, 255, 259–60, 276–8, 280, 305–6, 309, 346–50; technique 155–7, 231, 238, 239
Red-gloss 201
Red-ground style 57, 59–60, 62, 63, 68, 74, 77, 147
red ochre 234, 238
reduction 232, 236
Reed painter 348
Reichhold, K. 307, 338, 347
relative chronology 249–51, 258
relief decoration 146, 204–5; *see also* plastic accessories
relief line 149, 155, 172, 173, 234
relief sculpture 155, 160, 167–8, 172, 243
relief wares 237
religion 265–6, 280
remanent magnetism 258
reserved decoration 202–3; technique 329
restoration 267–73
Rhegion 150–1; attributed 346
Rheneia, purification deposit 30, 100, 101, 103–4, 106, 108–9, 255, 291, 353
Rhitsona 97, 303, 310, 349
Rhodes: finds 10, 33, 110, 131–2, 194, 198–9, 289, 291, 317, 320, 343; Museum 319
Rhodian 198, 199; Fikellura 123–4, 127, 130, 298, 317; Geometric 34–6, 293, 299, 317, 334; imitation of Attic Black-figure 46; impressed decoration 203; misattributed 299–300, 304; Mycenaean 5, 289, 296, 317; Protogeometric 10, 335; Wild Goat style 114, 117, 118, 124, 295, 297, 298, 317
Rhodian-Milesian 297
Rhomatos, C. 333, 342
rhyton 227, 329, 349
ribbing 191, 202
Richter, G.M.A. 301, 349
Ridgway, D. 343

Riezler, W. 307, 347
ring-vases 56, 106, 121
Ristoro d'Arezzo 275
rivets 240
Rizzo, M.A. 345
Roberts, S.R. 353
Robertson, C.M. 333, 337, 347
Robinson, D.M. 355
Roccanova painter 188
Rocco, A. 348
Rohde, E. 344
Roman wares 201, 202, 236, 352, 356
Romano, Giulio 275
Rome: Servian wall 294; Vatican
    Museum 276, 319; Villa Giulia
    Museum 51, 319
Rosette bowls 111, 298, 299
Ross, L. 284, 285, 308
Rotroff, S.I. 350, 352
rouletting 145, 204
Ruckert, A. 333, 339
ruddle *see* miltos
Rumpf, A. 291–2, 297, 300, 338, 345,
    354, 355
running dog 329
Running Man painter 125

sacred tree 329
St Valentin group 347
sakkos 329
Sakonides 80, 338
Salamis 286, 287
Salzmann, A. 286, 295
Sam Wide group 179, 287–8, 289, 348
Samaria 352, 354
Samian: definitions 329; Geometric 35,
    334; Orientalizing and Black-figure
    117, 123, 126–7, 134; Protogeometric
    10
Samos: finds 27, 33, 35, 110, 126–7,
    265, 342; group 58
Sams, G.K. 346
Sant' Agata de Goti 282
Sardis 10, 34, 36, 117, 131, 153; *see
    also* Lydian
Saticulan 309
satyr 72, 159, 170
saucer 227

scarabs 253, 353
Schäfer, J. 350, 352
Schefold, K. 343, 347
Scheibler, I. 338, 352
Schiering, W. 343
Schilardi, D.U. 355
Schliemann, H. 286, 289
Schmalz, B. 339
Schröder, B. 308
Schweitzer, B. 288, 290
Sciatbi 255
sculpture 1, 155, 160, 167–8, 172, 243,
    251
'second white' 169, 173, 330
Selinus: finds 286; foundation 252, 253,
    353
semicircles: pendent 10–11, 33; upright
    8, 12
Semper, G. 288, 289
Senatus Consultum de Bacchanalibus
    280, 309
Servian wall 294
Servius 277
Seta, A. Della 346
Severe style 284, 285, 330
sex, distinction by colour 58, 59, 72,
    86, 120, 127, 169, 173
shading 175, 191, 275
shapes 284–5, 351; copying 271–2;
    types 207–29
shaping 231
Shear, T.L. 353
Sheedy, K.A. 342
sheen 232, 237
sherds 208–9, 268–9, 272–3
Shuvalov painter 346
Siana cups 74–5, 78–9, 92, 123, 224,
    302, 338
Sichtermann, H. 349
Sicilian 17, 23–4, 30, 38, 40, 45;
    colonial wares 39, 62, 139, 281;
    generic name for Black-figure 280–1,
    283; misattributions 277–8; native
    Geometric (Siculan) 40, 139, 335;
    Red-figure 182–3, 188–9
Siculan 40, 139, 336
Sicyonian 336
Siebert, G. 352

Sieveking, J. 304, 305
sigillata 201–5 *passim,* 237–8, 241, 350
signatures 243–5, 260, 307, 354
silvering 145
Simon, E. 331, 347
simple krater 218
Sindos 258, 355
Sinn, U. 350
sintering 232–3, 236
Siphnian treasury 254–5, 355
Siphnos: attributions 339; finds 30, 31, 100, 103–4, 333, 339
Sipsie-Esbach, M. 332
sipyis 229
siren 42
Sisyphus painter 186–7
sites 323
situla 330
Situlae, East Greek 131–2, 300, 305
Six's technique 330
sketching 270
skyphos 223, 224
Skyros, Protogeometric 6, 11
Skythes 162–3, 260
slip 239, 330
Smith, C.H. 299, 301, 302, 306
Smith, H.R. 345, 348
Smyrna: Black-figure 115, 122–3, 128–30; finds 33, 110, 111, 254; Geometric 26, 33, 36; Museum 319; Orientalizing 109, 111, 115, 122; Protogeometric 10
snakes 20, 22, 60, 65
Snodgrass, A.M. 355
Solon 76
Sophilos 72–4, 76, 244, 302
S.O.S.amphorae 75, 86, 142, 288, 338
Sotades painter 171, 203
South Italian 23, 30; Red-figure 3, 182–92, 228, 239, 260, 276, 349
Sparkes, B.A. 331, 349, 351
Sparta 24, 26–7, 36, 93, 95, 352; *see also* Laconian
Spina 261
spiral, false 32
Spivey, N.J. 345
squat lekythos 173, 175, 190, 221
Stackelberg, Baron O.M.von 284

Stais, V. 301, 355
stamnos 32, 132, 173, 175, 219–20, 285
stamped decoration *see* impressed decoration
standard processes 231–7
standed bowl 224
Stark, C.B. 356
Stavropoullos, D. 286
Steinberg, A. 355
stemless cup 203
stemmed bowl 224
step meander 330
Stephani, L. 287, 350
Stibbe, C.M. 339
Stillwell, A.N. 348
stirrup vase 12, 37, 330
Stockholm group 101
Stoop, M.W. 354
stratification 249, 263
Strøm, I. 339, 340–1
Strong style 330
Studniczka, F. 291, 293, 297, 300, 302, 305, 308
study of vase-painting 275–311, 354–5
Sub- 330
Subgeometric 17, 23–4, 27–9, 31, 35–7, 40, 44–5, 48, 51, 56, 60–2, 88–9, 96, 100, 106, 110–11, 119, 134, 137, 141, 239
Submycenaean 6, 7, 9, 238, 258
Subprotogeometric 11, 16, 29, 33
Suessula painter 179
Swallow painter 260
Swinger, the 83, 338
Sybaris coins 283, 285
Sydney, Nicholson Museum 320
symplegma 330
Syracuse 88, 263; foundation 252–3, 353; local ware 138–9, 344; National Museum 319
Syria 23, 26, 41, 56
Szilágyi, J.G. 345

Talcott, L. 347, 351, 353
Talos painter 176
Tanagra 199
tankard 216
Taranto National Museum 319

Tarentum 24, 27, 183, 186–7, 191, 258; cup 91, 92
Tarquinia 39, 141, 182, 345
Tarsus 35, 119, 254, 352, 355
'tea cup' 225
Technau, W. 339
technique 61–2, 87–8, 231–41, 351–2
Tell Abu Hawam 253, 355
Tell Defenneh: destruction 255, 355; finds 110, 127, 129, 131–2, 255
Tell Halaf ware 237
Tenos 30, 31
terminus ante quem 330
terminus post quem 330
textiles 2, 17–18, 41, 289
Thapsos class 25, 333
Thasos: Chiot 122, 134, 343; imitation of Black-figure 135; 'Melian' 108, 134–5; Wild Goat style 118, 134
Thebes 97, 180, 339
Thera: finds 26, 30, 45, 100–1, 103, 109, 198, 286–7; Museum 319
Theran 31–2, 100, 106, 286–8, 303
Therasia 286
Thericlean vases 281, 330
thermoluminescence 257, 268
Thermon, metopes 51, 57, 167
thermoremanent magnetism 258
Thespiae, Polyandrion 255, 355
Thessalian 72; Geometric 16, 17, 23, 26, 29, 33; Protogeometric 7, 10, 11, 332
Thessalo-Cycladic 11
Thiersch, H. 302, 303, 337
Thompson, H.A. 339, 351
Thompson, M.S. 290
throwing 204, 231
Thucydides 46, 252, 253
Thurii 183, 188, 283
thymiaterion 330
Tiberios, M.A. 338
Tillyard, E.W.M. 309
Timoleon 188
Timonidas 58, 72, 244
Tischbein, W. 279
Tiverios, M.A. 356
Tleson 79–81, 242
Tocra 108–10, 122, 138, 338

tondo 75, 78, 92–3, 163, 172
Toronto, Royal Ontario Museum 320, 343
tracings 270
trade/traders 259–62, 264
Trendall, A.D. 309, 349, 355
tripod-pyxis 330
Triton 55
Troy 36, 168
trozzella 330
Tübingen group 128, 129
Turkey (museums) 319
turning 208, 231
Typhon 55
Tyrrhenian amphorae 73–6, 80, 147, 242, 261, 301, 337; definitions 282, 302

Uhden 276
Ukraine: finds 119, 348, 349; local wares 129, 157, 194, 199, 261
ultra-violet light 268
unguentarium 330
Ure, A.D. 339, 348, 351
Ure, P.N. 303, 310, 339, 351
Urla group 129
Urlichs, L. 295
urn 276

Vallet, G. 335, 343, 346, 355
Valletta, G. 276
Vallonarian amphorae 39
Vanderpool, E. 355
varnish 233
Vasari, G. 275
vase-painting 12, 37, 41; Canosa 199; history of study of 275–311, 355–7
Vatican 72, 82, 276, 319
Veii 30, 33, 39
Verdelis, N.M. 332
Vickers, m. 351, 352, 354
Vienna (museums) 320
Villa Giulia Museum 51, 319
Villa Giulia painter 171, 348
Villani, G. 275
Villanovan amphora 39
Villard, F. 332, 335, 344, 346, 354–5
Vineyard cup 123, 124

vitrification 232
Vlastos group 118, 343
Volterra 181, 182, 310
volute-krater 35, 170, 176, 218–19
votive 191, 330
Votokopoulou, I.P. 332
Voyatzis, M.E. 332
Vroulia/Vroulian 132–3, 299
Vulci 39, 121, 148, 180–2, 281–4, 292, 305
Vurva style 301–2

Wace, A.J.B. 290
Waiblinger, A. 342
Walter, H. 334, 342
Walter-Karydi, E. 333, 343, 345
Walters, H.B. 309
Warsaw National Museum 321
wash 330
Watzinger, C. 310
wave pattern 330
Wedgwood, Josiah 278, 279
Wehgartner, I. 345
Weinberg, S.S. 333, 336, 352
Welcker, F.G. 283
Wells, B. 332
West Slope ware 193, 195–6, 197, 198, 203, 211, 226, 350
Western Greek: Geometric 16–17, 27–8; Protogeometric 7, 12
wheel, potter's 231
Wheel group 31, 32
wheel-marks 268–9
white on dark decoration 17, 26, 38, 52, 137, 140, 192, 194

White-ground style 87, 157, 169–73, 237–8, 239, 347
White style 61–2
Whitelaw, T. 334
wickerwork, influence of 289
Wide, Sam 179, 287–8, 289, 347
Wild Goat style 42–3, 45, 93, 106, 109–24, 126–30, 132, 134, 138, 215–16, 218, 220, 228, 237, 239, 254, 290–1, 293–300, 343, 346
Winckelmann, J.J. 278
Winnefeld, H. 303, 309
Winter, A. 352
Winter, F. 300, 306–7
Wintermeyer, U. 349
Wissowa, Paul 302
Witte, J.de 284, 292, 306
Wolters, P. 302
wood, influence of 219, 223, 227
Woodhead, A.G. 354
Woolly Satyrs 170
workshops, size of 259
Würzburg, M.von Wagner Museum 318, 320

Xenophantos 260

Yiannikoyri, A. 350
Yntema, D. 335, 344
Young, R.S. 333, 338

Zahn, R. 292, 297, 300, 305, 308, 309–10
Zapheiropoulou, Ph. 339
Zervoudaki, E.A. 352
Zilverberg, M. 345

PLATES

A Cup: ht 14.7 cm.
10th cent. BC.

B 'Tea-cup': ht 9.2 cm.
10th cent. BC.

C Lekythos: ht. 15.5 cm.
Early 10th cent. BC.

D Oinochoe: ht 30 cm.
Late 10th cent. BC.

1 Attic Protogeometric

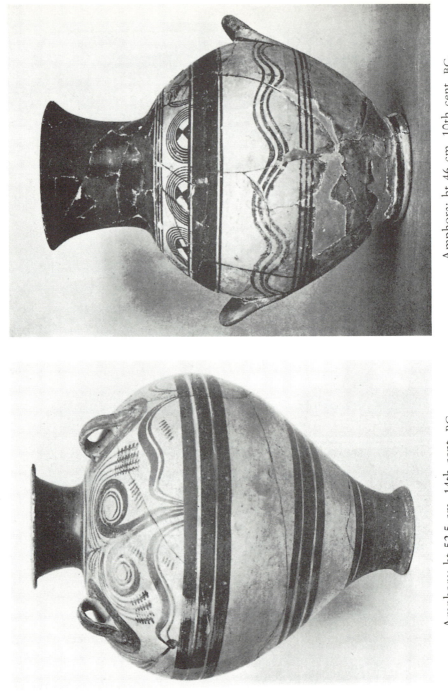

Amphora: ht 46 cm. 10th cent. BC.
2B   Attic Protogemetric.

Amphora: ht 52.5 cm. 14th cent. BC.
2A   Mycenaean

A. Amphora: ht 72.2 cm. c. 875–850 BC.

B. Amphora: ht 77.5 cm.
Middle or later 9th cent. BC.

3   Attic Geometric

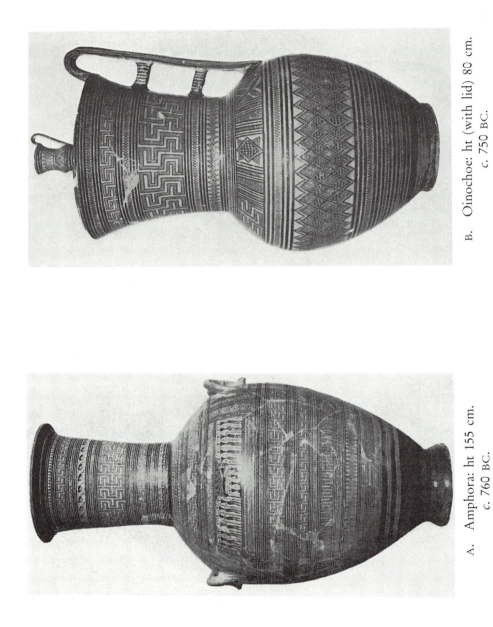

B. Oinochoe: ht (with lid) 80 cm.
c. 750 BC.

A. Amphora: ht 155 cm.
c. 760 BC.

Detail of Plate 4A
5   Attic Geometric.

Amphora: ht 28 cm, *c.* 700 BC.
6B   Theran Geometric

Pyxis: ht (with lid) 19.5 cm, *c* 740 BC.
6A   Attic Geometric

Hydria: ht 27.7 cm. Later 9th cent. BC.
7B Cretan Protogeometric B

Oinochoe: ht 21.9 cm. Late 8th or early 7th cent. BC.
7A Rhodian Geometric

Oinochoe: ht. 33.4 cm. c. 720–690 BC.
8C. Protocorinthian.

Cup: ht. 6.7 cm. Later 9th cent. BC.

Kotyle: ht. 10.5 cm. c. 740–30 BC.
8A, B. Corinthian Geometric.

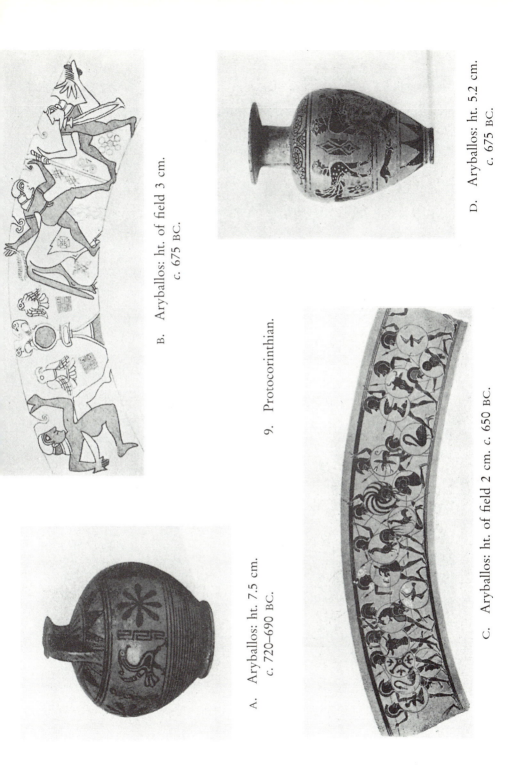

B.   Aryballos: ht. of field 3 cm.
c. 675 BC.

D.   Aryballos: ht. 5.2 cm.
c. 675 BC.

9.   Protocorinthian.

A.   Aryballos: ht. 7.5 cm.
c. 720–690 BC.

C.   Aryballos: ht. of field 2 cm. c. 650 BC.

A.   Kotyle: ht. 19 cm. *c.* 660 BC.

B.   Aryballos: ht. 7.8 cm.
c. 600 BC.

C.   Alabastron: ht. 9.7 cm.
c. 625–00 BC.

10.   Protocorinthian and Ripe Corinthian

Olpe: ht. 27.5 cm.
c. 640–25 BC.

11A.   Transitional Corinthian

Oinochoe: ht. 38 cm.
c. 625–00 BC.

11B.   Ripe Corinthian

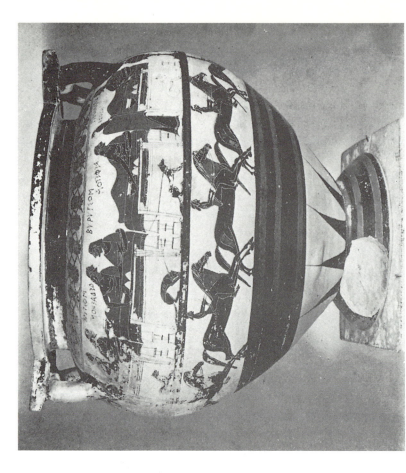

C. Column-krater: ht. 46 cm. c. 600 BC.

12. Ripe Corinthian

A. Kotyle: ht. of field 6 cm.
c. 580 BC.

B. Kotyle: ht. of field c. 6.5 cm.
c. 580 BC.

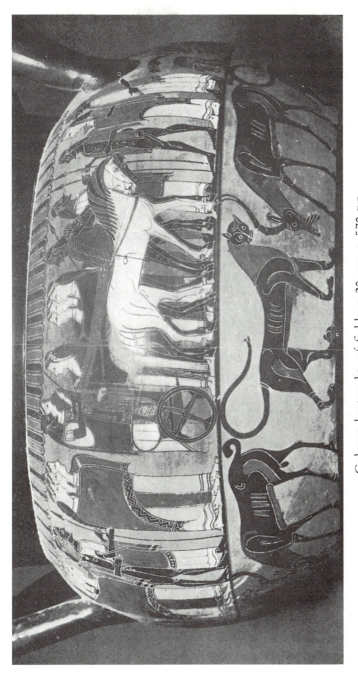

Column-krater: ht. of fields c. 20 cm. c. 570 BC.

13.   Ripe Corinthian

B. Krater: ht. 39 cm. c. 690 BC.

A. Hydria: ht. 52.5 cm. c. 700 BC.

14. Protoattic

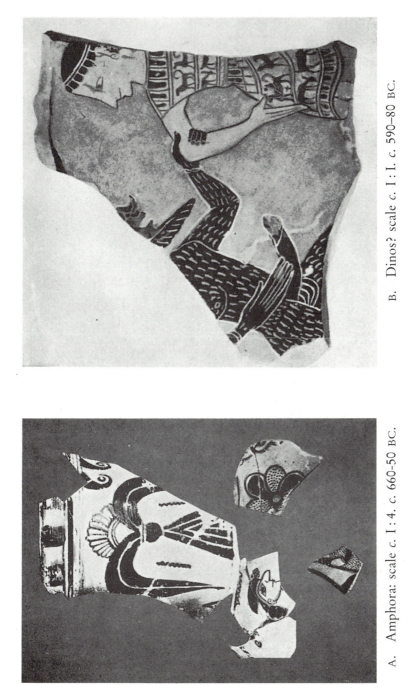

B. Dinos? scale c. 1 : 1. c. 590–80 BC.

15. Protoattic and Attic BF

A. Amphora: scale c. 1 : 4. c. 660–50 BC.

Amphora: ht. 108.5 cm. *c.* 660 BC.

16.   Protoattic

Amphora: ht. 122 cm. *c.* 615 BC.

17. Protoattic

Dinos and stand: total ht. 93 cm. *c.* 590 BC.

18. Attic BF

A.   Volute krater: ht. 66 cm. *c.* 570 BC.

B.   Detail: ht. of upper field 5.6 cm.

19.   Attic BF

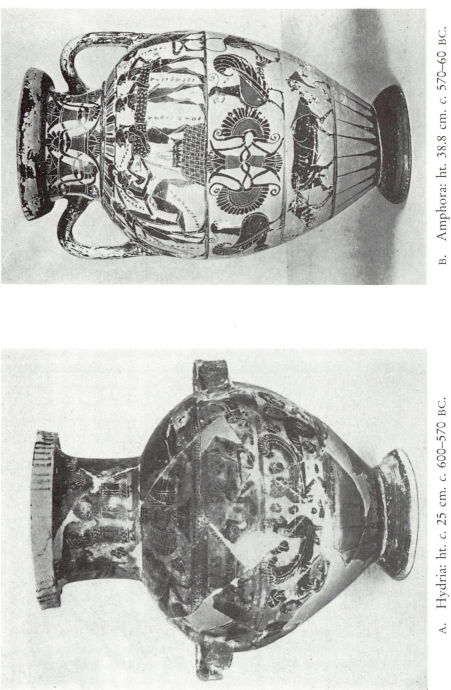

A. Hydria: ht. c. 25 cm. c. 600–570 BC.

B. Amphora: ht. 38.8 cm. c. 570–60 BC.

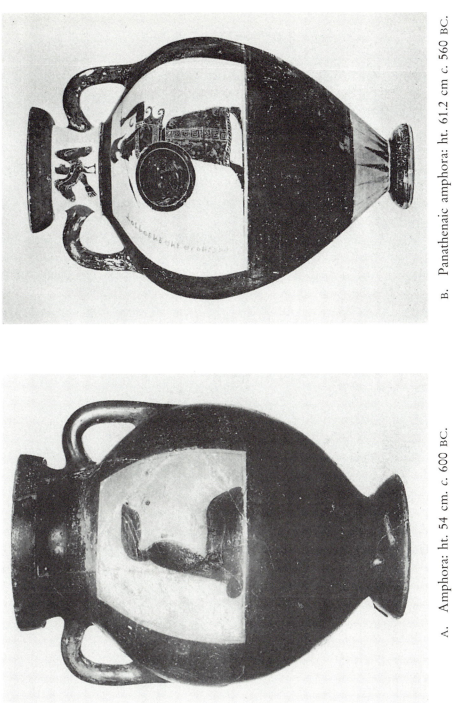

A.   Amphora: ht. 54 cm. c. 600 BC.

B.   Panathenaic amphora: ht. 61.2 cm c. 560 BC.

21.   Attic BF

Amphora: ht. 61 cm. *c.* 530 BC.

22. Attic BF

Amphora: ht. 33 cm. *c.* 530 BC.

23. Attic BF

A. Comast cup: ht. 9.5 cm. *c.* 580–70 BC.

B. Siana cup: ht. 13 cm. *c.* 570–60 BC.

24. Attic BF

A.   Lip cup: ht. 12.4 cm. *c.* 550–30 BC.

B.   Band cup: ht. 13.3 cm. *c.* 550–30 BC.

25.   Attic BF

A–B.   Cup: diam. (without handles) 22cm. Early 6th cent. BC.

26.   Laconian

A–B.   Cup: diam. (without handles) 17.8 cm. *c.* 550–40 BC.

27.   Laconian

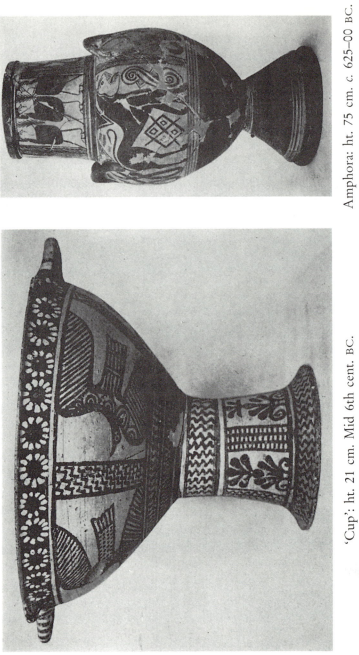

Amphora: ht. 75 cm. c. 625–00 BC.

28B. Eretrian

'Cup': ht. 21 cm. Mid 6th cent. BC.

28A. Boeotian

Details of Plate 29A

Cup: ht. 5 cm. c. 675–50 BC.

29D. East Greek: Bird bowl

Amphora: ht. 43.5 cm. Early 7th cent. BC.

29A–C. Cycladic: Linear Island group

B.   Oinochoe: ht. 36 cm. c. 625–00 BC.

A.   Oinochoe: ht. 30 cm. c. 630 BC.

A. Oinochoe: ht. of field c. 6.5 cm.
c. 625 BC.

C. Bowl: ht. of field 7.8 cm.
c. 615–00 BC.

D. Sarcophagus: ht. of field c. 17 cm.
c. 515–00 BC.

B. Krater: ht. of field c. 3.7 cm.
c. 600–575 BC.

31. Wild Goat style (C Chiot, D Clazomenian sarcophagus)

Amphora: ht. (as preserved) 31 cm. c. 540–30 BC.

Amphora: ht. 30.5 cm. c. 540–20 BC.

Cup: diam. (without handles) 23.5 cm. c. 550 BC.

33B. East Greek BF

Situla: ht. (as restored) 47.6 cm. c. 575–50 BC.

33A. East Greek Situla

Amphora: ht. 35.1 cm. *c.* 540–30 BC.

34.   Etruscan BF (Pontic)

Hydria: ht. 44 cm. *c.* 520–10 BC.

35. Caeretan hydria

Column-krater: ht. 45.7cm. *c.* 550–30 BC.

36. 'Chalcidian'

A.   Amphora: scale *c.* 4 : I. 500–490 BC

B.   Bell-krater: scale *c.* 2 : 3. *c.* 440 BC.

37.   Attic RF

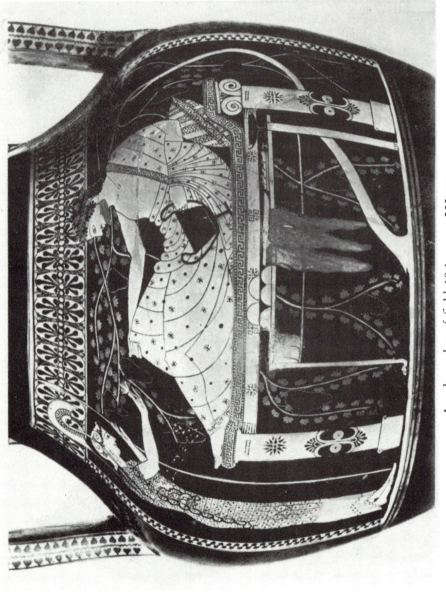

Amphora: ht. of field 18.1 cm. c. 520 BC.

38. Attic RF

Amphora: ht. of field 24.2 cm. 510–00 BC.

39.   Attic RF

Cup: greatest length of fragment *c.* 18.7 cm. 500–490 BC.

40.   Attic RF

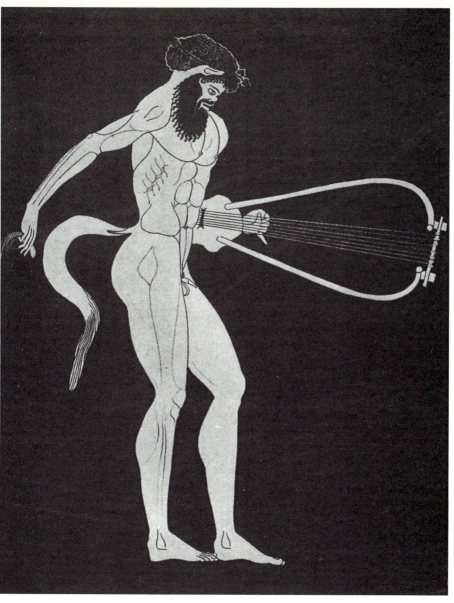

Amphora: ht. of figure 27 cm. *c.* 490 BC.

41. Attic RF

Amphora: ht. of field 24.7 cm. 500–490 BC.

42. Attic RF

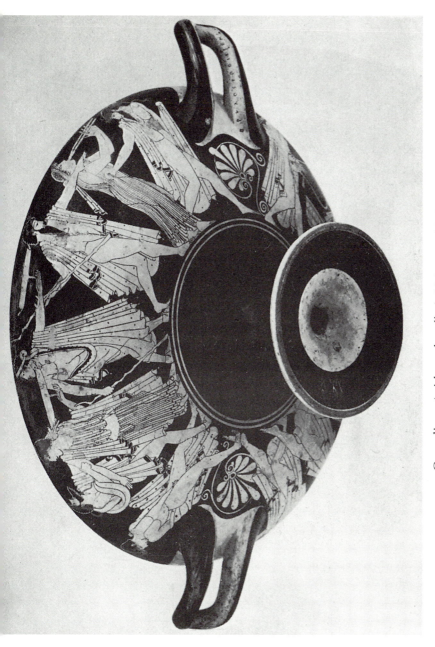

Cup: diam. (without handles) 32.2 cm. 490–80 BC.

43.   Attic RF

Bell-krater: ht. 37.1 cm. *c.* 470 BC.

44. Attic RF

Pelike: ht. 41 cm. 460–50 BC.

45. Attic RF

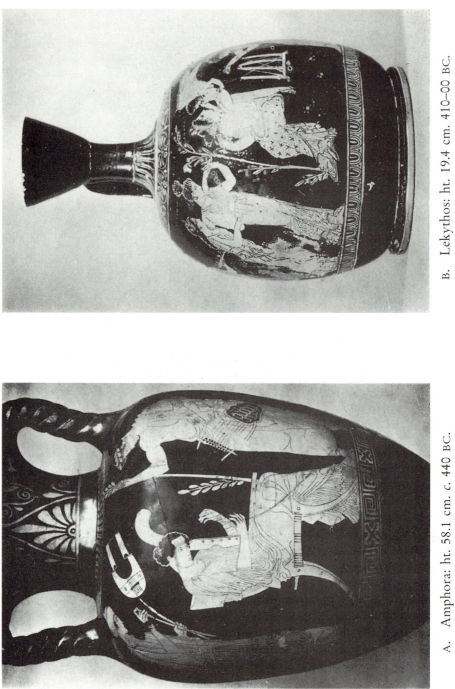

A. Amphora: ht. 58.1 cm. c. 440 BC.

B. Lekythos: ht. 19.4 cm. 410–00 BC.

46. Attic RF

Lekythos: ht. of field 9.2 cm. 430–20 BC.

47. Attic RF

A. Bell-krater: ht. 31.5 cm. 420–10 BC.

B. Bell-krater: ht. of second figure 15.4 cm.
c. 440 BC.

48. Attic RF

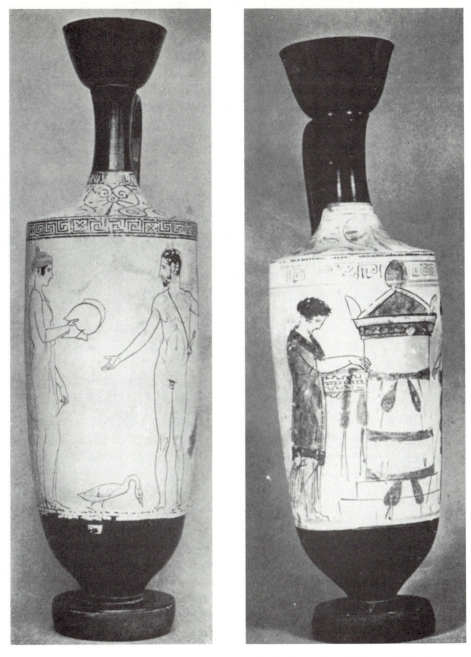

A. Lekythos: ht. 38.7 cm. 450–40 BC.   B. Lekythos: ht. 31.5 cm. 420–10 BC.

49. Attic WG

Pelike: ht. (as made up) 28.7 cm. *c.* 380 BC.

50. Attic RF

Pelike: ht. 42.5 cm. *c.* 350 BC.

51.   Attic RF

Volute-krater: combined ht. of fields *c.* 29 cm.
430–20 BC.

52A.   Apulian RF

B.   Bell-krater: ht. of field *c.* 17 cm. 440–30 BC.

52B.   Lucanian RF

Calyx-krater: ht. of field 28.5 cm. 360–50 BC.

53.   Apulian RF

Amphora: ht. 81 cm. *c.* 340 BC.

54.   Lucanian RF

Kotyle: ht. 29.5 cm. *c.* 330 BC.

55A.   Campanian RF

Bell-krater: ht. of field 16.3 cm. *c.* 350 BC.

55B.   Paestan RF

Amphora: ht. 17.4 cm. First half of 2nd cent. BC.

56A.   West Slope

Bell-krater: ht. 22.2 cm. Second half of 4th cent. BC.

56B.   Gnathian (Apulian)